THE FRENCH PRESS

THE FRENCH PRESS
Class, State, and Ideology

J.W. Freiberg

Foreword by Ernest Mandel

PRAEGER

PRAEGER SPECIAL STUDIES • PRAEGER SCIENTIFIC

Library of Congress Cataloging in Publication Data

Freiberg, J   W
    The French press.

    Bibliography: p.
    Includes index.
    1. Press--France. 2. Industrial relations--
France. 3. Government and the press--France.
4. Journalism--Political aspects--France.
I. Title.
PN5178.F75   074   80-25581
ISBN 0-03-058309-8

Published in 1981 by Praeger Publishers
CBS Educational and Professional Publishing
A Division of CBS, Inc.
521 Fifth Avenue, New York, New York 10175 U.S.A.

© 1981 by Praeger Publishers

All rights reserved

123456789   145   987654321

Printed in the United States of America

For Nicos Poulantzas (1936-1979)
friend and colleague who provided
valuable advice about the direction
of this research.

FOREWORD

The political, opinion-shaping power of newspapers, once widespread literacy has been achieved, has generally been estimated to be so large that the press has even been called "the fourth estate." It is true that the advent of newer mass media, reaching an even larger percentage of the total citizenry, has somewhat reduced that power. That decline, however, should not be exaggerated. Radio and television have generally tended to conform to what public-opinion pollsters and market researchers tell them to be "the public's consensus." They therefore operate more on the basis of opinion reflecting than of opinion shaping. And while it is true that they thereby also influence opinion, albeit more indirectly, in the sense of conformism and conformity, it should also be noted that their influence on their listeners' and viewers' minds is of a more fleeting character—at least as long as video cassettes and other new gadgets do not take over in the field of news programs. With regard to information and opinion formation, the old Latin formula, <u>verba volant, scripta manent</u> retains a large measure of truth.

So the question of a free and pluralistic written press, and of the possibility for the average citizen to have access to large-scale, contradictory, non uniform news and numerous different interpretations of it, remains of central importance in a democracy. The questions of whether the press is really free under bourgeois-parliamentary democracy, to what extent it remains so, and to what extent its freedom is endangered and eroded, are vital to all those for whom human progress is indissolubly linked to more human freedom.

It is, of course, a truism that freedom of the press—like all freedoms—can be defined in two quite different ways, negatively and positively. The negative definition of freedom of the press means the absence of legal and/or political prohibitions, the absence of censorship and of institutions a priori denying average citizens (or organizations of citizens) the opportunity of printing and diffusing their opinions. In that negative sense, freedom of the press means the formal right of all to publish whatever they wish, at least in the field of beliefs, opinions, commentary on events, and general information. (The right of individuals to defend their privacy against encroachments of sensation-hunting reporters does not conflict with that negative freedom, except in some borderline cases.)

The positive definition of a free press means the effective material capacity of individuals or groups of individuals to have their opinions printed and circulated. If it costs $10 million to found a daily newspaper, and many more millions to run it, the abstract "right" to do so—that is, the absence of any law or institution prohibiting it—will be of little avail for the overwhelming majority of the citizens. It will be like the right to become a millionnaire, when in fact less than 0.5 percent of the population accumulate such wealth.

Liberals have generally concentrated on the first definition and denounced any encroachment on a free press from that point of view. Radicals have tended to concentrate on the second definition, and have turned their fire on the obvious ties between the private property of the printing enterprises and the possibility this presents for control through ownership, hence rendering the press less than "free" for a large part of the public. For them, freedom of the press would mean, literally, free access to printing presses for all. Marxists, aware of the disgraceful happenings in the press and publication fields of the postcapitalist societies, should rightly combine both conditions as indispensable to a truly free press. By doing so, they would only be returning to the tradition of Marx and Engels themselves, who remained throughout their lives staunch opponents of censorship, in society as a whole as well as in their own political parties.

When one considers that 63 years after the October Revolution, the Soviet penal code still carries an article imposing heavy punishment for anybody who "slanders Soviet society and the Soviet state"—an editor of the critical magazine Poisky has just been condemned to three years deportation to a hard-labor camp for that dastardly crime and that crime only—one wonders whether Soviet society is really the most homogeneous in the world, as the Soviet leaders tirelessly proclaim. (A similar remark can be made about China, where the editors of four "dissident" newspapers have just been arrested.) After all, late bourgeois society, crisis-ridden and torn by deep class conflicts as it is, feels strong and self-confident enough, at least in the core countries, to allow anyone to "slander" it at will without paying a dime in fines, let alone being condemned to hard labor. And one must assume that in the eyes of the leaders of the capitalist class, radical, Socialist, and Communist criticism of capitalist society, currently printed in millions of newspaper copies, must appear at least as slanderous as does the criticism of Soviet society in the eyes of the Moscow leaders.

During the month of August 1980 more than one million Polish strikers explicitly demanded the abolishment of censorship and asserted their absolute right to publish their own bulletins and newspapers. That should make those die-hards who still believe that the limitation of newspaper publishing to those who toe the ruling party's line is justified at least sit back and think about whether this really has anything to do with defending the class principle or the proletariat's class interests in the press. It is my contention that the state's (and ruling party's) monopoly of access to the mass media, and its capacity to withhold from the average citizen (primarily the average worker) an enormous mass of information, let alone any news interpretation different from that of the ruling group, is one of the mainstays of that minority's monopoly of power. Soviet-style bureaucracies desperately need that monopoly in order to defend and protect their massive material privileges (among other things, preventing information about these privileges from becoming widely known to the mass of the citizens).

The monstrous hypertrophy of the state is however by no means limited to the Eastern-bloc countries. It is also very much a fact in the West. The assumption that private property and a market economy guarantee the consolidation and extension of human freedom has been cruelly contradicted by the evolution of bourgeois society since World War I (and had already been previously contradicted by that same evolution, at least in countries subjected to colonial conquest). Private property and market economy engender competition. Competition leads to concentration of capital, that is, concentration of economic power. Under monopoly capitalism that concentration of economic power becomes so great that it implies at least the capacity to completely subordinate the direct and daily functioning of the state to the needs of the ruling class, and to radically limit personal and democratic freedoms whenever their exercise tends to undermine the rulers' vital interests.

Paradoxically, one could turn Milton Friedman's assumption upside down: the more one wants to guarantee or restore unbridled economic freedom (market economy) when a growing number of people refuse to pay the price of a normal application of the "rules of the game" (by no means eternal economic laws but only the laws of functioning of a specific class society called capitalism), the more one has to use extra economic coercion to force the "remedies" of mass unemployment and massive cuts in real wages and social services down their recalcitrant throats. Under late capitalism, economic freedom and personal and political freedom (the guarantee of a minimum of democratic rights to all people) become increasingly incompatible with each other, at least in periods of protracted crisis. (And we are going to witness an increasing number of such periods of crisis in nearly all capitalist countries.) The last 15 years have tragically confirmed this in many semi-industrialized countries with long standing so-called democratic traditions, including Uruguay, Chile, and India (under Indira Gandhi's "emergency"). The next 15 years will raise a similar threat for the richest industrialized countries.

Journalists and newspaper publishers have been exceptionally hard hit by this new wave of destruction of basic democratic rights. Literally hundreds of them have been kidnapped, tortured, or brutally murdered in such countries as Brazil, Chile, Argentina, Nicaragua, El Salvador, and South Korea, to name just the most sinister examples. Nothing of this magnitude happened even after the rise to power of Mussolini and Hitler, under "classical" fascist conditions.

While these abominations are broadly recognized, denounced, and condemned—at least verbally (which does not keep the victims from being killed)—there is an even deeper threat to the freedom of the press. This arises out of the process of concentration and centralization of capital itself in the printing sector and the newspaper publishing industry, independently of the degree of survival of bourgeois-parliamentary democracy. Today one needs a preposterously large amount of capital to start and run a daily newspaper, and hence fewer and fewer individuals or organizations do actually run daily papers. Monopoly capitalism therefore leads to a growing monopolization of the daily press or, to put it in other words, to its concentration in fewer and fewer hands.

As a result of that evolution, access to broad information and critical and controversial interpretation of it have been radically curtailed for a large sector of the public in the West also. The most striking confirmation of that regression can be seen in the fact that the social-democratic mass parties in Western Europe—by far the strongest political force in that part of the world, averaging at least 35 percent of the popular vote—have been forced to abandon their daily presses in one country after another. Such official party newspapers are absent in West Germany, Britain, France, Holland, and Sweden, and this list is by no means complete or final.

The basic merit of Dr. Freiberg's book is to present this trend in great detail for a particular country, France. I know of no other book that has done such a thorough and painstakingly researched and documented inquiry on the state of the press in a given capitalist country.

Dr. Freiberg's conclusion about the growing monopolization of the press and its grave implications for the functioning of a democratic political system are all the more convincing in that France is by no means an extreme case in the West. In the United States, for example, there are large metropolitan areas with the number of inhabitants equaling small or even medium-sized European countries, where the citizens no longer have any choice as to what daily paper they will read or as to the editorial opinions to which they will be subjected. Ninety-seven percent of U.S. cities have a single daily paper, and when there are two, the owners are often the same and impose identical editorial policies.

In France, for a number of historical reasons, this final stage in the concentration process has not yet been reached. What is called in France la presse d'opinion (opinion-expressing press, as opposed to sensationalist or so-called general-information newspapers) somehow still survives, as witnessed in the Communist Party press and the special dailies like Libération and Le Matin on the Left, Les Echos and La Croix on the Right, with that exceptional and venerable institution of Le Monde, which is unique in the world, hovering over them all. In the provinces however, recently the stronghold of opinion shapers like La Dépêche de Toulouse, the slaughter has been more thorough than in Paris, for a variety of causes that Dr. Freiberg brings out shrewdly.

Furthermore, while the increasing preponderance of weekly papers as against dailies—in the face of television's instant information competition—seems a universal phenomenon, it should be stressed that French mass-circulation weeklies still correspond to major political and even ideological options, in contrast to North American or West German magazines of the general information type, as exemplified by Time or Der Spiegel. Nevertheless, the openly political character of the French newsweeklies tends slowly to decline also; Le Nouvel Observateur, however, remains more outspokenly leftist than, say, Der Spiegel (while moving increasingly to left-center), while L'Express, after having started as a left-center opponent of the Algerian war, is now outspokenly center or even center-right. Le Figaro has made a clear and unforeseen breakthrough as an articulate and sophisticated voice of the far-right sector, giving this political extreme a kind of intellectual respectability for the first time since the Liberation.

All this being said, however, it remains true that the variety of opinions to which a politically interested French citizen has access in the daily papers—and the French are the most highly politicized people of the world!—has been drastically reduced, compared with the prewar or post-Liberation situation, as Dr. Freiberg proves with an abundance of facts and figures. This bodes ill for the future of democratic freedoms in that country, if this dangerous trend is not radically reversed in the coming years. The fact that concentration of newspaper and printing-trade capital has operated in favor of such characters as Mr. Hersant only adds more spice to an already unpalatable dish. It is, of course, the trend itself that is most significant and perverse, not the individuals who are profiting from it.

Two questions, dear to structuralists and empirical sociologists alike, can be asked in conjunction with the process that is rooted in the very nature of capitalism; both are dealt with by Dr. Freiberg in a thorough way. First, is there somehow an intrinsic link between technological progress and the growing monopolization of the press? Second, is not the decline of the opinion-shaping press a consequence rather than a cause of the allegedly growing depoliticization of Western society, of the "death of ideology" (supposedly induced by the welfare state and the decline of social contradictions)? The second question can be reformulated more sharply: do quality newspapers disappear because it costs too much to run them, or because they find fewer and fewer customers?

The first questions I would answer with a cautious "yes, but." Yes, in the framework of capitalist market economy, rationalized by the profit motive underlying competition, increased technological sophistication and progress in the printing trade spectacularly increase the outlays necessary for running a daily paper. In that sense, electronics and the third technological revolution have dealt a staggering blow to the freedom of the press under capitalism. They have dealt no less a blow to trade-union strength in printshops, a fact Dr. Freiberg lucidly illustrates (thereby justly involving the labor process itself and the class struggle) in the analysis of the monopolization of the printing and newspaper publishing industries.

A fundamental fact of newspaper financing, however, well-known through many previous studies, shows the limitations of any argument that sees the monopolization of the press as an inevitable result of "technological fatality." No mass-circulation newspaper can be profitably run in and by itself today. Any daily paper, whatever the wealth of its owner, that would want to cover costs by sales alone would have either to cut costs drastically (that is, the number of pages published) or to increase its sales price considerably. In either case, mass circulation would disappear. So a self-financing, mass-circulation, daily paper has not only become difficult under the third technological revolution, it has become impossible. Daily mass-circulation newspapers can survive only if they receive subsidies from outside sources. (The sources of these subsidies in the French case are traced in detail in the present study.) In that case, however, there can of course be no question of the capitalist profit motive, or of the logic of technological progress under capitalism.

What capitalists engaged in the business of producing and selling daily newspapers really sell is advertising space. They "buy" readers of their newspapers at great cost in order to sell advertising aimed at these readers. The financial viability of these enterprises is in fact heavily dependent on their advertising incomes. Capitalist firms that are able, willing, or sufficiently interested to finance large-scale advertising campaigns, however, become increasingly destabilized (tending to be concentrated in mass-consumer goods, industries, and trading outfits. They are therefore deeply affected by the recurrent recessions of late capitalism—for example, the automobile industry is currently engaged in heavy advertising to overcome a severe crisis of overproduction and increased international competition—and the stranglehold of capital over the press thereby acquires a new importance. Therefore the increased monopolization of newspaper industry capital itself is magnified by the weighty influence of the principal advertisers, who are themselves, characteristically, monopolistic corporate firms. The fact that their accounts can be withdrawn at will, and are in any case not available to openly anticapitalist papers, makes the system function in a nearly flawless way in the interests of the propertied class.

This is not, of course, a fatal and automatic result of contemporary technological progress in the printing industry, separate and apart from the overall way in which late capitalist society functions. It is automatic only inasmuch as no decisive countermoves are undertaken to check the process. In most Western European countries the state subsidizes to varying extents political dailies (and weeklies) in order to insure a minimum of political pluralism. This system, however, tends to operate in favor of the large established parties, as against new or minority formations, and so adds the danger of political monopolies to that of economic monopolization.

One can, however, envisage a more fundamental democratic reform, under which private property of the large printing presses would be abolished. They would be run under the administration of an independent agency (in French, régie would be the most adequate concept), with strictly limited powers of a bookkeeping nature, and under severe constraints of workers' control and public access to the books. Any group of citizens, whether organized in political parties or not, would have such access in proportion to the number of signatures submitted (or votes obtained in elections plus signatures submitted). This means that given the limitations of existing equipment, a certain minimum of public support would be required for the right to run a daily paper, whereas a lower level of public support would give the right to run only a weekly, a biweekly, or a monthly paper. Special pages in existing daily papers would in addition remain open for smaller groups of individuals to express themselves freely. Press runs would be periodically adjusted to actual sales. The drop of sales below a given ceiling would then lead to the transformation of the daily into a weekly: and an increase of the sales beyond a given threshold would allow the editors of a weekly to publish a daily if they wished to do so. The sale price of all dailies and weeklies would be identical. Subsidies would originate from the profits of the other fields of activity of the printing industry and from the public echequer, since one is, after all, referring to a sector that can make a fundamental contribution to the maintenance of democratic freedom. Additional guarantees and constraints would be added to avoid abuses, corruption, or undue state influence.

Whether such a radical reform could ever be introduced under conditions of bourgeois-parliamentary democracy is dubious, but that is no argument against trying. We are firmly convinced that this will be the way in which freedom of the press will be guaranteed and expanded under socialist democracy. There is hardly any doubt that it would represent a qualitative step forward in ensuring both negatively and positively a free and pluralistic press system, compared with the way in which the press functions today, both in the East and in the West.

To make it possible to answer the second question (regarding the cause of the disappearance of quality newspapers), Dr. Freiberg has introduced the important notion of the two-tier system of the press. This is the concept that the function of the press, as part of the mass media and in an even larger sense as part of the whole "ideology-producing apparatus" of bourgeois society, is to reproduce the social division of labor which is tightly linked to the class division itself. Bourgeois society needs one set of quality newspapers to inform the ruling class and its leading managers in all fields of social activity. Simultaneously, it needs another set of newspapers to keep the masses docile. Therefore we have, side by side, quality newspapers like Le Monde and Le Figaro (the quality of Le Figaro declining rapidly, however) and mass-circulation sensationalist dailies like France-Soir. The fact that a majority of working-class readers, including those who vote for the Communist Party, are readers of the sensationalist papers and not of L'Humanité, or other CP dailies in the provinces, gives weight to the subtle analysis of Dr. Freiberg. He finds that working-class readers are not particularly as affected by the heavy doses of political indoctrination present under the superficially apolitical surface of the sensationalist press. Perhaps, then, the question is one of the depoliticization of the working class.

Several important reservations should, however, be added to such an overall analysis. In the first place, the sheer lack of journalistic quality in the opinion-shaping press, and hence its ability to cater to the needs and worries of the wage earners, is an important element in the situation. Generally, social-democratic and CP dailies have been boring and engaged in heavy-handed political indoctrination, very often opposed to the workers' real needs. Their decline in circulation in all those cases reflects less their depoliticization than their increasing skepticism about established mass parties and their policies, for which they continue to vote more for reasons of the lesser-evil type than for reasons of deep commitment. Periodically, explosive happenings show that France remains highly political, which of course demonstrates the relative impotence of the sensationalist papers to influence their readers in an ideologically significant fashion.

In the second place, the shift of a large part of the French working-class readers to sensationalist daily papers reflects the growing nervous strain and fatigue of late capitalism—evident in the process of production, in mass transportation, in air and noise pollution, to single out three fields among many others. The increased tension and fatigue make regular quality reading more difficult, and put greater emphasis on pure entertainment and such peripheral activities as the ubiquitous tiercé (state lottery), which is occupying more and more space even in L'Humanité.

In the third place, one cannot speak of any basic long-term trends in politicization/depoliticization, but rather of cyclical ups and downs. While it is undoubtedly true that the fifties and the sixties saw a reduction of sharp class conflicts as the result of the long postwar economic boom, it is also true that that whole period ended in the fireworks of May 1968, which were certainly no proof of a growing depoliticization. The dissullusions born from the lack of basic political change after May 1968, and the collapse of the Union of the Left's attempt to cash in on the May 1968 capital on a reformist basis, have certainly created a new wave of relative depolitization in the late seventies, now followed by a new, slow upsurge of political interest in the wake of the economic crisis and sharpened class conflicts produced by it. It is not difficult to show that these cyclical ups and downs are reflected in the fortunes of the opinion-shaping newspapers and in the relative influence of the sensationalist press.

Finally, even if the relation between levels of political interest and the weight of the monopolized, sensationalist, mass-circulation dailies is somewhat similar to the classical chicken-egg relationship, that is no reason to underestimate the negative long-term impact of bourgeois monopolization of the newspaper industry on the political destiny of the West. Dr. Freiberg is right to stress the fact that in a highly politicized country like France, the mass-circulation dailies have not—should one add, not yet?—succeeded in modifying their readers' electoral behavior. They have, however, succeeded in cutting their readers off from an increasingly important mass of current information, indispensable for orienting oneself in relation to increasingly complex national and international events. A sufficient amount of information is, after all, a necessary ingredient of class consciousness, which must be distinguished from the class instinct that is still present in the large majority of Western European wage earners.

So the antics of the monopolized mass-circulation dailies are not neutral from the point of view of the long-term evolution of the relationship of forces between the classes. They operate in favor of capital and at the expense of the working class, although in a more subtle and indirect way than through straightforward political indoctrination. And in some precise cases—racism and xenophobia being ominous examples—their effect on the political thinking of broader masses is already evident, due in part to the lack of adequate reaction from the mass parties of the Left. This balance sheet leads to the conclusion that a systematic countereducation, a large-scale counterculture based among other things upon adequate information, is an indispensable antidote to the dangers to democratic freedoms that grow out of the increasing monopolization, uniformization and stultification of the daily press. The classical labor movement was able to institutionalize such a counterinformation and counterculture. The labor movement in the full upsurge and restructuring of today and tomorrow will need to be able to repeat that performance at a much higher level of awareness and sophistication.

Ernest Mandel
October 1, 1980

ACKNOWLEDGMENTS

The research for this study was made possible through a fellowship jointly sponsored by the National Science Foundation and the Centre National des Recherches Scientifiques.

Earlier versions of the manuscript received careful attention from many colleagues whose constructive critiques served to inform me where improvements should be made. Among these, I am especially indebted to Robert Alford, Philip Antweiler, Manuel Castells, Peter Dreier, Susan Eckstein, Robert Gehret, Stanley Hoffman, John Horton, Deborah L. Kee, Ernest Mandel, Ralph Miliband, S. M. Miller, Harvey Molotch, Nicos Poulantzas, George Ross, Gören Therborn, Alain Touraine, Gaye Tuchman, and Michael Useem.

My base in France was the Center for the Study of Social Movements, of which I have been a member for a decade. I am deeply appreciative of the honor this represents, and for the material and spiritual support given me by the Center's director, Alain Touraine, its researchers and staff. Once back in the United States, the Sociology Department of Boston University, then chaired by Sol Levine, generously relieved me of certain duties so that I might concentrate on writing.

There is, of course, considerable technical typing, editing, and printing that goes into producing a book. Dozens of highly skilled individuals—many of whom I shall never know—have contributed. I would like to single out, however, the efforts of Nancy Newman, and of Lynda Sharp and Catherine Buckner at Praeger.

CONTENTS

FOREWORD by Ernest Mandel vii

ACKNOWLEDGMENTS xvii

LIST OF TABLES xxii

LIST OF FIGURES xxv

LIST OF ABBREVIATIONS xxvi

INTRODUCTION 1

    Toward a Critical Theory of the Media 2
    Property Relations and Authority Relations in the
      Press Enterprise 5
    Class Struggles Within the Press Sector 8
    The Capitalist State and the "Free" Press 11
    Modes of Journalism and Class Relations in Capitalist
      Society 14

PART I
PROPERTY RELATIONS AND THE PRESS ENTERPRISE

INTRODUCTION TO PART I 19

1   OWNERSHIP AND INFLUENCE IN THE PRESS
     ENTERPRISE 23

        Patterns of Ownership 23
        Authority Relations 33
        External Influences 39
        The Role of Monopolistic Advertising Corporations ... 41

2   MONOPOLIZATION IN THE FRENCH PRESS:
     THREE CASE STUDIES 50

        Jean Prouvost: The Last of the Grand-Style
          Press Barons 51

Chapter		Page
	Hachette: The World's Largest Publishing Multinational	57
	Robert Hersant: The Conquest of a Press Empire	64
	Conclusion	81
3	LE MONDE: AN EXPERIMENT IN WORKER PARTICIPATION	84
	The Development of Worker Participation at Le Monde	84
	Le Monde's Internal Contradiction: Worker Participation and Corporate Hierarchy	88
	Attacks on Le Monde	92
	Can Le Monde Survive?	96
	Advertising: Le Monde's Achilles' Heel?	99
CONCLUSION TO PART I		101

PART II
CLASS STRUGGLES WITHIN THE PRESS SECTOR

INTRODUCTION TO PART II		105
4	PRINCIPAL MANAGEMENT STRATEGIES IN THE PRINTING SECTOR	111
	The Current Situation of the Printing Sector	111
	Strategies of the Printing Bourgeoisie	117
5	THE PRINTERS: LAST DAYS OF A LABOR ARISTOCRACY	120
	The Structure of Anarchosyndicalism	120
	The Union at Its Acme	122
	The Longest Strike in French Labor History: Parisien Libéré	126
	The Printers' Ominous Future	135
6	THE JOURNALISTS: DECLINE OF THE POLITICS OF PROFESSIONALISM	138
	The Situation Among Journalists Today	138
	The National Journalist Union (SNJ)	141

Chapter	Page
The Politicization of the Journalist Unions	146
CONCLUSION TO PART II	152

PART III
THE CAPITALIST STATE AND THE FREE PRESS

INTRODUCTION TO PART III		157
7	THE STATE AS RULE MAKER AND ENFORCER	163
	The Status of French Press Law	163
	The Legislative Blockage of the "Press Statutes" Promised at the Liberation	166
	The Dialectic of Consent and Coercion	168
	State Financial Aid to the Press	169
	Ad Hoc Government Study Commissions	172
	Administrative Regulatory Agencies	174
	Ministerial Intervention	175
	Lawsuits Against Publications	177
	The Courts and the Leftist Press	177
	Censorship and Seizure	180
	Arrests of Journalists and Editors	183
	Violence Against Journalists	186
	Violence Against Press Enterprises	187
8	DIRECT LINKS BETWEEN THE STATE AND THE PRESS	189
	The State as an Active Agent in the Field of Information	189
	State Personnel Interlocks with the Press Bourgeoisie	199
CONCLUSION TO PART III		204

PART IV
MODES OF JOURNALISM AND CLASS RELATIONS IN CAPITALIST SOCIETY

INTRODUCTION TO PART IV		209
9	THE SENSATIONALIST PRESS	213
	Overt Depoliticization and Inherent Conservatism	213

Chapter		Page
	The Inherent Conservatism of the Human Interest Story	216
	A Shift to the Right	219
	Informational Vacuity	221
	The Crisis Orientation	224
10	THE PERSISTENCE OF AN INFORMATIONAL PRESS	227
	The Demise of the Political Party Press	229
	The Relative Success of the Far Left Press	231
	Conclusion	233
11	ON THE ROLE OF THE MEDIA IN CLASS RELATIONS	234
	The Role of the Media in Social Reproduction	237
	The Two-Tier Media System and the Legitimation Process	239
	Media Usage and Class Origins	240
	Social Class and the Use of Periodicals	244
	Is the Two-Tier Press System Part of a Two-Tier Media System?	246
CONCLUSION		252
A NOTE ON RESEARCH METHODS		254
APPENDIXES		259
BIBLIOGRAPHY		286
INDEX		306
ABOUT THE AUTHOR		321

LIST OF TABLES

Table		Page
1.1	Print Runs in the Largest Newspapers, 1945-69	24
1.2	Percentage of Daily Provincial Newspapers Printed by the Largest Firms	30
1.3	Differential Growth Rates of Advertising in Paris and the Provinces	42
2.1	Estimate of Hachette Gross Earnings, 1972-74	62
3.1	Who Owns <u>Le Monde</u>?	88
3.2	Financial Analysis of <u>Le Monde</u>, 1976	98
4.1	Growth in the Importation of Printed Material	115
5.1	Average Incomes of Full-Time Male Workers, 1976	125
5.2	Principal Strategies in the <u>Parisien Libéré</u> Strike	129
6.1	Changes in the Unionization Patterns of Journalists, 1970-79	150
7.1	Financial Aid to the Press by the French State, 1976	172
7.2	Seizures of the French Press in Algeria, 1957-60	183
8.1	Political Offices Held by the Press Bourgeoisie, 1977	201
9.1	The Political Spectrum of the French Daily Press, 1947 and 1976	220
10.1	The Disappearance of the Political Press, 1944-70	230
10.2	Extent of the Parallel Press: Numbers of Regular, Periodical Publications, 1973	232
11.1	Occupations of Readers of Four Major Parisian Dailies, 1975	242

Table		Page
11.2	Circulations of Sensationalist and Informational Newspapers in Paris, 1961-76	243
11.3	Classified Job Advertising in the Parisian Press, 1976	244
11.4	Regular Readership of Periodical Magazines, by Occupational Category, 1973	245
11.5	Television Watching, by Occupational Category, 1973	247
11.6	Television Programs Offered and Seen, 1973	248
A.1	Daily Circulation Controlled by Largest Press Groups, 1969	261
A.2	Origins and Life Spans of All General Information Newspapers Appearing in Paris, World War II to 1977	262
A.3	Newspapers Held Directly by the Industrial Bourgeoisie Just Before World War II	263
A.4	Newspapers and Newsweeklies Held Directly by the Industrial Bourgeoisie in 1975	264
A.5	Changes in Commercial Advertising in Parisian Dailies	266
A.6	Sources of External Financing in the Press and Publishing Industry	266
A.7	Hachette's Principal Press Holdings, Late 1976	267
A.8	Hachette's Principal Publishing Holdings, 1972	268
A.9	Book-Length Critiques of Le Monde	270
A.10	Summary of the Agreement Between the Parisian Press Owners Syndicate and the Comité-Inter (Negotiating Committee) of the Parisian Printers, July 1976	273

Table		Page
A.11	An Outline of Current French Press Law	275
A.12	Different Forms of Press Subsidies in European Countries	278
A.13	Examples of the Flow of State Personnel into Information Enterprises	280
A.14	The Political Spectrum of the Parisian Daily Press at the Liberation	282
A.15	The Political Spectrum of the Daily Press in 1976	284
A.16	The Content of Five Major Newspapers	285
A.17	The Education of Readers of Four Parisian Dailies, 1975	285

LIST OF FIGURES

Figure		Page
1.1	The Building of the Modern L'Aurore	26
1.2	The Structure of Advertising Agencies in France	44
2.1	The Press Empire of Jean Prouvost in 1975	52
7.1	The Range of Enforcement Modes Used by the French State in the Realm of the Press	170
8.1	The French State Monopoly over the Electronic Media	194
9.1	Evolution of Number of Pages Devoted to Various Rubrics, 1946-65	215
A.1	Organigram and Top Management of Le Monde, 1976	269
A.2	Structure of the Printers Union (Press Sector)	272
A.3	The Havas Advertising Empire, 1976	279

LIST OF ABBREVIATIONS

AFP	Agence France Presse: Major French news agency
AGPI	Agence générale de presse et d'information: News agency of Hersant press group
AJEF	Association des journalistes économique et financière: Specialized journalist association
BVD	Bureau de vérification de la publicité: Voluntary advertising control board of advertising agencies
CESP	Centre d'études des supports de publicité: Private agency which does reader profile studies of most publications
CFDT	Confédération féderale du travail: France's second largest union confederation; socialistic
CGC	Confédération général des cadres: Middle management union organization; extremely conservative
CGT	Confédération général du travail: France's largest union; linked to the Communist party
CNPF	Comité national de la patronat française: Owners organization, like the U.S. National Association of Manufacturers
CP	Communist party
Edi-Monde	Editions du Monde: Hachette subsidiary
FFSJ	Fédération française des sociétés des journalistes: Organization set up to coordinate different "journalist associations in enterprises across France
FFTL	Fédération française des travailleurs du livre: Anarchosyndicalist organization of the four printer's trade unions
FO	Force ouvrière: Conservative union federation
MRP	Mouvement républicain populaire: Resistance and liberation-era left Christian political party
NMPP	Nouvelles méssageries de la presse parisienne: Monopolistic press distribution subsidiary of Hachette
OJD	Office de justification de la diffusion: Private organization which verifies circulation of subscribing publications
ORTF	Office de radio diffusion-télévision française: Previous umbrella organization which administered and managed state-owned radio and television
RMC	Radio Monté Carlo: One of the principal peripheral, "private" radio stations broadcasting into France
RTL	Radio-Télé Luxembourg: Another peripheral station
SNJ	Syndicat national des journalists: Independent journalist union

SOCPRESS	Société française d'édition et de presse: Principal corporate unit of the Hersant press group
SOFIRAD	Société financière de radio-diffusion: State-owned holding company used to hold controlling shares of the peripheral radio and television stations
UEC	Union étudiant communiste: Communist student organization
UNSJ	Union national des syndicats des journalistes: Umbrella organization of the four principal journalist unions (SNJ, CFDT, CGT, and FO)
UNEF	Union national des étudiants français: The national student union; more important in anti-Algerian War demonstrations than in May 1968

INTRODUCTION

> The press is not an instrument of commercial profit; it is an instrument of culture. Its purpose is to give accurate information, to defend ideas, to serve the cause of human progress. . . . The press is free when it does not depend on either the power of government or the power of money, but only upon the conscience of its journalists and readers.
>
> Albert Camus
Combat, December 1944

> Incapable of realizing our dearest dream, which was to safeguard the press from the world of capitalism, what actually did come to pass made quick work of the idealists who thought they could run a press enterprise. In a capitalist regime, móney always imposes its way in the end.
>
> We see the resistance papers close down, one after the other, or, which is worse, we watch them taken over by big capital.
>
> Albert Camus
Combat, August 1954

Until the outbreak of World War II, the Parisian press was dominated by a handful of sensationalist newspapers, most of which were owned by major industrialists. Besides these politically conservative newspapers, one also found a small, but lively, center and left press, including official daily publications of both the Socialist and Communist parties. During the war, newspaper enterprises were forced to choose between collaborating with the Germans or shutting down altogether; most large enterprises chose the former.

At the same time, the resistance movement gave birth to its own press, a broad spectrum of clandestinely printed and distributed publications that attacked in print both the German invaders and their Vichy government collaborators. It was these teams of clandestine journalists who, at liberation, were given the confiscated printing plants of those papers which had collaborated during the war and who, as a consequence, set up and edited the liberation press. Among them was Albert Camus, who expressed the liberation dream for the press in his famous daily paper, Combat.

However, by the 1950s both the Parisian and the provincial press were once again dominated by large-circulation, sensationalist newspapers. The highly politicized publications of the 1940s were replaced by overtly apolitical, but inherently conservative, newspapers and periodicals which again were owned principally by industrial magnates and major corporations. By the 1960s these corporate press enterprises had been formed into major press groups in Paris; the remaining independent enterprises were forced to either close down or be absorbed, with only a few exceptions. In the provinces, a similar concentration process left vast areas of France with but a single newspaper with names such as "Ouest France" or "Sud-Ouest"—and quite appropriately so, since their monopoly did indeed cover these regions.

This study is about the social, economic, and political processes that permitted—I would even say determined—this transformation of the liberation press back to its prewar organizational structures and editorial policies. The French press of the 1970s is not unlike that of most other Western societies, but, in a very real sense, its history dates back only 30 years. In this brief time, the processes of concentration, monopolization, and depoliticization have accomplished what has elsewhere taken over a century. This study is an effort to analyze the actual dynamics of these processes as well as to theorize about their meaning in the broader framework of the structural transformations that characterize contemporary capitalism. The attempt, therefore, is to link theoretical analysis very closely with research findings, introducing the former at the rhythm required by the latter. Although it makes for difficult reading, this switching from theoretical considerations to detailed descriptions and back again is, nevertheless, necessary.

TOWARD A CRITICAL THEORY OF THE MEDIA

The major modern communication systems are now so evidently key institutions in advanced capitalist societies that they require the same kind of attention, at least initially, that is given to the institutions of industrial production and distribution. Studies of the ownership and control of the capitalist press, the capitalist cinema, and capitalist and state capitalist radio and television, must interlock historically and theoretically, with a wider analysis of capitalist society, capitalist economy and the neo-capitalist state. (Williams 1977, p. 136)

Williams is arguing that the media can only be understood in the broader political and economic interface between mass communication enterprises and more general social, economic, and political processes in advanced capitalist society. One cannot stay within the formal organizational boundaries of media institutions for the media have become linked too closely with other industrial sectors and penetrated too deeply by the capitalist state. Oscar Negt has argued, "The media do not constitute the core of a critical media theory" (1978, p. 64); only by studying the media's interpenetration with other corporate structures and the state will the functioning of the media enterprises themselves become understandable. Furthermore, the changing media organizational structures and output must be analyzed in terms of the economic and social transformations that characterize late capitalism. Stuart Hall, while admitting that there is a structural linkage between the growth of the media and "everything we now understand as characterizing 'monopoly capitalism'," proceeds to claim that these structural determinants of the contemporary media can be left to one side and exclusive attention given to studying the media as "ideological apparatuses" (1977, p. 12). Graham Murdock and Peter Golding criticize Hall's position, arguing, "On the contrary, the ways in which the mass-media function as 'ideological apparatuses' can only be adequately understood when they are systematically related to their position as large scale commercial enterprises in a capitalist economic system and if these relations are examined historically" (1973, p. 88).

In a seminal article, Nicholas Garnham (1979) has taken the Murdock and Golding position to heart and argued convincingly that a critical study of the media must move far beyond the reductionism and instrumentalism of Ralph Miliband (1969) and the determinism of Louis Althusser (1971) and Nicos Poulantzas (1975). These three theorists treat the media in a passing fashion as intentionally manipulated ideological weapons of a cohesive <u>ruling</u> (that is, not just dominant) class. The media, in Miliband's terms, are "<u>intended</u> to help prevent the development of class-consciousness in the working class and to reduce as much as possible any hankering it might have for a radical alternative to capitalism" (1969, p. 50, italics added). In the view of Althusser and Poulantzas, the apparatuses are necessarily <u>state</u> apparatuses, an analysis based on the classical Marxist differentiation between state <u>power</u> and state <u>apparatus</u> (which only together constitute the capitalist state). The state is seen as a power relation reflecting the balance of class struggle, the stakes of which are the control of the administrative and repressive state apparatus. Thus the media constitute only one item in a list of state apparatuses (along with religion, family, the educational system, and so on), which are seen as necessarily operating in the service of the dominant class and class segments.* Garnham has produced a powerful critique of the inadequacies of these reductionist perspectives on the media and has argued that a fruitful political economy of mass communications:

> shifts attention away from the conception of the mass media as ideological state apparatuses and <u>sees them first as economic entities</u> with both a direct economic role as creators of surplus-value through commodity production and exchange and an indirect economic role, through advertising, in the creation of surplus-value within other sectors of commodity production. Indeed a political economy of mass communication in part chooses its object of study precisely because it offers a challenge to the Althusser/Poulantzas theorization of the social formation as structured into the relatively autonomous levels of the economic, the ideological and the political. For the major institutions of mass communication . . . display a close interweaving <u>within concrete institutions</u> and within their specific commodity forms of the economic, the ideological and the political. (1979, p. 12, italics added)

I have cited Garnham at length because the present study cannot be understood outside of the perspective he espouses. From the Miliband or the Althusser-Poulantzas points of view, both see the media almost exclusively in terms of the ideological function of their output, there would be no logic to including in the present study such subtopics as the defensive struggles of the printers' and journalists' unions in the face of the new technology entering the sector. The printers, after all, have nothing to do with directly determining the content of any publication. However, what Garnham is claiming, and

---

*See Jan Ekecrantz et al. (1976) for an analysis of the Althusserian position on the media.

I wholly agree, is that to ignore studying the labor relations and shifting management strategies within the press <u>as an industrial sector</u> would be to ignore the fact that there may be, to quote Garnham, "a clear divergence between the functions of capital within the material process of mental production and the conscious, willed intentions of the capitalists or of their ideologues" (1979, p. 23).

There is, in other words, a historical specificity to the concrete mass media enterprises that both Miliband and the Althusserians pass over, thus precluding any investigation into the complex mediating processes that exist between the capitalist class per se and the ideology that appears in the media in advanced capitalist societies. This mediation is introduced by the partial autonomy of the media enterprises from the dominant industrial and financial enterprises, on the one hand, and from the capitalist state on the other. The media's degree of autonomy from these two spheres of power is an empirical question and clearly must vary in either a comparative or historical framework. The present study attempts to research concretely the political economy of the French press as an industrial sector. Only when we analyze such factors as the organizational transformation of the sector, the changes in fixed capital relative to living labor and the effect of this on labor relations and authority patterns within the enterprises, and the state's increasing penetration of the sector can we proceed to speak about the press's ideological impact on class relations.

I would now like to introduce briefly certain theoretical considerations underlying each part of the present study. These are elaborated and to some extent documented by the analysis in subsequent chapters.

PROPERTY RELATIONS AND AUTHORITY RELATIONS IN THE PRESS ENTERPRISE

During the German occupation of France (1940-44) certain elements of the bourgeoisie in general and of the press bourgeoisie in particular either directly collaborated or in any case conducted "business as usual," leading to a crisis of the state and a crisis of hegemony at liberation. The crisis of the state was evident in that the only accepted bourgeois party, the left Christian Mouvement Républican Populaire (MRP) found it necessary to share power with the Communists and Socialists. The crisis of hegemony was evident in that bourgeois ideological forms were temporarily discredited and ineffective. The bourgeois press, for instance, was by and large confiscated (more because it was bourgeois than because of direct collaboration in certain notable cases), and the press enterprises were given over to teams of journalists who had put out the clandestine press during the war, many of whom were Communists, Socialists, and left Christians. For the first three years following the Liberation, therefore, the press was dominated by papers with an anticapitalist perspective.

Left-wing dominance posed a clear threat to the bourgeoisie, especially since the left government of the era promised to place the press "outside of capitalism" by promulgating a press statute aimed at separating the editorial control of a paper from the ownership of the enterprise, nationalizing all printing shops, which were to be used equitably by teams of journalists, and prohibiting the formation of newspaper chains and press groups. Despite a series of close votes in the National Assembly, the bourgeoisie was able to avert various legislative efforts to pass such statutes, and after 1947, the bourgeoisie regained both political and ideological control in general.

Without the protection of the press statute promised at liberation, the capitalist "marketplace" soon began to eliminate the postwar, left-oriented press. The concentration process soon began to create newspaper chains and press groups; independent press enterprises, with some important exceptions, either were bought out and absorbed or went bankrupt. Especially hard hit were the engagé political newspapers: of the 27 right, center, and left political papers of the liberation era, only 3 remained by 1970. The political parties—which had a flourishing press at liberation—today have no public press whatsoever, with the partial exception of the Communists.

The concentration process in France follows that described by Bagdikian (1972) in the United States, Anders (1968) in Germany, Murdock and Golding (1973) in the United Kingdom, Hauser (1974) in Austria, Seppanen (1974) in Scandinavia, and Suzuki (1974) in Japan. In 1969, the eight largest press enterprises published 77 percent of all newspapers circulated in the United Kingdom, 71 percent in Austria, and 64 percent in Denmark. In France the eight largest enterprises only controlled 46 percent of all circulation, but of course this concentration was less advanced, having begun anew after the war (Nixon and Hahn 1971, p. 42). All of these researchers find similar factors at work leading to this general phenomenon of concentration of the press in advanced capitalist society. The four principal factors cited in this literature are all important elements in the French case: (1) the demise of papers in small towns and cities and the consequent dominance of the nearest metropolitan center in supplying information; (2) the monopolization of the aligned supply sectors (especially newsprint, press distribution, and printing equipment), which has led to soaring prices which small enterprises cannot absorb; (3) the role of monopolistic advertising agencies in patronizing only overtly depoliticized papers and shunning the small, politically involved publications; and (4) a general decline in the use of the press and in the profitability of press enterprises relative to the electronic media.

The literature on the concentration of the press also stresses that the press groups formed typically belong to members of the industrial bourgeoisie (Axel Springer in West Germany, Lord Thompson in the United Kingdom, Kurt Falk in Austria, and so on). This is precisely the case in France, where in 1975 major publications were held by the principal industrial magnates in wool (Le Figaro), textiles (L'Aurore), aviation (Jours de France), hospital equipment (Nouvel Observateur), and publishing (France-Soir), to name a few. The industrial bourgeoisie, this information makes clear, has regained its prewar domination over the Parisian Press. In the provinces, a different but equally powerful concentration process has produced a handful of monopolistic press enterprises, each of which dominates a vast geographical area with little or no competition.

The ideological importance of this restoration of the industrial bourgeoisie to its position of dominance in the press sector is quite clear, especially considered in conjunction with the successful campaign to eliminate all claims by journalists and their "journalist association movement" to participate in the formation of the political line and editorial content of the papers for which they work. In the 1970s, it was industrial magnates and monopolistic corporate units, who with only a handful of exceptions, owned the French press enterprises outright and controlled the decision-making hierarchy within each enterprise. When one sees this in conjunction with the fact that the French state controls the major news agency (Agence France Press) and the state's total monopoly on all television and radio in France, it becomes clear that the information media are strategic sites in the class struggle.

It is important to note that the principal strategy in the bourgeois-owned press enterprises and the state-controlled electronic media is not a direct effort at the political manipulation of the electorate. Rather the key ideological strategy in normal times is the depoliticization of everyday life; almost the entirety of bourgeois-owned or controlled media are highly sensationalist and more overtly involved in entertainment than in direct propaganda. This is noticeably more the case in France than in Germany (Alberts 1972) or in the United Kingdom (Murdock and Golding 1973), probably because of the highly politicized and polarized situation in France, and may well be the most effective strategy possible—outright conservative editorializing in the media would tend to offend the French political ear. When the chief of the editorial staff of the reactionary daily L'Aurore told me, "We are not a newspaper of the right, but of the center,"* it became clear to me that, in France, overt conservative rhetoric is essentially taboo.

This finding has important implications for the theory of ideology in advanced capitalist society, which all too often is conceived of from an instrumentalist and manipulative perspective. What the present study indicates, though, is that there are two strategies of bourgeois media ideology, one for normal times and one for times of crisis. During a crisis of the state, a political crisis, or a crisis of hegemony, the instrumentalist view is more nearly correct; in such times the more usual ideological strategy is abandoned in favor of a direct class polemic in the mass media. This happened, for instance, in France during the March 1978 legislative elections, when the pre-election polls predicted a victory for the united left. The bourgeois-owned press opened a bitter campaign which directly contradicted its usually low political profile. Such sudden eruptions of political ideology may be even more effective because of their rare use and last minute entrance into the fray.

During "normal" times (which, of course, are still times of class struggle), the principal ideological strategy operative in advanced capitalist societies involves three major aspects: (1) the depoliticization of the political process itself, turning the discussion from class relations to ephemeral issues and political personalities; (2) the depoliticization of everyday life by the encouraged nonapplication of political reflection to the work situation, media experiences, consumption patterns, and so forth; and (3) the multileveled encouragement of acquisitive consumerism. The mass media clearly play a key role on a tactical level in furthering this strategic effort to legitimize capitalist society by turning it into a depoliticized, atomized world of individual "consumers."

CLASS STRUGGLES WITHIN THE PRESS SECTOR

The concentration process in the press has led to the formation of ever larger corporate enterprises, which are today investing in electronic and printing equipment that has the capacity to eliminate a good portion of both the journalists and the printers required in the traditional press enterprise. This ascendancy of fixed capital over skilled labor power has several important implications, including both increased centralization of control within the enterprise (for example, an editor can call up any proposed article on a monitor

---

*Interview with Gilberg Guillminault, December 1, 1977.

screen and instantly make any desired changes) and between enterprises in one press group (for example, Robert Hersant can have material written in Paris under his direct supervision and then sent electronically to his entire chain of papers) as well as an increased profitability for the conglomerate, monopolistic firms capable of making these fixed capital investments. These changes give the conglomerate firms a competitive edge over the traditional shops and therefore become additional factors acting to increase concentration in the sector. The effect of this increased disjunction in the rate of profitability between the most and the least profitable enterprises in the printing sectors as a whole is to force the closing of the latter and the scrapping of their printing equipment. This increased concentration operates hand in hand with a partial "deindustrialization" of the sector; France has actually lost a considerable proportion of its productive capacity in printing. (This same phenomenon of monopolization leading to deindustrialization is also found in other industrial sectors, especially paper, steel, and textiles.)

With this partial dismantling of the French printing industry and the decreased need for skilled labor power at those shops equipped with the new electronic material, the rate of unemployment among printers has soared, and journalists have suffered a similar fate. But besides this quantitative decrease in the use of labor power there has been a concomitant qualitative decrease, that is, a massive "de-skilling" of many of the nournalists and printers who are fortunate enough still to have work. Journalists who once researched, wrote, and took responsibility for their articles are now being replaced by a "division of labor" that aims at an organizational coordination of more "specialized" workers, some of whom do research, others of whom write, while others rewrite. This division will allow greater control by editors and hence owners since articles will become the responsibility of the organization and no longer of a professional journalist. The printers who are being eliminated will be replaced with lowly skilled white-collar workers who will need only typing ability; after a text is typed into the photocomposition machines, the process is automated through the printing presses. Harry Braverman refers to the important political implications of this technological displacement of labor which "leads to the progressive elimination of the control functions of the worker, and their transfer to a device which is controlled . . . by management from outside the direct process" (1974, p. 212).

Hence the physical environment of workshops in modern industrial plants is radically different from traditional workshops, and in the press sector this difference is readily visible: the modern dust-free, photoelectronic, silent shop is in no sense the same environment as the ink-splattered, noisy, traditional print shop. Thus the ideological impact of the setting of the modern shops is almost diametrically opposed to what it was in the traditional shops. The physical layout and the new type of "mental" labor relations of production in the photoelectronic print shops structure an ideological setting in which the new "mental" labor workers (because of either their middle-strata* origins or their middle-strata socialization in the new relations of production) will not experience the polarization of capital and labor in the workplace that was characteristic in the past.

The French printing workshop (like those in many other industrial sectors) therefore will be decreasingly polarized along class lines and hence may well cease to be a significant site for transmitting the working-class tradition of voting for the left, and particularly for the Communist party, and communicating the political counterideology that has served to neutralize partially the dominant, pro-capitalist ideology of the educational system, the sensationalist media, consumerism, and so on. This hypothesis implies that the current evolution of industrial settings in advanced capitalist societies will serve as one of several factors making it increasingly difficult for the left to propagate counterideology and organize effective unions, on one hand, and viable political pressures on the other.

As several critics, especially John and Barbara Ehrenreich (1976), have pointed out, the absence of an analysis of labor's reaction to this degradation is a serious lacunae in Braverman's generally monumental work (1974) on the effects of monopoly capital on labor. In response Braverman himself claims (1976) that the reaction of the working class as a whole is difficult to analyze, due in part to the inadequacy of the conceptual apparatus currently available (especially the still impoverished analysis of the "new working class") and in part to the relatively long time spans over which such historical changes occur. Nevertheless, in the present study the reactions of the printers and journalists and their respective unions are quite clear.

---

*I use the term "middle strata" (see Therborn 1978) to avoid two problems with alternate terminology: (1) the term "new petty bourgeoisie" as used by Poulantzas (1975) does not adequately distinguish today's white collar labor force from the traditional petty bourgeois shopkeepers, and (2) the term "middle class" is self-contradictory, since a dialectical analysis is a <u>bipolar</u> class analysis; the necessary additional analysis of class segments and class strata enriches but does alter the primary contradiction in capitalist society between the bourgeoisie and the working class. White collar workers are seen in the present study as a stratum of the working class.

In the face of these threatening developments, the still powerful traditional unions in the press sector have become progressively more politicized. Both the journalists and the printers have had powerful unions through which they have struggled with the press bourgeoisie for better wages, hours, and work conditions. Until recently, these unions had a corporatist, professionalistic outlook. The major structural degradations in the positions of both journalists and printers, however, have led to increased activism on their part (in 1976, there were seven days when the entire French press was blocked from appearing by printer and journalist strikes) and increased involvement of both categories of press workers in France's major labor federations. This increase in political conflict in an industrial sector undergoing the structural changes mentioned above leads the owners of the corporate enterprises of the sector to call directly on the state to intervene; the complicity of the French state with the press bourgeoisie in recent years will be examined here closely.

Insofar as the future of the press will be a function of internal developments in the sector, one can only predict (1) increased concentration and monopolization; (2) press owners' increased control of both editorial and organizational aspects of press enterprises; (3) decreased use of labor, accompanied with a massive de-skilling of those who do remain; (4) the disappearance of both "journalists" and "printers" as labor categories, to be replaced by more "specialized" workers of increasingly middle-strata origins; and (5) the reduced ability of the new press workers to form effective unions with which to counter the increase in the rate of exploitation that will accompany the new equipment, pass on the working-class tradition of a left vote, and carry on the task of counterinforming themselves against the increasingly pervasive pro-capitalist ideology.

These are grim predictions. But I see few counterforces within the sector that are capable of neutralizing this evolution. If change is to come, if the French press is to be decentralized, demonopolized, and opened to the many perspectives and rich political debates of the postwar era, the changes will have to come from outside the sector. Only significant political change in the society as a whole can forestall the evolution of the press toward ever larger units controlled by a decreasing number of ever larger corporations.

THE CAPITALIST STATE AND THE "FREE" PRESS

The capitalist state has two principal tasks: the reproduction of the material conditions of production and the reproduction of the social conditions of accumulation that characterize capitalist society.

The French state's involvement in the media grows out of the second of these tasks, namely, the state's effort to contribute to the social reproduction of the existing conditions of production.

Claus Offe (1975, p. 127) has pointed out that the state's principal strategy is precisely to conceal its principal task of reproducing the inequalities of capitalism behind an ideology of equality: equal education, equality before the law, state responsiveness to all justified demands, and so forth. The capitalist state therefore presents itself as "neutral," and the guarantor of freedom of equality. One of the spheres in which it does so is, of course, its guarantee of a "free press."

Even though the conservative press is heavily dominant, there is in France a respectable left press, which is quite sizable and influential compared with the left press in most other advanced capitalist societies. Nonetheless, the contradiction buried in the principal ideological strategy of the capitalist state (the apparent protection of equality coupled with the real task of reproducing inequality) structures an ambiguity in the relation between the capitalist state and the "free press"—in France, as in every other capitalist society. While the French state does allow a free press (except during times of crisis), it intervenes heavily in the media to ensure that information is transmitted basically in the interests of the dominant class. In no other advanced capitalist state is the intervention of the state as pervasive as in France (see Smith 1977).

In France the state owns and controls the monopolistic press agency, Agence France Presse (AFP) and also maintains a complete monopoly on all electronic media in France, as Chapter 9 documents. Regardless of what the press does, therefore, the French state is in direct control of the reception and transmission of information by the AFP and the dissemination of this information over television and radio, which reach a far wider audience than do the print media. The French state is also the majority stockholder in one of the country's two monopolistic advertising agencies so it can also intervene decisively in the advertising sector.

State intervention in the print media is certainly more indirect than in the electronic media, but it is still quite considerable. Antonio Gramsci (1974) has described state intervention as being a "dialectic of consent and coercion," as is readily visible in the myriad of channels through which the French state intervenes in the "free press." At one extreme, the state grants important financial aid to the press and enforces laws assuring an egalitarian distribution of all publications, including those on the left. At the other extreme, as we shall see in detail, the French state has used censorship, seizure, suspension, and arrest of journalists and newspaper editors to force submission and compliance on the part of the press. The degree of direct intervention by the state in the content and political ideology of media enterprises increases dramatically during crises, as does the intervention of the capitalist state.

State intervention cannot be viewed simply since there are multiple logics structuring the state's purposes in its intervention. The so-called instrumentalist view of the state, which sees the state as nothing more than a tool of a unified dominant class, is therefore a clearly inadequate conceptual model. The capitalist state does, of course, attempt to act to further the long term interests of the dominant classes, but one must see that it does so with varying degrees of dependent representation of popular class interests, and that at times it produces legislation and policy opposed to the short term interests of particular dominant classes and class segments. In other words, the capitalist state serves, in effect, as a site of interclass struggle and negotiation, a sphere of political action where the interests of dominated classes can be partially institutionalized and realized. This potential is especially important in times of crisis of the state, as at the liberation, when important (though in the long-run inadequate) social-democratic legislation was passed that greatly altered the organizational and editorial makeup of the French press of the era.

But the capitalist state is not merely an arena of <u>interclass</u> confrontation; it is also a site of <u>capitalist intraclass</u> struggle and negotiation. As such, the state is informed by a second logic: the regulation of capitalist intraclass relations, whereby it acts to balance the sometimes directly opposed interests of different segments of the dominant class.* This intraclass function of the capitalist class has three sublogics.

First, the capitalist state acts to balance the sometimes contradictory interests of different industrial sectors. Policies that aid the bourgeoisie of one sector may well reduce the profitability of freedom of action of the bourgeoisie of other sectors. The capitalist state, therefore, attempts to promote the general interests of the bourgeoisie with respect to the particularistic interests of a given industrial sector. The state is charged with management of the capitalist economy as a whole; policies disproportionately favoring the bourgeoisie of a given sector eventually become contradictory to the profitability and viability of the economy as a whole.

---

*In fact, the multiple divisions in the dominant class make it more appropriate to analyze it as a "dominant power bloc," as I have argued elsewhere (Freiberg 1981).

Second, the state acts within a given industrial sector in favor of big capital over small and medium capital. Policies become more and more biased in favor of the highly concentrated, oligopolistic firms, leaving the remaining entrepreneurial corporate units to suffer the fate of the "marketplace."

Finally, state intervention is undertaken to protect and extend the interests and powers of state agencies and apparatuses per se. The capitalist state is itself a corporate structure, and it defends its self-interest while fulfilling its twin functions in class relations.

MODES OF JOURNALISM AND CLASS RELATIONS IN CAPITALIST SOCIETY

An analysis of the conflicting modes of journalism found in the French press raises the complex issue of the role of the press in ideological relations in capitalist society. Such an analysis must consider the press's double autonomy in a liberal society. On one hand, the content of the press is not directly structured by official agencies but is the product of a complexly mediated, partly autonomous industrial sector of privately owned enterprises. On the other, the ideological impact of the information (or non-information) presented in the press is mediated by a readership for whom the mass media are not the sole source of social, economic, and political information and analysis. Most critical research on mass communications ignores these bothersome complexities and utilizes simple deterministic models which assume that the media can be considered instruments in the hands of a unified dominant class for ideologically manipulating a banalized and thoroughly gullible population.

Given the absence of an adequate general model from which to study ideological relations, the scope of my remarks on the ideology is quite limited. Essentially, only one principal hypothesis is argued, namely, that the mass media contribute to ideological relations in capitalist society by participating in the reproduction of basic and pervasive <u>class divisions</u>. Along with other divisive culture institutions, especially the educational system, the media operate to differentiate the life experiences of different classes and class segments and hence play a role in producing social agents who are appropriately formed (and informed) for their differentiated social positions. In other words, part of the population must be readied for and kept satisfied with low-paying, low-prestige, strenuous, and sometimes dangerous occupations. At the other extreme, a smaller part of the population must be formed to execute the duties of management positions so as to further the accumulation of capital. They also must be prepared to <u>defend</u> the visible inequalities entailed by the capitalist mode of production, inequalities which are, interestingly, directly counter to the basic ideological principles formally espoused in the society's official discourse.

Analyses of the media's contribution to the reproduction process must always be undertaken within a framework that distinguishes the differential relations between the media and different social classes. To ignore this point is merely to produce a Frankfurt School-type of cultural critique which hypothesizes a general cretinization of the population as a whole by the modern media. Apart from its elitist perspective, this approach fails to recognize the empirical fact that different social classes choose widely different media experiences. One needs to account for <u>Le Monde</u> in France, the <u>New York Times</u> in the United States, <u>La Stampa</u> in Italy, and other dailies and serious newsweeklies in the advanced capitalist societies, not to mention the existence of informational films, television and radio programming, and so on. These nonsensationalist media products require treatment within a critical media theory for, whatever ideological function they fulfill for their elite consumers, they certainly do it in a radically different fashion than the sensationalist media do for their mass clientele.

The importance of the class differentials in media experience becomes clear when one adds to it the differences engendered by other culture institutions. Thus Pierre Bourdieu and Jean-Claude Passeron (1970) have argued that children emerge from the home with differential cultural and linguistic capital divided along class lines, and the study by Christian Baudelot and Roger Establet (1972) finds that the educational system tracks these children along two separate pathways determined largely by class origins. There are, of course, many other social and cultural institutions involved in this continual, multi-leveled reinforcement of the early differences structured by the home and school and reinforced by differential media experiences. The task of this process is not only to divide the future work force into future "manual" and "mental" laborers, but simultaneously to legitimize the existing differential in France between the wealthy and the poor. France, one should realize, <u>has the greatest inequality between the highest and lowest salaries and between the wealthiest and poorest individuals of any advanced capitalist society</u>.

It is difficult to assess the effectiveness of political ideology in the sensationalist press. One does not want to assume, as Stewart Ewen (1973) points out, that conservative media content has a direct linear effect on consumers. On the contrary, Miliband (1969, p. 236) has written of the mass media's historical inability to deliver the vote during elections. The present study finds precisely the same phenomenon: the reconquest of the left-oriented, politically active, liberation era press by the industrial bourgeoisie. The press's concomitant switch to a conservative (if overtly depoliticized) perspective, even though reinforced by the new presence of the consistently conservative perspective of the state-controlled electronic media, has in no way corresponded to any political shift in the French electorate.

This introduction has dealt in a cursory fashion with a great many theoretical points. The pages that follow contain highly detailed accountings of the actual processes by which the French press is being transformed, for it seems to me that future theoretical advances in political economy-oriented analyses of the mass media—and of ideological relations in general—must be based on detailed case studies.

PART I
PROPERTY RELATIONS
AND THE PRESS ENTERPRISE

INTRODUCTION TO PART I

Part 1 focuses on how the press is organized in France, that is, in an advanced capitalist society, studying three aspects of this question: (1) What is the nature of the patterns of ownership in the press sector? (2) To what extent is ownership of an enterprise synonymous with control of the editorial and political line of its publications? and (3) To what extent and through what channels are press owners influenced by broader segments of the dominant class?

Chapter 1 discusses the patterns of ownership that characterize the press sector and their development since World War II. The key phenomenon here has been the <u>concentration</u> of press enterprises, the simultaneous reduction in the total number of enterprises and the continual growth of the larger at the expense of the surviving smaller enterprises. In this aspect, France is like practically every other advanced capitalist society. What makes the French case valuable, however, is the fact that a revolution in press ownership in 1944 disrupted the concentration process in the prewar press. At the liberation, all but a dozen press enterprises were confiscated from their prewar owners and given over to teams of journalists who had distinguished themselves by publishing clandestine newspapers during the war. This transition changed the organization of press ownership in three important ways. First, the prewar press enterprises had been owned in large part by the industrial bourgeoise; after the war, the new owner-journalists were for the most part of middle-strata origins. Second, the prewar press enterprise owners were for the most part conservative, as was the political line of their newspapers; in contrast, approximately half of the postwar owners were Socialists, Communists, or left Christians. Third, the prewar press had begun to concentrate into press groups; the postwar press dissolved these corporate structures and was characterized by its small, independent enterprises.

In the three decades since the war, the ownership of the press has undergone a "restoration," which has been largely a product of the process of concentration. Not only has this process returned the ownership, and hence control, of most press enterprises to the bourgeoisie, but it has also favored the larger conglomerate enterprises over the smaller, producing an ever increasing control of the sector by monopolistic corporate units and multiple-enterprise press groups. In the provinces, the small liberation enterprises have closed or been absorbed by today's giant regional monopolistic newspapers with names like "Sud-Ouest," "Ouest France," and "Sud-Est"—precisely because they do indeed cover vast geographical regions of France, sometimes in a total monopoly. Unlike their Parisian counterparts, owners of most of these provincial press enterprises have accumulated this capital inside the press sector. I will refer to these owners in the press sector as the "press bourgeoisie."

In Paris the situation is more complicated since the major newspapers and newsweeklies, with only a few exceptions, no longer belong to the liberation-era press bourgeoisie but have been bought out by industrial and financial capital. The owners of the Parisian press are therefore not "press bourgeoisie" in the strict sense of the term but industrial bourgeoisie from other sectors who have purchased the liberation papers. A brief look at the situation of several major publications in 1975 underscores this point: <u>Le Figaro</u> was owned by France's major wool industrialist; <u>L'Aurore</u> (another major daily) by the major cotton magnate; <u>France-Soir</u> and <u>Le Point</u> (the largest circulation daily and an important newsweekly) by the world's largest publishing-related multinational corporation (Hachette); and <u>Nouvel-Observateur</u> (an important socialistic newsweekly) by the leading health-care goods industrialist, to name a few. In their role as press owners, these industrialists who penetrate the press sector with capital accumulated outside the sector will also be referred to as "press bourgeoisie," although the implications of this reconquest of the liberation press by the industrial bourgeoisie must be examined in detail.

Chapter 1 also presents a discussion of authority relations in the press enterprise. These <u>organizational hierarchies exhibit an induced reproduction of the general class relations that characterize contemporary capitalist society</u>. That is, property relations determine authority relations in the enterprise, which in turn shape both the financial and editorial aspects of each enterprise. One of the dreams of the liberation had been to separate these two functions, having journalists and editors responsible for the editorial content of their newspaper and removing this power from the realm of capital. <u>Le Figaro</u>, for example, was run in this manner from 1944 until 1969; today, however, all power to determine its content and political line has been centralized in the hands of its controversial owner, Robert Hersant.

Finally, Chapter 1 examines the links between the press sector and the dominant class as a whole. What becomes apparent is that although the press bourgeoisie has both the right and the organizational structures needed to determine and control the content and political line of its publications, it is influenced at the same time by broader interests of the dominant class through a series of necessary exchanges. The press bourgeoisie obtains the advertising income,

PART I: PROPERTY RELATIONS / 21

loans, and information sources it needs to run its enterprises; in return, broader segments of the dominant class obtain the ideological support they need on both specific issues (support on topical social and political problems) and general issues (support of their social and political worldview).

Chapter 2 presents three case studies of monopolistic press groups chosen to illustrate different types of monopolistic practices. First a recently dismantled traditional press empire is examined. Built with capital accumulated external to the press sector and based on an anachronistic, labor-intensive structure, this press group was little more than a collection of publications owned by interlocking holding companies, and its atomistic structure necessitated a good deal of administrative and technical duplication, as each press enterprise was a separate entity. In contrast to this nineteenth-century model of a press group, the corporate structures and strategies of two capital-intensive corporations in the press sector are also examined. By far the largest corporate unit in the press sector is Hachette, perhaps the world's largest publishing-related multinational, with major holdings in the paper industry, the printing industry, press distribution, and retail sales of written material as well as its publishing enterprises. It is therefore a powerful vertical monopoly capable of protecting its profitability by manipulating its intersubsidiary dealings. The power of this major corporate unit is enhanced by its interlocks with one of France's major banks, which itself, we shall see, is deeply involved in both the press and the electronic media. Robert Hersant's recently constructed newspaper chain is also based on a capital-intensive strategy. Its chief logic is maximal centralization permitted by sophisticated new electronic technology.

The transition from the labor-intensive press empire of Prouvost to the capital-intensive empires of Hachette and Hersant provides the material for a case study of the effects on the work force of the unemployment and de-skilling of workers brought about during such developments. The constantly increasing concentration of the press in ever larger corporate units and their incessant replacement of living labor with fixed capital investment in new technology leads to what Harry Braverman analyzed as the progressive elimination of the control functions of the workers and their transfer to management (1974, p. 212). The details of the strategies and struggles internal to the press sector will be analyzed in Part 2, after we have traced the monopolization process on the organizational level.

Chapter 3 presents a study of the organizational anomaly of the press sector: the worker-participation structure of Le Monde. The argument is made that Le Monde's editorial independence and recent conversion to an openly socialistic position must be understood as a direct function of its worker-participation organizational structure. Le Monde's attacks on capitalist society are possible only because it is owned by its journalists, editors, and clericals. Furthermore, this exceptional organizational independence has been maintained only by a series of successful defensive moves against incessant attacks from those whom Le Monde threatens. These attacks are analyzed as concrete moments of class struggle; Le Monde's dissidence is a threat not only to the ruling conservative government but to the delicate balance of class relations that characterizes contemporary France.

1
OWNERSHIP AND INFLUENCE IN THE PRESS ENTERPRISE

PATTERNS OF OWNERSHIP

In looking at the ownership of the French press, one wants to account for the <u>structure</u> of ownership as well as the <u>identity</u> of its present-day owners. In other words, one first needs to account for the changing topography of ownership itself due to the extensive concentration of press enterprises that has occurred since World War II. Then one can investigate the class origins of individual and corporate press owners as well as the origins of the capital they invest in these enterprises.

The Concentration Process

The press sector in France has been undergoing active concentration since the turn of the century. While the total French print run is roughly comparable to what it was in 1914, there has been a consistent erosion of the number of publications. Whereas there were 60 Parisian and 242 provincial daily newspapers in 1914, in 1975 there were only 10 and 75, respectively (<u>Presse Actualité</u>, May 1977). The average paper today therefore has a far larger circulation than papers in the past. In the provinces the magnitude of this shift is particularly impressive: there are less than one-third the number of provincial titles today as in 1914, while the provincial press prints 85 percent more copies than it did then. Hence the average provincial newspaper today has a circulation fully 600 percent higher than did its pre-World War I equivalent. However, it is

TABLE 1.1

Print Runs in the Largest Newspapers, 1945-69
(thousands)

Year	4 Major Parisian	All Other Parisian	20 Major Provincial	All Other Provincial
1945	991	3,463	2,537	4,977
1969	3,066	1,530	5,377	2,145

Source: Guillo Lohan, "Les Concentrations dans la presse quotidienne et leurs incidences sur les marchés de l'information et de la publicité" (Thèse, Université de Paris I, 1970).

the very largest of the remaining titles, principally, that have enjoyed this massive increase in average print run, as the data in Table 1.1 indicate.

While the circulation of the four largest Parisian papers has more than tripled (and the 20 largest provincial papers more than doubled) since World War II, the circulation of the remaining titles in both groups has fallen by 50 percent. Concentration of the press works in two directions: while it swells the larger titles, it shrinks the smaller.

The concentration process moves swiftly, as the French case makes perfectly clear. Although the events of the occupation and liberation reversed the concentration process, in the 35 years since the war, the Parisian press has returned to its prewar status. Today, as then, it is dominated by a small number of large circulation, highly sensationalist newspapers. In 1930, the four largest Parisian papers together put out 68 percent of the total number printed. Liberation authorities confiscated these four papers, altering the situation dramatically; in 1945, only 22 percent of the Parisian print run was produced by the four largest papers. By 1968 the prewar pattern had been reestablished: the four largest papers accounted for 67 percent of the Parisian total, and by 1975, fully 73 percent (Presse Actualité, February and May 1977).

Seen in a European perspective, press concentration in France is in fact quite similar to that in other countries. Between 1960 and 1970, France, Italy, Great Britain, and Sweden all lost about 16 percent of their general-information daily papers. In West Germany and Denmark, fully 33 percent of all newspapers disappeared during this same period (UNESCO Statistical Year Book, 1971, p. 181). Press concentration in France is actually moderate compared with other European countries (see Table A.1) due to the fact that the liberation gave birth to a whole new generation of independent papers.

It should also be noted that while the concentration process reduces the number of press enterprises, efforts are made occasionally to launch new dailies. In 1972 there were only eight newspapers, and one of these, Combat, closed down in 1974. However, several new small circulation papers started up: Libération (1973, independent left), Le Quotidien de Paris (1974, socialistic), Le Quotidien du Peuple (1975, Trotskyist), Rouge (1976, Trotskyist), and Le Matin de Paris (1977, socialistic).* One effort at opening a large circulation daily, J'Informe (1977, conservative), was a short-lived financial disaster. In any case, these efforts do indicate that new papers can be born, thereby attenuating to some extent the concentration process, which drives independent enterprises out of business.

Press Concentration in Paris

Of the 31 dailies published in Paris in March 1939, only ten reopened after the liberation, and only three of these still existed in 1975. The new enterprises that began at the liberation proved to be extremely short lived: 16 of 26 Parisian papers beginning after the war were closed within three years, and three more soon followed. As for newspapers that have been opened in recent years, the mortality rate is extremely high. Seven attempts lasted less than one year, including three very well-financed efforts (see Table A.2).

These enterprises have disappeared in several ways. Many closed, unable to compete for advertising with the larger enterprises. Others, often with appreciable circulations, were bought out and merged with larger papers in an attempt by the larger enterprise to take advantage of their already established readership. The contemporary newspaper, L'Aurore, for example, is a graveyard of earlier titles (see Figure 1.1).

Most surviving newspapers owe their continued existence to their inclusion in a press group, a system which allows unprofitable dailies to be supported by the more profitable periodical publications of the group and also to receive occasional direct injections of funds from the interested individuals and institutions who stand behind the groups. In 1977, of the eight principal Parisian dailies, only one,

---

*Of these, by 1979, only Libération and Le Matin de Paris remained as daily newspapers.

FIGURE 1.1

The Building of the Modern L'Aurore

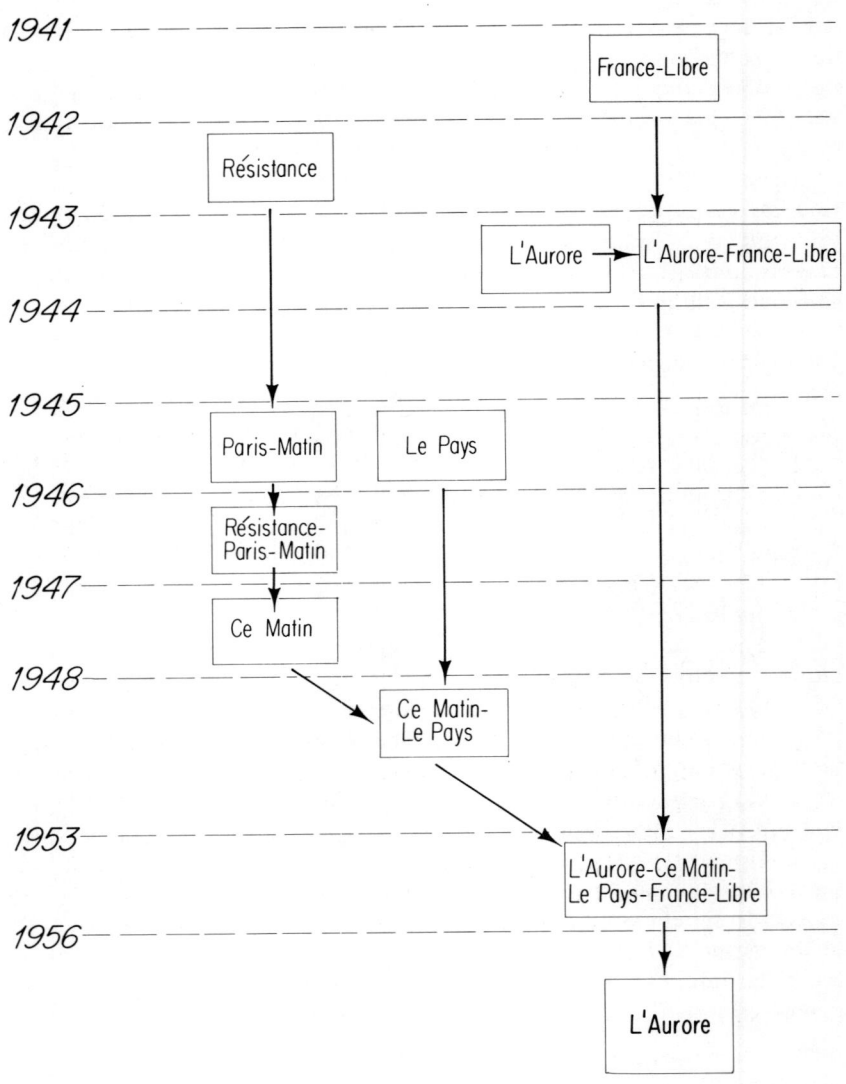

Source: Presse Actualité, March 1974.

Le Monde, existed outside of such a group. Even the viability of the Communist party paper, L'Humanité, was based on the same principal as the bourgeois-owned papers: the CP press group published four dailies and more than a dozen major periodicals.

Within the press groups, the allied publications not only help support the dailies directly (all major Parisian dailies except Le Monde reported a yearly deficit for 1975 and 1976), they back up these dailies in numerous other ways. They are the Parisian equivalent of the provincial monopolistic structures* for they allow the group to use similar patterns of centralization: group-owned advertising-booking agencies, shared printing centers, shared billing offices and distribution means, and so on. Furthermore, they provide a powerful bargaining position for dealing with advertisers, who are sold packages of advertising in the group's journals. In the classic pattern, this allows these press groups a competitive edge over independent units.

These press groups vie with each other like any competing giant corporations. For example, there were fierce battles in a region just to the south of Paris between two of the largest press groups, with tactics including undercutting advertising pricing, making special offers (often at a loss) to delivery and retail establishments, and offering specially tailored deliveries. Eventually these two competitors negotiated a truce that arranged for guarantees of noncompetition, the opening of a new shared printing plant, and an agreement to work together to pressure eight local independent publications out of business (Bellanger 1974, p. 436).

Press Concentration in the Provinces

The provincial press as a whole was greatly affected by World War II. In 1939, 63 percent of all papers were printed in Paris, while in 1945 this figure dropped to 38 percent, and by 1975 to 35 percent. Why? To begin with the German occupation was more harsh within than outside Paris, and many of the clandestine papers were printed elsewhere (Paxton 1972, p. 223). Non-Paris-based journalist teams thus got an opportunity to open local papers, many of which became enfranchised at the liberation. Furthermore, the many shortages

---

*By "monopolistic" I imply that a given newspaper has no significant set of competing dailies in a given region. This is often the case in contemporary advanced capitalist societies, particularly the United States, where 97 percent of cities have only one newspaper (Nixon 1968). See Eversole (1971) and Tuchman (1974).

that plagued liberated France made it difficult to ship the Parisian press quickly enough to meet the deadlines for provincial distribution. Most important, however, was the fact that the significance of local news mushroomed in the provinces as the degree of provincial industrialization and urbanization shot up from its stunted prewar levels.

By 1958, most of the liberation press in the provinces had been silenced, and, with a few exceptions, only large-scale press enterprises remained. At this point, an entirely new round of concentration began, linking the remaining large provincial papers to varying degrees and in varying ways. One particularly nefarious type of linkage was the "advertising pooling" arrangement, whereby large provincial papers formed de facto monopolies on advertising. That is, they negotiated agreements to coordinate their composing and printing of advertising. The common advertising-booking agencies they formed were then able to sell space to advertisers for the group as a whole. Since the same ad was reproduced identically in all the papers, it was only composed once. Hence it cost less to produce per paper and so sold at a lower price, undercutting the price at which independent newspapers could afford to sell their advertising space. Once begun, this type of merger spread over the whole of France in just a few years.

At the very forefront of this movement stood Robert Hersant, who nearly three decades later would stand at the helm of two of Paris' largest daily papers but who, at the moment, remained an obscure personality. Rich from his successful automobile magazine, he bought a series of small, financially failing liberation newspapers in the center of France, which he affiliated into a larger paper, Centre-Presse, to accumulate a circulation adequate to begin to interest advertisers. An idea was born. In similar fashion, the socialist Paris-Normandie in Rouen linked with several small local papers to form a group. In 1962, another group formed in Alsace; three small papers announced a new, combined circulation of 153,000 copies. In the South, Gaston Defferre's socialist Le Provençal of Marseille, joined with two conservative papers. In 1963, three major groups were formed in the Bordeaux, Lyon, and Grenoble areas; each group's new circulation was above 400,000. This concentration increased the pressure on the remaining (locally monopolistic) papers; their survival depended upon concentrating into similar groups in order to share expenses.

This process snowballed, and ever larger units were formed. In 1966, Ouest-France, in Rennes, which already had a wide circulation, set up a group totaling over 900,000 in circulation. The next year saw the formation of an even larger conglomerate, "Province No. 1," which spread over 19 departments and had a circulation of 1.2 million. Province No. 1 involved the merger of two major press enterprises, which set up the following corporations to pool their affairs for greater profit: a common news agency, a common print shop, and a common advertising-booking agency.

Certain tactical maneuvers typical of the monopolization process are highly visible in this particular merger between two monopolistic papers: <u>Le Progrès de Lyon</u> and <u>Le Dauphiné Libéré</u>. <u>Le Progrès de Lyon</u>, which dates back to 1859, was one of only ten provincial papers allowed to reopen after World War II. In the past it had been close to both the radical and socialist movements, and had carried articles by Louis Blanc, Gambetta, Emile Zola, and Jean Jaurès. It was one of the earliest papers in France to warn about the rise of fascism. As it grew after the war, however, it progressively lost its political voice and became increasingly sensationalist and depoliticized. In 1963 it absorbed the two daily papers of St. Etienne, and soon afterward it bought out two more daily newspapers in Marseille. The more it expanded, the more directly it competed with its rival, <u>Le Dauphiné Libéré</u> of Grenoble, which was similarly absorbing papers surrounding its zone of action. A fierce period of conflict followed, with price cutting, early morning undercutting deliveries, threats to advertisers, and the like. Finally, the finances of <u>Le Dauphiné Libéré</u> were overextended by a costly offensive move: it had opened a new printing center at the very edge of Lyon. The escalation of the war had gone too far for the bookkeepers: discussions were opened between the two giants (each with a circulation of about 600,000 copies), and the negotiations proved fruitful. Four common printing centers were opened, and the journalists of the two enterprises, with considerable layoffs, were reorganized into an independent agency that would supply articles not only to those two papers but to any other interested paper in the area. In the changeover, more than three hundred employees and printers were fired (<u>Presse Actualité</u>, December 1966). The story is not atypical; that of <u>Sud-Ouest</u>, for example, runs quite parallel. By 1969, it was all but impossible to run an independent paper in the provinces. Nine major provincial press groups accounted for almost 75 percent of the daily circulation; the 15 largest enterprises accounted for practically 90 percent (Guillo Lohan 1970, p. 94).

The process of concentration was encouraged by the practices and structures of France's two dominant, monopolistic advertising corporations: Publicis and Havas. Together they handled the advertising for 50 major provincial dailies and for fully two-thirds of the papers and press groups with circulations above 100,000. They acted as a spur to concentration by disfavoring the independent papers, preferring to supply more profitable advertising to the centralized advertising-booking agencies of the major press groups. In 1969, for example, the nine largest regional groups received

TABLE 1.2

Percentage of Daily Provincial Newspapers
Printed by the Largest Firms

	1951		1973	
Enterprises	All Papers Printed	Press Enterprises	All Papers Printed	Press Enterprises
4 largest	24.6	3.7	39.3	9.5
8 largest	39.1	7.4	56.7	19.0
12 largest	49.7	11.0	75.3	28.0

Source: François Denoël, "La Presse Quotidienne," Les Cahiers Français (October-December 1976).

504 million francs of advertising, as opposed to what all the other papers of provincial France together received, which totaled only 165 million, less than one-third as much (Guillo Lohan 1970, p. 96). Given this quasi-monopoly by the largest regional groups on advertising income, it is hardly a surprise to find that by 1973 more than three-fourths of the daily papers printed in the provinces were produced by the 12 largest firms (see Table 1.2).

Who Owns the Press Enterprises?

Since editorial power is determined, in the final analysis, by relations of ownership within each enterprise, attention must be given to precisely who these owners are. A given member of the press bourgeoisie, of course, can be financially active in other sectors, and in fact many of the current "press bourgeoisie" are industrial magnates in non-press-related fields. This pattern of industrial bourgeoisie owning the major newspapers has developed twice in recent French history, indicating that control of the media is an important priority for the French industrial bourgeoisie.

During the Third Republic most of the major papers were held by the most important industrial entrepreneurs of the time, including the Comité des Forges steel trust, presided over by the powerful Wendel and Schneider families. Other major papers were owned by Prouvost (wool), Depuy (paper) and Darblay (wheat) (see Table A.3).

Only three major newspapers escaped their grasp: <u>Le Petit Journal</u> (which was failing quickly and only circulating 175,000 copies), <u>Le Matin</u> (also failing and only printing 300,000, a mere fraction of the 1.5 million it had printed in 1917), and <u>L'Echo de Paris</u> (in even deeper trouble, its entire staff of journalists having quit in order to produce <u>L'Epoque</u>, a far right journal that welcomed in the German invaders) (Albert and Terrou 1974, p. 97). Thus, with very few exceptions, the press enterprises of the Third Republic were directly owned by major industrial magnates.

<u>The Events of the Liberation</u>

The confiscation of these papers at the liberation was in part a response to their collaboration, but it was also a political decision on the part of the liberation authorities to remove the industrial bourgeoisie from its position of direct domination of the press. One clear example of this policy was the case of <u>Le Temps</u>, a paper which had closed down when Nazi troops entered the "Free French Zone" in 1942, and which had in no way collaborated. Nevertheless, there was never any question in de Gaulle's provisional government, which was made up of an alliance of the Socialist, Communist, and left Christian (MRP) parties, of allowing the enterprise to reopen. Partly this was a function of <u>Le Temps</u>'s conciliatory position at the time of the prewar Munich accords, but mostly it was because the paper was owned directly by the Wendel and Schneider steel interests.* Hubert Beuve-Méry, who founded <u>Le Monde</u> on the presses of <u>Le Temps</u> after the war, claims that an arbitrary mechanism was developed for confiscating <u>Le Temps</u>: November 26, 1942, was selected as the final date for all papers in the southern zone to have been closed down.† This date was chosen purposely, Beuve-Méry (1956) argues, because <u>Le Temps</u> had shut down on November 29.

After the liberation, the confiscated enterprises were given to the left-oriented teams of journalists who had put out the clandestine press during the war. Many of these individuals were aware that there would be new efforts by the industrial bourgeoisie to gain

---

*Until 1942, German occupation was of only the northern half of France, with the puppet Vichy regime of Maréchal Pétain ruling the south. Enterprises were considered to have collaborated if they continued publication under direct German occupation.

†See Stanley Hoffman's analysis (1974) of the real versus the "official" version of the liberation.

control in the field of printed information, and therefore they pressured the state to promulgate the protective press statutes that had been promised at the liberation. Several early efforts failed, and after 1947, with the general bourgeois restoration well advanced, such legislation could no longer be passed. The fate of the liberation press was determined: they were sentenced to die in the capitalist marketplace. One by one as the liberation papers found themselves in financial troubles, the industrial bourgeoisie bought itself back into the press. By 1975 the situation showed at least as intense a penetration of the press sector as before the war. Major papers were held by various magnates, each dominant in the industrial sector where he had originally accumulated his capital: Jean Prouvost (wool), Fernand Béghin (paper), Marcel Boussac (cotton and textiles), Marcel Dassault (aviation), and so forth (see Table A.4).

Thus, by 1975 the Parisian press had once again fallen largely under the direct control of elements of the industrial bourgeoisie, though there were several unsuccessful efforts of other industrial bourgeoisie to penetrate the sphere of the press. In 1956 the Dupuy family (paper and oil) attempted to open a major daily paper, Le Temps de Paris, which never caught the public's eye and failed, at a loss of many millions. In 1965 Marcel Dassault attempted to open a major newspaper, Vingt-Quatre Heures, which was also an immediate failure. Finally, in 1977, came J'Informe, backed by the Michelin family, among others. Like the two papers mentioned above, it was set up to compete directly with Le Monde,* and it suffered the same fate.

Given my hypothesis of the past and present domination of the press by the industrial bourgeoisie, it seems worthwhile to investigate why these efforts by major industrial figures failed. All of them had more than adequate initial capital and excellent prospects to attract advertising since their backers enjoyed a wide range of contacts in the business world. But these papers failed to attract readers, and no matter how much pressure is put on advertisers and advertising agencies, they cannot justify for long placing ads in a paper that attracts little readership. We will later see that newspapers have class-specific readerships, and among the evening papers, the working class had its France-Soir, while the liberal bourgeoisie and the new middle strata had their Le Monde. We also know that newspaper readers tend to be loyal to a paper to which they have become habituated (Presse Actualité, February 1978).

---

*See the analysis below of the class content of these efforts to reduce Le Monde's effective socialist-oriented journalism.

It is probably the case, therefore, that to open a new newspaper, one must appeal to a newly developed class segment or, at the very least, a new political faction. The new leftist papers, for example, have a readership that was created politically during the May 1968 events. Similarly, the relative success of the recent socialistic daily Le Matin is due probably in large part to a readership forged by the efforts of the "union de la gauche," a united front of the Socialist, Communist and Left-Radical parties, during the mid-1970s. If this hypothesis is correct, it implies that one does not easily open a successful daily paper with a strategy of luring a readership from other papers by advertising campaigns; instead, one must spot a readership (that is to say, a sociologically defined readership) that has no paper.

AUTHORITY RELATIONS

The importance of investigating the patterns of ownership that characterize the press sector is clear: press enterprises are managed like any capitalist enterprise: with legal ownership comes the right to make all final decisions, including editorial policies. Also, the class origins of the individual agents filling the hierarchically ranked positions demonstrate an induced reproduction of the class relations of the society as a whole. In contemporary France, for the most part, press owners are either industrial bourgeoisie from other sectors or press bourgeoisie who have built large press groups. Directors and editors-in-chief, in turn, tend to come from the intelligentsia, which is drawn from the upper middle strata (Bertaux 1977). Journalists come from still more modest middle-strata backgrounds and have far less education than directors of papers; in 1970, only 17.6 percent had finished any post-high school studies (Cayrol 1973, p. 223). Finally, the printers are without exception from working-class origins. Of course, practically any capitalist industrial setting exhibits this pattern of class relations in its relations of production with equal fidelity. These relations, however, take on an acute and particular importance in the press (or other media), where there is production not only of surplus value, but also of the information through which bourgeois domination over representations of society is assured.

The Subordination of Journalists:
The Censorship Process

Journalists are in a juridical position of subordination, equal in status to any other employee, with no more and no less protection from arbitrary decisions by their employers. The one exception to this is the "right of conscience" (clause de conscience) which comes from a 1935 law permitting a journalist to quit a paper with an appreciable indemnification if that paper undergoes major changes in editorial policy or change of management. This law is of interest because it sets a precedent recognizing the right of a journalist not to be forced to write what he does not believe. Nonetheless, the right to quit does little to change the fact that the editorial policy of French papers is strictly set by their owners; the right of conscience only assures the disappearance of those who would be the dissidents. Although the clause was originally a product of an idealistic journalist demand, its principal historical function has been to aid the industrial bourgeoisie in their reconquest of the liberation press. Later, we shall see, for example, how Robert Hersant has used this mechanism to eliminate most left-oriented journalists from the newspapers he has taken over, en route to replacing them with more conservative journalists of his own choosing.

In any press enterprise, a hierarchy is set up to inspect articles.* The structuring of authority in the press industry is particularly capable of enforcing this multilayered censorship without its seeming to be done directly across the owner-journalist line because, except at the very highest levels, the hierarchy is composed largely of journalists who have worked their way up through years of trustworthy service. One enters as a reporter whose main responsibility is to reword what comes in over the wire services. Then, if all goes well, one becomes a full-fledged journalist in the "service" (field) of one's interests. Here one covers minor events, until one is eventually called on to write increasingly important articles. In time one might become the assistant department head (sous-chef), that is, be put in charge of three or four other journalists who cover one portion of the field handled by one's particular department. These several assistants report to the department head (chef de service), who in turn reports to the editors and finally to the editor-in-chief. As one works one's way up this ladder, one is handed authority little by little, and one moves progressively from the production of articles to the rereading of articles by those beneath oneself in the hierarchy. Most editorial censorhip, thus, is done by one's colleagues a step above, who can hardly be called—and are seldom thought of—as "management." Yet, they do operate to police the content of articles as per the norms set, in the final analysis, by the press owners.

---

*See Gaye Tuchman's (1978, pp. 31, 156ff.) discussion of this phenomenon in the U.S. newsroom.

Important articles are read by the whole hierarchy, and changes can be made at successive levels. Philippe Simonnot, ex-journalist at Le Monde, published an intriguing account of this multileveled rereading:

> I had proposed for a paper of mine that was to appear on page one a title that used the active form of the verb. It was transformed by the department head to the passive form, and then changed back to the active form by the editor-in-chief, and so in the end it appeared as I had originally written it.
> Thus, at each stage of rereading, the hierarchy was able to manifest its power in a purely formal manner. Form alone, the control of it, allowed the exercising of power in "a pure state," since it was really of no importance if the title appeared in the active or passive. On the contrary, what was important, even essential, was to demonstrate to one's subordinate one's power over him. (Simonnot 1977, p. 113)

After selecting the journalist at two different levels (both hiring and assigning him), and after censoring his articles through a multileveled filtering system, top management has two further means of intervention. First, there is the decision as to which articles will appear and which will not: there are always more articles written than there is available space. Selection allows further filtering. Second, a tight control is maintained at the highest levels over the choice of headlines.

In the story of Philippe Simonnot this whole operation becomes highly visible. His problems actually began because of an article that was not censored; unfortunately for him, it passed through the usual hierarchy and appeared on March 8, 1976. Simonnot was Le Monde's expert on petroleum matters, and this particular article was a moderately revealing study of how the French state had pressured certain oil interests to form its nationalized firm Elf-Aquitaine. Simonnot had obtained some of his information from a classified government document in which he found an explanation of the entire affair written by a government functionary. His undoing was that the censorship channels at Le Monde had no way of knowing the origins of his information and therefore had no reason to censor his article. Within days the minister of finance and the prime minister himself were demanding revenge: the firing of Simonnot.

Three different but reinforcing moments of censorship were operating in this case: (1) corporate pressures (the oil interests were embarrassed by the revelation and were no doubt pressuring the finance minister); (2) state pressures (the finance minister and even the prime minister were embarrassed by the fact that a functionary of theirs had allowed Simonnot to get to this information, and they, too, were directly pressuring for rectification; and (3) organizational pressures (Le Monde's director was embarrassed that his internal organizational channels had allowed such an article to appear, and he saw no choice but to cut Simonnot off to avoid threatened state retaliations at Le Monde).

A recent sociological study of censorship in the French press found that according to the journalists of the three local papers of the city of Lille, relatively little direct censorship actually occurs; most changes made on the editorial level are minor. This does not mean, however, that there is little censorship, only that it operates principally in another fashion:

> The intervention of the hierarchy leads to a pervasive attitude which journalists call "self-censorship," that is, a method to prevent later criticism by deforming or prestructuring information. Self-censorship is the conformity of the journalist to the line imposed by those who manage the journal by adapting information to their expectations. (Le Journalist, January 1977)

The communication from the owner to the journalists of the political and social line of a given publication takes place principally through informal channels. But occasionally an editor commits to paper the limits of what journalists may and may not write, and one such document fell into my hands. I refer to a circular signed by the editor-in-chief of Ouest-France dated November 22, 1976, and addressed "to all journalists." It gives a flavor of the quite direct editorial policies that journalists must respect and tells them in no uncertain terms just what are the appropriate social positions, politics, and taboo topics for Ouest-France:

> We live in a world which, more than ever, has a need to hear calm news [une information sereine] to which one can refer, and which only adult journalists, that is to say, responsible journalists can produce. . . .
> Our references to the Church must clearly signify that we cannot, given the difficult times in which the Church finds itself, speak of the Church like any other title of the regional press. . . .
> The more open we are, the more we must know what we stand for, that is, Christian Democrats searching to help mankind to open up and to avoid the risks of political

adventures which, from whichever direction they come, might compromise the exercise of elementary liberties.

A stunning example of the subordinate position of journalists comes from the Time-like newsweekly, L'Express. An internal petition supporting Socialist François Mitterrand in his presidential bid against Republican Valery Giscard d'Estaing received 109 signatures out of 120 journalists. Nevertheless, they were not permitted to write an article even hinting at their support of the Socialist candidate; the weekly was solidly behind the Republican candidate chosen by its owner (L'Humanité, May 17, 1974). Another example from the same magazine is provided by sociologist Maurice Duverger, now a major editorialist at Le Monde. He writes that he quit L'Express in 1965 because its owner, Jean-Jacques Servan-Schreiber, "demanded a total orthodoxy of all who wrote for his magazine" (Duverger 1977, p. 111).

This pattern of total centralization of control of newspaper content is not broken by the few instances of noncapitalist, or non-ordinary-type capitalist publications. Le Monde is the case I know best. Although this journalist-owned paper is free of the division between owners and journalists, control in the paper is as centralized as in any other paper. Decisions of any importance are never taken without checking up to the next higher level.*

Hierarchy and Authority in the
Communist Party Press Group

The press group of the Communist party, whether taken as a whole or publication by publication, exhibits a strict centralism. The CP is totally opposed to journalist participation, and in fact their analysis directly parallels that of the press bourgeoisie on this point. In a recent interview, the director of the CP's press and information office stated, "If the journalists at Le Monde decide to have a certain political line, it makes sense only because they happen to own part of the paper. But if the paper belonged to Mr. X or Mr. Y, then it would be up to him to decide"† (Presse Actualité, January 1978). CP

---

*Interviews with Jacques Fauvet, June 6, 1977, and Jean-Marie Dupont, January 21, 1977.

†This rationalization for the centralized control of CP publications contradicts the usual CP position on the rights of workers to manage the enterprises in which they work.

control over L'Humanité is direct; the director, Roland Leroy, is a member of the Political Bureau of the CP, and the editor-in-chief, René Andrieu, is in constant contact with Georges Marchais, who heads the party as a whole. The paper receives daily written communications from the Political Bureau (Presse Actualité, January 1978).

In a recent interview, J. P. Gaudard, head of the economy section at L'Humanité, was asked about the degree of latitude he enjoyed writing for the paper: "As far as party policy goes, I have absolutely no latitude. The work of elaborating the issue is done by the economy section of the party. . . . I am more involved in an ideology than I am in the trade" (Harris and Sédouy 1974, p. 52).

Occasionally, party publications have strayed from the centrally defined line, and the reaction has always been swift. In the 1960s, for instance, Clarté, the periodical of the Communist Student Union (UEC), began to run debates between members of its editorial committee. Three different tendencies emerged besides the party line: an Italian CP (proto-Eurocommunist), a Trotskyist, and a Maoist. By no stretch of the imagination was this forum going to be allowed in a party journal: within three months only the official line remained. Another case is Louis Aragon, director of the highly acclaimed journal, Les Lettres Françaises. When Aragaon reacted vehemently to the Soviet invasion of Czechoslovakia, the highly respected periodical disappeared within several months because of "financial difficulties" which had not been noticed theretofore (see also Caute 1964). In similar fashion, Démocratie Nouvelle, directed by Paul Noirot, was openly pro-Dubcek. Shortly after the Prague events of 1968 the periodical was closed for "financial reasons."*

The CP is actually caught in a dilemma. It is no surprise to find a party press, any party press, highly centralized, tightly controlled, and mostly propagandistic. On the other hand, such publications are only of interest to party militants; they are not going to attract a general readership. The failure of the party press of every political party in France demonstrates clearly that people will not buy a newspaper to read political propaganda. They want either information or entertainment: party propaganda is neither.

---

*There are several other major examples one could add, for example, Vendredi of Guehenno, or the eclectic and brilliant publication, Action, begun as a clandestine paper by Pierre Hervé. France Nouvelle and La Nouvelle Critique suffered similar fates in 1978.

EXTERNAL INFLUENCES

I have argued that it is the owners of press enterprises who have both the legal right and the operational apparatus to control the content of their publications. Although this is true with respect to the people who actually write and compose the paper, it is a simplification with respect to the external environment in which the press owner must operate. A press owner must take numerous external sources of influence into account in determining the political and social line of his publications, and, insofar as these external influences play a role in determining the publications' content, the press owner is somewhat restricted.

It would be impossible to account for all the external influences operative in this way. What I would like to do, however, is point out several of the major pathways of external influence by examining in some detail the concrete dealings between the management of a press enterprise and the external economic, social, and political environment. This method allows us to predict some specific channels of intervention through which segments of the dominant classes external to the press enterprise are able to gain influence over the editorial and political positions taken by particular publications.

Press owners—or their upper-level managers—have four principal activities: (1) they handle issues concerning financial stability (reading financial reports that tell them about corporate debts, sales, costs of production, advertising, and so on); (2) they are in constant contact with the local elites (the leaders and spokesmen in economic, social, and cultural spheres);* (3) they receive calls from and meet with the local and national political officials; and (4) they deal with internal organizational matters (considering proposed organizational changes, promotions of individuals, actively heading the multileveled censorship and authority structures, and, in most cases, maintaining an active upperhand in decisions about content, especially in jealously guarding the right to determine headlines and access to the front page).

In carrying out their responsibilities, the press bourgeoisie must deal with a host of individuals and organizations external to the press enterprise itself. Specifically, the owners must work with

---

*The phenomenon of "local elites" (<u>notables</u>) is important in Paris, but it is carried to the extreme in the provinces, where a small set of powerful individuals exercises a remarkable control over all spheres of social and political life, including the press (Servan-Schreiber 1975, p. 365).

banks, advertising companies, powerful individuals from social and cultural groups, and also local and national political figures. All of these dealings involve <u>exchanges</u>, of either finances or influence. Each of these external exchanges produces a given amount of leverage by which pressure can be put on the press bourgeoisie to influence the content and political ideology of their publications. Besides the specific ability of bankers, advertisers, elites, and politicians to influence the press, one wants to investigate the <u>class content</u> (and particularly the intra-dominant-class dynamics) of this external influence on press enterprises.

It is during these exchanges between the press bourgeoisie of particular enterprises and the financially, socially, and politically powerful, who represent broader interests of the dominant class as a whole, that the general perspective and special interests of other segments of the dominant class enter into decisions about content and political ideology. In other words, the press bourgeoisie is not independent of other, broader segments of the bourgeoisie when it determines editorial policy. Take for example the discovery of massive real estate scandals in the early 1970s; the one major Parisian paper to avoid all reference to these was <u>Le Figaro</u>, which during this era printed fully 400 percent more real estate advertising than the nearest competitor (<u>Presse Actualité</u>, February 1978).

Furthermore, the press bourgeoisie's dependency on other segments of the dominant class is not simply a function of financial intercourse comparable to that of other industrial sectors. The press bourgeoisie is in the strategically vulnerable position of needing a daily inflow of interviews, stories, leads, hints, disclosures, and the like. Insofar as state personnel, social elites, and culturally prominent individuals channel this information to certain publications and withhold it from others, they can seriously affect how up to date and well informed a newspaper is. Most directly vulnerable are the nonsensationalist, "informational" publications; by their very nature they cannot simply reproduce the news agency dispatches that come in over the wire services but need to locate further information and corroboration to elaborate the typically sparse news dispatches. Insofar as these informational publications take an investigatory or critical posture on a given issue, they find themselves progressively disfavored with respect to submissive publications, which edit the news dispatches and news releases little, if at all. This process is particularly effective in France, a country with an extreme degree of state and industrial secrecy. These channels are, therefore, under considerably more control than in other countries, and this is surely one reason why in France there is essentially no "investigative reporting" whatsoever: today's disclosure would simply mean tomorrow's ostracism. There is no more central difference between U.S. and

French journalism than this, as Tunstall has emphasized (1977, p. 24).

THE ROLE OF MONOPOLISTIC ADVERTISING CORPORATIONS

> La publicité est con
> La publicité nous prend pour des cons
> La publicité nous rend cons*
>
> Graffiti, Paris subway, 1977

A newspaper, unlike most products, is sold twice. On the one hand, it must sell to the public, and we shall see how shifting publics can spell success or doom for different papers and even different modes of journalism. On the other, a newspaper must sell to its advertisers. In 1977 Le Monde sold on the street for F1.60, about 32¢ at the time; had it had no advertising income, it would have had to sell for twice that amount (Presse Actualité, February 1978). Even a fraction of such a price increase would have greatly cut readership, as happened to a lesser extent with every small increase in the past (Presse Actualité, May 1977). As a rule of thumb, slightly over half of the income of the average press enterprise is derived from advertising revenues. This figure goes as high as 81 percent for Le Figaro (Brunois 1973, p. 81). Clearly, therefore, most newspapers and periodicals are financially dependent on advertising income.

Advertising revenues come from two separate sources: commercial advertising and classified advertising. Measured in milimeter/columns, commercial advertising in recent years has been declining in most papers, and dependency on fewer advertising accounts has increased.† There are fewer accounts in each economic sector precisely because of the concentration-monopolization process; furthermore, each of these remaining accounts is a larger corporate unit. These fewer, larger corporate units therefore enjoy increased potential leverage over the press owner, since the competition to capture the remaining accounts intensifies. This competition is further increased by three other pressures on the Parisian press:

---

*Advertising is asinine. Advertising assumes we are asinine. Advertising makes us asinine.

†Le Monde internal document dated February 22, 1977; Presse Actualité, February 1978. See Table A.5.

TABLE 1.3

Differential Growth Rates of Advertising
in Paris and the Provinces
(millions of francs)

	1967	1976	Percent Change
Parisian dailies	345	775	+180
Periodicals	735	1400	+190
Provincial dailies	600	1730	+288

Source: Presse Actualité, February 1978.

the general "underdevelopment" of advertising in France,* increased competition with other media,† and increased competition with the provincial monopoly press enterprises (see Table 1.3).

Advertising presents a dilemma for the press: advertisers demand a certain degree of ideological input, yet in present-day France

---

*French advertising, while impressive in absolute terms (NF 8.7 billion in 1977), is actually the smallest percentage of GNP of any industrialized society. In 1968, advertising amounted to 2.9 percent of the GNP in West Germany, 2 percent in the United States, 1.2 percent in the United Kingdom, but only 0.68 percent in France (Cayrol 1973, p. 99). So, relative to other advanced capitalist societies, it is that much harder to find advertising income, especially during economic downturns. In 1975, for example, the top ten advertisers spent 6.3 percent less on advertising than the year before. This volatility can pose difficult financial problems for press enterprises, particularly for independents or small press groups (Le Monde, May 24-25, 1977).

†The written press in France benefited for many years from the state's original decision not to have paid advertising on television. When this was changed in 1968, the relative share of advertising revenues in the press dropped as that of television rose. In 1967, advertising expenditures in the press, television, and radio were 75, 0, and 24 percent, respectively. By 1976 those figures had changed to 50, 26, and 24 percent, respectively (Le Monde, May 24-25, 1977).

it is advertising that allows an enterprise to be independent from state aid and, equally importantly, to sell at a popular price. Nowhere is this dilemma more apparent than in the case of two socialistic publications: <u>Le Monde</u> and <u>Nouvel Observateur</u>. It is only their notable success in attracting advertising that has given them the fiscal basis to remain independent enterprises. In turn, it is clear that only their independence has allowed them to take openly pro-socialist political positions in recent years.

The Monopolistic Structures of the Advertising Industry

The advertising industry, like other external supplier sectors with which the press enterprises must deal, is highly monopolized and concentrated. A highly monopolized sector tends to induce structural pressures toward concentration on those sectors with which it has economic exchange. This phenomenon can be seen clearly in the important effects the French advertising sector has had on the new press born in France in 1944. It is impossible to examine the processes involved without taking account of the corporate conglomerate that dominates the sector, Havas.
Just after World War I, the advertising wing of the Havas agency was formed, and within a decade it had organized a formal monopoly agreement with the five major press enterprises of the period (Albert and Terrou 1974, p. 96). By about 1930, Havas had exclusive advertising rights for more than 200 newspapers and had 75 subsidiaries in the provinces to manage its affairs. In an interesting study of this period, one researcher has detailed the life and death power over papers that this prominence gave to Havas (Toscan du Plantier 1974, p. 96).
What developed out of the early Havas procedure was an advertising practice totally different from that in the United States or most other Western countries. There are four separate levels to the system, or, to put it differently, two separate middlemen, as shown in Figure 1.2.
Most newspapers and periodicals do not sell their own advertising space. They hire an advertising-booking agency (<u>régis</u>) to do this for them, and they tell the agency how much space they would like to sell and at what price. In turn, the ad-booking agency deals with either advertisers directly or the advertising agencies that handle the accounts of major firms.
Advertising in France is dominated by Havas and a second corporate giant, Publicis. In many European countries, it is U.S. capital that dominates the advertising agencies; France is the exception, for U.S. penetration into this sector accounts for "only" about

FIGURE 1.2

The Structure of Advertising Agencies in France

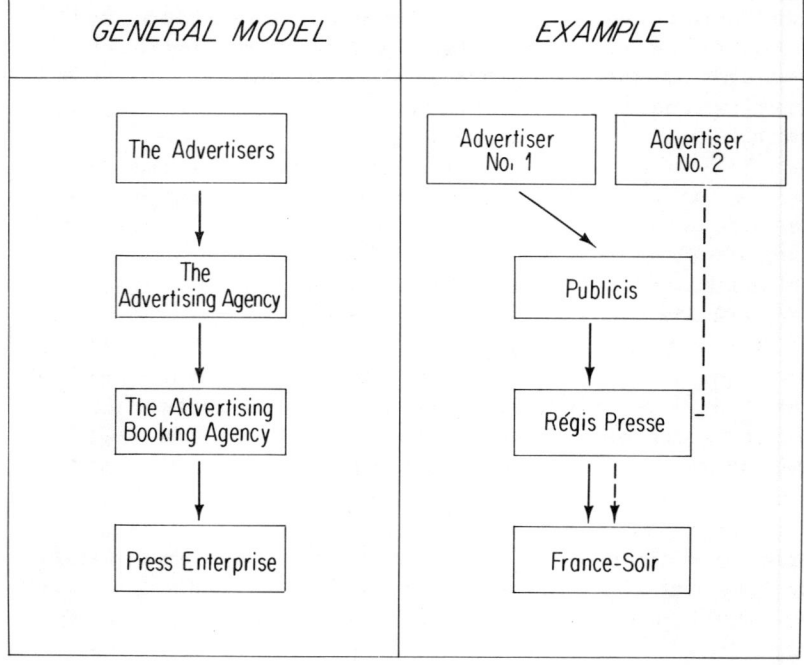

Source: Compiled by the author.

one-third of the industry.* The two firms do about 20 percent of all advertising agency business and about 25 percent of all advertising-booking agency business (Bellanger 1976, p. 352). But even these impressive figures do not indicate the full power of these monopolistic corporate units; consider also the following: (1) Havas bridges the private sector-public sector division, since the French state owns 56 percent of it;† (2) each of these corporations has a vertical monopoly in that each has a subsidiary advertising-booking agency; Havas has a wholly owned subsidiary, Havas Régis, while Publicis owns 66.5 percent of Régis-Presse, with the remainder held by the corporate giant of the press sector, Hachette (L'Humanité, March 26, 1974); and (3) these two ad-booking agencies have an almost total monopoly in the provinces: between them they book 90 percent of all advertising placed in the provincial press (L'Humanité, March 26, 1974). So powerful is the control of the advertising sector enjoyed by these two vertically integrated monopolistic firms that even the otherwise quite conservative government report drawn up by the ad hoc "Drancourt" commission warned of the "monopolization tendency in advertising."‡

The Induction of Monopolization:
Advertising's Impact on the Press Sector

As the advertising industry has become increasingly concentrated in recent decades, it has become one more monopolized sector with which a given press enterprise must deal. This increased concentration in advertising has, in turn, aggravated the concentration

---

*The internationalization of the U.S. advertising industry forms an important element of the contribution of the mass media to U.S. imperialism, as has recently been argued in some excellent studies, especially Schiller (1971), Mattelart (1976), Read (1976), and Tunstall (1977). For a brilliant critical study of advertising, see Ewen (1976).

†This state involvement derives from the nationalization of Havas after the war, the firm having been convicted of collaboration. At that time, the news agency functions of Havas became what we know as "Agence France Presse," while the advertising agency functions maintained their prewar name (Archambault and Lemoine 1977, p. 200).

‡The Drancourt commission reported that in 1969 the top five of the 325 French-based advertising firms accounted for 35 percent of all business in the sector (Bellanger 1976, p. 354).

of the press, since advertising agencies favor the large circulation papers over the small and the concentrated provincial newspaper conglomerates over the remaining independent enterprises.

To illustrate how the induction process occurs, let us consider three important suppliers to the press sector whose respective industrial sectors are themselves highly concentrated. Paper, presses, and delivery services can be purchased only from corporations which enjoy a near monopoly in their respective sphere. The absence of competition in these sectors allows these corporations to set prices for the maximum limit the market will bear. But apart from this classic use of monopoly control in a sector, a second factor has recently proved equally important: the monopolization of a sector is often accompanied by a partial deindustrialization of that sector, that is, the progressive closing of less competitive (small- and even medium-capital) firms in a sector during the monopolization process leads in some cases to an absolute decrease in the sector's productive capacity. At certain times this reduction in capacity affects regions of a country, at others it affects entire countries, which are progressively deindustrialized in one or several industrial sectors. The Common Market has served to exacerbate this process, and the effects in the printing and press sector are quickly traced. The French paper-producing industry, for example, has been largely dismantled, causing the importation of Scandinavian pulp to increase dramatically (CP 1976, p. 13). This deindustrialization of the paper industry has been accompanied by a meteoric rise in the cost of paper (in one recent year, the price rose 84 percent) as well as a serious drain on French international balance of payments (Presse Actualité, May 1977).

The soaring prices and curtailed availability of supplies are disproportionately more difficult for smaller enterprises than for larger corporate units for several reasons. First, supply costs form a larger proportion of expenses in smaller enterprises than in larger and are hence harder to absorb. Second, advertising makes up a smaller proportion of income in the small independent enterprises, and since this is where price increases can be passed along most easily, they are at a relative disadvantage once again. Third, small enterprises operate at a lower rate of profit than their more capital-intensive competition; hence any reduction in profitability is felt sooner. These are the types of concrete pressures that induce concentration from monopolized sectors into other industrial sectors with which there is exchange.

How Advertising Affects Editorial Policy

Advertising also has a direct impact on the social and political content of publications. One researcher has argued that it is pressure from advertising agencies that has been the principal factor in reducing all but a few French publications to their current sensationalist mode of journalism. Advertising agencies, he claims, have openly insisted that publications be aimed at the "lowest common denominator" in their audience (Cayrol 1973, p. 113). This process has greatly changed the newsweeklies: L'Express, for example, was revamped from a politically involved Radical party* journal of the 1950s to a slick, middle-of-the-road Time format precisely in order to expand its advertising income (Presse Actualité, September 1971).

Manufacturers themselves respond to uncensored editorial content of publications with which they do business. Astra margarine removed its ads from a paper that ran an article on the superiority of butter; La Croix lost clothing ads when it dared editorialize that an overemphasis on clothing was spoiling the spiritual purpose of First Communions; an automobile manufacturing plant stopped advertising in a paper that reported on a strike at the assembly plant (AJEF 1972, p. 18). Press enterprises attempt to prevent this reaction by self-censoring their articles. For example, Ralph Nader wrote in 1971 that some months before he had been invited to France by Paris-Match to give expert testimony on a comparison of French cars with regard to automotive safety. Nader did the study and even received the page proofs, but the article never appeared since, as in American investigative reporting, he had included the brand names in the report (AJEF 1972, p. 20).

Advertisers also intervene in the content of the press by getting certain articles written that would not otherwise have appeared. For instance, French journalists and their families are often invited to visit foreign countries, with the expectation that in return they will write articles about their host countries. Some recent examples are a week in India to learn about new beauty products, a five-day tour of Europe organized by several chemical companies, three days in the United States organized by General Electric, four days in Italy organized by Olivetti, a week in Guyana to learn the merits of French rocketry, a week-long Mediterranean cruise with a three-hour lecture on a new anti-pollution product, and a week in Japan organized by Honda (Boris 1975, pp. 25ff.). These articles are surrounded by paid advertising taken out by the sponsoring countries' tourist board. A special supplement on a country appears that otherwise would never have been undertaken. Advertising and reporting are inextricably merged in those supplements for only a handful of French publications

---

*Despite its name, the Radical party is a conservative, center party.

set off advertising with the word "publicité," as required by law. Furthermore, such pseudo-articles constrain the press enterprise to censor actively articles directly critical of the local regime, climate, and so on.

Journalists are also constantly being invited to expensive lunches and dinners, at which time an issue of the day is discussed with a representative of a corporation or a ministry involved in a topical issue. Highly specialized journalists sometimes become "presse attachés" for a corporation in the field of their expertise. Michel Droit, for example, was for years chief of the important literary supplement Figaro Littéraire, while at the same time he was presse attaché for a large publishing firm, Presses de la Cité (AJFS 1972, p. 26). Specialized journalists also form professional organizations, which typically become closely linked with the corporations in the field they cover. It is therefore no great surprise to find on the membership list of the Association of Aeronautical Journalists the name of the public relations manager of Marcel Dassault's aviation corporation (Boris 1975, p. 25).

Through such means as these, advertisers and advertising agencies extract from the press bourgeoisie—and to some extent from journalists—the power to set certain limits and expectations on the content of the publications in which their advertising is placed. In return, the press bourgeoisie receives the advertising that makes up 50 to 60 percent of the average French publication's income, without which they could not survive.

These remarks have attempted to outline the specific institutional channels whereby the advertising industry is able to influence the structure and content of the press. One could also observe the increasing penetration of banks into the press sector, as external financing of the press enterprises and the publishing sector in general has mushroomed in recent years (see Table A.6). The theoretical point, however, would be identical: it is through contacts such as these that the press bourgeoisie and their journalists enter into exchange relations with other segments of the dominant class. The ideological demands made by advertising agencies and banks, to mention but two spheres of exchange, are no doubt more often implied than negotiated in detail. Yet they are effective because the press bourgeoisie is in perennial need of advertising, loans, and other considerations, and therefore it cannot be insensitive to a set of ideological boundaries structured by the interests of the advertising agencies, banks, and other institutions with which it does business.

This is not to imply that the press bourgeoisie is in a completely dependent position; on the contrary, press owners do have a relative autonomy in taking positions on particular issues. Advertisers need the press as much as the press enterprises need the advertising income; the fact that one can outline the efforts of the advertising corporations to increase their influence over the content and political ideology of the enterprises with which they do business does not imply that the pressure they can create is not mediated by many other considerations on the part of the press owners.

2
MONOPOLIZATION IN THE FRENCH PRESS: THREE CASE STUDIES

There are three information empires of the postwar Parisian press that stand head and shoulders above the many smaller collections of titles. These monopolistic organizations are of three distinct types.

One, that of Jean Prouvost, was constructed with industrial capital Prouvost accumulated from his monopoly holdings in the wool industry. The other two, Hachette and Robert Hersant's newspaper chain, have developed from a base within the press and publication sector. Hachette's vertical monopoly spans the full realm of industrial subsectors related to the press: it is not only the major publisher of periodicals and books in France but also has a near monopoly on the distribution and sale of all printed material in France and a broadly based international distribution operation as well.

Robert Hersant's horizontal monopoly consists of a chain of newspapers collected during the last twenty years throughout France plus the 1975 purchase of Le Figaro and the 1976 acquisition of France-Soir. Whereas Prouvost's empire was labor intensive (every publication had a separate organization and personnel), Hersant's modern version is capital-intensive, consisting of fully electronic print shops located throughout France, which print his local papers as well as Le Figaro in the morning and France-Soir in the afternoon.

The Prouvost empire became progressively incapable of making an adequate return on investments because its labor-intensive mode of organization involved numerous duplicated costs. The press group also had no way to escape the precipitous decline in advertising income that accompanied the sudden and deep recession of 1974-75. Hachette, in contrast, was capable of passing through the crisis relatively unscathed; many ends of its widely diversified holdings are protected from economic downturns, including press delivery and school supply subsidiaries.

The new Hersant empire represents an important trend in capital-intensive printing and publishing. His strategy, in contrast to that of the Prouvost group, involves a radical reduction in his personnel expenditures, which he accomplishes by an accelerated centralization of all possible aspects of his operation. In 1975, when the anachronistic Prouvost empire was sold off, the two principal purchasers were Hachette and Hersant.

The following case studies of these three differing monopolistic press structures present many details of their development and internal organization. By viewing the specificity of each case, we can trace the multiple logics of the monopolization process. It means little to say that the three press empires are all "monopolistic." In fact, they operate in radically different ways, each of which must be analyzed separately.

JEAN PROUVOST: THE LAST OF THE GRAND-STYLE PRESS BARONS

Through a maze of holding companies and dummy corporations, Jean Prouvost and his perennial partner, Fernand Béghin, acquired and launched many of the most prestigious titles of the French press. The extent of the empire is known today only because in 1975, when Prouvost was in his early nineties, he was forced by the banks that had extended him credit to sell the greater part of his holdings. Several useful studies on the interlocking of his various publishing and holding companies have been produced by union militants. Figure 2.1, culled from three such studies, is far from complete, but it does contain the principal publications and holding companies and also indicates where the Prouvost group interlocks with the corporate holdings of other press bourgeoisie.

The figure indicates that the group was based on those corporations which actually published the various journals, while associated corporations were set up to provide subsidiary supplier companies, such as SNIP (an advertising agency), Bénélux de Régie (an advertising-booking agency), and SDF-Néogravure (a vast complex of printing plants). It is instructive to look carefully at the interlocks present in this printing subsidiary. Besides Prouvost and Hachette, other stockholders in 1975 included the Banque de Paris et de Pays-Bas (hereafter referred to by its nickname, Paribas*), as well as one of France's

---

*Paribas was the eighth largest bank in France in 1975 (Morin 1974, p. 293).

FIGURE 2.1

The Press Empire of Jean Prouvost in 1975: Holding Companies and Interlocks with Other Corporate Press Bourgeoisie

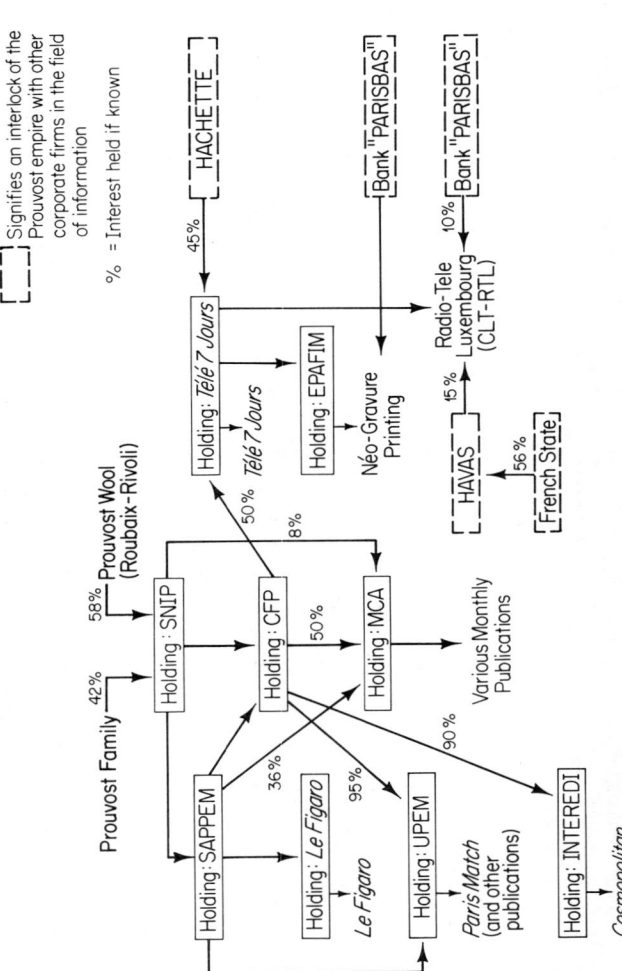

Notes: Several minor holding companies have been omitted for the sake of clarity. There were many other holdings, no doubt, that are not known.
SNIP= Société Nouvelle d'Information et de Publicité; CFP= Compagnie Française des Periodiques; SAPPEM= Société Anonyme Parisienne de Publications et d'éditions modernes; UPEM= Union de Publications et d'éditions modernes; INTER-EDI= Société Internationale d'édition et de diffusion; MCA= Marie-Claire Album.
Sources: Journal des Journalists (CGT), no. 10 (1976); Presse Actualité (March 1976).

two monopolistic paper corporations, whose president was Fernand
Béghin, Prouvost's partner at Le Figaro. Through Télé-7 Jours,
Prouvost and Hachette also owned major shares of the private radio
and television stations in Luxembourg (CLT-RTL), which broadcast
into France. Here, they are joined by Havas and, once again, the
Banque Paribas. Paribas is also a major shareholder in Hachette and
therefore enters into CLT-RTL at least twice. Since 56 percent of
Havas is held by the French state, the corporate interlocks bridge the
public and private spheres.

Prouvost at Le Figaro

The war and liberation were difficult times for Jean Prouvost;
Paris-Soir was confiscated, and Prouvost himself was tried by the
High Court of Justice and convicted of conspiracy against the state.
He went into hiding and was sought by the national police for over
three years. The bourgeois restoration of 1947 (which was greatly
aided by the intervention of the U.S. government in the form of the
Marshall Plan) had several major effects in France, including the
ousting of several communist government ministers and the scission
in the CGT.* It also saw many wealthy industrialists cleared by the
courts with findings of "insufficient evidence." It is true that many of
these industrialists, who continued to do business and make profits
under Vichy, also gave money to the Resistance, and it is no doubt
impossible (and irrelevant) to try to determine retrospectively whether
they were motivated by a sense of nationalism and a disgust with Nazi
and Vichy practices or if they were merely hedging their bets. Prouvost, in any case, in 1943, delivered a valise of cash for the Resistance
movement to one Michel Debré (a future Gaullist prime minister). At
the time, the Resistance was cut off from London and in dire need of
funds. Nevertheless, many did not want to accept money from Prouvost.
Eventually, however, the testimony of Debré helped clear him (Perier-
Daville 1976, p. 43). Still, the question remains: how did he arrive
at the glorious revenge of obtaining the prestigious Le Figaro?

In 1934, François Coty, Le Figaro's owner, chose Pierre
Brisson to run the paper's acclaimed literary section. Brisson later
became director of the paper itself and greatly increased its scope
and quality in the years leading up to the war by bringing in such

---

*See Le Monde of May 9, 10, 12, 1967, for a fascinating analysis
of the role of U.S. labor movements in financing and encouraging the
scission in the CGT.

brilliant contributors as André Gide, François Mauriac, Georges Duhamel, and even an occasional article by Jean-Paul Sartre.

In 1940, after a narrow personal escape from the occupying Germans, Brisson arrived at Lyon, in the Free French Zone, and set up Le Figaro. Under the Vichy regime there was strict control over the press; to avoid this, Brisson attempted to produce a paper that was starkly apolitical. He refused to strike out at the Jews and the Resistance, he did not publish anti-Semitic or anti-Resistance propaganda, nor did his prestigious daily condone the actions of the Nazis and Vichy. This formula worked from June 1940 until November 1942, but it left the paper with little advertising and a limited circulation. How to balance the budget? Brisson called on Prouvost, who loaned the paper 1 million francs through Paris-Soir, which had reopened in Paris and was openly collaborating. The future link was made.

When Coty died, the paper became the property of his widow, who spent the war safely in the United States, where she married a Mr. Cotneareanu. Just after the liberation, Brisson reopened the paper in Paris and received a telegram from Mme. Cotneareanu directing the paper to take a strongly pro-U.S. view on international matters, that is, support the Atlantic Alliance forces (Perier-Daville 1976, p. 28). Brisson immediately wired her a response in which he explained that the post-liberation press regime was significantly different from before the war, and that it was he, as director of the paper, who had received the permission to resume publishing from the authorities. At this point, given the liberation press laws, Brisson could have cut off all of her legal claims to the paper, but his politics did not allow him to do so. For, although he voted Socialist and proudly told everybody so (he called himself a "républicain libéral, c'est-à-dire démodé), he was in favor of a journalism that was "outside of capitalism, but in agreement with it." He therefore proposed to Mme. Cotneareanu that Le Figaro be divided into two separate companies, one concerned with the financial management and the other with the editorial production of the paper. Mme. Cotneareanu was by no means ready to accept this recommendation, but after a decision in Brisson's favor by the Commercial Court (Tribunal de Commerce) in 1948, she had no choice but to negotiate. Brisson convinced her in 1950 to sell half her holdings in the paper to Jean Prouvost (in partnership with Fernand Béghin), which she did for the paltry sum of 1.5 million old francs, along with the right to buy the other half later. This right was later exercised in 1964 for NF 200,000, an equally absurd price given that Le Figaro produced a net profit of NF 140,000 that year alone, on a gross of NF 140 million (Nouvel Observateur, January 21, 1965).

In 1950 a management agency (Société Fermière) was set up to run the editorial end of the publication for a period of nineteen years. Brisson became president of both companies and thus ran Le Figaro under a total, but apparently happy, dictatorship until his death in 1964. During this period, the paper reigned supreme among the bourgeoisie and upper middle strata; its circulation was twice that of Le Monde, and its advertising income was stupendous. In the NF 140 million mentioned above for the year 1964, fully 120 million were from advertising and only 20 million came from sales.

During these years, Brisson defined a conservative but open and intelligent line for Le Figaro. In contrast to Le Monde, it was opposed to neutralism for France and strongly in favor of the U.S. alliance. It was anti-communist, but not irrationally so, as were L'Aurore, Le Parisien Libéré, and France-Soir. On most domestic issues the paper was pro-de Gaulle, and here it was aligned with Parisien Libéré against Le Monde and L'Aurore. The editorials were in favor of a continued French presence in Southeast Asia and North Africa, although with far less fanaticism than in Parisien Libéré and L'Aurore; Le Monde was outrightly opposed to French colonialism. Basically, then, Figaro was nationalistic and conservative, yet there were particular issues on which Brisson stood up and broke with this line. Thus he came out against the French participation in the joint French-Anglo invasion of Suez. This position cost him readers, as he knew it would, but he was a moral man who stood up for his beliefs. He exhibited what the French call "the moderate liberalism of the classical right."

This was the grand period of the postwar press, grand in that the political and editorial lines of the best of the Parisian papers were set by the directors and not by the press bourgeoisie who would, in the years ahead, regain control of all the papers except Le Monde. It was Brisson (not Prounst) who determined the line at Figaro; Pierre Lazareff (not Hachette) made the editorial decisions at France-Soir; Robert Lazurick (not Boussac) ran L'Aurore; and Hubert Beuve-Méry wrote stinging editorials at Le Monde under the pen name "Sirius." So in reading back through the yellowing issues of these papers from the late 1950s and very early 1960s, one finds a still vital and lively press which was invariably split on major questions and presented arguments from opposing perspectives. This was true to a certain extent in the provinces as well; for example, with François Hutin at Ouest-France. Yet, when these great journalists died or retired, the editorial independence they enjoyed disappeared with them, except where it was structured into legally binding organizational patterns; but this was so only at Le Figaro and Le Monde.

Brisson's death in 1964 left only five years remaining of the legally separate editorial controlling body at Le Figaro; soon it became clear that it would be difficult to convince Prouvost and Béghin to maintain the division between editorial and financial responsibilities. In 1965 a "journalist association" was formed to further this effort, and negotiations with Prouvost began. Looking back, it is obvious that Prouvost was merely running down the clock, waiting for the termination in 1969 of the legally divorced editorial and ownership functions. When the spirit of May 1968 entered the well-known building at the Rond Point of the Champs Elysées, a 24 hour "warning" strike was held; it was the first peacetime day Le Figaro had not appeared since the mid-1860s. Prouvost, however, refused to sign an agreement to continue the two separate entities, unless (1) he was president of both, and (2) the Société Fermière functioned in merely an advisory capacity to the owning corporation.

When Charles de Gaulle resigned on May 1, 1969, political turmoil descended upon France as the political parties formed alliances for the ensuing presidential elections. In the midst of this political fracas, the journalists at Le Figaro went out on strike. The journalists received numerous letters of support, even one from Fernand Béghin, who parted company with Prouvost over the issue. In fact, Prouvost's position quickly became an outspoken defense of the rights of ownership. He was joined by Georges Pompidou, who, desperately needing Le Figaro's active support, wanted the strike settled as quickly as possible, and who, unlike de Gaulle, had no sympathy for the idea of "participation." The powerful printers union was also opposed to the journalists; in classic CGT and CP fashion, they refused to support any participationist structure, which they saw as confirming the rights of ownership. The journalists, finding themselves with considerable public sympathy but few strategically useful allies, were forced to call a temporary "honorable" peace on May 23, when the Commercial Court (Tribunal de Commerce de Paris) assigned a judicial administrator to run the paper and make suggestions to the court about the necessary transition. Assigned for three months, he actually stayed for two years.*

By 1971, the picture had changed sharply for the worse. Béghin had sold his shares to Prouvost, who had a preemptory right to buy them. In addition, the government commission that had been appointed to study the journalist association movement that had grown from the Le Figaro and Le Monde experiences outrightly condemned such corporate participation configurations. While the report expressed a feeling that some reform was needed, it did not feel that the participation scheme of the journalist association movement was the best

---

*He also wrote a useful book on Le Figaro (see Brunois 1973).

way to handle it. Le Monde, it held, was an exception, not a model. The report bluntly stated that the transfer to the journalists of part of the ownership of a paper would simply "create supplementary rigidities" (Lindon Report 1970, p. 90).

By 1975, the Prouvost empire had begun to lose its financial viability. As a labor-intensive collection of titles, it was not able to protect itself against inflation, changing consumer demands, and recession, as were the more broadly based, highly automated and centralized empires of Hachette and Hersant. When the Prouvost press holdings were sold, Hachette bought most of the periodicals, and Le Figaro went to Robert Hersant. Prouvost's empire was dead. Hersant's was crowned, Hachette's enlarged. Le roi est mort! Vive le roi!

HACHETTE: THE WORLD'S LARGEST PUBLISHING MULTINATIONAL

The Development of the Hachette Empire

Louis Hachette was born in 1800 to an affluent family; he attended the finest high school (Louis-Le-Grand) and France's most prestigious college, The Ecole Normale Supérieure. During his student days he made a small investment in a Latin Quarter bookshop, "Brédif," from which grew the largest publishing-related corporation in the Western world.

The introduction of trains provided the first great opportunity for Brédif. Station bookshops were instant successes, with most of their business being handled by a single distribution company that had received permission to open the kiosks. The events of 1848 gave Louis Hachette his big chance. In return for his early support of Louis Napoleon, elected president of the republic in 1849, Hachette was granted the exclusive right to this market. For the first of many times, an opposing firm was reduced to a mere customer.

By 1882 Hachette held a formal, exclusive contract with the train companies to supply and manage 750 bookstalls. This agreement guaranteed Hachette's fiscal stability, and also put the firm in a position to censor literature as it saw fit. In the very year it opened, Hachette banned 18 works (Enkiri 1972, p. 13). The next year writers began to rise in protest, and petitions were signed against these practices; among the signatories were Henri Rochefort, Octave Mirabeau, and Guy de Maupassant. Clémenceau openly attacked the trust in the National Assembly, calling it a "monopoly" (Enkiri 1972, p. 13).

The introduction of mass public education in 1883 provided the second great opportunity for the Hachette family to build its dominant position in the publishing sector. The firm managed to become the almost exclusive supplier for all of France of school books and school equipment in general: teaching material, blackboards, desks, and the like. To this day, Hachette is still the reigning giant in this field of guaranteed, recession-proof, subsidized sales.

During the last years of the century, Hachette bought out the "messageries," which carried out the distribution of the Parisian newspapers, and soon became the exclusive distributor of the daily press. Meanwhile, in 1906 the Parisian subway company also signed an exclusive contract with Hachette for its underground press kiosks. By the end of World War I, Hachette was a major corporation.

After the war, the Hachette family decided to augment the company's capitalization with outside capital. At this time the Banque Paribas received two seats out of seven on the Board of Directors (Conseil d'Administration), which it has held ever since. Horace Finaly was both president of the bank and an administrator of Hachette; henceforth the two corporations would be intricately interlocked. With the new capital this association brought in, Hachette moved to expand its monopoly on distribution. Press enterprises that used other distributors became prey for its revenge, since Hachette owned the kiosks where their papers were sold (Enkiri 1972, p. 32).

During World War II, Hachette continued to do business as usual and made profits on the sales of such Nazi propaganda journals as *Signal*. Hachette, therefore, ran into the same problems at the liberation as did Jean Prouvost. Condemning words can be found even in a National Assembly speech by the young Jacques Chaban-Delmas, later a Gaullist prime minister (replying to Francisque Gay of the MRP): "I think we were together enough in the Resistance that it would be superfluous for me to tell you about how insulted I am to hear you accuse me of being a defender of the renaissance of the Hachette trust" (Enkiri 1972, p. 36).

In September 1944, Hachette's distribution buildings were sequestered by the liberation authorities; the notion was to turn the "messageries" into a public service. Hachette's strategy in the face of this confiscation was quite remarkable: they opened a rival company, "Expéditive," partially financed by a loan of F40 million from the Banque Paribas. Hachette ran its new company like a well-managed David; it was only a matter of time before the poorly run, nationalized Goliath, still staffed by loyal Hachette cadres, would become untenable. As various press enterprises ran into financial trouble, Hachette made loans on condition that they allow Expéditive to handle their distribution. The long printers strike of 1947 financially undermined many of the undercapitalized liberation enterprises, and many turned to Hachette. As it became more and more apparent that the organizational structure of the nationalized company was doomed, a long and revealing debate was held in the National Assembly. When the vote was tallied, Hachette prevailed. The Bichet law provided for the establishment of a nationally chartered cooperative, the NMPP (Nouvelles Messageries de la Presse Parisienne). This legislation confirmed Hachette's ownership rights to the entirety of its original holdings and arranged for Hachette to rent these to the NMPP. Hachette was given 49 percent of the stock in this nonprofit corporation, and a cooperative of all participating press enterprises held the remaining 51 percent.

Hachette in the 1970s

It is safe to say that, between the two major cooperatives it controls, Hachette's distribution system handles over 90 percent of the distribution of the national press. Some notion of the ultra-profitability of this operation can be surmised from the fact that, since the liberation, the cost of the transportation of goods in general has risen 505 percent, and by 1975 the cost of the transportation of the press had soared 1,824 percent (Bellanger 1975, p. 403). Of the 41,700 points of sale, Hachette directly owns 11,000. For its own publications it thus combines the publisher's profit, the transporter's profit, and the retail profit. In 1971 the gross sales of the NMPP chain amounted to almost F35 billion (Enkiri 1972, p. 62), of which a "forfeit" of 1 percent goes to Hachette, above and beyond the rental of Hachette's buildings, trucks, and other distribution equipment. In 1975, of the F5 paid at a newsstand for L'Express, only F2.85 were returned to the journal, with the other F2.15 going for distribution costs and retail profit, that is to say, principally to Hachette (Le Monde, September 17, 1974). Hachette is in the enviable position of collecting the monies from the sales of the press, subtracting its fees, and returning the remaining funds to each publisher. In 1972 Hachette paid Le Monde only 51.4 percent of the face value of the papers handled. By 1975, this figure had dropped to 46.9 percent.*

What is particularly amazing about the Hachette vertical

---

*This figure comes from a Le Monde internal document. In the several months I spent at Le Monde, a great many internal documents were made available to me. Seldom were they titled, and occasionally they were not even dated; I doubt if they could be found now, even just a few years later. Given the nature of Le Monde's mode of operation, I felt strong reason to trust the accuracy of the documents, so I cite them accordingly.

monopoly is how difficult it is to escape. For instance, one would guess that its role in subscriptions would be minimal; one would assume that each enterprise would prepare its own publications for mailing. This is not the case. One finds "Presse-Routage," a wholly owned subsidiary of Hachette and the world's largest in its field, handling 60 percent of all Parisian subscriptions. Its customers include 17 dailies, 66 weeklies, 152 monthlies, and 88 others. Only Le Monde, Le Figaro, and L'Humanité, among dailies, have their own distribution system for subscriptions.

In Belgium, a Hachette subsidiary, Agence et Messageries de Presse (AMP), imports, exports, and sells through a chain of newsstands. It accounts for 17 percent of all distribution of books, 27 percent of dailies, and 40 percent of periodicals in Belgium (L'Humanité, March 26, 1974). Hachette is in fact the world's largest international distributor of published materials. Hachette has subsidiaries in 33 countries in Europe, Africa, the Americas, and Asia (Le Monde, April 26, 1974). In 1974, Hachette's total international gross was almost F1 billion, about one-fourth of Hachette's total of about 4 billion that year (Correspondence de la Presse, February 21, 1975). In a full page ad in Le Monde, Ithier de Roquemaurel, chairman of the board and chief administrator of Hachette (and a great-great-grandson of Louis Hachette) entitled his article "A Tool of the Interpenetration of Cultures." It would be hard to put it better. Such, at any rate, was the opinion of the Brussels Commission, which in 1974 opened investigations into Hachette's international "monopolistic practices" (Le Monde, July 26, 1975).

Hachette's Press and Publishing Holdings

Hachette's press group has gone through some major changes in recent years, as the rate of profit has decreased progressively due to higher costs of paper, distribution (!), and printing. By 1976, only about 6 or 7 percent of Hachette's capital was in the press (L'Expansion, September 1976). The sale of France-Soir also helped "depoliticize" Hachette which, as a monopoly corporation, was high on the list of firms to be nationalized by the "Programme Commun" of the united left. Nonetheless, in 1976 Hachette still had at least a dozen major subsidiaries, each of which published numerous periodicals (see Table A.7). Their total circulation was over 5 million copies per week, and they included one of France's five major newsweeklies, Le Point. In 1979, Hachette was in the market to purchase a major share in Le Parisien Libéré (Presse Actualité, June 1979).

In 1973, Hachette's press operations amounted to 10 percent of all publications, 17 percent of all distribution, and 32 percent of all exportation of books and periodicals in France. In this same year, its involvement in the world of books amounted to 18 percent of all publications, 23 percent of all book distribution, and 24 percent of all book exportation (L'Humanité, March 26, 1974). As Hachette itself describes its publishing holdings: "In the domain of the book, the range of Hachette stretches from school books to paperbacks (2,000 titles, 30 million copies sold per year), from art books to police novels, through books for the young and general literature" (Le Monde, April 26, 1975). Hachette's publishing holdings include such major houses as Fayard, Gasset, Hachette-Literature, Stock, Albin Michel, and a dozen more (see Table A.8). But Hachette does not restrict its investments to the written word. It is also a major stockholder in radio and television stations insofar as these are open to private capital. We have seen how Hachette was a partner of Jean Prouvost in Radio Télé Luxembourg. Hachette also recently made use of its close ties with Prime Minister Chaban-Delmas and was given the exclusive rights to join the state radio and television company in the preparation of video cassettes made from the extensive libraries of the state-owned channels (Enkiri 1972, p. 156).

Hachette was also involved in the printing sector, as one might suppose. As was mentioned earlier, Hachette owned 50 percent, with the Banque Paribas holding part of the rest, of the vast printing plant, SDF-Neogravure, but Hachette also controlled another chain of important printing shops through its subsidiary, "Brodard et Taupin." Hachette was equally hard at work in the advertising sector, holding 33.5 percent of the stock of "Régis-Presse," which served as the group's principal advertising supplier, and also held extensive quantities of speculative real estate (Le Monde, June 23, 1964; Presse Actualité, February 1974; and especially La Vie Française, November 17, 1973). All of this probably only scratches the surface since in France it is easy to conceal holdings through interlocking subsidiaries, of which Hachette had 150 (La Vie Française, March 21, 1974). The total value of its assets can only be estimated. La Vie Française/Opinion established its gross earnings as shown in Table 2.1.

In 1975, Hachette's press earnings alone grew to NF 893 million, and the income for the group as a whole rose to 4.5 billion; in 1976, the group grossed 4.9 billion (Presse Actualité, January 1977 and February 1978). By 1977 the total gross earnings of the 105 corporations known to be Hachette subsidiaries (wholly owned) were well above 5.7 billion—with press earnings of 1.4 billion (Presse Actualité, September 1978). According to François Morin's recent study of the largest corporations in France, Hachette, which operates in an economically unimportant sector, ranked an impressive 68.

TABLE 2.1

Estimate of Hachette Gross Earnings, 1972-74
(millions of francs)

Sector	1972	1973	1974
Press group	583.1	646.4	664.5
Book publishing	607.6	661.5	798.8
MMPP	718.3	807.0	920.4
International	360.2	412.4	493.1
Other activities	670.2	701.2	781.1
Total	2,939.4	3,228.5	3,657.9

Source: La Vie Française/Opinion, July 3, 1975.

Who Owns Hachette?

Ownership is never easy to ascertain in France, even for much simpler corporations. Several studies put the family holdings at 8 to 10 percent (Presse Actualité, January 1976), while others estimate it rather higher (Morin 1974, p. 127). Certainly the family remains the single most powerful group, since they continue to dominate the board of directors. The Banque Paribas holds 6 to 7 percent and itself has important interlocks with other major corporations that hold Hachette stock: the Union of Swiss Banks (5 percent), the Union of Parisian Insurance Companies (5 percent), and the Banque Worms (3 percent) (Presse Actualité, January 1976). Both Paribas and Hachette have extensive holdings in media related sectors (paper, printing, press and book distribution, advertising agencies, and so on). Sometimes both have supporting holdings in one corporation; for instance, Hachette owns 8 percent and Paribas 10 percent of the important media complex, Radio-Télé Luxembourg. Both corporations also have extensive international holdings; in June 1978, for example, a Paribas investment subsidiary (La Compagnie financière de Paris et des Pays-Bas) bought 20 percent of the capital of the Power Corporation of Canada. This company's subsidiaries have a virtual monopoly on the French language newspapers published in Québec (Presse Actualité, September 1978).

Given the importance of the interlocks of Paribas and Hachette, it is certainly no surprise that these fiscal graftings induce exchanges of high-level personnel between the two corporate entities. Edmond

Fouret, for example, was simultaneously president of Hachette and an administrator of Paribas. Often the personnel of these two corporations are also linked closely with the state apparatus, particularly through Gaullist channels. Henri Deroy, for instance, was an administrator of Hachette and also Goveneur du Crédit Foncier de France (Chairman of the National Bank for Housing Construction and Mortgages) from 1945 to 1955. He was also an administrator of Paribas Corporation (New York) and of Paribas International S.A. Or take the case of Emmanuel Monik, who was Inspecteur Général des Finances (Chief Inspector of the Ministry of Finance) and later Secrétaire Général (Executive Director of the Central Bank) of the Banque de France. Later he became administrator of the international investment wing of the Paribas bank complex (Compagnie Financière "Paribas" International). In 1952, he became vice president of the executive committee of Hachette (Enkiri 1972, and Durand 1974).

A dozen other personnel interlocks between the state and Hachette could be described.* In and of themselves, however, they only demonstrate what is reasonably obvious: major industrial corporations are tightly linked with major financial institutions and the state. But it is important to see that the graceful coordination of such corporate giants as Hachette and Paribas is not a function of the individual elites who hold the interlocking positions. On the contrary, the places these agents fill are merely the product of the corporations' structural and financial linkages. Similarly, there is a structural determination to the relative success of this corporate alliance in penetrating personnel into important state apparatuses. Hachette is not only a monopolistic corporation (that is, dominant in its sector); it is also a monopoly capital corporation (the sixty-eighth largest corporation in France). It is therefore part of the most powerful segment of the dominant class, and hence, predictably, it would be involved in the ruling functions of the dominant class.

One does not, however, want to simplify the subtle mechanisms

---

*Take the case of Simon Nora, who has held numerous government positions, including membership in the cabinet of the minister of finance (1953-54), after which he was in Mendès France's cabinet. Following this he was a special assistant in the cabinet of Chaban-Delmas, an administrator of Hachette's "Télétudes," and simultaneously an administrator (for Hachette in all probability) at the Compagnie Luxembourgeoise de Télévision. He later became the general manager (directeur-général) of Hachette. When he was replaced in 1974, it was by another ex-cabinet member of Chaban-Delmas, Gérard Worms (L'Humanité, March 27, 1974).

by which corporate giants influence the state. In fact, they can exert this influence only up to the point where they become a threat either to the more general interests of the dominant class as a whole over which the state presides or to the autonomy and legitimacy of the state apparatus itself. This limit to the influence of any single corporation was highly visible in a recent Hachette-related scandal which was one central factor leading to the resignation of a prime minister.*

Hachette's broad industrial base puts it in an entirely different position from the anachronistic Prouvost empire. Its corporate diversification renders it practically immune to the recessionary setbacks that cut advertising income so drastically and plague the more traditional press groups. Hachette's educational and book publishing and its monopoly on distribution render it safe from the changes in readership trends that undermined the fiscal stability of the Prouvost press group. Furthermore, whereas inflation threatens the small press groups and is proving ruinous to the remaining independent papers, Hachette's multileveled vertical monopoly allows it to pass on the inflated prices through its system and thus escape the reduction in profitability other firms feel. Hachette, it seems, represents a viable monopoly structure that has only one potential threat: nationalization. With the defeat of the left in the 1978 elections, when nationalization of Hachette had been a _formal_ part of both the Socialist and Communist parties' programs, that threat is no longer on the short-term political horizon.

ROBERT HERSANT: THE CONQUEST OF A PRESS EMPIRE

> The first time I meet the journalists of a paper I have just bought, I ask them permission to leave to take a piss. The

---

*In 1971 Prime Minister Chaban-Delmas helped plan an exclusive agreement between Hachette and the state-owned radio and television corporation for future retailing of video cassettes of state-owned material. Simon Nora and Gérard Worms of Hachette engineered the agreement through their past contacts at the state-owned media corporations. When a senator named Diligent (!) threatened to expose this illegal use of personnel interlocks, President Pompidou, already displeased over other issues, asked for Chaban-Delmas' resignation (Enkiri 1972, p. 121, and L'Express, August 7, 1972).

second time, I leave to piss without saying anything. The third time, I piss on them.

Robert Hersant
Quoted in Nicolas Brimo, <u>Le Dossier Hersant</u>

Robert Hersant has become France's William Randolph Hearst. In the last several decades he has amassed a wide range of newspapers and periodicals and created a dominating press empire. His story reads like a novel, although I like to think of it as a military campaign. Hersant first became known to history on August 26, 1940, when the collaborationist daily, <u>Le Matin</u>, ran the following article:

THE YOUTH CORPS HAS INAUGURATED
ITS NATIONAL CENTER OF PROPAGANDA

The Youth Corps, the French Guard and the National Collectivist French Party yesterday inaugurated the opening of their national propaganda center, while their leaders, Pierre Clémenti, Charles Lefebvre and Robert Hersant briefly announced that the goals of the movement are, above all, anti-Jewish and anti-Mason. (Brimo 1977, p. 25)

This organization had its offices at 28 Avenue des Champs-Elysées. Hersant personally took part in confiscating this property from the Lang Company, just as he did in procuring for himself an apartment at the expense of the Rosenthal family (Brimo 1977, p. 20). One also catches glimpses here of the criminal side to Hersant's actions even during his open collaboration: in September of 1940, the Paris police opened an investigation against him on charges of extortion (Brimo 1977, p. 20).

Forced to leave Paris for the "Free French Zone" in the South, Hersant tried his hand under Vichy. He obtained a grant of F600,000 to open and direct a "Maréchal Pétain Youth Center" at Brévannes. He also obtained funds to open his first publication, <u>Jeunes Forces</u>, an organ replete with Pétainist ideology. But again the criminal side appears: his youth center at Brévannes apparently had a surplus of jam, which was in short supply during the war, and Hersant entered the black market. In mid-1943, he was convicted on charges stemming from this affair and was sent to prison for the first time. He served this sentence in Rouen; later in life he would have a total monopoly over the newspapers of this city and a close working relationship with its mayor.

After the liberation, Hersant was <u>convicted</u> of collaboration and sent to prison. Like Prouvost, he was condemned to "indignité nationale"; but not having the personal wealth of Prouvost, Hersant had to wait until the general amnesty of 1952 to have his record cleared. During the years that followed, Hersant and his brother opened several small publishing companies in Paris. There followed other criminal convictions stemming from these business dealings, and, besides fines, Hersant once again was faced with the bitter experience of prison (Brimo 1977, p. 29).

By 1976, Robert Hersant stood at the top of the second largest press empire in France; his press holdings produced a combined gross income of F1.1 billion per year. He had 8,000 employees, 1,100 of whom were journalists. He owned or had controlling interest in 12 dailies (including the important Parisian dailies <u>Le Figaro</u> and <u>France-Soir</u>), 9 weeklies and biweeklies, and 11 monthlies. His publications had a total circulation that reached 4.5 million readers; about 20 percent of Frenchmen who read a daily or periodical read one of his (Pons 1977). By 1980 he also had taken over the daily <u>L'Aurore</u>, thereby giving him control over 47.2 percent of the Parisian daily press (<u>Presse Actualité</u>, September 1979). This rags-to-riches story is certainly worth following in detail.

First Steps Toward an Empire

"Mr. Hersant, which of your newspapers is your favorite?"
"The next." (Pons 1977, p. 251)

The Campaign in Central France

The high interest in automobiles and automobile culture after World War II led Hersant to found his first publication, <u>L'Auto-Journal</u>. The considerable profits from this were invested in the <u>Centre-Presse</u>, which was built from a collection of 11 small liberation press enterprises in central France. These small newspapers (in Dordogne and Perigord) had limited circulations of about 10,000 each and by the mid-1950s were having trouble balancing their budget. As they were fused into local editions of <u>Centre-Press</u>, they were instantly depoliticized; those that had taken controversial positions became indistinguishable from those which were already sensationalist before Hersant's arrival.* By pooling many of the functions of

---

*The <u>Eclaire du Berry</u> (Chateauroux), for instance, was transformed from a pro-socialist daily to a bland local edition of <u>Centre-Presse</u>. In Brive, <u>Le Gaillard</u> and <u>Brive-Informations</u> were in constant disagreement with one another on political and social issues until Hersant bought them both in 1960 and fused them into <u>Centre-Presse</u>.

this newspaper chain, Hersant created a profitable, moderately large-circulation (130,000 in the mid-1970s) operation which provided him with the necessary funds for the next stage of his expansion.

The Campaign in the North

After the liberation there were three newspapers in the very north of France: Nord-Eclair (Christian Democratic), Nord Matin (originally Réveil du Nord) (Socialist), and La Voix du Nord (center left). By the mid-1960s, Nord Matin, 40 percent of which was owned by a workers' cooperative, was in desperate need of an influx of capital to replace its outdated printing presses. Enter Hersant, stage right. He became the principal stockholder on condition of a dissolution of the workers' cooperative, although he did have to agree to the formation of an internal committee that would have editorial control for 25 years. Within one year, however, this committee was staffed with pro-Hersant journalists, and the paper no longer took pro-Socialist positions (Pons 1977, p. 125).

By 1971 Hersant had convinced his local competition, Nord-Eclair, to share advertising and a combined journalist staff. In 1974 he became principal owner of Nord-Eclair, although again only under stringent conditions: Hersant was given 35 percent of the voting shares, while 25 percent was held by the journalists, and 40% by chosen trustees. By 1975 he had arranged adequate support among the trustees to control the editorial line of the once liberal paper.

Hersant now controlled both newspapers of Lille and set out to achieve a similar monopoly in Le Havre. Such monopolies guarantee a press owner considerable influence with both local politicians and businessmen, who are dependent on newspapers for campaign support and advertising space. In Le Havre, France's principal English Channel port, Hersant purchased a controlling share of the stock of Havre Presse. The second newspaper, Havre Libre, was a socialist publication of an interesting sort. Set up in late 1944, its administrative council was structured to be one-third Communist, one-third Socialist, and one-third MRP. When Hersant began negotiations to join Havre Libre to Havre Presse in 1969, the journalists of both enterprises went out on a long but unsuccessful strike. Hersant obtained only a minority of shares in Havre Libre but was given control of its printing and technical operations (Pons 1977, p. 142). Eventually he will own the enterprise outright, since he has first right of refusal in all future stock transactions, and the newspaper's pro-socialist line will surely be altered.

Hersant's First Major Conquest: Paris-Normandie

Paris-Normandie was an openly Socialist newspaper formed in Rouen after World War II by members of the MRP and Socialist party.

The original shares were acquired for the symbolic sum of F100 apiece, with the trustees agreeing to maintain the political line of the newspaper, and reinvest all profits in the enterprise. This policy allowed Paris-Normandie to maintain a financially stable operation and even to purchase new printing presses without outside capital. It seemed safe from Hersant's insatiable appetite.

Hersant was born in Rouen and had attended school with Jean Lecanuet, a Gaullist who was elected mayor. Lecanuet had no greater opponent than the editor-in-chief of Paris-Normandie, Pierre-René Wolf, who consistently editorialized in favor of the Socialist opposition. Lecanuet, aided by the coincidence of Wolf's hospitalization, did all he could to convince the aging shareholders to sell their interests to Hersant.* Hersant was offering as high as F300,000 for packets of stock that had originally cost 300, and Hersant already held 33 percent of the stock before Wolf learned of these illegal underground purchases. (One of the social-democratic ordinances of 1944 held that all investments in the press required a full and complete disclosure of the origin of all funds.) Outraged, Wolf left his hospital bed to write a stinging editorial in the newspaper (January 20, 1971) disclosing all this, but to no avail. By 1971 Hersant controlled 60 percent of the votes, enough to alter the legal structure of the corporation so that he could put it under his personal control. In 1972 Wolf died, a broken man, and Hersant's takeover was complete; for the first time, his tactics became national news. Pierre Viansson-Ponté wrote in the May 17, 1972 issue of Le Monde: "What we see going on in Rouen is cynical, brutal and intolerable . . . fifteen, twenty papers all owned by one man: this is a monopoly. From the financial monopoly, one quickly crosses over into a monopoly on opinions."

In May 1972, both the journalists and printers at Paris-Normandie went out on strike to protest the takeover. The outpouring of popular support on the national level made Hersant feel the pressure of a concentrated counterattack for the first time. He settled quickly with the printers, promising them the job security and raises they demanded (Le Monde, May 28-29, 1972). After eight days, the journalists agreed to what seemed like a fair proposal: the promise of "editorial independence, no reduction in their number, and open con-

---

*We are able to follow events so closely only because of a pamphlet published by the dissident journalists of the enterprise (Livre Noir de Paris-Normandie, 1975). (Hersant later successfully sued them for publishing stolen documents.) Lecanuet later became minister of justice, and Hersant was later to control two major Parisian papers, which again would be able to support each other.

ditions in which to perform their professional duties" (Brimo 1977, p. 65). In fact, Hersant did not keep even one of these promises, and in a letter dated June 4, 1974, he formally rejected the accords themselves in a letter to his journalists.

It is worthwhile to notice Hersant's tactics after the takeover since they were used in later conquests. First, he replaces any left-oriented or pro-union journalists (<u>Presse Actualité</u>, June 1976).* At <u>Paris-Normandie</u> this included a change in the editor-in-chief, the principal heads of all departments, and a total change of 44 out of 115 journalists (<u>Presse Actualité</u>, November 1976). His new editor-in-chief instituted an abrupt switch from the paper's socialist tradition; the new editorial policy could be seen in the headline the day after the Pinochet coup in Chile: The Army Did Its Duty.†

Second, Hersant turns any cash assets of the newly conquered enterprise into further investments in other enterprises and borrows heavily on the fixed capital assets. Most of the cash raised from <u>Paris-Normandie</u> was used to aid another aspect of his campaign in the North: an effort to purchase as many periodicals in the area as possible. By 1976 this campaign had captured 14 different weeklies and biweeklies in this region for Hersant's press group; the investment totaled over F5 million (Brimo 1977, p. 66).

Third, when Hersant takes over a press enterprise, the advertising and news agency input are switched to Hersant's wholly owned subsidiary advertising and news agencies. One finds progressive numbers of pages that appear in other titles of the group, not only advertising and "service" pages (television listings, comics, and so on) but also news articles written by his news agency, AGPI (Agence générale de presse et d'information), and editorials as well. This consolidation allows a progressive reduction in the number of journalists used, which, along with other duplication-eliminating centralization, allows an appreciable increase in each publication's profitability, hence giving Hersant the competitive edge over the more labor intensive surviving independent enterprises. But of course it allows simultaneously a greater degree of centralized monitoring of the political and social content of articles and editorials.

---

*Of course he could not do this in the enterprises in which he was forced to sign agreements forming internal editorial committees.

†One should note that Wolf's <u>Paris-Normandie</u> had openly supported the Allende victory in 1970.

The Conquest of Paris

When an aging Jean Prouvost liquidated his press empire in 1975, Hersant was selected among other interested parties to be allowed to purchase the most influential conservative newspaper in all of France: Le Figaro.

Why was Hersant chosen? Other interested but vetoed parties included Jean-Jacques Servan-Schreiber (owner of L'Express and head of the Radical party)* and Simon Nora, past counselor to Jacques Chaban-Delmas. Gaullist Prime Minister Jacques Chirac, however, was in the best position to influence both Prouvost and the lending institutions, and he had been quoted as saying "Le Figaro nous intéresse beaucoup" (Nouvel Observateur, June 30, 1975). Furthermore, François Ceyrac, head of the powerful "Comité National du Patronat Français,"† was of a similar mind, stating "The only solution for us is Hersant" (Nouvel Observateur, June 30, 1975). The decision to sell Hersant the politically important newspaper, therefore, was taken in the highest political and corporate circles so it is not surprising that when Hersant went to the banks to borrow the large sums necessary for the purchase, he succeeded.

According to Denis Perier-Daville, president and founder of Le Figaro's journalist association, there may have been some displeasure in Gaullist circles with Le Figaro.‡ Although it was still a solidly pro-government paper, as it had almost always been, it was "liberal" in that there had been room for divergence in it. In fact, the political ideology of the front page with its big name columnists like Raymond Aron and François Mauriac, was sometimes contradicted by other articles by unknown journalists writing on inside pages. An increasing number of journalists saw themselves as socialists. Once, when Jean d'Ormesson wrote a particularly conservative article, 50 journalists signed a petition demanding that it either be blocked or its counter-perspective represented with a pro-Mitterand article. In addition, the journalists were highly unionized and formed a strong journalist association. Given that the journalist association was proposing to raise money to purchase a sizable portion of the

---

*The Radical party, despite the sound of its name in English, is a moderate, anti-socialist, center party.

†An owners organization not unlike the National Association of Manufacturers, except that the CNPF owners are from larger firms on the average than the NAM owners.

‡Interview with Denis Perier-Daville, February 12, 1977; confirmed by interview with François Boisarie, June 14, 1977.

stock (Perier-Daville 1976, p. 181) and the traditional importance of Le Figaro in mobilizing the traditional political right in France, there was good reason for the Gaullists to attempt to assure themselves of the prestigious daily's future evolution.

Hersant at Le Figaro

In any case, Hersant was chosen, and he paid about NF 70 million for the venerable newspapers. There were several unexplained aspects of the raising of this capital, although several investigators agree on the four largest of the contributing banks.* Two are of particular interest: the Banque Nationale de Paris, which is state-owned and therefore could easily have been influenced by the prime minister, Jacques Chirac; and the Banque Vernes, in which Marcel Dassault, a principal stockholder, could have wielded enormous influence (Pons 1977, p. 211).†

The borrowing power of the Hersant group is awesome. In 1975, the main holding company, SOCPRESS, had F61 million in long- and medium-term loans, yet the group managed to receive the 10 million needed for the purchase of Nord Eclair. Then, besides the 38 million borrowed to finance the Le Figaro purchase, Hersant also had to award indemnities to a high percentage of the journalists who

---

*There seem to be three principal mysteries in this purchase. (1) Some reports claim that the payment was made in cash in 500-franc notes brought into the bank in two large suitcases (Pons 1977, p. 210). "Espèces," however, is an ambiguous term and could also have been referring to a bank check. (2) Hersant, unlike other potential purchasers, had knowledge of a real estate transaction involving the traditional Le Figaro building on the Champs Elyseés. By offering to move at once, he collected a cash indemnity of NF22.5 million and a monthly saving of 3.5 million. The real estate transaction involved a British firm (Heron Corporation) and Hersant's industrial mentor, Marcel Dassault (Pons 1977, p. 211). (3) Hersant claimed he was able to use NF10 million liquid which he found in the cash reserve of Le Figaro to help purchase the paper (L'Expansion, September and November 1976). It seems a bit strange to use the assets of a corporation to help purchase that same corporation.

†See Le Canard Enchainé of October 27, 1976, for documentation of the close personal and political linkages between Hersant, Marcel Dassault, and Jacques Chirac. L'Express of August 25 also provides information on the Dassault-Chirac links. See also L'Unite, November 12, 1976, and L'Humanité March 28, 1977. Given these three men's importance in their respective fields, this information has important implications.

left at his takeover under the "right of conscience," and who, under this clause, were owed indemnities based on their seniority totaling another F20 million. In this period, Hersant also spent 30 million for his regional printing centers and another considerable sum to switch over to facsimile and offset printing in his Parisian plants. Furthermore, six months after these loans were established, Hersant was able to go back to the banks for the cash needed to fund his 50 percent purchase of France-Soir (Pons 1977, passim; Brimo 1977, passim; L'Expansion, September and November 1976). The degree of this borrowing power is probably more a sign of government support for Hersant's projects than an indication that the banks have suddenly developed new confidence in a minor and fading economic sector like the press. These loans indicate a willingness on the part of major financial institutions to tie up considerable capital in order to assure a dominating presence in the press. The motivation is not profit but control of the media.

When Hersant bought Le Figaro he promised the principal editorialists (Raymond Aron, Jean d'Ormesson, and others), and the journalists in general, that the daily editorial business of the paper would be run not by him but by those already in charge. By late 1976, that is, just over one year after the purchase, Aron, d'Ormesson, and all the other original members of the "Daily Editorial Management Committee" had been replaced. Hersant had broken his agreement, as he had previously at Paris-Normandie. As he puts it, "Money is stronger than honor" (Pons 1977, p. 162).

The atmosphere at Le Figaro in 1976 was best described by the concise phrase of one of the journalists I interviewed there: "C'est le Chile." Of the 293 journalists at Le Figaro at the time of Hersant's arrival, over 160 had resigned by 1976, and over 30 more had been fired. The right of conscience is supposed to operate for only three months after a new owner purchases a paper, but Hersant has declared openly that it is permanently available. His willingness to bear this expense is a product of his wish to remove from Le Figaro, as from all of his papers, all left-thinking journalists as well as all union militants.* In 1977, still more journalists left (Le Monde, April 13, 1977). Those who quit included the heads of such central departments as international politics, French politics, general information, education, and law. The editor-in-chief was forced out, as was his assistant. These departures were followed in 1977 by the departures of Raymond Aron, Jean d'Ormesson, and Xavier Marchetti, who had made the mistake of thinking they could work for

---

*Interview with François Boisarie, June 14, 1977.

Hersant. When Aron left, he wrote a major article in the newsweekly Le Point (June 1977) condemning Hersant.

These enforced departures at Le Figaro have allowed Hersant to appoint an entirely new staff to write the news the way he sees fit. For instance, Charles Rebois, the new head of the French politics department, is formerly from Hersant's own news agency, AGPI (Presse Actualité, June 1976). A second example is the case of Louis Pauwels, who entered AGPI in September 1977; two months later he was on "loan" to Le Figaro as editor-in-chief (Presse Actualité, January 1976). One of the few men who actively helped from the inside in Hersant's takeover of Le Figaro was Yann Clerc, a reactionary journalist-administrator who in 1976 headed the conservative journalist union attached to the right-wing national organization, Confédération Générale des Cadres (CGC). The policy on union membership was clear: any journalist hired by Le Figaro was expected to join the CGC. Hersant relentlessly repressed other journalist unions. In 1976, of the nine journalists Hersant asked permission to fire, six were elected union delegates. The labor inspector refused to permit this political firing of several of these delegates; several months later, however, the minister of labor himself overturned the injunction of the lower office.

In 1978 Le Figaro was not what it had been before Hersant took it over. Its renowned editorialists and finest journalists were gone. He had greatly reduced its pagination to cut costs, thus reducing as well the room available for articles.* The poorer quality of the general articles as well as the editorials was quite evident, and Jacques Sauvageot of Le Monde claimed that Le Figaro was no longer a serious intellectual competitor, that is, where previously Le Figaro had been mentioned every day in the morning meetings of Le Monde's editorial team (which looks at what was reported in the morning papers), by 1978 it was not at all rare to go a week without Le Figaro being mentioned.†

Hersant himself wrote an article in the paper in March 1976. Never before had an owner of Le Figaro demanded that his own article be published in the paper. Even more conservative administrative personnel such as Jean d'Ormesson attempted to block it (Presse Actualité, April 1976). Hersant's article was in response to one published a week earlier by Raymond Aron in which Aron stated that the advent of Eurocommunism was important and provided some

---

*Interview with Jean d'Ormesson (Executive Editor), March 7, 1977.
†Interview with Jacques Sauvageot, April 1, 1977.

real problems for the international cohesion of Communism. Hersant's reply, "L'Empire et L'Eglise," exhibits a 1950s hysteria on the subject:

> The USSR, having become sure of herself and dominant, now intends to free herself of the constraints of Yalta, and substitute for the control of national boundaries, the internal control of the European nations. She has available to her, for doing this, the active participation of the Communist parties in power. This is the stage before they actually take over power. (Le Figaro, March 11, 1976)

Even this single appearance of Hersant as a contributor is representative of the general turn to the right of the political ideology of Le Figaro. The days of a Le Figaro with a more liberal set of inside articles were gone. For example, the law column had previously supported conscientious objection and condemned the death penalty; by 1977, all traces of Le Figaro's enlightened conservatism had vanished.

The editorial turn to the right of the prestigious daily, however, was eclipsed by Hersant's creation of Figaro-Magazine, a slick weekly averaging well over 100 pages, which was included, for a supplemental charge, in the Saturday newspaper beginning in September 1978. In this weekly supplement, Hersant's editorialists consistently wrote from a reactionary position equalled only by Minute, and by Carrefour of the Amaury press group. The magazine editorialized in favor of a nineteenth century type of capitalism free of government controls, supported the presence of French troops in several African countries, and struck out at the policies and leaders of both the Socialist and Communist parties. This "journal du combat" was included as a supplement rather than sold as a weekly in order to benefit from a loophole: as a "daily" it paid less taxes than did the weeklies. It was not long before the Political Press Association registered a protest with the authorities, but to little immediate avail (Presse Actualité, May 1979). Actually, Hersant had had market tests done on the feasibility of selling Figaro-Magazine as a separate weekly, but it failed utterly, selling only 3000 to 3500 copies in the Parisian area (Presse Actualité, January 1979).

Besides the nonmarketability of Figaro-Magazine on its own footing, its effect has no doubt been watered down by the plethora of recent Figaro supplements: a Sunday edition (since September 1979), a weekly 8-page economic supplement (since November 1979), and a 150-page Figaro-Madame woman's magazine (included along with the political magazine in the Saturday edition since April 1980). The shortage of sales of Figaro-Magazine led to a reduction in its editorial staff in late 1979 (Presse Actualité, January 1980). Hersant nor anyone else could long ignore the fact that the more overtly political a contemporary publication is, the more difficult it is to sell.

Nevertheless, the appearance of Figaro-Magazine was an important event for the French right, and cannot be confounded with its lack of profitability for Hersant. During the 1960s and 1970s the conservative intelligentsia of France found very few suitable publications in which to write. Most right wing publications contained such vitriolic anti-Algerian racism, for example, to render them unacceptable vehicles for the conservative intelligentsia; such was the case with Minute, for instance. With the advent of the "New Philosophers" (Bernard Henri-Lévy, André Glucksman, et al.) in the mid-1970s, and especially the movement of conservative intellectuals known as La nouvelle droite, the absence of respectable publications on the right made itself keenly felt. Hersant's appointment of the respected Louis Pauwells as director of Figaro-Magazine hence played an important role in creating such a journal, and in legitimating the writings of the neo-conservatism which developed in France after the debacle of the united left in 1977.

Hersant at France-Soir

Pity Jacques Buob, a journalist who left Le Figaro at the approach of Hersant and found a job at France-Soir, when no one would have imagined that only a year after the highly controversial purchase of Le Figaro Hersant would again be in the market (and the banks) to purchase a second Parisian paper.

France-Soir had the widest circulation of any French paper; over 1.1 million copies were sold daily in 1968. During the 1958 Algerian crisis, some issues sold more than 2 million copies. The paper, although it belonged to Hachette, was in fact managed by its editor-in-chief, Pierre Lazareff, until his death in 1972.* He was perennially pro-government, and yet the newspaper, as well as its director, dealt little with open political reporting or analysis.

In 1975, the paper's deficit was F18 million; sales were off 8 percent for the year in Paris and 20 percent in the provinces. By 1976, the circulation had dropped from its acme by 50 percent. Hachette tried several different technocratic and corporate-type

---

*See the obituary by Pierre Viansson-Ponté, Le Monde, April 22, 1972.

directors, but they could not reverse the trend, and understandably so, given the changing occupational structure of Paris, which was losing working-class population while expanding in the new middle-strata workers who, as we shall see later, seldom read such sensationalist newspapers. Hachette invested F5 million in one last major advertising campaign and made a final round of personnel and format changes. Nothing worked. Hachette was ready to sell.

One researcher reports that at a working lunch in Paris, Hersant met with Prime Minister Jacques Chirac, Marie-France Garaud (advisor to Pompidou and then Chirac), and Jacques Douce (chairman of the board and chief administrator of Havas Advertising Agency, 56 percent of which is owned by the French state) to work out the details of the sale (Brimo 1977, p. 99). It was clear that Hersant's name could not be used; the purchases of Le Figaro and, before that Paris-Normandie were still fresh scandals. In June 1976, Hachette announced that it would sell France-Soir to Paul Winkler, president of a successful photo and design agency, and director of the Hachette subsidiary, Edi-Monde. For F49 million, Winkler bought Paris' largest, if not most profitable, daily. This was in early July. In early August, Winkler announced that he had taken Robert Hersant as a 50 percent partner. When a strike was threatened, Winkler agreed to hold off for a short while. Other offers were made by Claude Perdriel,* a socialist, and Jean-Claude Smadja, a liberal, as well as several others. The prime minister, along with others, made every effort to discourage these would-be left minded purchasers (Brimo 1977, p. 99). On August 17, the sale became final; that day a long and well-organized strike began.

As the strike wore on, the journalists began to disagree among themselves. One of the later strike votes carried by only 98 to 81. But, as at Paris-Normandie, most influential in ending the eleven-day strike was the desertion of the printers' union. One of the great problems of French printers in 1975 was that better than 60 percent of all printed material was printed outside of the country (Communist Party, 1976, p. 17). Winkler offered to repatriate the printing of several of his periodicals, and the peace was won. The timing was ideal; the strikes and demonstrations had drawn little attention, even though they were large and militant, for in August Paris is essentially closed.

Winkler/Hersant offered the usual indefinite right of conscience to the journalists; all were welcome to leave, and, as always, many

---

*Claude Perdriel, along with Jean Daniel, owns and manages the important socialistic weekly, Nouvel Observateur.

did. (One group went to Claude Perdriel with the idea for a daily paper, and it is they who eventually made up the backbone of the successful new socialistic daily, Le Matin.) Hersant's usual repression on editorial, political, and union levels soon followed. Department heads and editors were replaced by the new administration.*
Hersant's direct editorial intervention became apparent when the September 18, 1976 issue appeared with a "signature strike," wherein no journalist allowed his or her name to be affixed to an article in protest of the censorship of major articles, especially one on the aerospace industry magnate, Marcel Dassault, which had been so thoroughly altered (censored) that the journalist who wrote it refused to allow it to be published at all (Presse Actualité, November 1976). Other major articles were altered entirely in editorial rewriting, most noticeably one which criticized the Parisian police (Presse Actualité, November 1976).

Hersant at L'Aurore

If Hersant found it necessary to hide the first steps of his France-Soir takeover behind Paul Winkler because of the uproar over his previous purchase of Le Figaro, he had to be even more careful in his takeover of L'Aurore barely two years later. The purchase of L'Aurore from July to November 1978 by an unknown holding company, the subsequent resignation of the principal directors, editors, and journalists of L'Aurore, and their replacement with individuals from the Hersant press group did not go unnoticed, however, leading as it did to public protests by the journalists of L'Aurore, widespread discontent in the Parisian press in general, discussions in the Parlement, and an American-style interrogation of President Giscard d'Estaing at a press conference held on November 21, 1978.

During this press conference, Giscard was essentially forced into declaring himself in favor of maintaining pluralism in the press, to which end he would ask the prime minister to have the important Economic and Social Council prepare an in-depth study on the press. The council appointed a commission headed by Georges Vedel, the honorary dean of the Faculty of Law and Economy of the University of Paris, and the commission proceeded to produce a long report in May 1979. This report, while suggesting revisions in state aid aimed especially at helping the advertising-poor political press and proposing the formation of a "commision des opérations de press," which

---

*Interview with Paul Parisot, June 14, 1977.

would serve as a state agency to which interested parties could contest a proposed takeover move, ended with the unrealistic conclusion that, since "the future of the press is in the hands of the press itself to determine," only the "capacity of cooperation between press enterprises" could lead to a solution to the problem of concentration (Journal Officiel, August 7, 1979).

In the meantime, Hersant had consolidated his indirect takeover of L'Aurore, which had been an unprofitable enterprise for some years, although the second daily of the group, Paris-Turf (exclusively covering horse racing) always made up the deficit. The cotton and textile magnate owner of the two papers, Marcel Boussac, had fallen on hard times and had sold the two publications to an unknown holding company, Franpresse, in 1978. Soon after this sale, dealings between Franpresse and SOCPRESS, a Hersant holding company, led to an agreement for a "technical cooperation" that presaged the consolidation of the advertising personnel of the four papers (L'Aurore, Paris-Turf, Le Figaro, and France-Soir), the eventual printing of the former two at the new printing shop being built in a northern suburb of Paris for the latter two (La Plaine Saint-Denis—at a cost of NF 120 million, more evidence of Hersant's vast borrowing power), and the use of Hersant's facsimile network by the two papers.

The speculation of a Hersant takeover raised by these agreements was augmented one month later after the resignations of Francine Lazurick (director of L'Aurore since the 1968 death of her husband, Robert, L'Aurore's liberation-era director), Dominique Pado (co-director of management and political director of L'Aurore), José Van den Esch (principal political editorialist), and Gilbert Guilleminault (chief of the editorial staff). The Franpresse holding company immediately appointed Pierre Janrot, the editor-in-chief of Hersant's France-Antilles since 1976, to take over these administrative functions. Of the old L'Aurore hierarchy, there remained only one person, Roland Faure, who was assured by Franpresse that he was to stay on as political director and chief of the editorial staff. Faure stated in a nationally aired radio interview (November 3, 1978) that the appointment of Janrot did not imply that Hersant had taken over L'Aurore for "if he had, L'Aurore would have had to continue without me." It was only one month later, however, when Faure resigned.

By November the journalists of L'Aurore held press conferences and wrote the president of the Republic for help, and Faure published a letter in Le Matin condemning the Hersant takeover. But it was too late. By January 1979, L'Aurore printed the "daily calendar" in common with Le Figaro, and by February there was a combined production of the employment section. All four papers were blocked by several printers' strikes during this time, but the aim of these was solely to hold Hersant to his 1978 promise to maintain 65 percent of the technical personnel of the previously separate printing operations. By March the photocomposition of L'Aurore was being done in the rue du Louvre Figaro building, and a combined team was producing the employment ads and stock market reports for both Le Figaro and L'Aurore. More Hersant personnel flowed into L'Aurore: Marc Rouzier (editor-in-chief of Hersant's news agency, AGPI) became assistant chief of the editorial staff, and Jacques Guillené-Brulen (editorialist at Le Figaro) became editor-in-chief for foreign news.

The journalist unions at L'Aurore (SNJ, CFDT, FO) had their lawyers join the L'Aurore clandestine takeover to the existing lawsuits against Hersant for infraction of the anti-trust laws of 1944, but it is doubtful that the courts will soon take decisive action on these (see below). In the meantime, the absorption of L'Aurore continued: by July the sales departments were joined, and by December 1979 all L'Aurore's remaining journalists were operating in the Figaro building, while 45 (of the original 70) had been fired. After November, only four pages of L'Aurore (foreign and domestic political news) were written by a separate staff; the remainder of the paper was written by the Figaro staff.

In the firing of the surplus L'Aurore journalists, Hersant, as one would expect, included the union delegates. (He had earlier fired Claude Prunier, the SNJ delegate, and vice president of the national SNJ, only to have the work inspector find the firing purely political and disallow it.) The layoffs of these delegates essentially eliminated union activism in the remaining L'Aurore personnel—if, indeed, it still made sense to conceive of L'Aurore as a separate entity. Hersant had succeeded again and now with Le Figaro, France-Soir, and L'Aurore controlled three enterprises accounting for 47.2 percent of the daily Parisian press in 1979.

Notes on Some Struggles Against Hersant

Hersant has met challenges along the way but has not been noticeably affected by them. Part of the reason is that he has used his press empire to construct a minor political career for himself, beginning with an "American-style" campaign that brought about his election as a deputy to the National Assembly in 1956. His collaborationist past and criminal background, however, led to the formal invalidation of his original election, although a subsequent reelection gave him the seat. He used this office (which he finally lost in 1978) more to gain political contacts for his press empire (and an immunity from prosecution) than for any political designs per se, as he openly stated in a major interview (L'Expansion, November 1976).

One anti-Hersant uprising involved the courageous struggle of two brothers who owned L'Eveil Normand, a small, healthy weekly publication which Hersant wanted to add to his list in the Normandy area. It was a pitched battle, with Hersant buying little weeklies from the surrounding area and trying to force advertisers and readers to abandon L'Eveil. Eventually, the Meaulle brothers became a national symbol of the struggle against Hersant (Le Monde, December 9, 1973).

Another attack on Hersant has come from the main consumers' association, L'Union Fédérale des Consommateurs, which federates about 80 local consumer groups and publishes the large-circulation, Consumer Guide-style Que Choisir? It has used the right of class action suit, recently won in French law, to challenge Robert Hersant. François Ruberol, president of the association, explained that Hersant was being sued for breaking the 1944 press laws and, in particular, for not putting his name on the papers he publishes. The logic, as Ruberol put it, is that courts may well go along with making Hersant live up to this minor provision of the law and that once he does so he will be susceptible to indictment for owning more than one daily newspaper.*

The journalist unions and their common federation have struck back at Hersant, not only through strikes at the papers he has taken over but also in initiating lawsuits against his monopolistic practices. The CGT-affiliated journalist union began a lawsuit in January 1977, which was followed by a second suit instigated in February by the journalists affiliated to the socialist "Confédération Française du Travail" (CFDT), the conservative "Force Ouvrière" (FO), and the independent Syndicat National des Journalists (SNJ). Edmond Maire, general secretary of the CFDT, explained that the purpose of the suit was to break "the greatest risk, that of the ever-increasing silence that surrounds current concentrations, and impedes research on the processes involved, and thus contributes to the progressive loss of the freedom of information" (Le Monde, February 8, 1977). The suit of the CFDT (France's second largest union federation) asked that Hersant's papers be sequestered, and Edmond Maire's direct involvement gives an idea of how serious the situation would have been for Hersant if the left had come to power in the 1978 legislative elections.

---

*Interview with François Ruberol, December 16, 1976. See also Que Choisir, December 1976, and Le Monde, November 11, 1976.

These lawsuits are moving extremely slowly, however, and there was little progress until November 1978, when Hersant was summoned before an examining magistrate. Nearly a year later, the magistrate declared the lawsuits of the consumers' union and the journalists' unions admissible. The concentration of numerous dailies in the hands of one man, wrote the judge, "is of such a nature as to threaten the free existence of the profession and, consequently, to gravely injure the collective interests of journalists" (Presse Actualité, November 1979). It will take a considerable amount of time, however, for any final ruling to come down from the courts.

Hersant's activities have spurred huge marches in Paris attended by 100,000 demonstrators (Presse Actualité, September 1976). There have been meetings of the union delegates of the many different papers he owns. There have been angry speeches in the National Assembly and even a debate in the Assembly in April 1975 (for which Hersant and other press-owning deputies such as Jean-Jacques Servan-Schreiber, Marcel Dassault, and Gaston Defferre were conspicuously absent) (Le Monde, April 18, 1975). In the final analysis, these approaches have done little more than the insults and revelations of Le Canard Enchaîné, which insists on referring to him as "HERR SANT" (November 3, 1976). The only real threat to Robert Hersant's press empire in 1976-77 was the avowed intention of the left political parties to utilize the provisions of 1944 to break up his newspaper chain should they come to power. With the defeat of the left in 1978, Hersant's empire seemed safe. It was technically sound, being based on the most modern equipment and processes. It was also financially and politically sound: he had strong links with the banking community and the conservative political parties. In the late 1970s one could only conclude that Robert Hersant would remain a central figure in the French press for the foreseeable future.

CONCLUSION

These three case studies of differing patterns of monopolistic practices highlight several major points. Prouvost's labor-intensive model of press empire was no longer viable by 1975, given the high costs incurred by its multiple noncentralized press enterprises. Future press groups can be expected to be capital-intensive, which will allow them to (1) greatly diminish the quantity of labor needed from journalists and printers; (2) radically de-skill the remaining workers; (3) reduce the power of the journalist and printer unions by this quantitative and qualitative reduction; and (4) greatly centralize their operations. The press enterprises that can make these changes first will have a far higher productivity than the remaining labor-intensive enterprises; thus the former will grow even larger and more centralized as the latter fail under the increased pressures.

Such monopolistic firms as Hachette and Hersant may soon be the only corporate structures capable of dealing successfully with the aligned industrial sectors from which the press must purchase its supplies. The paper, printing, photo-electronic equipment, and related sectors have themselves undergone monopolization and are dominated today by one or several usually multinational corporations. The monopolistic practices of these dominant corporations form an environment that tends to reproduce itself inside the sectors with which it comes into contract; thus those practices pressure the press sector to concentrate even further.

We have seen that the press sector is itself endowed with a major multinational conglomerate, Hachette. Certainly this corporation will remain dominant in the sector, since it takes an extremely large capital outlay to attempt to compete with the dominant firms in one single sector; it would be essentially impossible to accumulate adequate capital to begin a multiple-sector effort to set up a new vertically integrated conglomerate.

Hachette's vertical interlocks give it the broad base it needs to survive the periodic business cycles endemic to capitalist society. These crises, such as the recent 1974-75 recession, operate to purge economic sectors of small and medium-size enterprises and thus are actually beneficial to monopolistic corporations. A vertically integrated corporation like Hachette is virtually sheltered from economic crises since it is constantly doing business between its different branches and subsidiaries. Furthermore, it is extremely broad-based, with many sectors immune to crisis (school supplies, press distribution, printing for government bureaucracies, and so on).

Robert Hersant's monopolistic practices are of a significantly different kind than Hachette's. Hersant's horizontal holdings consist of press monopolies in various cities (for example, Rouen, Le Havre). These give him control of both local information reporting (since there is no local radio or television in France) and local advertising. With the unusually high profits available from this monopolistic position, Hersant has begun the process of the total electronic centralization of his press empire. Eventually, the greatest part of all his papers will be written and composed in Paris and sent by the facsimile process to the regional printing plants he has set up across France.

This centralization gives Hersant (and the Parisian dominant class to which he is closely linked) a new degree of control over the production and circulation of information in the provinces. The political importance of this became clear in the 1978 legislative elections, when democratic socialism was on the ballot; Hersant used his papers in an outright propaganda campaign against the left.

Together these three studies make it clear that the reconquest of the liberation press has once again placed the industrial bourgeoisie in control of the written press and, to some extent, of the electronic media. They also tell us about the multiple logics of corporate monopolization strategies and remind us that our analytical tools will need to be capable of distinguishing between various corporate strategies.

It is no longer possible to study "mass communications" without investigating the details of the conglomerates and multinationals that are dominant in the field. Recently, Schiller (1971, 1973), Aronson (1973), Read (1976), and especially Mattelart (1974b, 1976) have begun to make serious contributions toward the development of appropriate methodologies for studying the political economy of communication corporations.

These studies also make it clear that the state is closely linked with the monopolistic firms in the press sector, confirming the notion that while there is a relative autonomy of the state over the various segments of the dominant class, the state still is more likely to intervene in favor of the most powerful segment of the dominant class (monopolistic corporations in the various sectors). Thus only as a general pattern can we say that the state intervenes to preserve the relative balance of opposed dominant class segments. In the press, in any case, the state has consistently intervened in the interests of the monopolistic firms. A bit later I shall look in detail at the specific channels of state intervention, but first I will turn to study the independent enterprise that breaks most of the patterns established in the discussion to this point: Le Monde.

3
LE MONDE: AN EXPERIMENT IN WORKER PARTICIPATION

THE DEVELOPMENT OF WORKER PARTICIPATION AT <u>LE MONDE</u>

<u>Le Monde</u> developed directly from a pre-World War II newspaper, <u>Le Temps</u>, which had been an opposition paper during the nineteenth century. Although <u>Le Temps</u> certainly was not an antigovernment publication, it had the courage to displease the government on particular issues, and this paradigm set the stage for its postwar successor. <u>Le Temps</u> passed through various hands until it reached a director by the name of Louis Mill, who fell upon hard times. At his death, a court looking into his estate discovered a closely guarded secret: he had long since secretly sold 50 percent plus one shares. Although this discovery was made in 1931, it was not until two years later that a union weekly discovered and published the identity of its controlling owners: the Comité des Forges, the steel trust.

<u>Le Temps</u> was sequestered at the liberation, although it had in no way collaborated. It had closed down on November 29, 1942, while the liberation authorities chose November 26 as the mandatory closing date. Clearly <u>Le Temps</u> had been confiscated to remove it from the control of the Comité des Forges; such was the spirit of the liberation.*

---

*See Hoffman (1974) for an analysis of the forces at work during the liberation to glorify the left and stigmatize elements of the bourgeoisie.

Le Temps served as the model for Le Monde: small headlines, no photographs, and specializing in a serious and even scholarly coverage of social, political, and diplomatic affairs. It is no surprise that the continuity was so great; along with Beuve-Méry at the prewar papers, one could find 30 of the 31 journalists writing for the new Le Monde (Chatelain 1962, p. 35). The fact that the journalists were originally employed by Le Temps and that they had in no way collaborated was important later in legitimating their claim to be made partial owners of the enterprise.

Hubert Beuve-Méry, Le Monde's creator, represents the very essence of the nonsocialist, but progressive Christian-liberalism that was important between the wars. In fact it is impossible to understand the libertarian, progressive position of Le Monde under Beuve-Méry or the socialistic position under his successor Jacques Fauvet without noting that the enterprise's upper editorial staff is almost without exception made up of people who were politically formed in the "democratic Christian" or "left Christian" movements of prewar France. These movements often linked to the important national movement "Action Chrétienne Jeunesse Française," were made up of an anti-clerical laity which demanded that the church remove itself from secular affairs. This movement, which spawned important demonstrations before World War II, played a major role in the Resistance. At the liberation, many voted for the progressive MRP, while others became libertarian socialists. It would be difficult to overestimate the influence of left Christian militantism on Le Monde.*
In a recent book on Le Monde, Jean-Noël Jeanneney and Jacques Juliard (1979) have gone so far as to compare Le Monde's internal processes to those of Port Royal, and Beuve-Méry's probing journalism to the ethic of Jansenism.

From 1934 to 1938 Beuve-Méry was a correspondent in Prague for Le Temps. By 1938 and the Munich agreements, Le Temps was a pro-government paper linked to the Foreign Ministry, and it predictably supported the accords. Beuve-Méry resigned in protest and during the latter part of the war took active part in the Resistance. After the war he was called upon by General de Gaulle to set up a prestigious, internationally respectable newspaper on the site and

---

*Besides Beuve-Méry and Fauvet, Jacques Sauvageot (head administrator), André Fontaine (head of foreign politics), Pierre Viansson-Ponté (head of French politics), Pierre Drouin (head of the economy section), and Jean Planchais (chief editorialist on military matters), in other words, all of Le Monde's top editorialists, were active before World War II in the left Christian movements.

with the equipment of Le Temps. He was not trusted solely with the
new paper but was joined by F. Funck-Brentano, one of the earliest
advisors to de Gaulle in London and a member of his postwar cabinet.
Joining the two was René Courtin, another trusted Gaullist. Each of
the three held equal shares, and various other associates held smaller
parts. This structure worked well enough until 1948, when the question of France's relationship with the United States became topical
and highly political due to the accelerating Cold War.

A split occurred in Le Monde around this issue: René Courtin
supported French entry into the Atlantic Alliance (as did J. J.
Servan-Schreiber, then at Le Monde), while Beuve-Méry took the
opposite position, arguing that what was involved was a rearming of
Germany. Beuve-Méry editorialized in favor of a strongly armed,
neutral Europe that was not heavily reliant on the United States
(Jeanneney and Julliard 1979, p. 83). These views were hotly contested in government circles, and Courtin and Funck-Brentano
refused to continue to write for the paper (Thibault 1978, p. 225).

By 1951, Beuve-Méry was harshly criticized for his "neutralist" position by both government officials and the conservative press.
He stood fast, nonetheless, until Courtin and Funck-Brentano publicly
attacked his editorial policy. At that point he handed them a letter of
resignation, which they accepted. The reaction, however, was immediate: left political leaders strongly condemned the government for
intervening in the press, readers formed special committees of
support, and the journalists organized into a group, which they called
the Société de Rédacteurs (journalist association) to coordinate their
action in support of Beuve-Méry. They threatened to strike if he
were removed from his duties as director of the publication. The
journalists even contacted the president of the republic, Vincent
Auriol, and asked him to intervene with a specially appointed commission. These pressure tactics and Beuve-Méry's gamble paid off:
he was reinstated with full powers.

Two months later, Beuve-Méry announced structural changes
that were intended to preclude the possibility of such an attack from
the outside: there would be an augmentation in the shares of the Le
Monde corporation, with the new shares to be given to the journalist
association to hold in trust. They were given 28 percent of the stock,
which, like all other stock in Le Monde, is not transferable to one's
inheritors but passes to one's successor at the paper. Beuve-Méry
had thought of the idea previously, but it was the support of the journalists during the crisis that led directly to his decision.*

---

*Interview with Hubert Beuve-Méry, March 14, 1977. See also
Duverger 1977, p. 144.

Throughout a series of ideological and financial attacks on Le Monde (see below) the paper's journalists supported Beuve-Méry unfailingly. Today's hierarchy at Le Monde is almost exclusively composed of those who stood by their editor-in-chief during the early years. Continual efforts to reduce Le Monde's success and independence failed, but they convinced Beuve-Méry that he must go even further to protect his paper from the grasp of big capital. In 1968, at this retirement, Beuve-Méry chose his successors: Jacques Fauvet (editorial director of the paper) and Jacques Sauvageot (director of financial matters). But more importantly, he also increased the participation of the journalists to fully 40 percent, and gave another 9 percent to the middle level administrators (cadres) and the clericals. He also offered shares to the printers, but they turned them down along the classical CGT lines of refusing participation schemes in capitalist industry. In the 1970s the ownership breakdown was as shown in Table 3.1.

The structure of Le Monde thus provided for fully 49 percent of the stock to be held by employee associations, with 40 percent belonging to the journalists. The patterns of daily management, however, have little to do with this, as the journalist association meets only on occasion, as does the Conseil de Surveillance, which is, by statute, presided over by the president of the journalist association.* In its daily functioning, Le Monde was run like all other French papers: from the top down. Neither Beuve-Méry nor his designated successor, Jacques Fauvet, have permitted "minority papers," although Le Monde's columns are open to outside viewpoints that vary widely on the issues of the day. When the paper itself takes a stance, it is decided upon by the editor-in-chief. As Jacques Fauvet wrote:

> A newspaper without a "patron" is a being with no character; it is better to have a bad one. To give such a paper a patron is to bring it a modicum of unity, that is to say, of life, despite the natural and necessary diversity of a team. (Chatelain 1962, p. 188)

---

*For a more detailed analysis of Le Monde's internal structure, see the organigram in Fig. A.1.

TABLE 3.1

Who Owns Le Monde?

Shareholder	Percentage Share
Personnel	
Journalist association	40.0
Cadres	5.0
Employees	4.0
Management	
Jacques Fauvet	7.0
Jacques Sauvageot	4.0
Individuals*	
Hubert Beuve-Méry	10.0
Jean-Jacques Beuve-Méry	5.5
Eleven other "moral guarantors"	24.5
Total	100.0

*Complex rules fix limiting conditions under which these shares can be bought by other individual associates. In any case no one can hold more than 25 percent of these, or 10 percent of the total shares.
Source: Internal document of Le Monde, dated April 15, 1973.

LE MONDE'S INTERNAL CONTRADICTION: WORKER PARTICIPATION AND CORPORATE HIERARCHY

An independent corporate structure based on worker participation that must survive in a highly monopolized capitalist society is continually threatened by the very nature of its contradictory existence. Externally, its socialized relations of production will draw automatically hostile reaction from the traditionally structured corporate units with which it has intercourse. Internally, the workers themselves have been through family, educational, social, and previous professional experiences which have in no sense prepared them to participate in a socialized enterprise. Under Beuve-Méry and Fauvet, Le Monde functioned like a capitalist enterprise in every way, with the exception of dividing bonus money equally at the end of the fiscal year. All editorial and organizational decisions were made by the director, or, after Beuve-Méry's retirement, by the co-directors. Anyone lower on the hierarchy found himself incapable of action, since the norm was to clear all decisions above. Under Beuve-Méry this went relatively unquestioned, especially since the overwhelming majority of journalists belonged to the independent and quite apolitical SNJ union and saw themselves as professionals.

The contradiction at the heart of Le Monde was set into action by the events of May 1968, which, after all, raised the same questions on a national level. This was the year Beuve-Méry retired, and he only exacerbated the problem by making two seemingly contradictory decisions. On one hand, he increased the direct control of Le Monde's workers to an effective majority; on the other, he appointed Jacques Fauvet and Jacques Sauvageot with the full and complete authority of the chief executive officers of any capitalist corporation.

Le Monde's circulation had soared during the 1960s, from 167,000 in 1961 to 352,000 after the May events (Presse Actualité, May 1979). Beuve-Méry had always run the enterprise on a shoestring, and indeed his fiscal conservatism had proved beneficial for the young enterprise. But by 1968 the independent enterprise was both fiscally sound and desperately in need of additional journalists. Of the several dozen journalists who were added after Fauvet's appointment, nearly all had been deeply involved in and affected by the May events. Since the daily was editorially supportive of the student positions, this new generation of Le Monde journalists were in effect encouraged to carry on their student activism within the enterprise. These new journalists avoided the apolitical and corporatist SNJ and joined the CFDT-affiliated union. As CFDT journalists, they saw themselves as salaried workers, not as underprivileged professionals, as had their older counterparts who still controlled the stock-holding journalist body, the "journalist association." The CFDT journalists, furthermore, joined with CFDT clericals and CFDT cadres to form a CFDT bloc.

This new formation posed a serious threat to the journalist association, which is predicated upon the management rights of ownership, whereas the CFDT position is based upon the management rights of workers. As the vice president of the journalist association (a member of the CFDT) told me, "For now we will play the journalist association card; if that fails to provide a more democratic input into the structure of authority, then we will use the CFDT directly."*

---

*Interview with Philippe Labarde, January 21, 1976.

It was clear to everyone in the mid-1970s that this contradiction could become explosive at the rapidly approaching retirement of Fauvet, which as it was had been set back to provide time for a solution. Beuve-Méry had had the authority to determine the format of his succession and the wisdom to retire early enough to allow him to remain on in an advisory position to oversee the transition. But Fauvet no longer had either the moral nor the juridical authority to impose a future on Le Monde's organizational structure; it was clear that it would be necessary to derive a consensus if a devastating split between the two generations of journalists was to be avoided. The younger journalists insisted that the prestigious daily's third-generation administration should reflect its socialized organizational structure and pro-socialist editorial positions: total authority should not be put into the hands of one or several individuals again. The older and more moderate journalists, on the contrary, felt that a newspaper needed strict and clear lines of authority since there really was not time in the four hours available to write and edit the most important articles and editorials for a committee structure to work.

By 1978 the enterprise was floundering in its inability to solve these problems rooted in its contradictory nature, and it was clear that time was running out. A broad consensus was reached, however, for a unique individual, Jean-Marie Dupont, to undertake an in-depth critical study of the enterprise and its problems. Dupont had the trust of all, partly because of his frank and engaging personal nature, partly because of his singular background. The administrators trusted him because of his effective assistant editorship of the social affairs desk and because of his background as a militant left Christian ("catho de gauche"). The older journalists had confidence in him because he had been secretary general of the national SNJ and an extremely effective president of Le Monde's journalist association, guiding it gracefully through the difficult years when the CFDT challenge to the association was growing. The younger journalists, in turn, supported Dupont largely because of his national reputation as a (pre-1960) student militant; he had been president of the Lille branch of the important National Student Union (UNEF) and had then been chosen president of the national organization itself. Finally, even the militant printers of the enterprise trusted Dupont, partly because of his union activism, but especially because of his working-class origins.

Dupont's final report was devastating. He argued that both the tone and structure of Le Monde's administrative organization were maladapted to the important challenges facing the enterprise. Power was far too centralized in the two executive directors, causing the organization to exist on a day-to-day basis, with absolutely inadequate long-term planning. Dupont attributed Le Monde's inability to make decisions about modernizing its print shop and streamlining its archaic business offices (cadres) on this hyper-centralization. Fauvet and Sauvageot kept the report secret for a month, so severe were its criticisms. In the end they acceded to one of its major suggestions and formed a "management team" (équipe de direction) around them, including the editor-in-chief, two assistant editors-in-chief, the assistant director of finances, the director of the print shop, and the director of advertising. Dupont was named secretary general of this management team, which was to meet every week and discuss all decisions.

Besides beginning the arduous task of undertaking modernization of the print shop (which involved a successful round of delicate deliberations with the printers unions), the management team negotiated a set of ground rules for the choice of a successor to Fauvet. Although the team would continue its weekly meetings and involve itself in editorial policy as well as organizational decisions, a new single director of the publication would be chosen democratically by the 200 editorial staff members of Le Monde.

In early 1980 began a long process of divisive internal struggles to determine Fauvet's successor. Six months, two general assemblies, and five official ballots later, Claude Julien, director of the monthly Le Monde Diplomatique, emerged the victor. He will serve alongside Fauvet for a rather long time and will not take over the position as such until January 1983.

Before taking this position, Julien had served as head of the international desk for the daily, where he had specialized in coverage of the United States (he had studied at Notre Dame University and speaks flawless English) and in reporting on Latin America. As director of Le Monde Diplomatique, his choice of articles and personal editorials reflected this double interest: he wrote excoriating critiques of U.S. foreign policy and particularly of U.S. domination of Latin America. He openly supported revolutionary struggles in Latin America, criticized U.S. participation in the overthrow of Chilean democracy, and generally turned the monthly publication into what the French call "un organ de combat." Its columns were continually open to the left, and critics of all aspects of capitalism, colonialism, and imperialism found an important forum. There was, for example, extensive coverage of the contribution of "cultural imperialism" to contemporary international relations (see Schiller et al. 1974).

Le Monde, however, is not Le Monde Diplomatique, and to gain the 60 percent of the votes necessary for victory, Julien made important promises to some of Le Monde's more moderate journalists not to impose his radical views on other journalists and editorialists. Furthermore, he made major concessions in a letter to the journalist association to renegotiate a more collegial style of management, moving away from the top-down format. Nevertheless, Le Monde clearly is continuing the movement to the left already evidenced in Fauvet's succession to Beuve-Méry. As Nouvel Observateur (June 9, 1980) phrased it, the change from Fauvet to Julien is a transition from a "progressive Christian-democrat" to a "pro-Third-World left Christian."

ATTACKS ON LE MONDE

Le Monde is a threat for two reasons. First, the paper itself has taken an openly pro-socialist stance since Jacques Fauvet became its director in 1968; even before that, the paper often took positions that were directly opposed to government policy. Second, under both directors Le Monde has been an open forum for a remarkably wide range of opinions; dissidents and outcasts from both the right and the left have a national podium from which to speak. Although Le Monde, like the rest of the French press, does no investigative reporting, it does accept position papers critiquing everything from government programs to Communist party policies.* Le Monde has therefore been threatening at different times to both the Communist left and the Gaullist right; it is no surprise to find that it has been criticized from both directions.

Attacks on Le Monde have taken two major forms: ideological attacks (criticisms in other papers, pamphlets, circulars, and books) and financial attacks (efforts to buy out the paper and attempts to set up a competitive paper to cut off Le Monde's advertising). It is worthwhile to take a look at several instances of each type of attack. These attacks on Le Monde are not simply instances of laissez faire capitalist competition; they are concrete movements of class struggle between elements of the French bourgeoisie and an important newspaper that has become increasingly anti-capitalist.

Ideological Attacks

"Le Monde was born on the nineteenth of December, 1944. Five days later the attacks began" (Chatelain 1962, p. 49). The left was

---

*After the loss of the 1978 legislative elections, Le Monde printed critiques of the CP written by Party intellectuals such as Jean Elleinstein and Louis Althusser.

the first to criticize the new paper, finding it a direct successor to
Le Temps, the prewar paper controlled by the steel trust (L'Humanité, December 24, 1944). It was not long before the right took over
the attack, as Beuve-Méry's paper became more and more outspoken
in favor of an armed neutral Europe.

More recently, Le Monde's controversial support of the student
demonstrations during May 1968 was almost equally displeasing to
both the right and the Communist left. The Gaullists considered Le
Monde's position "anti-French" (La Nation, September 23, 1968),
the far right labeled Beuve-Méry the "Red Star" of France (Rivarol,
June 8, 1970), while the Communists accused the prominent daily of
being "leftist" (L'Humanité, May 21, 1970). Raymond Aron, writing
in Le Figaro (June 23, 1975) excoriated Le Monde for contributing
to "the destruction of liberal society."

The press bourgeoisie's distaste for Le Monde is well expressed
by Jean-Louis Servan-Schreiber, a central figure in the L'Express
group, and director of L'Expansion, France's largest circulation
business publication: "On the national level, Le Monde is the institution which supports the malcontent journalists, and always prints
the nearly daily communiques which the strikers publish" (Servan-
Schreiber 1972, p. 188).

These criticisms in the press are in themselves no great threat
to Le Monde's independence and survival. But of course they operate
in concert with many other pressures on the enterprise. For example,
a series of pamphlets have been published attacking the paper. In
1952, the Bulletin of International Political Study and News published
a newsletter entitled, "Le Monde, The Communist Auxiliary." This
circular claimed not only that Le Monde had given aid to Communist
propaganda organizations but that the paper was "equally dangerous
for its absences and silences" (Chatelain 1962, p. 184). In 1970,
Jean Cau published an attack at Le Monde's pro-left positions, entitled, "Le Monde: Or Objectivity in Question" (Bellanger 1976,
p. 233). Both of these pamphlets were anonymously sent to Le Monde's
advertisers, thus transferring the attack from the ideological to the
financial level.

In 1976, a similar attack on Le Monde was launched, and I was
able to investigate it in some detail. This time the pamphlet was
written by a minor novelist, Louis de Villefosse. His pamphlet,
"Le Monde and its Methods," was published by a front organization,
the Association for a Critical Reading of the Press, which in fact
was run out of his home. The letterhead sported several major names,
including Eugene Ionesco, Julien Freund, and Jacques Ellul.* This

---

*Jacques Ellul claimed, however, that de Villefosse had mis-
used his name (Interview with Jacques Sauvegot, April 1, 1977).

94 / THE FRENCH PRESS

pamphlet, like its predecessors, was sent to Le Monde's advertisers; enclosed was a letter typed on a plain page with no letterhead whatsoever and followed by an illegible signature. It read, in full:

> Dear Mr. President,
> We found the name of your enterprise among the major advertisers in the classified ads and help-wanted sections of the paper Le Monde.
> Did you know that Le Monde, besides its well-known political tendencies, constantly threatens the very basis of free enterprise? (1)
> Hoping that you will think carefully about this matter, I am, Mr. President, yours sincerely,
> L-------M------- (illegible)
> (1) There are other papers with good circulations, and better return for your money, for your search for management personnel.*

In 1975 a widely circulated "Information Letter" of the Group for Social Study and Research (no address and anonymous) contained a careful analysis of advertisers in the Communist and "para-Communist" press. It asked advertisers to withdraw their support from Le Monde and boycott other advertisers that did not do so. There have been other similar attacks at Le Monde's advertising, sometimes involving the considerable expense of free mailings of books attacking the paper. By 1977, there were four major book-length critiques of Le Monde, one from the Communist left, one from the Gaullist right, and two from ex-Le Monde reporters (see Table A.9).

None of these ideological attacks has done serious damage to Le Monde. Taken as a series, however, they show that the paper is constantly under attack. It is not easy to determine the appropriate response; when Beuve-Méry, Fauvet, and Dupont (then president of the journalist association) all responded on the front page to the attack of one of these books, most people felt that they only served its purposes by advertising the attack. In any case, if the attacks remained purely ideological, they would have little effect; the problem, however, is that they operate to reinforce the direct financial attacks.

---

*Jacques Sauvegeot, co-editor of Le Monde, gave me a photocopy of this pamphlet during the interview of April 1, 1977.

Financial Attacks

Financial attacks other than the efforts to cut off Le Monde's advertising have taken two principal forms. First, there have been several efforts to buy out Beuve-Méry and the journalists who write the paper. In 1953, for example, Beuve-Méry was invited to lunch with "one of the magnates of French industry" and was offered several million francs to "develop" his paper, with only one stipulation: that it "become a bit more national." When he refused this offer, the money was given to a small financial daily, L'Information, in an effort to build it up into serious competition with Le Monde. Over NF 4 million were lost in this venture, as the circulation of the paper never went beyond 70,000 copies. The project was funded by the postwar equivalent of the Comité des Forges, the "Groupement de L'Industrie Siderurgique" (the steel industry lobby) (Chatelain 1962, p. 131).

The lesson from this expensive failure was evidently not well learned, for there have been several other efforts to tone down Le Monde's influence by creating competing papers. In 1956, Le Temps de Paris was funded in part by the "American Association for Free Enterprise" along with its French equivalent and additional industrial and financial corporations such as Michelin, Esso Standard, Bank Worms, the Milk Trust, and Jacques Dupuy and family (Chatelain 1962, p. 145). The paper lasted only 66 days and lost a total of several million new francs. The new enterprise had offered to double the salary of any Le Monde journalist who would switch: only 3 of 70 consented. Advertising billboards were taken out all over France and in the United States as well; they asked specifically for advertisers to change newspapers. As L'Humanité correctly noted, "It is especially Le Monde which is aimed at. The masters of Le Temps de Paris have decided to kill it . . . its positions on different issues of internal and foreign politics are too liberal" (Chatelain 1962, p. 144).

In 1977 the same experience was repeated. A new afternoon daily called J'Informe was created by the pooled finances of several major industrialists.* This newspaper lasted only 77 days, and lost

---

*Involved were Jean Clazel (industrialist), Jean Bourrellis (public works contractor, of the Michelin family); Gerard Pedraglio (management of Publicis advertising corporation); Michel Montenay (oil-importing magnate); Willemot-Roussel (metallurgy industrialist); and a representative of the Banque Paribas (Presse Actualité, September 1977 and January 1978).

some NF 30 million in the venture (Presse Actualité, January 1978). Although it printed 350,000 copies the first day, its readership soon stabilized at a mere 20,000 (Le Monde, September 20, 1977).

All of these various attacks—ideological and financial—have failed thus far to influence the independent journalism of Le Monde. No doubt they have cost it a certain amount of revenue loss through the years, but so far the paper has been able to hold its own financially. Whether it can continue to do so remains to be seen; in 1977, for the first time, the paper only barely broke even (Presse Actualité, January 1978). It is important to examine in detail just where Le Monde's financial weaknesses are in order to help predict whether Le Monde can continue to survive as an independent enterprise.

CAN LE MONDE SURVIVE?

From 1967 to 1977, Le Monde has been read more and more in the provinces as well as abroad. During this decade the paper's circulation has increased 49 percent in Paris (to 194,000); 115 percent in the provinces (to 162,000), and 82 percent (to 81,000) abroad. The foreign sales of Le Monde in 1977 made up fully 19 percent of its circulation. In 1966, 52 percent of the paper's circulation was Parisian; by 1978 increases elsewhere have reduced this figure to 44 percent (Le Monde 1978).

Le Monde's 1.35 million readers make it the most widely read of all Parisian papers, as compared with France-Soir's 1.29 million and Le Figaro's 0.88 million. Le Monde's public is extremely young; 57 percent are 34 or younger. This gives Le Monde a decided advantage over Le Figaro, whose readers are the opposite extreme. What is news is that it is not at all obvious that today's young Le Monde readers will switch to Le Figaro in their middle years as they age and prosper, as the last generation did. The widened political differential between the two papers and the noticeable fall in the intellectual quality of Le Figaro since Robert Hersant took it over will probably serve to keep most of Le Monde's readers loyal to the paper of their youth. If I assume that most of Le Monde's readers will indeed prosper, it is because of who they are. Fully 33 percent of them are upper-level managers, and another 25 percent are middle-level managers. Many readers are professionals: lawyers, engineers, and especially teachers of all levels (CESP 1975).

In the meantime, Le Monde has grown into a large corporation, with 1,250 employees split almost evenly between the 600 printers, foremen, and other blue-collar workers and the 650 white-collar employees: administrators, clerks, secretaries, and, of course, journalists. The 183 journalists were extremely young (half of them

under 40) and unusually well educated by the standards of French
journalists (more than two-thirds of them holding higher education
diplomas).

Financially, the picture in 1976 was more mixed than it had
been in the past. This was not the fault of insufficient advertising; in
fact, advertising income had kept pace with the growth of the staff.
In 1976 advertising revenues were up 12 percent over 1975, to
NF 150 million.* On the other hand, the average edition of Le Monde
in 1976 was 11.4 pages longer than in 1966, so the newspaper was
far more expensive to produce.

Le Monde's increasing financial difficulties are therefore
primarily a consequence of increased costs to the paper; circulation
and advertising having grown at a healthy pace. Nevertheless the
rate of profit has slipped precipitously in recent years: 1972, 8.2
percent; 1976, 3.5 percent; 1977, -1 percent; and 1978, 1.5 percent.
This is higher than for most enterprises, which typically lost money
during the year; Le Monde, however, has no press group nor external
source of funding to support itself. Table 3.2 gives an analysis of
inflow and outflow through the enterprise. Should Le Monde ever
slip into the red, for several consecutive years, even if the loss per
year were only a relatively small amount of money compared to the
NF 274 million gross income (1976), the problem would be difficult
to confront, as Le Monde's expenses are very difficult to compress.†
Le Monde cannot elect to cut down on the number of pages (to reduce
printing and paper costs) since this involves cutting back either advertising or written space. If circulation dropped because of decreasing coverage a downward adjustment of advertising would follow, and
Le Monde would find itself in a negative spiral.

In sum, Le Monde is feeling the pressures of trying to exist
as an independent enterprise in the midst of the monopolistic environment of its suppliers, distributors, and competition. Le Monde's
financial survival, given these external pressures, is largely out of
the control of the enterprise itself. Healthy increases in circulation
and advertising income have not offset the increasing costs set by
the monopolistic supplier firms on one hand and the powerful union

---

*This compares with Le Figaro's astounding NF 271 million
income and France-Soir's 195 million (Presse Actualité, February
1978).

†This information was gathered from a number of interviews
at Le Monde with personnel in the accounting and analysis office,
representatives of the journalist association, and management, and
yearly reports (Rapport des Gerants).

TABLE 3.2

Financial Analysis of Le Monde, 1976

Item	Amount
Expenditures	
Total, per copy	NF 1.37
Journalism	21.2%
Printing	33.5%
Paper	24.1%
Administration and general	21.2%
Income	
Total, per copy	NF 1.42
Sales	38.8%
Advertising	61.2%
Net profit, per copy	NF 0.05

Source: Le Monde: Dossiers et documents (January, 1978).

demands of the printers, journalists, and other white-collar employees on the other.

Clearly, Le Monde must succeed on its own, year by year, if it is to survive since it is not built into a press group or backed by an external source of capital. Le Monde's small set of satellite publications* grossed only NF 14.6 million in 1976, a small sum when contrasted to the daily's yearly gross of 260 million (Le Monde, "Dossiers et documents du Monde," 1977). The daily must therefore live on its own income, 61 percent of which, in 1976, came from advertising. The principal threat to Le Monde, therefore, comes from a reduction in advertising, since the paper's circulation seems

---

*Selection hebdomadaire (a weekly summary); Le Monde diplomatique (an excellent monthly diplomatic commentary); Le Monde des philadelistes (for stamp collectors); Dossier et documents (a monthly specializing in in-depth coverage of varying topics); Le Monde de l'education (monthly covering educational matters); and Weekly English Selection (appears as the center section of the Manchester Guardian Weekly).

linked inextricably to the new middle-strata workers, who will make up a stable, if not necessarily expanding, fraction of the French work force for the foreseeable future. (In 1962 France had 2.4 million "cadres"—administrators and managers. By 1976 this group had swelled to 4.2 million.)

ADVERTISING: LE MONDE'S ACHILLES' HEEL?

There is no question that a 5 to 10 percent drop in advertising would be devastating for Le Monde, as its top administrator, Jacques Sauvageot, has claimed on numerous occasions. But there is good reason to believe, other things being equal, that it would be difficult for such a downturn to be the product of a purposive campaign against the important daily. In the first place, with the exception of only a few direct clients, Le Monde's advertising comes through commercial advertising agencies. It would be difficult and unusual for an ad agency to decide on its own to avoid placing its business with a given publication that has proved a successful medium in the past. An ad agency places its accounts in the most appropriate publication for a given product and consumer target, and, as there are major studies done each year by several independent firms measuring the audience characteristics of individual publications, manufacturers are well aware of which newspapers and journals are read by the section of the public they wish to target. Le Monde's penetration of the upper reaches of the new middle strata is of undeniable importance for advertisers; so any political distaste of Le Monde's positions would be neutralized in large part by advertisers' need to reach the newspaper's elite readers. In any case, no one individual advertising client of Le Monde accounts for more than 1 percent of the paper's commercial advertising income, or 0.6 percent of the total advertising.* Classified advertising is, of course, essentially immune to manipulative efforts since its base is so broad.

Le Monde is certainly a remarkable paper, in both its editorial integrity and its organizational structure. It seems likely to retain its prominence in the future if it can make a graceful transition from the Fauvet directorship to that of Claude Julien. It should have a continued success in attracting advertisers, especially when the drop in the quality of Le Figaro is taken into consideration. Furthermore, Le Monde lives richly now, in complete contrast to the Protestant ethic of the Beuve-Méry days, when journalists took the bus

---

*Interview with Michel Colas, December 20, 1977.

and everyone earned little. Today, the salaries at Le Monde are far higher than at any other paper, for employees as well as journalists. If times were to become more difficult, some financial slack could be taken up; there is a high spirit at Le Monde, and people are proud and pleased to work at this respected enterprise. When the paper next comes under renewed attack, and judging from the numerous episodes recounted earlier it surely will, or when the enterprise suffers a drop in advertising income due to a serious downturn in the business cycles that characterize capitalist society, the solidarity among Le Monde's various work groups that has been present in the past will probably emerge once again. Nonetheless, one must see that Le Monde is becoming increasingly anachronistic. It is an independent press enterprise in an economic sector where the essence of survival has proven to be concentration and centralization. Le Monde's greatest problems, therefore, will probably be more a function of its outmoded economic structure than of the ideological and financial attacks launched by those it threatens.

CONCLUSION TO PART I

Part I has attempted to document the changing corporate structure of the press sector in France. The concentration process, turned back by the events of the liberation, has once again produced a highly monopolized sector sporting such corporate giants as Hachette and Hersant. The monopolization processes within the sector have been induced and exacerbated by an identical process in its supplier sectors (especially paper pulp, printing equipment, press transportation, and advertising).

This concentration and monopolization process has radically altered the class character of press ownership. At the liberation, the press enterprises were given over to journalists, who put out the clandestine wartime publications. By the 1970s, most Parisian newspapers were once again owned outright by either flamboyant industrial magnates (whose fortunes were made in other industrial sectors), or by huge monopolistic press sector firms. We have looked at the exception to these patterns, the remarkably independent enterprise, Le Monde.

The importance of the ownership patterns became clear when we observed the authority relations operative within the press enterprises. "Freedom of the press" turned out to mean simply the freedom of the press owner to determine the editorial policy and political line of his publications. It is important to note, however, that even press owners do not enjoy an unlimited editorial autonomy. They are subject to pressures from the bourgeoisie of other sectors (particularly their supply sectors), as well as from government officials. Thus their editorial positions reflect not merely their particularistic interests, but the more general interests of broader segments of the dominant class.

All of the above has been documented before: Bagdikian (1972) analyzed the process in the United States, Murdock and Golding (1973) in the United Kingdom, Anders (1968) in West Germany, Seppanen (1974) in Scandinavia, and Suzuki (1974) in Japan. None of these earlier studies, however, see the press sector as a site of class conflict, and so none carry out an analysis of the effects on labor organization and unionization of these major structural shifts in the sector. In Part II, the present study will turn to a detailed look at the efforts of the printers and journalists to fight against the concentration, centralization, and monopolization tendencies, which for them translate into a progressive decrease of jobs and de-skilling of workers.

PART II

CLASS STRUGGLES WITHIN THE PRESS SECTOR

INTRODUCTION TO PART II

The struggle for control of the press between the small independent enterprises and the larger corporate units, which have in fact taken the upper hand, must be seen as a moment of intraclass as well as interclass struggle. The intraclass dynamics can be found in the sector's transition from small and medium to large capital: the smaller enterprises produce a constantly decreasing share of the total circulation and receive a diminishing portion of the total advertising income, while the corporate, monopolistic units have had the opposite fate.

In its interclass dynamics, the transition has led to the virtual disappearance of the small enterprises run by the wartime clandestine journalist teams, who were of modest social origins and who expressed varied sorts of pro-socialist tendencies. In the surviving larger enterprises, there has been a loss of nearly all editorial control by journalists and even editors; the liberation dream of a separation between management and editorial functions, or, as it was expressed at the time, between "financial capital" and "intellectual capital," has been utterly smashed. Part 2 traces another level of the changing interclass dynamics brought about by the concentration and monopolization processes in the sector, namely, the vast changes in labor and labor relations within the sector. Given the magnitude of the changes in the means of production due to the concentration process and the ever increasing predominance of fixed capital investment over living labor power, it is hardly surprising that there has been a very significant transition in the relations of production.

Harry Braverman (1974) has addressed the relationship between the monopolization process and its effect on labor and labor relations in his monumental work on the topic. His thesis is that the constant search for increased productivity (that is, a higher rate of profit than the average enterprise in a given sector) leads the capitalist to invest progressively in more fixed capital equipment capable of diminishing his wage costs (p. 206). In order to remain competitive, other enterprises in the sector must follow suit, and the decrease in job slots soon becomes generalized throughout the sector. Of course, only the larger firms have the capital to purchase the new productivity-raising equipment; hence, the productivity of these corporate firms is soon far superior to that of the smaller enterprises, which are incapable of the necessary capital expenditures. This unequal development only further fuels the monopolization process; eventually the small firms are forced either to manage with low rates of profitability or to charge comparatively high prices for their products and risk an erosion of consumers.

Braverman argues that the industrial reorganization in the technologically upgraded enterprises also has serious consequences for those workers fortunate enough to retain their jobs. First, there is a rapid de-skilling of this personnel as their work functions become progressively fractionated and their once highly skilled crafts become reduced to machine tending (pp. 200, 208 ff.). This de-skilling allows once highly trained and well-paid craftsmen to be replaced by less-skilled labor and leads to a progressive elimination of the control functions of the worker over his production activities and their transfer to management (p. 212). This transfer in turn exacerbates the separation of "mental" from "manual" labor, that is, it divorces the conceptualization of work processes from their execution (pp. 239, 315), rendering the work force increasingly dependent upon both technical expertise and management. Since the working class is excluded from the former category by the selective education system and from the latter by its lack of capital, the entire process operates to increase both the immediate control of management over the work site (pp. 170, 212) and the long-term structural inability of labor to run an industrial sector without the technical and organizational skills monopolized by management (p. 425). In almost every industrial sector, workers themselves are far less capable of operating that industry today than they were 50 or 100 years ago (p. 231).

Braverman presents a powerful set of hypotheses, and Part 2 of this study examines these in the case of the French press and printing sector. There is, however, a great absence in Braverman's model, as several of his critics have noted (see Ehrenreich and Ehrenreich 1976; and Johnson 1978). Braverman does not trace the effects of these altered labor relations on the unions and union activities of the workers involved. In fact, he views the entire process more in terms of structure than of struggle. As Johnson (1978, p. 42) states, "The heart of the labor process is the struggle between capital and labor. . . . The relations of classes, as they work themselves out in historical settings, dialectically interrelate with the structural determinations that Braverman analyzes." For instance, Braverman does not see that the capitalist has a second motivation behind increasing machinery and decreasing living labor: the quantitative and qualitative reduction of labor eliminates the effective strike threat in the work place. The present study will examine this extremely important point in great detail. Labor does not passively accept these structural changes, as Braverman himself knows: in a footnote he quotes a vice president of General Motors who "pointed out that in 10 plant reorganizations conducted by the G.M. Assembly Division after 1968, 8 of them produced strikes" (p. 197n) Braverman fails to assess the counterstrategies available to unions or the politicization of unions and union federations to which the progressive displacement and de-skilling of labor lead. The following chapters attempt to account for the political reactions of both journalists and printers to the structural transformations being introduced into the press sector.

The following highly condensed analysis of the press (and the printing sector in general) pinpoints a number of the recent transformations in production relations that Braverman discusses. They fit together to tell an important story about contemporary class relations in advanced capitalist society.

As fixed capital investment has risen progressively in the larger enterprises of the sector, journalists and printers have been replaced more and more with new generations of photoelectronic equipment. As a result, the productivity of these large corporations has increased relative to the productivity of the sector as a whole, and they have acquired a more competitive edge. With increased earnings, the cycle is begun anew, as these firms continue to buy out the few remaining independent press enterprises and increase their investments in new technology for other aspects of their operations, thereby further increasing their profitability and competitive edge with respect to lower-technology shops. This process also has important implications for ideological manipulation: the major corporations active in this movement closely interlock with monopolistic corporations in related industrial sectors and hence are pressured by these supplier firms to structure the news in the light most favorable to the interests of those major corporations. Furthermore, the new technology allows an increased centralization of administrative and editorial control so that entire press groups and newspaper chains can be administered—and censored—from a single, central location.

Increased concentration of and investments in fixed capital have been accompanied by a sharp decrease in the overall productive capacity of the French printing industry. As we shall see, this downturn parallels the decrease in productive capacity in the French paper industry as well as the steel, textile, and other industrial sectors. This process is inseparable from the internationalization of these industries, as ever greater proportions of printed material and newsprint are imported from abroad, to the serious detriment of France's international balance of payments. (The creation of the Common Market (EEC) must be seen in light of its utility to big capital, its main political supporter.) The decrease in French productive capacity in the printing sector is due to the closing of dozens of small and medium print shops (the largest of which were quite appreciable), which all had perfectly serviceable equipment. This equipment is removed from the sector (sold as scrap metal, actually), thus decreasing the total capitalization of the sector and raising the profitability of the surviving corporate enterprises relative to the sector as a whole.

Both the increasing investment in labor-eliminating equipment and the dismantling of productive capacity have led to a sharp increase in unemployment among both journalists and printers in recent years. In 1976 both groups had unemployment rates of about 14 percent, among the highest rates in any industrial sector. These figures promise to climb sharply, as a recent government report suggested even further industrial dismantlement and massive layoffs.

For those journalists and printers fortunate enough to retain their employment, the increased reliance on new technology has led to noticeable de-skilling. Journalists who research and write articles are being replaced by more "specialized" re-write persons, as the division of labor begins to remove the responsibility for articles from individual journalists. The result has been an increased control of content by editors and hence owners, since the articles are constructed on a corporate model rather than written by a professional journalist. Similarly, whole categories of printers, whose work in the lead-based print shop was highly skilled, are being replaced by white-collar employees who need only typing skills. Other skilled printer's tasks are being eliminated altogether.

This increased use of new technological developments leads to a relative increase in white-collar labor and a concomitant decrease in manual labor. The fact that this shift occurs simultaneously with the de-skilling mentioned above clarifies the manipulative nature of the "mental" versus "manual" labor distinction, which forms one of the ideological mainstays of advanced capitalism. Highly skilled manual labor is in fact far more mental than lowly skilled "mental" labor (and is, appropriately, usually far better paid as well). In any case, the relative increase in white-collar labor has important implications for collective action and organization. There has been an interpenetration of the upper levels of the new white-collar labor force and the lower levels of management which acts to blur the class distinctions so clearly present in the traditional lead-based print shop. The new educational requirements for the white-collar positions, for example, are not radically different from those of lower management, and one could hypothesize that the consumption values of the two groups are far more similar today than were those of traditional management and traditional labor.

The elimination of a great part of the traditional blue-collar work force from the print shop and their replacement by lowly skilled individuals of middle-strata origins significantly diminishes the political and social polarization along class lines and so will have major reverberations on unionization in the sector, especially when one considers the fact that the traditional printers in Paris have run a closed shop. The printers, even with their anarchosyndicalist traditions, had been one of the original unions for form the Communist Party-linked CGT. Furthermore, although membership in the CP varied greatly from category to category of printers, a great portion of them voted for CP candidates in local and legislative elections. For these reasons, among others, the relative increase of white-collar labor in the print shop introduces significantly different production relations which act, in the final analysis, to increase the degree of control held by management. In the press sector, the "modernization" process operates to allow a more direct manipulation and control of information by the press bourgeoisie.

It is, of course, possible that the new white-collar workers of the press sector will create new forms of activism and new labor demands. On the other hand, they will be fewer in number relative to management than in the past, and their lower skill levels will make them more replaceable. Furthermore, the printers will have a radically different work situation: the white lab coats and the dust-free rooms of an electronic print shop produce an entirely different situational ideology than did the working-class blues and the noisy workshops of the traditional lead-based print shop.

The reaction of the still existing traditional unions to this threatening situation has been to become progressively less corporatist and more politicized. Until recently, the journalists and printers have been unionized in professionalistic unions more interested in high pay and accompanying privileges than in class struggle. The major structural degradations in the positions of both printers and journalists described above have not been accepted quietly, however, and the struggles launched against these changes have increased the contact of both journalists and printers with the national labor confederations. A new activism has appeared: in 1976 alone, the entire French press was barred from appearing more than half a dozen days by printer and journalist strikes; these job actions were supported by both national union confederations, the CGT and the CFDT.

To attempt to explain the decreasing corporatism and increasing politicization of both the printers and the journalists in relation to these current structural changes, one wants to step back and briefly consider the press enterprise as one branch of the printing sector as a whole in order to view the profound reorganization of this entire sector and clarify the structural exigencies acting on the press bourgeoisie. When they in turn alter production relations in their individual enterprises in respect to these exigencies, they create the pressures and conditions that in turn produce the increased activism and politicization of both the journalist and printer unions. This is why, contrary to Braverman's otherwise insightful analysis, it is impossible to analyze transformations of class <u>structure</u> without simultaneously analyzing transformations of class <u>struggle</u>.

4
PRINCIPAL MANAGEMENT STRATEGIES IN THE PRINTING SECTOR

Press enterprises are only one category of printing enterprises. In looking at the broader situation in which the sector as a whole finds itself, we can pinpoint structural pressures that have led the press bourgeoisie to make various decisions about technological transformations. These transformations, in turn, have important repercussions for the industrial relations inside the press enterprise. We shall begin with an overview of some of the general patterns of the current situation in the printing sector and then examine the particular strategies used by the press bourgeoisie to raise their productivity and simultaneously reduce the bargaining power of both printers and journalists.

THE CURRENT SITUATION OF THE PRINTING SECTOR

Originally, printing shops were small, petit-bourgeois enterprises, and this is still visible in France: 7,500 shops have from 1 to 50 employees, while only 350 shops hire more than 50 printers. The corporatism of the printers is derived, in part, from this artisanal background (Presse Actualité, June 1968). Newspaper print shops are among the larger shops; printers there work shorter hours and earn better salaries than they would in the smaller shops (INSEE 1974, p. 54). This relatively favorable situation for the printers in large shops produces a greater structural pressure on the management of these shops (including all press enterprises) to introduce modern equipment in order to increase their productivity. Opposing efforts by the powerful printers union to refuse any technologically induced layoffs, however, guarantee that the sector will be polarized with considerable conflict, as has indeed been the case in recent years.*

A Labor Monopoly: The CGT in Paris

The printing industry is highly Parisian, with just under 50 percent of all French printers working in the large printshops in and around Paris (INSEE 1974, p. 43). Partly through good strategies on the part of past leadership and partly through historical accident (the CGT was asked to send out printers in the first days of the liberation), all Parisian printers are syndicated to the CGT. As would be expected, this situation of monopoly has given the CGT a powerful negotiating position with respect to the owners of the printing sector. In fact, Parisian printers in general earn a salary from 14 to 24 percent higher than do non-Parisian printers (Cahiers d'étude de presse 1963, p. 24), and printers in the press subsector earn fully 30 percent more than their provincial counterparts (INA 1976, p. 10). In 1975, it cost NF 3,500-5,000 to compose one page of France-Soir in Paris, for example, while the same process cost the Républicain Lorrain only NF 714 (INA 1976, p. 10).

These high wages are only one aspect of what the powerful printers union, the Fédération Française des Travailleurs du Livre, has obtained. It has also been able to impose a CGT label on every printed copy of every publication, and it also hires, fires, and supervises its own workers. That is, a printer is not hired by management; it is the central FFTL office that sends out the necessary personnel. In other words, a newspaper asks for the number of printers it needs on a given day, and the central picks whom it wishes. The print shops gain the advantage of not having to pay a full staff on days when the paper prints fewer pages, but the CGT gains far more. As printers change papers reasonably often in their career, they do not feel bound to a particular enterprise. Paternalistic management becomes all but impossible, and union solidarity within the FFTL is structurally reinforced.

---

*This pattern is typical throughout advanced capitalist societies. Printers have recently held long and powerful strikes in the United States, London (London Times), Sweden, and Belgium. In the United States, the 114-day strike in 1962 and the 89-day strike in 1978 at the New York Times sensitized many Americans to the identical issues.

The Increasing Concentration of Printing Enterprises

The printing sector continues to experience an accelerating concentration and centralization of enterprises, as is typified by the concentration of press enterprises in Paris and the provinces. There are several reasons behind this trend. First, the amount of fixed capital in the average printing shop increases by roughly 10 percent per year.* In 1961, the average print shop's fixed capital per printer was about NF 29 million, while by 1972 it was about 57 million (INSEE 1974, p. 13). The total fixed capital of the press and book publishing subsector as a whole has risen from NF 4.8 billion in 1959 to 14.5 billion in 1972, while during this period hundreds of individual enterprises have closed (INSEE 1974, p. 14). At the same time as the amount of fixed capital needed to run a competitive shop has increased so dramatically, the hourly productivity in the average shop has fallen by about 5 percent annually since 1961 (INSEE 1974, p. 14). Furthermore, this low hourly productivity for the printing industry as a whole is exaggerated in the press enterprises, which have only one-half the hourly productivity of the printing industry as a whole (INSEE 1974, p. 53). In a traditional lead-based press enterprise, four principal spheres of work must be done sequentially each day: (1) make the lead text; (2) set it in a page form; (3) press out a master and mold a lead cylinder around it; and (4) place this on the presses and print the papers. Since a daily newspaper must be able to include the latest developments in the news, the printing is done as late as possible; so certain sets of printers must wait until others have finished. Hence, much idleness—and a low hourly productivity.

All press enterprises must come into constant contact with monopolistic corporations in associated sectors, and their dependency on these multinational or market-controlling firms accelerates concentration within the press sector. For instance, all print shops are subject to pressures to increase fixed capital assets (new generations of technology) emanating from the monopolistic corporations that control the supplies they must purchase: IBM and Harris (photocomposition); Kodak and Agfa Gevaert (photoengraving); Dupont de Nemours (photosensitive plates); Empain Schneider (Creusot-Loire offset printing presses); Banque Paribas and Banque Suez (paper), and so forth.†

---

*This "average" figure surely hides an important difference between monopolistic and independent print shops.

†Press interview with Roger Coquélin, FFTL, November 29, 1976.

In calendar year 1974, the price of newsprint climbed fully 84 percent (CP 1976, p. 13). By 1977 paper cost more than twice what it had three years before (Le Monde, January 21, 1977). This price increase cannot be a product of increased demand, since there has been no increase in French newsprint usage in the last decade (Bellanger 1976, p. 335).

In France the paper industry is dominated by two major corporate groups, each linked with major banks—Banque Paribas and Banque de Suez. Acting as a spokesman for the paper industry, its principal entrepreneurial magnate, Fernand Béghin, argued in a recent editorial that the recent price rise was due to the Scandinavian suppliers of pulp raising their prices dramatically. He pleaded with the French state to allow a comparable rise in the price of domestically produced newsprint (Le Monde, January 21, 1977). In fact, only 18 percent of the production of these two dominant French corporations is of newsprint, the rest of their production being devoted to other paper products. Why? Because the state, through a remnant of the 1944 social democratic legislation, regulates the price of newsprint, and hence profitability is higher in other paper items that the state does not control. The production of newsprint in France fell from 436,700 metric tons in 1960 to 260,000 metric tons in 1976 (CP 1976, p. 13). During the same period, imports of newsprint rose from 170,000 to 320,000 metric tons (Mattelart 1976, p. 272). Naturally, this increased dependence has had serious consequences for the French balance of payments (Presse Actualité, May 1977). In brief, with the multinationalization of the paper industry, French productive capacity has not only been monopolized: it has been largely dismantled, leaving France vulnerable to the price rises set by pulp-exporting countries.

The Dismantling of the French Printing Industry

In 1972, 30 percent of all periodicals and 40 percent of all magazines edited in France were printed outside of the country (Lecat Report 1972, p. 21). Fully 203 periodicals were printed abroad: 125 in Italy, 60 in Belgium, and several in Holland, Spain, and Luxembourg (CP 1974, p. 24; Presse Actualité, September 1976). Two-thirds of all mail order catalogues were printed abroad, as were numerous publications of state bureaucracies and agencies: the Renault catalogue, all automobile registration forms, national lottery tickets, Air France magazines, and all publications of Havas (Le Monde, September 6, 1977). Ironically, even several CP journals were printed abroad (Le Monde, March 17, 1977).

TABLE 4.1

Growth in the Importation of Printed Material
(millions of NF)

Material	Commercial Balance	
	1962	1972
Journals and magazines	-10	-36
Books	102	-57
Catalogues	18	-200
Photographs	0	-30
Total	+110	-323

Source: Institut National de la Statistique (INSEE), "Industries polygraphiques, press-édition" (Paris: INSEE, 1974), p. 23.

Just how serious this externalization of French printing is becomes evident when one looks at some figures for the importation and exportation of printed material, as shown in Table 4.1.

By 1975, the yearly balance-of-payments deficit was NF 396 million, and in 1976 it jumped to 617 million (Presse Actualité, May 1977). This represents a considerable amount of printing: the printers union estimates that the return to France of all of this printing would create about 10,000 printing jobs and restore the industry to full health. The trend, however, is going in the other direction, with imports rising 18 percent annually since 1962 (CP 1976, p. 24).

The effects of this exportation of French printing are striking. In the mid-1970s, one found closed print shops of varying sizes and modernity throughout France. About a dozen of the major shops were occupied by their workers at the first notice of their impending closure, but since the factories were going to be abandoned anyway this tactic had little effect. The closed Chaix printing plant in northern Paris is one example. The plant is a vast complex of buildings which house enormous quantities of equipment ranging from traditional lead-based to the most modern heliogravure equipment. This plant has been permanently closed and in 1976 was occupied by its former printers. The hundreds of presses served only to run off a few thousand strike posters; the major book-printing presses were silent altogether. Two full years of occupation changed nothing. The same was true at Chaufour in Vitry and Helio-Cachan in Chilly-Mazarin. The vast Georges Lang print shop, which had 2,800 workers in 1968, closed down in 1978. Victor Michel, Draeger, and even what was left of the massive Néogravure were also ready to collapse (Le Monde, September 6, 1977).

There are two basic arguments as to why this process happens.* The management version is that there is cheaper labor abroad. This, the CGT claims, is false: printing unions have always been and are currently as strong elsewhere in Europe as in France. Management also claims that in other countries fewer workers are employed per machine so costs are kept down. False, replies the CGT; recent studies have shown the numbers to be comparable, if somewhat differently divided. There are fewer strikes, claims management; again the CGT does not agree. The CGT point of view is that the process is a product of capital's search for the highest short-term profit. The Florence conventions of UNESCO in 1950, the CGT says, assured free circulation of all educational, scientific, and cultural material, such as journals and books. There is no duty on these items among the member countries of the Common Market. Through a loophole in this agreement, the French press bourgeoisie is able to send copies of a magazine printed abroad directly to the homes of subscribers in France with no duty to pay, since it involves printed material. Furthermore, there is an especially low international postal rate for sending the publications.

There is a further and more important use of this duty-free, international mailing of printed material. French publishers who print abroad order bulk paper from Scandinavia to be delivered to a third country where the printing is to be done. No duty is paid on the paper coming into these countries since it is technically "in transit" and will be leaving within an allotted time (that is, printed and mailed to subscribers in France). There is therefore no tax paid anywhere on the paper, a considerable saving for the press bourgeoisie.† The financial advantage of this system is reflected in the extent to which it is used: about two-thirds of all subscriptions to journals are printed and mailed from abroad (CP 1976, p. 16).

Only the stronger printing firms can survive the combined factors of accelerating fixed capital investments, lower productivity and lower return on capital, pressures from monopolistic competitors and suppliers, and the disappearance of clients who decide to

---

*Interview with Roger Coquélin, FFTL secretary, on June 1, 1977.
†Interview with Roger Coquélin, January 1, 1977.

publish abroad. Between 1972 and 1974, 81 (non-press) print shops closed (CP 1976, p. 8). Those that do survive often do so thanks to an increased dependency on the financial capital of banks. Recent years have seen sharp increases in both short- and long-term external financing, as the twin factors of concentration and deindustrialization (including externalization) have forced surviving plants to attempt to increase their productivity (and hence profitability) radically by investing in the very latest technological developments (INSEE 1974, p. 15).

STRATEGIES OF THE PRINTING BOURGEOISIE

In the face of these exigencies, the owners of the larger printing enterprises have mapped out a survival strategy based on four principal tactics: (1) increase productivity by introducing the most modern equipment; (2) devalue fixed capital in nonsurviving firms by rendering it obsolete; (3) decrease the number of printers needed; and (4) deskill the work process for the remaining printers.

The effort to increase productivity in the printing sector involves the adoption of photoprinting processes and the massive investments this necessitates. It is important to see that there is nothing obvious about the need to make these changes, and certain firms, such as Le Monde, have decided to wait and see what the future brings, both technically and socially, before making the changeover. In fact, in France there is actually a surplus of many types of new equipment. Among offset printing presses this surplus runs to 30 percent, while two-color offset presses are underused by 44 percent, at the same time that 15 percent are being added per year.* However, this is looking at the issue on a societal level as opposed to the enterprise level, which in a capitalist society is the only operative level in investment planning.

The devaluing of capital is accomplished by forcing smaller, less competitive firms out of business and by favoring such a rapid turnover of new generations of equipment that the equipment of the closing firms cannot be reused (profitably) and must be sold for scrap.

In the printing sector, this entire process is quite visible. The monopolistic firms have introduced the new electronic equipment, thereby increasing their productivity at the expense of the independent enterprises which cannot afford to replace their lead-based

---

*Interview with Roger Coquélin, June 1, 1977.

equipment. When these smaller firms have closed, their heavy equipment, although perfectly adequate, is of no value since the monopolized supplier firm industries have an interest in no longer producing repair parts for the lead-based machinery. Sometimes the equipment scrapped is of remarkably new vintage; this was the case at Néogravure, at Chaufour, and especially at Chaix. It must be stressed that the equipment at Chaix was perfectly serviceable, were profitability not the only motivating factor in the economy. This devaluing of capital, or, in plain terms, destruction of perfectly serviceable and extremely valuable equipment, is a serious drain on socially productive labor. It serves the interests of monopolistic firms by countervailing the tendency of the falling rate of profit, but for the society as a whole it is purely destructive and wasteful. At Chaix, for example, the material, all of which was in good working order, cost NF 50 million, but was sold for scrap at NF 3 per kilo (Le Monde, September 6, 1977).

The introduction of photocomposition material brings with it a reduction in both the quantity and skill level of the labor needed from printers. The bourgeoisie of the printing sector sees a double opportunity here: first, to reduce their considerable labor costs and, second, to break, once and for all, the CGT monopoly's powerful hold on the Parisian printing industry. Between 1969 and 1974, more than 13,000 printers were laid off permanently (Presse Actualité, March 1976). This sudden, massive unemployment and the reaction it provoked among the printers led to the appointment of an ad hoc government commission, the Lecat Commission, which concluded that 3,000 more printers would have to be laid off each year between 1974 and 1980 to bring employment in the field into line with the needs of the new equipment. In sum, the report supported the future firing of fully 25 percent of all printers then working. It also called for an increase in printing capacity of 25 percent during this same period, a capacity to be met by the introduction of more photocomposition and offset equipment. The report, in brief, all but openly called for increased monopolization in the field of printing (CP 1976, p. 24).

The current changes in the printing industry, however, lead not only to a quantitative decrease in labor but also to a qualitative change. Before the turn of the century and the introduction of the linotype machine (itself pushed at the time by the salesmen of the American corporations that produced them (Will 1976, p. 135)), it took six to ten years of training to become a competent typesetter. After the linotype machine, it took only two years to learn either to type out the text on the machine or to place the blocks it produces in the metal forms that make up the pages. Today, with the introduction of the photocomposition machine, no training is needed whatsoever. The only skill necessary is typing: one simply types in a text, and out of the back of the machine comes a perfectly justified (even right-hand margin) text ready to be taped to a mock-up page, of which a photocopy will serve to key the printing presses. As one researcher writes, in summarizing an interesting study on the transition, "The making of a paper is changing. Fluorescent glass tables, films, and white lab coats are replacing the print shop tables, lead, working-class blues and noisy linotype machines; it is no longer a workshop, but a laboratory" (Cahiers Français 1976, pp. 21-27). The principal thrust of this de-skilling of French printers is brought into focus by a study of the introduction of photocomposition in the Canadian press, which concluded, "The introduction of photocomposition in Toronto dailies in Canada led to the breaking of the printers union and the assigning of the work to non-trained and non-union secretaries" (Dumas 1972, p. 30).

5
THE PRINTERS: LAST DAYS OF A LABOR ARISTOCRACY

THE STRUCTURE OF ANARCHOSYNDICALISM

> We have good union activists in all parties, and many belong to no party whatsoever. Until recently, one of our very best union men was a Royalist.
>
> Mr. Dubois, chief of the printing press section at <u>Le Monde</u>

One of the major traits that typifies an anarchosyndicalist union is its jealously guarded autonomy with respect to union federations and particularly to the high centralization of national labor confederations. This does not prevent Gaullist and Republican governments from referring to the printers as "the Red union," nor did it keep Georges Pompidou from once claiming that there were three unions to break: the printers, the dockers, and the air navigators. What is so threatening about these unions is the degree of prolonged struggle they are able to wage and the fact that their respective near-monopolies in their vital fields allow their strikes to be extremely effective. The printers union is a remarkably powerful organization; later we will look in detail at a recently concluded twenty-nine-month strike, during which it took on and defeated one of the most retrograde and powerful personalities of the press bourgeoisie. Yet it is a dying union whose members are both ready to fight and aware of their impending doom.

Anarchosyndicalist unions are structured to provide maximal local decision-making power. Their organizations serve more to coordinate and negotiate with management; they are not sites where delegates meet to make decisions. Each level in the organization jealously guards its operational autonomy with respect to the higher level.

At the center of the printers organization are five unions which have total autonomy and are really quite different (see Figure A.2). The proofreaders union is by far the most anarchosyndicalist, although the typographers union is similarly oriented. At the other extreme is the printing press operators union, which is far more politicized and integrated into the national federation, the FFTL. This difference can be seen in the wide differential in membership in the CP of their respective printers. At Le Monde, for example, whereas 30 percent of the press operators are members, only 5 percent of the typographers and none of the proofreaders are members of the Party.* Within the current breakdown of printing work, there is a clear differential of CP membership along lines of mental versus manual labor: the heavier the manual work, the higher the membership in the CP.

The five unions participate, on the national level, in the Fédération Française du Travailleurs du Livre. The FFTL is a legally formed body, with elected representation not only from the five Parisian unions but from their regional and provincial equivalents as well. The FFTL was one of the first labor federations to form in France, dating back to the end of the last century when such organizations were actually still illegal.

The printers organized into a national federation in 1881, and along with carpenters, lithographers, cooks, and several other labor groups formed the Confédération général du travail (CGT) in 1895. Each of these constituent unions was jealous of its autonomy; this concern became part of the CGT and was written directly into its charter. Article 37 reads: "The CGT, based on the principle of federation and freedom, assures and respects the complete autonomy of the organizations which conform to the present statutes (Bruhat and Piolot 1966, p. 50).

There is an important operative autonomy in decision making between the organizational levels of anarchosyndicalist unions; in the present case, the five printers unions maintain considerable independence with respect to the FFTL, as does the FFTL to the CGT. Printers feel far more bound to their specific union (say, the typographers union) than to the FFTL. In turn, the FFTL is more affiliated to than it is integrated into the CGT. When the leadership

---

*Interviews at Le Monde.

of the printers union becomes overly involved in CGT affairs, it risks opening a split with its mass base, since the anarchosyndicalist tendencies are far more prevalent among the rank and file than among the leaders. Many printers I spoke with expressed little love for the CGT, although they were all appreciative of the reliable fighting the CGT was doing for their cause in the <u>Parisien Libéré</u> strike. Anarchosyndicalism implies a one-way relationship: the printers are glad to have the CGT monopoly, to make full use of it, and to have the CGT's help in times of struggle. At other times, they see no need to heed CGT calls for strikes and demonstrations to help other unions in other industrial sectors. Exactly the same pattern is true, in an even more marked fashion, of the relation between the printers and the CP. We have seen that there is a great differential in the Communist membership of the five FFTL member unions. It is impossible for the FFTL to take political positions directly, so great is the divergency in political perspective of its base. Even the CGT must keep its distance from the CP, although Georges Séguy and other top members of the CGT are members of the CP central committee.

On the shop level, each union sends a delegate to the inter-workshop committee, which coordinates issues within the print shop. This arrangement is particularly important, since the workshop set-up in Paris bars management from any direct contact with the printers in the press enterprises. If management has any complaints, they must speak to the delegate to the inter-workshop committee or to one of the elected technical foremen. Here the labor aristocracy of the printers achieves a remarkable autonomy from the repressive authority relations that typify the capitalist work place. The printers union has won and defended the right to be responsible for the organization of the print shop; in gaining this position, the union has precluded management's paternalistic and always somewhat authoritarian presence in the work place. This has been a critical factor in maintaining the solidarity of the printers to both the federation and the CGT.

THE UNION AT ITS ACME

In many ways the mid-1970s were a turning point for the nearly one-hundred-year-old printers unions. With the monopolization, concentration, and dismantling of the printing industry, the printers' unemployment rate has soared. From this point on they can only fight a defensive battle; most of their demands are aimed at saving the employment of those individuals <u>currently</u> working; there is no hope of preserving these positions for future generations of FFTL printers. Some efforts, of course, are being made to ensure that FFTL personnel be retrained to function as the operators of the new photocomposition material in the future. But regardless of the class origins of the technical and clerical personnel who will work in tomorrow's print shops, these workers will not be unionizable in the same way that the traditional printers have been.

At the height of its power, the CGT monopoly in Paris provided the union with the structural possibility of demanding and winning considerable advantages. The press bourgeoisie called upon the state to break up this closed shop situation, and in 1956 the so-called Moisant law was passed. This statute illegalized closed shops, holding that employers could not legally consider anything about an employee's union membership in the hiring process. There is no question but that the thrust was aimed directly at the printers. As one respected historian has noted: "This position, while it seemed to aim at the employers, actually was designed to break the hiring monopoly of the printers union in the press print shops" (Bellanger 1976, p. 125). The law, however, has had no effect whatsoever; it could not in and of itself reduce the favorable relations of force that the CGT enjoys in Paris. The printers, therefore, negotiated numerous advantages for themselves:

First, the union has been able to define the notion of "service." Printers do not work by the hour but are sent each day on a "service," which means that they will work a maximum of five hours (with a half-hour break) or until the work they are hired to do is finished. The notion of service, however, was also very beneficial to the press bourgeoisie in earlier days, when newspapers varied widely in their pagination from one day to the next and special editions were put out on a moment's notice at a major event. Instead of a given print shop having to hire and keep enough printers to print its maximum needs and therefore not using this labor on lighter days, the institution of "service" allowed each enterprise to ask the union central for precisely the labor they would need for a given day. Today, newspaper pagination and editions are far more regular, and the press bourgeoisie now condemns the printers for an institution they themselves encouraged in past years.

Second, the union is able to bargain with all the papers at once, since conditions must be equal in all shops, given that the printers can be switched from one shop to another as the union directs. The union deals with the owner syndicates of the press bourgeoisie rather than bargaining with the idiosyncracies of particular owners and particular print shop situations. In return, the press bourgeoisie has had the advantage of negotiating from a position of unity and coordination.

Third, the union not only supplies the men to each print shop but also supplies the foremen ("cadres techniques") to oversee their work. These foremen are initially elected by fellow printers; once elected, they are trained for the job and assigned to a given paper. This procedure has provided a shield between the printers and management at each print shop, a shield which has almost completely eliminated paternalism. Even the social security and retirement benefits for each printer are worked out and managed by the union central rather than the print shop(s) for which the printers have worked. This structural separation of printers from management has had the secondary advantage of maintaining union solidarity at a maximal level. Under this structure, a printer's <u>job</u> is in one (or several) individual enterprise, but his <u>career</u> is in his union. Seniority in the union is accompanied by certain advantages, and hence by a self-interested loyalty.

Fourth, the CGT printers enjoy impressive bargaining power throughout France but especially in Paris, where they have a total monopoly. This labor monopoly has allowed the union to negotiate some extremely favorable work norms, including detailed definitions of work intensity, the limitation of a typographer to working on a single publication (which prevents his open time from being employed by the enterprise to set type for a second publication), and a strict definition of extra wages for overtime work.

Fifth, perhaps the most direct way to see to what extent the printers have benefited from their powerful structural position and long-term union solidarity is by looking at their salaries. These vary quite a bit among different printers unions. In 1970, the average Parisian typographer or linotypist earned NF 49,000 per year, as opposed to 61,000 for the lead-mold makers and 38,000 for the printing press operators (Brunois 1973, p. 138). The extremely high figure for the mold makers is due to the fact that their actual work time was so short (about 2.5 hours per day in a Parisian newspaper) that many of them were able to work in both a morning and an evening paper and therefore to increase the average salary. More recently, with the disappearance of so many print shops, very few printers find supplementary work.

A recent government study showed that 20 percent of printers earned between NF 30,000 and 50,000, with 80 percent earning more than 50,000 annually (Toussaint 1976, p. 41). An executive at Hachette stated recently that at the time Hachette sold <u>France-Soir</u> in 1976 the average annual salary of printers at that paper was NF 63,000 (INA 1976, p. 10), or 5,250 per month, as compared to the average salary for printers in the provinces of 3,800. The only way to put these figures into perspective is by comparing this income with the schedule of average incomes in France given in Table 5.1.

TABLE 5.1

Average Incomes of Full-Time Male Workers, 1976
(new francs)

Occupation	Net Monthly Salary
Upper management	
Administrative	9,600
Technical (engineers)	7,520
Middle management	
Administrative	5,369
Parisian printers	5,250
Technical	4,035
Foremen	3,965
Employees	2,870
Skilled labor	2,570
Specialized labor	2,160
Unskilled labor	1,780
Overall average salary	3,118

Source: Le Monde, L'Année economique et sociale, Paris: Le Monde, 1976, p. 55.

The average printer's salary in 1976 ranks well within the average salaries received by management. It is out of all proportion to other salaries in the traditional working class. In 1976, only 10.8 percent of all monthly French salaries were higher than NF 5,060.(Le Monde 1976, p. 54).

Taken together, all these advantages certainly place the printers among the so-called labor aristocracy, and the union's "economism" is therefore not difficult to understand given the success of its past struggles.

The anarchosyndicalism of the union can be best observed in the details of the strategies and tactics the union brings to bear in a major strike action. There is no better case to do so than the thirty-month strike at the Parisien Libéré, to which we now turn.

THE LONGEST STRIKE IN FRENCH LABOR HISTORY: PARISIEN LIBÉRÉ

The Combatants

Le Parisien Libéré is a sensationalist type newspaper, where soft news overwhelms hard news; the paper has principally a working class readership. Before looking in detail at the strategies and counterstrategies used by the two sides in this colossal struggle, I want to spend a moment discussing the combatants. In any specific instance of industrial struggle, the many levels become confused; in the case of the Parisien Libéré, for example, even the personality of its owner, Emilien Amaury, became a vital factor.

The printers union was introduced in general terms in the preceding section; here I want to examine the concrete methods used by the union in its defensive struggle. The keystone of this empirical solidarity was the funding it was able to gather: all Parisian printers gave 10 percent of their salary every month, enough to provide roughly 80 percent of the salary of the more than 500 Parisien Libéré printers out on strike. Given that this financial solidarity was forthcoming for 29 months, this internal support totalled over NF 60 million. Other funds were raised through benefits, demonstrations, sales of posters, and sales of the FFTL's 350-page published version of the strike, Amaury's Putsch.

Besides this financial underwriting, which allowed the FFTL to carry out a protracted strike, great use was made of another aspect of the printers' anarchosyndicalism, namely, the high percentage of activist involvement during a strike. About 30 percent of all printers in Paris consistently participated in an endless series of demonstrations, occupations, break-ins, commando raids on Amaury's private delivery trucks, and the like.*

Furthermore, the printers union could count on both CGT and CP support. The highly anarchosyndicalist position of the union toward the CGT was quickly overcome by the material and political help the CGT was able to provide during the lengthy strike. The same is true to a lesser extent for the CP, whose dependable militants were extremely valuable to the union during the two and one-half years of action. In some ways, the heat of the confrontation united

---

*Interview. Given the sensitive nature of some of the information to follow, I will occasionally refer to an interview without disclosing the name of my informant(s). I have attempted to confirm reports by checking with independent informants.

the printers union and the CGT. In fact, some printers expressed fears that the union might become overly politicized and have difficulty returning to its corporatist patterns. On the other hand, Emilien Spaziro, an FFTL officer, felt that the union had gone through a self-critique and had rejected its past corporatism.* In any case, in view of structural developments affecting the printing industry, the politicization of union members will probably continue to grow.

Opposing the printers was Emilien Amaury, owner of the Parisien Libéré and of the press group of which it is a part. Amaury had had no formal education to speak of; before he entered the advertising business at age 25, the only thing he had really done well was amateur boxing. The printers were taking on a man who, as a boxer, was known for lasting out the entire fight: he had never been knocked out! (Echo de la Presse, December 4, 1967) If the printers union was known for engaging in strategically sound and tactically powerful struggles, Amaury had a similar reputation.

Amaury had led a double life during the war. On the one hand, he had worked comfortably enough under the Vichy regime, in which he held the position of director of the Office of Family Budgets from 1940 to 1944. Before the war he had been in advertising, and the contacts he had made helped him to found the Office of General Advertising, which was in charge of distributing the advertising budget for both the minister for the family and the underminister for youth under the Vichy regime. The office did more than NF 50 million worth of business from 1941 to 1944, and there is no question but that Amaury made handsome profits (FFTL 1976, p. 24; Faucier 1964, p. 290). On the other hand, Amaury loaned his apartment to the Comité National de la Résistance for its clandestine meetings during the war, and he gave money to the clandestine papers (Presse Actualité, June 1975). So while he was successfully doing business as usual, he was also building up a dossier to document his involvement in the Resistance.

From the liberation until 1947, Amaury served as director general of the state-owned Havas Advertising Agency. In 1947, he left this position to devote full time to his principal newspaper, Parisien Libéré, and succeeded in changing the statutes of the paper from a worker-controlled corporation (SARL) to a formal stock corporation (SA). As soon as he took control, Parisien Libéré changed quickly from its liberation format to a progressively more sensationalist and overtly depoliticized, while implicitly reactionary newspaper. During this period he was able to clear his name of

---

*Interview with Spaziro on September 11, 1976.

collaborationist charges and was even awarded the Rosette de la Résistance. He was also a Commander of the Great Maltese Cross of the Veterans of Foreign Wars of the United States in Europe (!) (FFTL 1976).

Amaury's press group consisted of a second Parisian newspaper, L'Equipe (which covers sports exclusively) and daily papers in Anger and Le Mans, as well as numerous magazines, including his reactionary, openly racist (anti-Algerian) political monthly, Carrefour. This was the third largest press group in France in 1976, grossing NF 350 million yearly and employing 1,500 (La Croix, August 18, 1977).

Amaury enjoyed struggling with the unions, which he condemned continuously, along with Algerians, drugs, Communists, birth control pills, and other assorted evils in the headlines of Parisien Libéré. He consistently refused to bow to union demands, which occasionally led to short strikes at his plants (Le Monde, May 21, 23, 1969).

Strategies and Tactics of the Great Strike

The "strategic confrontations" of this struggle are outlined in Table 5.2. Each party had a small set of central strategies, and the other produced counterstrategies to offset these. There is something to learn about the inevitably concrete nature of class struggle in particular confrontations by examining the development of these strategies and counterstrategies.

The struggle began in early 1974 when Amaury quit the Parisian Press Owners Syndicate and joined the Regional Press Owners Syndicate. Amaury had fought off a decrease in his circulation (due to the "deproletarianization" of Paris) by purchasing small press enterprises in bedroom communities around Paris (where the Parisian working class had moved). All of these editions were typeset and printed in Paris; nonetheless, Amaury claimed that since a great part of his circulation was "regional" (that is, not Parisian yet not provincial) and since he belonged to the Regional Press Owners Syndicate he was no longer bound to contract with the Parisian printers but instead with the (far less powerful) regional printers. Amaury wanted to make this claim so that the regional, rather than the Parisian, work norms would apply. Since he intended to make massive layoffs, the difference between the two was of critical importance.

In June several strikes broke out at the Parisien Libéré when negotiations were stalled. Then, in May 1975, Amaury laid off 200 typesetters, while simultaneously attempting to launch a house union to overthrow the FFTL-CGT reign. A strike broke out at once.

TABLE 5.2

Principal Strategies in the Parisien Libéré Strike

Printers Union (FFTL)	Amaury/Parisien Libéré	Comments
Principal Strategies	**Principal Counterstrategies**	
Block production and sale of Parisien Libéré to force Amaury to negotiate the lay-offs he had made	Avoid the blockade by closing the Parisien Libéré print shops and "regionalizing" the paper by opening print shops just outside of Paris	Amaury's surprise opening of the new shops in two weeks is a stunning victory. In the long run, however, the strike cuts his circulation 61 percent and his advertising income 31 percent.
Use spectacular actions to attract public attention to (a) pressure for negotiation and (b) lessen state/police intervention	Use the nationally followed Tour de France bicycle race, the new Parisien Libéré, and handouts to put across the management perspective	FFTL victory. A series of remarkably innovative tactics catches the imagination of the population. Large solidarity developed for the printers.
Strike the entire press to (a) force the isolation of Amaury, (b) push for industry-wide accords at the same time, and (c) structure the eventual inclusion of the Parisien Libéré in the accords	Be the only paper in Paris and one of only five in France to appear on the 15 total-strike days called by the printers. Claim it is the printers who are the cause of concentration and monopolization	FFTL victory. The Parisien Libéré strike helps put through the general accords, which in turn guarantee the future employment of the Parisien Libéré printers. Except at the Parisien Libéré, the monopoly stands intact.

TABLE 5.2 (continued)

Printers Union (FFTL)	Amaury/Parisien Libéré	Comments
Principal Counterstrategies	**Principal Strategies**	
Block the "scab" paper through calling a strike in the CGT-affiliated newspaper distribution corporation. Publicize the illegal 49-person mini-companies, and the fanatical anti-unionism of Amaury	Break the CGT monopoly among printers and the SNJ majority among journalists by hiring Force Ouvrière printers and starting a house journalist union. Create multiple 49-person companies to avoid representation and committees	Does lead to union pluralism at Parisien Libéré, but does not affect the CGT monopoly elsewhere. Agreement later bans the 49-person structure. Amaury forced to create his own distribution company at great expense; commandos attack and destroy.
Neutralize state intervention through general CGT, CP, and SP solidarity	Rely on state help for ideological support, police protection, and court decisions	The state intervened with police and ideology for Amaury, but in the end with money to make the negotiation possible.

130

From the seventh to the twentieth of May, no <u>Parisien Libéré</u> appeared. This was standard FFTL strategy: block the production and appearance of the paper and the owner must eventually negotiate since newspaper sales and advertising income lost on a particular day are sales lost forever. But, completely unbeknownst to the printers, Amaury had a brilliant double-edged counterstrategy prepared. Since the second and major thrust of his counterattack necessitated perfect secrecy, he made the first campaign particularly visible. This involved arranging to have the <u>Parisien Libéré</u> printed in Belgium and trucked into France. On May 21, the first Belgium-printed edition appeared. The printers, taken totally by surprise, turned all of their attention to stopping this Belgium edition. Besides attacking the delivery trucks and destroying their contents, commando raids were carried out on several of the Belgium printing plants (<u>Parisien Libéré</u> 1976, p. 100; FFTL 1976, p. 57). At the same time, negotiations were undertaken by the French printers with their Belgian equivalents toward producing an international policy on the matter; eventually these proved successful.

While the printers union was committing its entire attention to the anti-Belgium operation, Amaury was carrying out his principal counterattack on the printers strike and occupation. In late May he purchased two building sites—large existing warehouses—and had new cement floors and other basic construction work begun at once. At the same time he began two other processes that normally would take the better part of several years. First, he applied to the cities of Saint-Ouen and Chartres for permits to construct printing plants. Given the rococo bureaucratic extremes of French municipal authorities, even individuals applying for the most mundane of requests need months to accomplish their objectives. Since Amaury obtained his permits in a matter of weeks, and especially since Saint-Ouen initially turned down his request, it is probable that he enjoyed governmental help at the highest levels.

Second, the equipment necessary for a complete press printing shop is not quickly obtained as a rule. It is extremely costly to produce and so is typically made to order. It is also massive and only shipped and installed with serious long-term planning and usually lengthy delays. It can often take up to two years, yet Amaury hoped to accomplish it—<u>in secret</u>—in three weeks. He was fortunate: two Marinoni offset printing complexes were for sale; one was still at the manufacturer in the United States, the second was in Sweden. How to get them to Paris in anything less than a delay of half-a-year? Airmail. Amaury actually had several hundred metric tons of equipment shipped to him airmail; one estimation of the cost of this air freight alone is put at NF 30 million (FFTL 1976, p. 59). It was no problem for him to arrange for Force Ouvrière printers to provide the scab labor, and the state agreed to provide the security police Amaury would need to protect his new printing plants. He was back in business.

Imagine the surprise and dismay of the printers: they were occupying the print shops of the paper, they had successfully cut off the Belgium production of the paper, and suddenly one morning the paper appeared in full quantity at all the newsstands! A brilliant strategic move for Amaury, but at what cost? Could he ever hope to recoup the perhaps NF 75 million he had committed to setting up the new shops? Of course, a technological changeover would have eventually been necessary at some time. Did he perhaps provoke the strike in order to be able to make the transformation in one fell swoop?

The printers had a tactic in reserve. Almost all distribution of the French press is handled by the state-regulated distribution company, the NMPP. It so happened that the CGT had a strong majority in the NMPP, and thus it was not difficult to arrange a solidarity strike. While carrying on distribution as normal for the other papers, the NMPP workers refused to handle the <u>Parisien Libéré</u>. Amaury had a newspaper but no way to deliver it.

Amaury countered this tactic by hiring delivery trucks, while quickly purchasing a fleet of his own. The tactic, however, called up one of the quintessential facets of the anarchosyndicalist printers: direct action. The formation, <u>at the base</u>, of independent action units was immediate. These guerrilla-like commando units set out each night to locate and destroy Amaury's delivery trucks. Some of the trucks were escorted by police vans, and those of course could not be touched. But it was not possible to provide protection for each of the hundreds of trucks needed for both the Parisian and regional deliveries. Amaury's unmarked delivery trucks turned to tactics of constant route changing and high speed driving. This proved only partially successful: many were intercepted by the commandos, and they destroyed not only the papers but often the truck as well. One militant commando "colonel" with whom I spoke had personally set more than a dozen trucks on fire and dumped others into the Seine. Several times the printers brought a night's catch of delivery trucks to the Champs Elysées, which they left literally knee-deep in torn-up copies of what they considered to be scab editions of their paper.

Another principal strategy of the printers was to keep the strike highly visible to the general public. There were two reasons for doing this. First, a supportive public opinion would help pressure the state to push Amaury to arbitration. Second, and more immediately important, repressive state intervention in favor of Amaury was hampered by the highly public nature of the strike. Given that both the Socialist and Communist parties were strongly opposed to the recent maneuvers of the press bourgeoisie (Hersant's purchase of <u>Le Figaro</u> and <u>France-Soir</u> and the continuing concentration of the press in general) and given that the united left was polling about 50 percent of the French vote, the state could not legitimate a violent suppression of workers in the press sector. High visibility can be an effective defense.

It is difficult to describe adequately the highly innovative tactics employed by the printers to keep the strike before the public eye. The following list illustrates some of the tactics carried out by the <u>base</u> of the printers union, often without any communication to the central FFTL officials and just as often to the total chagrin of the tactically conservative CGT:

The Parisian Stock Exchange was invaded by about two hundred printers who disturbed trading for half an hour. The action received national coverage, as press photographers had been forewarned. Two employees of the stock exchange died of heart attacks as a result of the chaos. Police cleared the exchange with considerable violence.

Amaury was the organizer of a major sporting event, the "Tour de France," a series of bicycle races to which the French are addicted. The television coverage is extensive, and the printers managed to borrow a fully equipped camera truck and make a five-minute appeal for their cause.

Several hundred printers climbed the thousands of steps to the top of Notre Dame Cathedral and from the principal balcony unrolled a banner reading: NEGOTIATIONS AT <u>PARISIEN LIBERE</u>! It was a simple matter to close the doors behind them; the cathedral is as impregnable today as in Quasimodo's day.

The oceanliner, <u>S.S. France</u>, in mothballs in the North of France, was occupied for five days with appropriate signs draped over her sides.

In early 1977, Raymond Barre, prime minister, attended a secret dinner held at <u>France-Soir</u> by Jacques Hersant, son of Robert. Several other personalities of the press bourgeoisie and governmental circles were present. The printers learned of it, and a commando unit of 100 filed quietly up the back stairs and burst into the room, disarming Barre's bodyguard. Barre, a daring and persuasive man, immediately gave in to their desire to debate the <u>Parisien Libéré</u> situation. A one-hour argument ensued in which he defended his position while the printers held to theirs.

Another central strategy of the printers was to strike the entire Parisian press, including <u>Le Monde</u>, which was openly on the printers' side, and even <u>L'Humanité</u>, which, of course, was totally pro-FFTL. The idea behind these strikes was that the press bourgeoisie would help pressure the state to bring Amaury to the negotiating table. In 1975 there were seven strike days, in 1976 there were six, and in 1977 there were two more before the strike was negotiated. This total of fifteen strike days was financially difficult for many papers, as a good deal of their expenses had to be paid (journalists' salaries, rent, and so on) despite the foregone income that could never be recouped. The strategy pressured the press bourgeoisie in another way as well: it served as a general threat and helped bring the press owners syndicate to sign a general agreement regulating the transition of the remaining enterprises to the highly automated equipment of the future (the General Accords of July 1976).

The final component of Amaury's strategy was based on the consistent support he received from the state, which took several forms. First, Amaury was conspicuously successful in the courts. As early as June 1975, a superior court (Tribunal de Grande Instance) ruled that the occupied print shops be emptied immediately. However, due to the pressures put on the state by the CGT and the left political parties, it was not cleared by the police until after a later court decision in 1977. Amaury was equally successful in avoiding court-ordered sanctions; his numerous convictions for violation of labor codes, for example, were never pressed (FFTL 1976, p. 65).

Second, the police were particularly visible in their role of guarding Amaury's new print shops. They also provided guards for the delivery trucks and could be seen in front of his home. In all, the state spent a small public fortune protecting Amaury's private interests.

Third, friends in high places proved valuable to Amaury. As previously mentioned, the licenses he obtained in two weeks to build his major print shops in Saint-Ouen and Chartres would have required many exasperating months of battle without support at the highest level. Sometimes this intimacy was plain; news photographs from the annual Tour de France showed Amaury sitting between Giscard d'Estaing, president of the French Republic, and Michel Poniatowski, minister of the interior.

Fourth, there was heavy-handed, pro-Amaury state intervention in the so-called Mottin Report, which was issued by a government-appointed arbitrator who for several weeks had met with representatives of both sides. His report was so biased in favor of management that it bears little resemblance to the final negotiations that were at long last worked out between the printers and the management of Parisien Libéré in 1977.

Who won this colossal struggle? According to the FFTL, it was a "victory of exceptional importance" (Le Monde, August 18, 1977). L'Humanité's headline the next day, August 19, 1977, was: "VICTORY AT LE PARISIEN." The management of Parisien Libéré claimed that it was "a great date in the history of the press" and noted that "yesterday's accord was a result of a compromise" (<u>Correspondence de la Presse</u>, August 17, 1977). The minister of labor, Christian Beullac, called it a tie, "a compromise without victor or vanquished" (<u>Le Monde</u>, August 18, 1977).

Although <u>Parisien Libéré</u> indeed won several of the rights for which it had struggled (the right to hire its own printers, union pluralism in the print shop, and recognition as a regional paper), management cannot possibly claim this a victory. Consider the following statistics. Besides a 30 percent drop in advertising income between 1974 and 1976 (CESP 1976), the circulation of the paper fell from 786,000 in 1974 to only 310,000 in 1976 (<u>Presse Actualité</u>, May 1977). This sustained loss of 30 percent of its advertising income and 60 percent of sales income coupled with the immense expenditures referred to earlier must have made the strike financially devastating for the enterprise. No doubt it survived only on the strength of other publications in the group and of outside money and collateral derived from Amaury's real estate holdings. Furthermore, given the decline in circulation of sensationalist papers in Paris, it is highly doubtful that the circulation of the paper will ever reach even 350,000 copies again. The great strike was over, and if the printers had survived it with relatively minimal losses restricted to one paper, the <u>Parisien Libéré</u> would take decades to recover financially from the direct and indirect effects of the longest strike ever waged in French labor history.

THE PRINTERS' OMINOUS FUTURE

There is no better way to assess the relations of force between the press bourgeoisie and the printers union than to look at the negotiated agreements signed in 1976. In entering into the negotiations, the printers hoped to provide a future plan to reduce the "wild" effects of the unemployment that would be created by the introduction of the new photocomposition, facsimile, and computerized equipment. This consideration is missing from the Braverman (1974) analysis. At least in the case of the printers, labor is highly aware of the "degradation" process he describes, and they attempt to do what they can about it. In the present case this amounted to a creative admixture of negotiating and striking; one lent credence to the other, and the printers saw them (correctly) as complementary. On one hand, the strike served as a warning to the press bourgeoisie of the need to negotiate transitional labor relations for future technological transformations. On the other, the negotiations served to outflank the <u>Parisien Libéré</u> management: the printers knew that if a general agreement could be reached, the particulars of the strike outcome would be tempered by protection built into the broader agreement. The printers saw very clearly that their profession was undergoing profound changes and that their union would be structurally deprived of the relations of force it had held with respect to the press bourgeoisie for the last century. The time for negotiation, they knew, was while they were still in a strong bargaining position.

As the printers union clearly told all members in the material distributed to them on the agreement, "an accord is always the result of a compromise." Certainly the agreement reached, which had become the actual guiding document for the modernization of the Parisian press, reflects interests of both management and printers (see Table A.10). The agreement plans for a reduction in labor hours but assures those printers currently working that they will not have to pay personally for this elimination of their functions. On the other hand, the agreement does not, in fact could not, safeguard the role of the union in the years ahead. When the current generation of printers has retired and been replaced by the technicians of tomorrow—regardless of whether this personnel has been derived in part from reconverted printers—unionization in the sector will have been significantly altered.

In the modern print shops of tomorrow, the personnel will be largely of middle-strata rather than working-class origins. Even if today's unions are able to have their younger members and children fill some of the slots of tomorrow, the structural determinants of the modern print shop will cut this group off from its working-class origins. It will not be possible to organize and unionize the middle-strata workers of tomorrow's print shop as in years past. In addition, the higher the organic composition of press capital, that is, the more fixed capital present relative to labor power in the average enterprise, the harder it will be to strike, even if the workers are motivated to do so. Skeleton crews of management personnel can run the electronic equipment of tomorrow far more easily than they can the traditional machinery of today. Furthermore, the low level of skill required to run modern printing equipment means that it will be increasingly easier to replace striking workers in the future. For these reasons, among others, the days of the powerful printers union are numbered and the printers' future dim.

The 1976 agreement only eases the plight of the present <u>individuals</u> caught in the transition period. But tomorrow's printers will be far fewer in number, further de-skilled in relation to today's printers, and essentially middle-strata, whether by class origin or retraining, and therefore probably less powerfully unionized than today.

There is, however, a political consequence of this quantitative and qualitative reduction of printers. They have begun to forsake the corporatism that typified their trade for nearly a century. One can expect at least the present generation of printers to remain active members of the CGT, and, even more certainly, one can expect them to be a solid part of the left, whether of ephemeral alliances such as the "union de la gauche" of the 1970s or of the traditional left political parties.

6
THE JOURNALISTS: DECLINE OF THE POLITICS OF PROFESSIONALISM

THE SITUATION AMONG JOURNALISTS TODAY

Journalism is a withering profession in contemporary France. Unemployment has soared and stood at 14 percent in 1975, among the highest for any profession in the entire country. This represented a 70 percent increase over the preceding year (Presse Actualité, March 1976). Some of this unemployment results from the closing down of press enterprises, while much of it is due to the centralizing (pooling) of journalist functions by the Parisian press groups and the regional press monopolies. We have seen, however, that both the closing of shops and the centralization of control at work are products of the concentration of the press sector.

For those journalists who did have work, salaries varied widely between the Parisian journalists and their poorly paid colleagues in the provinces (Toussaint, 1976, p. 18). Furthermore, salaries varied enormously within Paris, according to two principal criteria.

First, the journalists working for leftist and Communist press enterprises were working for what the French call a "militant's pay." In 1976 this amounted to NF 2,300,* whereas the minimum wage was NF 3,500 in the "grande presse."† This donated labor was a major factor in maintaining the fiscal solvency of these enterprises.

---

*Interviews with René Andrieu of L'Humanité, May 5, 1977, and José Garçon of Libération, February 10, 1977.
†Including the enterprises publishing the "socialistic" elite press, such as Le Monde, Le Nouvel Observateur, etc.

Second, within the "grande presse" enterprises, the wide range of salaries from novice to editor-in-chief reproduced the extensive inequalities in income typical of France. Positions at the top, and their attendant incomes, are obtainable through two principal pathways: (a) elite education (relative to the mass of journalists), which, in the final analysis, is dependent on class origins, or (b) advancement in the organization, which is dependent on successful self-censorship of one's own writings combined with effective editorial policing of the writings of the lower-level journalists for whom one becomes responsible. Given that one is policing along lines determined by relations of ownership, it is again <u>class factors</u> that are determining access to the powerful positions and handsome incomes in the profession of journalism. Parisian editors-in-chief, to take the extreme case, made over NF 10,000 (Toussaint 1976, p. 18) per month in 1976, a salary earned only by the very highest administrative managers (<u>Le Monde</u> 1976, p. 55).

French journalists are experiencing de-skilling, if in a somewhat less dramatic fashion than their associates in the print shops. The concentration of the press has led to a sharp increase in the division of journalistic labor, which in turn has brought about both de-skilling and overspecialization.* One researcher has argued that the de-skilling has "proletarianized" the journalists involved (Lepape 1972, p. 173). In the most modern of papers, he points out, more than half of the journalists do not write; rather they are involved in the physical and technical processing of information. Add to this the fact that the journalists in the field in these "rationalized" papers do not write their stories but merely telephone or telex in their information, which is then written up by a second journalist and often rewritten by a third to provide the "objectivity" of another viewpoint. What this process leads to, among other things, is a rewriting of all articles in the perspective of management, since no single journalist is really sufficiently associated with an article to defend it from the changes wrought upon it. In some extreme cases, Lepape reports, there is a new type of subjournalist being trained to do some of the

---

*Jean Padioleau (1976, p. 265) has argued that although specialization among journalists leads to better documentation in articles, these "experts" are proletarianized as they are professionalized. One finds this in the new interaction norms of the newsroom, where today's journalists worry more about the exclusivity, placement, and length of their article than about its social and political content. He concurs with Tuchman (1972, p. 660 ff.) that the "rhetoric of objectivity" becomes more important than researched corroboration itself.

tasks that journalists usually do, for example, the light rewriting of wire service stories. He writes that whereas most card-holding journalists of today have attended a two-year degree program at a graduate school of journalism, the "employée de presse" can be trained in merely a few weeks (Lepape 1972, p. 170).

Overspecialization causes journalists to lose the ability to write synthetic accounts of how the events in their subspecialty relate to more general events. Furthermore, highly specialized journalists become increasingly dependent on their narrow sources of information and therefore must play an increasingly less critical role with respect to these sources. Journalists' exaggerated dependency on the corporations and bureaucracies they cover pressures them to report what they are told (Boris 1975, p. 26). What appear to be journalist-composed articles, therefore, are often merely rewordings of official corporate and government discourse. The "free press" in such instances is merely masking the communication of propaganda.

It is important to see that this dependency of journalists and the press on corporate and government sources does not hold in the relations between journalists and left political parties and labor unions. These latter organizations have trouble finding adequate media coverage and thus cannot afford to withhold information because their previous releases were not presented as they had wished. They may well try to influence journalists to present their information in a given manner, but they are not in a structural position to enforce their preferences. Journalists, therefore, stand in a structurally different relation toward spokesmen of the dominant class than they do toward spokesmen of the working classes.

Increased unemployment among journalists has seriously reduced their bargaining power with the press bourgeoisie, as became evident in a recently concluded five-year renegotiation of the journalist work codes (Le Monde, October 30, 1976). In the reworking of the official work codes the journalists won no significant victories. In fact, what is more indicative of their deteriorating position is the nature of the demands the journalist representatives put forward—which were successfully opposed by the press bourgeoisie. The journalists wanted to add a clause to an existing section on "professional ethics": "The refusal of a journalist to submit to pressure to write contrary to the truth, to his convictions or to his conscience can in no case be considered as a professional error." This was quite vehemently and successfully opposed. Even more directly denied was the journalists' request to set up a legally constituted electoral college of journalists in all enterprises. In its place, the press bourgeoisie merely conceded that "the agreements for the enterprise committee, and the delegates of the personnel to it, will take notice of the <u>specificity of journalists</u> in the press enterprise" (Le Journaliste, September 1976, emphasis in original).

Despite the still respectable salaries for those journalists able to find jobs, the position of journalists in France is rapidly declining. As one journalist union militant summarized the trend, "Amaury and Hersant are crushing the editorial teams and reducing them to powerlessness and servility" (Fédération française des sociétés de journalistes 1976, preface). Journalists' reaction to this deteriorating situation can best be seen in a detailed look at the structure and recent actions of their unions.

THE NATIONAL JOURNALIST UNION (SNJ)

Early History of the SNJ

The first journalist union, the SNJ, was created in 1918. During this same year, the union negotiated a code of professional ethics and work norms which, with several revisions, today provides the accepted standards covering the field. It is interesting to note that the organization of journalist activism led to a concomitant organization among press owners. In 1925, the National Federation of French Newspapers was formed, and in 1929 it began negotiations with the journalist union. The owners syndicate, however, successfully blocked the passage of any official work codes until 1935, when the National Assembly passed into law a Work Code for Journalists, which included such provisions as:

1. The definition of a journalist and the creation of the official identity card and the committee to regulate their issuance.
2. A guarantee of a fair salary as well as the copyrights for journalists for all that they write.
3. The creation of an annual vacation of one month to five weeks.
4. The creation of the "<u>clause de conscience</u>," whereby a journalist can decide on his own to leave a paper which, because of a sale or a new editor-in-chief, is in the process of changing its perspective or political ideology. He receives a sizable severance benefit for his having to leave a situation that is compromising to his honor, reputation, or, in a more general fashion, his morals (Lindon Report 1970, p. 12).
5. Establishing a special taxation situation for journalists such that they pay taxes on only 70 percent of their gross income.

The early SNJ's activism was therefore quite successful in improving the lot of the French journalist. The right of conscience clause has no equivalent in any other field; it is one thing to protect a worker financially when he is laid off his job, but it is quite another to require the enterprise to pay benefits when a worker leaves voluntarily. The logic of this exception to French labor law proved to be of use to the journalist association movement in later years. It provided the basis for the movement's claim that the relationship of a journalist to his paper is not identical to that of the usual worker to his enterprise.

The SNJ and the Journalist Association Movement

The logic of the right of conscience clause was reinforced by the events of the liberation, particularly by the assignment of the confiscated papers to teams of journalists who had proved themselves during the days of the clandestine press. As the liberation editors and their papers were progressively squeezed out by the concentration and monopolization tendencies in the late 1940s and 1950s, the SNJ began to speak of journalists as the "moral inheritors" of the ideals of the liberation press.

This feeling was brought to a head by two critical events. First, the 1950 court decision, which set up the "Société Fermière" (management company) at Le Figaro, clearly supported the SNJ's argument, namely, that there are two resources on which a paper must draw: "intellectual capital" and "financial capital." Second, 1951 was the year of the principal attack at Le Monde, which led to the brief resignation of Beuve-Méry, and his eventual transfer of 28 percent of Le Monde's stock to the newly formed journalist association. The journalist association movement was also aided by de Gaulle's interest in "participational" organizational structures. All these factors together allowed the formation of a powerful movement which spread throughout France. At the head of it stood Jean Schwoebel, president of the journalist association at Le Monde. By 1967 there were 19 member associations in different enterprises, and together they formed the French Federation of Journalist Associations (FFSJ). This group joined together principally to promote a list of demands including (1) the public's right to information, (2) the rights of journalists to participate in the editorial policy and selection of editors within their enterprises, and (3) legislation that would guarantee both of these. The movement continued to grow and at its peak included some 30 enterprises, including all the major Parisian dailies except L'Humanité, some of the principal Parisian periodicals, and 17 regional or provincial papers, including the very largest, Ouest France and the conglomerate, Province #1 (Schwoebel 1968, p. 155).

The Public's "Right to Information"

Schwoebel and his federation argued that the public service nature of information was inherent in the liberation ideals for the press and that to recapture these dreams it was necessary to recognize the "right to information." This right, he insisted, was similar to the right to education or the right to health (Schwoebel 1968, p. 46). André Paysant, professor at the University of Caen, has argued that this claim to the right to information represents a third phase in the claims for the press: first was the establishment of the freedom of the press in 1881; second were the liberation demands for a press free of both state and capitalist intervention; and the latest is the claim on the part of journalists and consumers that the public has a fundamental <u>right</u> to be openly and adequately informed (<u>Après Demain</u>, December 1973, p. 17). Someone of no less stature than Pope John XXIII made an identical claim in his remarkable <u>Pacem in Terris</u>, when he stated, "All human beings have a right to objective information" (Schwoebel 1968, p. 46). It is worth looking in detail for a moment at the principal practical implications of this claim for the <u>public's right to information</u>, since these demands, I would predict, foreshadow future developments in the coming decades. These implications include:

1. Free access for the public to the sources of information.
2. Public powers' obligation to communicate openly all the information they possess, reducing the place of secrecy to a strict minimum.
3. Right of a journalist to keep his sources secret.
4. Access to the mass media for organizations representing all points of view, along with an enlarged right to respond to charges or accusations.
5. Protection against the encroachment of concentration and monopolies.
6. Public financial aid to ensure the right to information, including special aid to small newspapers presenting political perspectives.
7. The definition of the rights and duties of journalists along lines of the 1971 Munich meetings of the European Journalists Union, which claimed the right to share in the editorial and appointment procedures (Fédération Française des Sociétés de Journalistes 1976, p. 42).

The principal claim of the journalist association movement was that journalists have a moral right to participate in the principal decisions of the enterprises in which they work. However, Schwoebel stresses, "it is not <u>as workers</u> in an enterprise that we ask for participation, but as members of a difficult and dangerous profession charged with a mission of public interest" (Lepape 1972, p. 239; emphasis in original). Thus the leadership of the movement openly claimed that it in no way meant to challenge the rights and prerogatives of capital. "The journalist associations are not looking to overthrow the classic commercial structures but merely propose to adapt them to the particular and important mission of the information media" (Lepape 1972, p. 238). Schwoebel even goes so far as to state openly, "The journalist associations are not looking to replace those in authority in the formation enterprises . . . authority is indispensable" (Schwoebel 1968, p. 174).

Schwoebel's movement caused enough consternation that eventually a parliamentary commission (the Neuwirth Commission) was formed to hear the movement's demands and complaints. Schwoebel reported before this commission that all enterprises should mandatorily have journalist committees holding at least 34 percent of the voting (that is, non-interest-bearing) capital in private firms and 26 percent of the voting capital in the board of directors of public information corporations (Bellanger 1976, p. 301). Furthermore, Schwoebel pushed for the passage of a "Statute of Press Enterprises," which had been promised at the liberation but never delivered (Lindon Report 1970, p. 15). Schwoebel also proposed the formation of a "National Information Foundation" to be financed by the state but managed by journalists and eventually by representatives of the consumers of the information media as well. This organization would guarantee financial existence to all information organs that published material in the public interest. Schwoebel carefully distinguished the role of this proposed institution from the process of nationalization: "We are opposed to a reform that would consist of nationalizing the print shops in order to make them available to journalist teams under the more or less direct surveillance of the state . . . a press at the service of an ideology and a regime" (Lepape 1972, p. 239). These hearings eventually led the National Assembly to form in 1969 the Lindon Commission on the Problem of Journalist Associations.

The journalist association movement, although it attempted to please everyone, in fact pleased no one. Through the years it received an increasingly hostile reaction from press owners, the state, and, finally, even the journalist unions themselves. Together these three sources of opposition crushed the movement.

The press owners did not accept Schwoebel's argument that the movement was not challenging the traditional "hierarchy" in the press enterprises. On the contrary, the press bourgeoisie felt directly threatened, since Schwoebel proposed that press enterprises be regulated by such provisions as: (1) no liquidation of an enterprise that would lead to the private recuperation of invested sums; (2) a limit on dividends; (3) profits necessarily reinvested in equipment; and (4) reserves and any excess going to the personnel (Lepape 1972, p. 140). The National Syndicate of Regional Press Owners wrote in a pamphlet that there was no instance in "Western democracy" of such financial restrictions on enterprise owners, nor such exaggerated claims to participate in management functions (Bellanger et al. 1976, p. 303). They mailed this pamphlet to all members of Parliament, urging them to oppose any legislative effort to commit to law the demands of the journalist association movement.

One by one, the press bourgeoisie struck back in enterprises where the movement had been able to establish itself. The counterattack took various forms. In the 1970s, many associations were joined by journalists who later, once they enjoyed positions of authority, took conservative stances and turned the associations into little more than house unions (this happened at both <u>Le Figaro</u> and <u>Paris-Normandie</u>) (Perier-Daville 1976, pp. 181 ff.; and "Livre noir de Paris-Normandie" 1975). Other papers, which had stalled until they saw which way the state would respond to the issue, realized that they were no longer under pressure to yield to the demands of their journalists. At <u>Paris-Jour</u> the president of the journalist committee was simply fired. Even the Socialist press bourgeoisie kept their distance from a <u>Le Monde</u>-type restructuring of their enterprise. Even Claude Perdriel of <u>Nouvel Observateur</u> allowed only a token (5 percent) participation of the journalists association in 1979. The journalists protested to the point of publishing articles in <u>Le Monde</u> openly pointing out the contradiction between Perdriel's traditional notions of labor relations and the "Socialist and democratic aspirations which led to the creation and development of the magazine" (<u>Le Monde</u>, January 12, 1977).

The state jointed the press bourgeoisie in opposing the movement. If "participation" had been an important concept in de Gaulle's social policy, it certainly was not present in the regime of Georges Pompidou, who once referred to the journalist associations as "soviets," which did little to help their public image.* Even more damaging, however, was the report of the Lindon Commission, set up by the Parliament specifically to look into the issue of the journalist associations. The Lindon Report saw the movement as a direct challenge to capitalist social relations:

> Challenging the current role of advertising is as damaging to the concrete position of the journalist associations as

---

*Interview with Denis Perier-Daville, February 12, 1977.

> is their challenging of the property rights of the press
> enterprises. In both cases, one is led to think that in
> order to reform the press, one must take action on
> other levels against the current economic system. This
> perspective makes the reform seem more difficult than
> it really need be. (Lepape 1972, p. 243)

Finally, the journalist unions themselves developed and changed to the point where they too opposed the journalist associations. In the early days of the movement, the claim was that the thrust of the associations was on a different level from that of the unions. Syndicalism, said Schwoebel, opposes the journalist to the owner of the enterprise; it is a sphere of class struggle. The journalist movement, on the contrary, links the journalists and owners as partners: "intellectual capital" and "financial capital" (Schwoebel 1968, p. 142).

THE POLITICIZATION OF THE JOURNALIST UNIONS

The independent union's movement to the left began in 1968. This politicization was spurred by two principal factors: the onset of rapidly accelerating unemployment, and the politicization of many of the young journalists during the events of May 1968. For years the split between the older, more conservative members of the union and the younger members had been widening; by the early 1970s it was highly visible. The old guard elected its last president in 1973; he campaigned on the slogan, "Autonomous unionism is not apolitical, but the refusal of partisan politics" (Perier-Daville 1976, p. 104). By the following year the president-elect of the independent union had his base among the young, pro-socialist journalists, as was quickly reflected in the open politicization of union positions. The following official union press release comments on a series of public outcries by the press bourgeoisie, who were experiencing a financial squeeze during the trough of the 1974/75 recession. It is clearly written in terms of political economy:

> When have they warned the public powers about the real
> dangers which threaten the information media; the dis-
> mantling of the paper industry, the reconstruction of a
> monopoly in distribution (Hachette), and the control of
> the manufacture of printing equipment by multi-national
> corporations? (<u>Correspondence de la Presse</u>, April 23,
> 1975)

The new SNJ, as the citation illustrates, refuses to divide

union issues from political issues or, for that matter, from a political economy of advanced capitalist society. This new ideological position was matched by a rejuvenated political activism: in 1977 the SNJ called for a national strike to combat the "evolution of technical material, the acceleration of concentration and the aggravation of these by pressures from both capital and political powers" (Le Monde, May 11, 1977). The traditional SNJ had always felt such actions "beneath its professional dignity."*

This turn to the left of the SNJ, and of journalists in general, also permeated the main journalist schools. In 1970, the School of Journalism at Lille expelled 17 students who had boycotted the class of a right-wing history professor because they considered his presentation overtly reactionary. This retaliatory action by the administration then led to a solidarity strike by the student body as a whole, which was joined in turn by a solidarity strike at the prestigious Center for the Education of Journalists in Paris. The strikes lasted two full weeks and were joined by the School of Journalism at Bordeaux. The strike committees of the three schools put out a joint communiqué explaining their position, and giving evidence of the new political consciousness among journalists:

> Why unite? The press is not neutral; it diffuses each day the ideology of the ruling class. The press owners hope to perpetuate this state of affairs in educating, in the schools, docile and submissive journalists. We must refuse the role of the cop of the bourgeoisie and provide ourselves the means with which to fight in the journalism schools, and then in the press enterprises. UNITE! PREPARE TO FIGHT! (Barou 1972, p. 78)

The new independent union (SNJ) forms part of an organization (the National Syndicate of Journalist Unions) that affiliates it with other journalist unions, including the CFDT- and the CGT-affiliated chapters. This organization takes openly pro-socialist positions. In the 1974 presidential elections, for example, it came out semi-officially for the candidate of the united left, François Mitterand (Archambault and Lemoine 1977, p. 181). In 1977, a delegation of the union federation met with the executive bureau of the Socialist party, and issued a joint communiqué containing an analysis of the media and a condemnation of "the increased penetration of capital

---

*Interview with Dennis Perier-Daville, February 12, 1977.

and political power, leading to new limitations on the information media" (Le Monde, February 6-7, 1977).

This shift in the political thrust of the SNJ is important in that it indicates significant pro-socialist sympathies among a very strong majority of the young, post-May 1968 journalists. The student activism of the May events molded the political sensitivities of an entire generation, and it is this which has melted away the professionalistic ideology of traditional journalists (see Touraine 1970a).* Given the changes in the politicization of journalist unions, one can hypothesize that had the journalists—not the press bourgeoisie—had control of the editorial policy of their publications, they would certainly have supported the left in the decisive legislative elections of 1978. This is why it has been necessary to study the industrial relations internal to the press sector: it is a concrete site of class struggle, where, since the war, the bourgeoisie has won major battles. Nevertheless, the journalists' identification with the general causes and struggles of the working class has increased the journalists' political awareness of the critical importance of the mass media in class relations. This change is evident in the shifts in the autonomous journalist union analyzed above, but it is even clearer in the increasing role in the media of the two principal French labor federations, the CFDT and the CGT. It is therefore worthwhile to close this discussion of class struggles of the journalists with a brief look at three other active journalist unions: the CFDT and the CGT on the left, and the counteroffensive of pro-bourgeois professionalism on the right, the CGC (Confédération général des cadres).

The End of Corporatism: The CFDT and the CGT

The CFDT itself developed from a Christian union, the Confédération française des travailleurs chrétiens (CFTC), which was

---

*One cannot approach modern France without familiarizing oneself thoroughly with the May events. In English, one can consult Daniel Cohn-Bendit (1968), Obsolete Communism. The Left Wing Alternative; Daniel Cohn-Bendit et al. (1968), The French Student Revolt; Barbara and John Ehrenreich (1969), Long March, Short Spring; Henri Lefebvre (1969), The Explosion; Allan Priaulx and Sanford J. Ungar (1969), The Almost Revolution; Patrick Seale and Maureen McConville (1968), Red Flag. Black Flag; J. J. Servan-Schreiber (1969), The Spirit of May; and Alain Touraine (1970a), The May Movement.

formed in 1919. This union developed out of a late nineteenth-century predecessor that was central in the "social Catholicism" movement of that era. The orientation was later changed to Christian Democratic and more recently changed again to become the pro-socialist labor confederation of today. The union claims that it made the last switch in the late 1950s (Maire and Juillard 1975); to the public mind the change came about in the heat of the events of May 1968.

Today the CFDT is strong in the more modern sectors of the economy (banking, chemistry, metallurgy, teaching, the state gas company, and the post office), while it is weak in the extractive and primary industries where the CGT reigns supreme (printing, mining, docking, and transport). The membership of the CFDT, if we take 1948 as base 100, slipped from 131 in 1963 to 126 in 1967. After the May events, the membership has grown steadily: today the union has just about 1 million members, in contrast to the 2.5 million of the CGT.

Perhaps the two most distinctive ideological innovations of the CFDT are its insistence on "autogestion," or self-management, and its extension of the critique of capitalist exploitation to include domination and alienation. Through self-management, the CFDT proposes eventually to socialize the means of production, while avoiding the direct assigning of these enterprises to the state. The union is far from clear as to what the specifics of running such a decentralized nationalization program would be like.

The CFDT analysis of the press calls for long-term structural changes. The union openly states, "No one has any hope left for the amelioration of the current capitalist structures in the press" (Le Monde, May 22-23, 1977). The CFDT has the following structural transformations in mind: (1) the socialization of the means of mass communication, especially the monopolies; (2) the management of press enterprises by journalists, other workers, and the consuming public; (3) the sharing of advertising money by all enterprises; and (4) the creation of nonprofit enterprises with access of the public to the communication media.* Whereas the CFDT currently creates an autonomous "intracollegial" section of journalists and other workers in each enterprise, the CGT operates only on a centralized basis that does not recognize the authority of individual enterprise sections.

In this contrast, one finds diametrically opposed notions of representation. In the CGT, a representative is elected and as a delegate makes decisions as he sees fit. In the CFDT, however, the

---

*As elaborated at the CFDT National Council Meeting of March 6, 1976.

TABLE 6.1

Changes in the Unionization Patterns of Journalists, 1970-79
(percentage)

Union	Journalist Card Commission 1970[a]	1976[b]	Elections 1979
SNJ	53	38	37
CFDT	25	23	26
CGT	14	13	12
CGC	—	16	16

[a] Based on 52 percent vote (6,307 of 12,032).
[b] Based on 57 percent vote (8,541 of 14,914).
Source: SNJ, "Analysis of National Congress Elections of 1976," Paris: SNJ, 1976; and Presse Actualité, June 1979.

representatives are expected to represent in the full sense of the word and therefore are required to check with the base constantly to find out what the prevailing opinion is on a given issue. In order for the base to guide its representatives intelligently, it must be thoroughly informed on all issues. This difference between the two unions shows up in all industries but is particularly interesting in the press since it entails quite different notions of what appropriate corporate structures for the information media ought to be like in a socialist society.

The CFDT seems to have an important future ahead of it, given the current situation in French labor relations. One sees this, for example, in the makeup of the union's members: one-third of the present members joined in 1975-77, and their average age is only about 30 (Le Monde, May 24-25, 1977). Nevertheless, CFDT membership has not increased proportionately to other unions in recent years, as Table 6.1 indicates.

The figures in Table 6.1 imply that as the independent SNJ has moved to the left, it has lost many of its members to the right, namely to the CGC. By 1976, given that the SNJ, CFDT, and CGT unions operated in a unified fashion, three-fourths of all French journalists were affiliated to a pro-socialist union.

Dependent Professionalism: The CGC

As the figures in Table 6.1 indicate, the journalist affiliate of the Confédération Generale des Cadres (CGC), which did not exist in 1970, drew fully 16 percent of the vote in 1976. This union affiliation is possible because, technically speaking, journalists are considered "cadres" (Bellanger 1976, p. 437). The first president of the union left no doubt about the CGC's opinion of its fellow journalist unions: "We don't want to be another journalist union, but THE OTHER union, opposed to the politicization of the UNSJ, to its demagogy, to its errors, to its tyrannical ways" (Archambault and Lemoine 1977, p. 180; emphasis in original).

In February of 1977, Jacques Chirac, as president of the RPR (Gaullist Party), went to pay a courtesy visit to Yvon Charpentie, president of the CGC. On the subject of political rights in the enterprise, both agreed on the need to limit "meetings, leafletting, talks and debates in the enterprise" (Le Monde, November 11, 1977). (This statement raises an issue of primary importance to which we shall have reason to refer in Part 4, namely, a working hypothesis that the workplace is one of several principal sites where the traditional working class learns of social and political events from a socialist perspective. See below.)

If the CGC had direct and friendly relations with the Gaullist party, it also related well to the National Committee of French Manufacturers (CNPF). A CNPF communication from the central committee of the CNPF to the operators of metallurgy enterprises, dated November 5, 1976, and urging these operators to help implant the CGC and the FO in their enterprises, fell into the public sphere. "The reformist union people are our partners in many particular instances" (L'Humanité, June 8, 1977).

CONCLUSION TO PART II

Part I argued that the bourgeoisie has retaken control of the press since the liberation and that the monopolistic firms (big capital) have grown at the expense of the independent enterprises (small and medium capital). Part II has attempted to focus on the class dynamics internal to the press enterprises, <u>for if the bourgeoisie has regained ownership of the press, it must still struggle with the highly organized unions of printers and journalists</u>.

The journalists have been a far greater threat than the printers on the level of control of editorial policy and political content. Through the journalist association movement they spread the <u>Le Monde</u> logic of journalist participation in the ownership and control of their enterprise. We have seen how this movement was stunningly crushed by the press bourgeoisie and the state, not without a certain helping hand from the journalist unions themselves.

These unions are today the last combatants in the information media for the liberation dream: the separation of the management of editorial policy and content from financial capital. Fully three-fourths of journalists were organized in the three left journalist unions in 1976, which struggled against the increasing concentration of the press by (1) calling strikes of the entire French press; (2) organizing huge street demonstrations; and (3) pressing the state to indict Hersant for his illegal multiple-newspaper ownership. All of this activism indicated an increased politicization of journalists, although there was little evidence that the activism was slowing the ever increasing monopolization process in any significant way.

In estimating the future of the French press on this issue of journalist control of editorial policy, one is asked to decide which of two principal variables will be dominant: the structural reorganizations in press capital, or the political activism of the journalist unions. Of course, both factors have important linkages outside the press sector.

The concentration of the press and the increasing replacement of living labor (both journalists and printers) by new, technologically advanced equipment is inseparable from the general monopolization tendencies of advanced capitalist societies. As long as the process of economic concentration occurs in the environment in which the press must operate, that is, in the various supplier industries upon which it is dependent, it makes little sense to imagine the economically dependent press sector as somehow being able to avoid these tendencies.

In a similar fashion, the increasing politicization of journalist unions, if it is to have any lasting influence, must increasingly become part of the general political movements of the working classes. Within the information sector, the newly politicized journalists will only be as politically viable as the union federations and political parties to which they are linked are powerful. Should the left come to power, it will have these agents within the press and electronic media enterprises, and hence a new effort at realizing the liberation dream—the public's right to information—could be made. But as long as the left remains a divided opposition, these agents can fight merely defensive battles; and, given the reduction in the numbers of journalist personnel as well as the continuous de-skilling and degradation of their job tasks, the battles will become progressively more difficult to win.

PART III
THE CAPITALIST STATE AND THE FREE PRESS

INTRODUCTION TO PART III

The explanatory power of theories of the capitalist state is greatest when the concept is defined neither too narrowly nor too broadly. The capitalist state is too <u>narrowly</u> conceived when it is identified with its formal, public institutions: such a conception of the state leads one to investigate the increasingly extensive penetration of the contemporary state in the economy inadequately. At the other extreme, the capitalist state is too <u>broadly</u> conceived when it is identified with any and all social processes involved in the reproduction of capitalist conditions of production and accumulation, as Antonio Gramsci (1971), Louis Althusser (1971), and Nicos Poulantzas (1975) tend to do. Gramsci (1971, p. 244), for instance, writes, "The state is the entire complex of practical and theoretical activities with which the ruling class not only justifies and maintains its dominance, but manages to win the active consent of those over whom it rules."

In between these two extremes, we can formulate a concept of the "state" that allows us both to move beyond the blinders of the institutional type of analysis and yet still to distinguish between state spheres and civil spheres of social reproduction. The capitalist state, one finds empirically, is far from the <u>only</u> active element in the reproduction of capitalist social relations; the dominant class has other means to promote the extended reproduction of the material and social preconditions upon which its position is dependent. The privately owned press, we shall see, is not an "ideological <u>state</u> apparatus," as Althusser and Poulantzas claim. The degree to which the state is involved, in any case, is an <u>empirical</u> question.

In capitalist society, the state can be seen as a configuration of formal institutions and programs as well as informal channels of control and influence which together have two principal tasks: the reproduction of the material conditions of production, and the reproduction of the social conditions of accumulation of capital.

The reproduction of the material conditions of production involves an increasing intervention by the capitalist state in the development of productive forces and the making of decisions about irreversible directions to be undertaken in the subsidization and socialization of the extensive costs of various infrastructural investments. Claus Offe (1975) and Poulantzas (1975) have both discussed the increasing presence of the state in directing and managing the overall material reproductive activities of the economy and the concomitantly increased exposure of the state to crisis as this role increases. The state is increasingly vulnerable to political crisis resulting from economic miscalculations and enforced austerity during the periodic crises of overproduction and underconsumption.

More concretely, the state intervenes in substantive ways in material reproduction. Its role in the infrastructure of production is to produce the material and social preconditions for the production system. Developing the material preconditions of the production system involves constructing and operating transportation systems, communication systems, urban space, and so on. Maintaining the social preconditions of production involves many active interventions, such as forming a stable financial infrastructure, currency system, and so forth and creating programs to aid in the social reproduction of labor power itself (education system, health care systems, and so on).

The state is also present in the reproduction of the social conditions of accumulation. In the case of the capitalist state, this presence means analytically that the state must attempt to defend a multileveled system of inequality based on the expropriation of surplus value by the owners of the private means of production. In direct contradiction to this is the central element of the ideological discourse of the capitalist state, which openly proclaims the state's commitment to equality, that is, equal educational opportunity, equality before the law, and so forth. In a remarkable paragraph, Claus Offe brings out just this point:

> The idea is that only if (and only as long as) the capitalist state manages, through a variety of institutional mechanisms, to convey the image of an organization of power that pursues common and general interests of society as a whole, allows equal access to power and is responsive to justified demands, the state can function in its specific relationship to accumulation. This is equivalent to saying that the state can only function as a capitalist state by appealing to symbols and sources of support that conceal its nature as a capitalist state; the existence of a capitalist state presupposes the systematic denial of its nature as a capitalist state. (Offe 1975, p. 127)

The institutions and policies of the capitalist state play central roles in both the reproduction of the material preconditions of production and the reproduction of the social preconditions of exploitative private accumulation. The sometimes contradictory policies put forth by different agencies remind us that the state is neither an instrument nor an independent subject, but a site where intra- and inter-class struggles and negotiations take place.

PART III: THE CAPITALIST STATE & THE FREE PRESS / 159

The primary logic of the capitalist state is seen in its intervention in favor of the general interests of the dominant class as a whole rather than the various segments of the working class. This is simply to say that the principal goal of the capitalist state is to assure a continuity in the material and social preconditions for the extrapolation of surplus value by privately owned enterprises. This does not imply, however, that a purely "instrumentalist" view of the capitalist state is adequate, for as soon as one assumes that the state can be conceptualized as a tool in the hands of the dominant class one's analytical model proves inadequate to trace the highly complex nature of both modern state intervention and the important intraclass struggles within the dominant class.

The advantage of conceiving the capitalist state as a site of interclass struggle is that one is led away from instrumentalist assumptions toward concrete studies detailing the specificity of working-class penetration of the state. In the case of France it is absolutely essential to make a historical (as opposed to an a priori) determination of class struggle within the state, since there has been significant variation in the degree of penetration and institutionalization of working-class interests in different eras. In the present study, for instance, it is only possible to understand the press of the liberation period and the anti-big capital, social-democratic press legislation passed at the time in the framework of an analysis of the strong presence of the left in the National Assembly and in state ministries just after World War II.

Furthermore, it is an empirical question as to what extent the penetration of the state by working-class interests represents merely a dependent participation. Several theorists have argued that the very nature of the capitalist state analytically predetermines the subordinate nature of working-class participation in political processes (Offe 1974; Touraine 1975). The position of the French Socialist and Communist parties and their equivalents throughout Europe, however, is that there is at least an adequate autonomy of the capitalist state to warrant working-class activism in electoral politics (Poulantzas 1975; Therborn 1978). In any event, such questions must be studied in the light of concrete case studies, as in the following analysis of the participation of the working class in the state commissions and agencies involved in the press sector. The dependent nature of this participation cannot simply be assumed: the challenge is to document the concrete political practices whereby the capitalist state is able simultaneously to allow participation of various classes and class segments and yet remain the principal operational sphere in which the reproduction of capitalist social relations takes place.

The capitalist state is not only an arena of interclass confrontation where intervention policies and practices are produced, which, while designed to be in the long-term interests of the capitalist class, are often protective and supportive of working-class interests on specific matters. The state is also a site of <u>intraclass</u> struggle and subsequent intervention, where the often opposed interests of different segments of the capitalist class confront each other. The state acts <u>to balance the often contradictory interests</u> of different economic sectors with the goal of promoting the general interests of the class as a whole. In order to carry off this balancing act, the capitalist state <u>must</u> have available a <u>relative autonomy</u> from each sector in order to be able to oppose occasionally the interests of any given sector when indicated by more general, long-term goals. In many cases this operational space is inadequately maintained, and, while this failure may serve the particular interests of a given economic sector, such an abrogation of the state's relative autonomy can lead to both delegitimation of the image of the state's "neutrality" in the eyes of the working class and dissension among various segments of the capitalist class.

There is a second, crosscutting logic to contemporary intraclass struggle besides these intersector conflicts: the confrontation within each sector between big (monopolistic) capital, and small and medium (competitive) capital. Here the French state, like other contemporary capitalist states, clearly intervenes in favor of the former and hence promotes the historical trend toward ever greater monopolization within each sector. In the press sector, the French state has promoted the concentration process by legislation and policy favoring large corporate structures over independent enterprises. Furthermore, recent state policies have favored capital-intensive reinvestment over labor-intensive labor processes, thus openly favoring increased unemployment among workers as well as the de-skilling of those fortunate enough to maintain their jobs. This has happened not only in printing, as we saw in Part II, but in such other sectors as textiles, coal, and steel during the mid-1970s. This state action in favor of concentration has thus served as a major spur to the monopolization process, which has involved some very serious economic transformations for the French economy in the sectors involved, including the reduction of the French productive capacity in each of the above-named sectors and the ensuing need to increase imports of the products involved. The French state is therefore deeply involved in the process of the internationalization of capital, a policy which benefits the multinational firms at the expense of the small- and medium-capital national firms in a given sector.

The third principal logic of the capitalist state apart from its intervention in respect to interclass and intraclass struggle is seen in its promotion of its own corporate self-interests. The relative autonomy of the capitalist state from the multiple segments of the capitalist class provides an operational space within which the state institutions and agencies find the opportunity to promote their own interests, as such, that is, their expansion and increased authority. Claus Offe (1974, p. 347) has argued that this "institutional self-interest" on the part of the state is conditioned by the fact "that the state is denied the power to control the flow of those resources which are indispensable for the use of state power." Offe is arguing that the prohibition of the capitalist state from organizing production according to its own political criteria, coupled with the fact that the state is dependent on private production from which its fiscal resources are derived, leads to the development of a set of state policies aimed at self-preservation. This fiscal dependency of the state apparatus on the successful functioning of the accumulation process means that the capitalist state does not merely heed assigned tasks in social reproduction but simultaneously follows its self-interests in safeguarding the production process and stabilizing the political relations within which the entire economic process occurs (O'Connor 1973).

One of the key elements of the ideological discourse of the liberal capitalist state has historically been the "free press." This claim has not simply been discourse since in fact most such states, including France, have indeed allowed a formal freedom of the press. Furthermore, the failure of the contemporary, so called Socialist states to match this achievement has only served to increase the legitimating impact within capitalist societies of the existence of a formally free press. What one wants to investigate, however, is whether a contradiction exists between the formal freedom of information and the laissez-faire policies that only encourage serious and continual erosion in the substantive pluralism in the mass media.

Ralph Miliband (1969, p. 219) has stressed the fact that in no field are the claims of democratic openness and political competition more valid than in the field of communication; in advanced capitalist society, the press, the television, and other mass communication media are "not normally monopolized, and subservient to, the ruling political power." There are, he points out, pressures on the press from ministers, state agents, and others, but these "qualify, not nullify" the formal freedom. The problem, Miliband theorizes, is that the notion of pluralist openness and free competition is misleading because the economic and political context in which the media function assure that they will be predominantly "agencies for the dissemination of ideas and values which affirm rather than challenge existing patterns of power and privilege, and thus weapons in the arsenal of class domination" (Miliband 1969, p. 236).

Although there is truth in Miliband's point about the misleading notion of defining "pluralism" solely in terms of the permissiveness of the state given the ability of the "market" to reduce dissident voices in the privately owned media, he underplays the role of the direct intervention of the capitalist state in the media, particularly in the European case. The following chapters attempt to document in detail the multiple interventions of the French state in the media, both those it holds directly and those in the private sector. For the sake of organizing this material, this intervention has been organized into four separate categories.

To begin with, the state sets the definitions of the limits of the autonomy of the press in its promulgation of press law. Perhaps the most clear distinction between U.S. and French press law is that in France the state reserves the right to reduce seriously this autonomy during declared states of national emergency.

Second, the state acts to enforce these formal rules as well as the unwritten rules of power politics. Here one witnesses concrete examples of the dialectic of force and consent. In other words, a broad range of means of intervention is available to the state in its enforcement of limits on the written press.

Third, the state intervenes as an active agent in the field of information production and distribution. The French state owns the major French news agency as well as at least a controlling interest in all radio and television broadcasting stations in and around France. The French state, therefore, is strategically placed in that it plays a major role in both the processing and dissemination of information.

Finally, we will see that the state also intervenes through the activities of its personnel. Here we can trace a series of public sector-private sector interlocks that have placed former state agents in powerful positions as directors of major corporate units that dominate the information industry.

7
THE STATE AS RULE MAKER AND ENFORCER

THE STATUS OF FRENCH PRESS LAW

Although a formally free press regime was created by legislation in France in 1881, there remain certain striking contrasts between these press laws and those of the English-speaking countries. The "étatism" for which France is renowned is all pervasive; there are few spheres of social relations in which the interests of the state do not take priority. Not surprisingly, this is also the case in the relations between the state and the press: the French state explicitly reserves unto itself the right of defining "exceptional states of affairs," during which press freedoms can be suspended. During a legally declared state of war or emergency, all freedom of the press recognized by common law is suspended, and the executive branch and especially the military authorities have full authority to forbid publication, censor content, and seize publications. The law calls for a return to normal press law at the end of the exceptional state.

Even in nonemergency times, however, the French state maintains significant rights of intervention. A publication can be seized when so ordered by a court or by the administration (the minister of the interior or, at the local level, the "préfets"). Court-ordered seizure is intended to be used against provocation to commit criminal acts, acts of rebellion, "outrages to proper morals," or exposure of private lives. This broad applicability has allowed serious abuses, as will be documented. Administratively ordered seizure depends merely upon a declaration of a "clear and present danger."*

---

*Publication can also be suspended for up to three months for (1) printing false news in bad faith, (2) troubling the public peace, or

One also wants to notice a very recent law (Article 16 of July 7, 1974) which permits "the government to, at any time, broadcast all declarations and communications which it deems necessary." These emissions are to be clearly labeled as government communications. This permeability of the French electronic media to immediate editorial takeover should be contrasted with the United States, where the privately owned media corporations have an ability to limit and conceivably block access of the government to their microphones. It is in this legal underpinning to the relative autonomy of the electronic media enterprises in the United States where "investigative reporting" takes root. Journalists can operate in an investigative posture vis-à-vis the government only insofar as their enterprises have an adequate autonomy from the state to protect them from the consequences of doing so.

While the above laws provide the juridical basis for repressive state intervention, there are other laws codifying the state's role as guarantor of the free press. Some of these date from the 1881 laws setting up the current press regime; most others are from the liberation era. Some of the legislation from the more recent period is of a social-democratic nature, such as the provision for a state-regulated cooperative effort in newsprint acquisition (which guarantees that all publications, small or large, have equal access and pay equal prices for their newsprint). Another important postwar law guarantees an unbiased sale and distribution of all publications in the NMPP (Nouvelles méssageries de la presse Parisienne) cooperative distribution system. In concrete terms, this means that in any one of the tens of thousands of newsstands in France one can purchase <u>L'Humanité</u> or even <u>Libération</u>. This is important because the distribution of the press is in no way dependent on the politics of a given distributor or newsstand operator.

These two pieces of social-democratic legislation can only be understood in terms of class relations. This legislation, one must remember, was <u>extracted</u> by the powerful postwar left political parties from a bourgeoisie still in political and ideological crisis from its acquiescence to—and in some cases active participation in—the Nazi occupation. As class relations have shifted back to the prewar situation of domination by the bourgeoisie, most of the legislation from the liberation era has been abrogated, although some, as in the examples mentioned above, is still enforced. This legislation operates

---

(3) provoking military disobedience or criminal activity. Foreign publications can be suspended for "propaganda of foreign origin which threatens national security" (Terrou 1962, p. 106).

as a minor fetter to the concentration-monopolization process, but despite continual pressures to modify these statutes from corporate interests, such as the paper industry bourgeoisie, the state has been reluctant to do so. Here we see a case of the state opposing the interests of the bourgeoisie of a particular industrial sector in order to serve the more general interests of the dominant class as a whole by maintaining a legal facade of being the guarantor of the "free press." In other words, in these two pieces of legislation, the state is acting to serve the long-term interests of interclass and intraclass social stability by promoting at least a minimal ideological pluralism. In doing so, one also wants to see that the capitalist state is also serving its own corporate interests by advertising its benevolent neutrality in the sphere of information. The cynicism of this posture can be found in the fact that such social-democratic legislation aiding small enterprises and politically extreme publications to survive is overwhelmed by other state policies that purposively aid the concentration process.*

Another striking contrast with press law in English-speaking countries is in the legislation prohibiting the publication of any judicial, governmental, or military information that has not been expressly cleared for publication. This practically eliminates the legal <u>possibility</u> of doing "investigative reporting" in the American style that discloses state scandals or wrongdoings. In contrast to the U.S. Supreme Court ruling allowing the <u>New York Times</u> to publish the "Pentagon Papers," which contained formally classified information, French courts have never allowed the French press to adopt a muckraking posture toward the state. Furthermore, it is extremely difficult to be critical of the president of the Republic, since any article which calls into question his honor or dignity can lead to a lawsuit. President de Gaulle was especially fond of this little piece of repressive machinery; he used it 118 times, while Pompidou resorted to it only seven times. Giscard d'Estaing has recently stated that he would not use it at all, which, while admirable, confirms the point being made (<u>Presse Actualité</u>, January 1980). Clearly, the lack of "investigative reporting" in the French press, therefore, is not simply a function of the absence of such a tradition, as some claim. On the contrary, the absence of the "tradition" is, in good part, a product of French press law. Not only is the press explicitly banned from probing into judicial, governmental, and military information, but it is similarly banned from

---

*See Gaye Tuchman's (1978, p. 162) discussion of the artificiality of the state's support of pluralism in the press in the United States. In particular, she demonstrates the <u>purposive</u> inadequacy of the Newspaper Preservation Act.

probing into the private lives of public officials. Furthermore, in France, unlike the United States, the truth of charges the press raises cannot serve as a legal defense. In the United States, a newspaper can charge anybody with anything; even if the charges are false, the paper is safe from libel charges as long as it did not <u>knowingly</u> print what turned out to be false. In France, on the contrary, once a paper enters a taboo area, neither the truth of its claims nor its good faith can protect it from prosecution.

Two further pieces of French press law contrast sharply with the English and American systems.* The first is the "right of rectification," whereby any public functionary who is criticized in a publication has the right to insert a response for free. In fact, every French citizen enjoys this protection under the second law, known as the "right of response." Any individual or organization named in any article, even if not in a negative manner, can within one year's time demand that the publication place the responding article on the same page in comparable length. In fact, this right is used extensively, and it makes for extremely interesting mini-debates, bringing up opposing perspectives on given issues.

THE LEGISLATIVE BLOCKAGE OF THE "PRESS STATUTES" PROMISED AT THE LIBERATION

State intervention can be passive as well as active. By <u>not</u> intervening, the state can choose to favor certain interests over others, and this passive mode has been one of the principal tactics the French state has used to avoid fulfilling the promises extracted from it during the liberation era. In 1944 it seemed certain that a set of statutes would soon be produced to protect the press from being recaptured by big capital; it is important to understand how this legislation came to be blocked.

In 1928 Léon Blum, head of the Socialist party, had called for the creation of state-owned press print shops to be made available on a guaranteed egalitarian basis to teams of journalists of all parties (Le Populaire, April 1, 1928).

Just after the liberation, the French state confiscated the press enterprises of all collaborating papers as well as certain enterprises that had not collaborated but were owned by the industrial bourgeoisie and turned them over to various teams of clandestine journalists. The exact legal status of the nationalized firms was not finalized at that

---

*For additional material on French press law, see Table A.11.

time; later this omission would prove to be the legal loophole through which the industrial bourgeoisie would regain control of the written press.

During the years immediately following the liberation, numerous legislative bills were introduced that attempted to codify and legalize the participation of journalists in the management and ownership of their enterprises. Gaston Defferre, the socialist mayor of Marseille and owner of its two principal newspapers, introduced one of these bills in 1946, when he was secretary of state for information. His plan called for the creation of joint stock companies in press enterprises, with one-third of the voting capital to be held by cooperatives representing the salaried workers. This measure was voted down in the National Assembly, as were three other legislative attempts to protect the press of the liberation from the stark realities of the marketplace.

These legislative efforts ran into opposition on two fronts. First, they were a threat to the industrial and financial bourgeoisie, who clearly had every intention of buying their way back into the press. The bourgeoisie's eager reentry into the sector is visible, for instance, in the undercover maneuvers of Hachette in its purchase of the largest of Parisian dailies, France-Soir. This newspaper had begun as a wartime clandestine publication entitled Défence de la France; however, in a search for new capital, it turned to the corporate advertising magnate, Marcel Bleustein-Blanchet. The capital the latter invested in the enterprise, however, was not his own; he was merely acting as a front for Hachette. So Hachette became the secret owner of France-Soir long before it was clear what the legal status of the press would be (Le Monde, August 24, 1976). Certainly we can assume, therefore, that Hachette, among others, was lobbying strongly against the legislative efforts mentioned above.

Second, these legislative attempts were opposed by the Communist party, which had an appreciable number of deputies in the National Assembly (Bellanger et al. 1975, p. 363). The Party has always opposed "participation" schemes, which it considers as affirming the rights of ownership as opposed to the rights of workers. Furthermore, the Party was certainly thinking about its own press enterprises, which were quite extensive at the time. The CP, like the press bourgeoisie, has never shown any interest in seeing journalists decide upon editorial policy or political positions; in the Party's enterprises, the central offices of the Party itself make all political decisions.

The legal status of the sequestered papers remained unclear for several years; in 1946 this problem was temporarily settled by the creation of a state holding company. This move was intended as a first step in the eventual nationalization of all press enterprises, which, according to the Socialist and MRP versions of the liberation dream, were to be rented out on an equal basis to teams of journalists representing all political tendencies. For a variety of reasons, the holding company functioned badly, running up substantial yearly deficits. It soon became apparent that it would not long survive, and the only question was whether some alternate shelter from the incursions of outside capital would be legislated to harbor the fiscally marginal independent enterprises.

The Moustier Law of 1954 ended all idealistic hopes. The law simply arranged for the legal transfer of the ownership of each nationalized press enterprise to the editors-in-chief then in charge, with no stipulations whatsoever as to how they were to organize their press enterprise. In effect, then, state property was given to private individuals, who were free to sell their interests in the enterprises as they saw fit. The revolution in the press was over; the counterrevolution had been confirmed. Once again press enterprises were corporations no different from any other corporation: capital reigned supreme.

Since 1954 there has never been a serious consideration of the "Statut de la Presse" promised at the liberation, although the issue was raised, and quite vociferously so, by the journalist association movement. It is important to see in this the presence of class conflict: the refusal of the state to produce legislation to provide journalists with editorial decision-making power is an instance of class-based state intervention. This state policy of *not* producing legislation has been an active state policy, supportive of the particular interests of the press bourgeoisie and of the more general interests of the dominant class as a whole.

The hypocrisy of the state's position is often blatantly visible. Only in 1979, when Hersant owned and controlled Le Figaro, France-Soir and L'Aurore, the government began to speak about the possibility of creating a "press enterprise commission" to forestall the elimination of the smaller enterprises. Jean-Philippe Lecat raised in the Senate the possibility of levying a tax on TV advertising to raise funds to support a "presse d'opinion." The irony, of course, is that there was no longer any such press to protect.

THE DIALECTIC OF CONSENT AND COERCION

Through the promulgation of press law as well as associated state activities, the "rules of the game" for the press are set forth. The state enforces these formal and informal rules through a variety of mechanisms. One can analyze this enforcement as a dialectical interplay of leadership and repression.* This is what Gramsci referred to as the "dual perspective," "the dialectical unity of the moments of force and consent in political action" (1971, p. 161). Here Gramsci takes up a traditional Italian theme, coming from Machiavelli's discussion of the two ruling modes available to the Prince:

> You should understand, therefore, that there are two ways of fighting: by law or by force. The first way is natural to men, and the second to beasts. But as the first way often proved inadequate one must needs have recourse to the second. So a prince must understand how to make a nice use of the beast and the man. (Machiavelli 1961, p. 99)

The analytical notion of the "dual perspective" also leads one to investigate the dialectic of the two moments in <u>any given instance</u> of enforcement. It is never possible to have one totally devoid of the other, although one can distinguish enforcement in which consent predominates, and, conversely, one knows when force prevails. Behind "consent" lie power relations of which all are aware. Conversely, coercion is equally dependent on consent—minimally the consent of the agents of coercion to carry out their orders.† If we take the dialectical couple of force and consent as a continuum, we can analyze the range of different modes of enforcement used by the French state. Putting the most consensual state posture at one extreme and the most coercive at the other, one arrives at the arrangement shown in Figure 7.1, which also serves as an introduction to the discussion of each of these varying types of state intervention.

STATE FINANCIAL AID TO THE PRESS

The most minimally coercive form of state intervention in the press is found in the yearly financial aid given to press enterprises.

---

*By this I do not mean to imply, however, that successful social reproduction is a product of only consent and coercion. In other words, the absence of overt coercion does not necessarily imply "consent." The populace also complies out of resignation, ignorance, concentration on personal survival, for example.

†This was so clearly depicted in the case of Iran. One of the world's most modern armed forces was rendered <u>irrelevant</u> when the crisis of the Shah's hegemony became acute in 1978, and his army delegitimized his command.

FIGURE 7.1

The Range of Enforcement Modes Used by the French State in the Realm of the Press

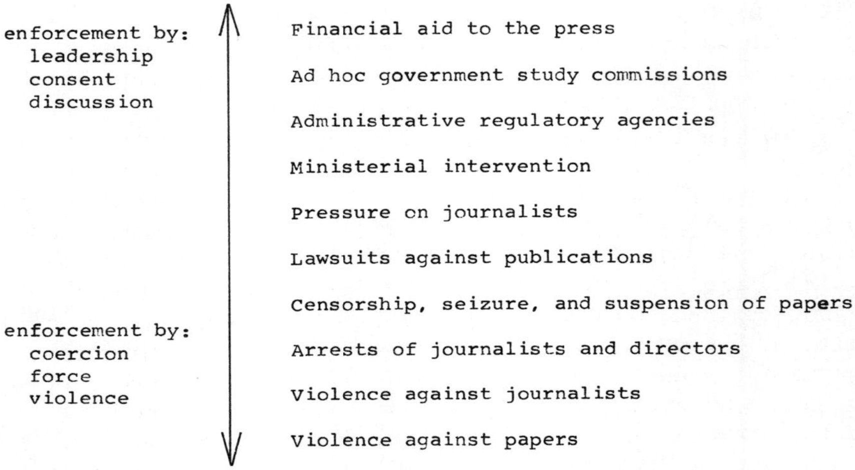

enforcement by:
  leadership
  consent
  discussion

  ↕

enforcement by:
  coercion
  force
  violence

- Financial aid to the press
- Ad hoc government study commissions
- Administrative regulatory agencies
- Ministerial intervention
- Pressure on journalists
- Lawsuits against publications
- Censorship, seizure, and suspension of papers
- Arrests of journalists and directors
- Violence against journalists
- Violence against papers

Source: Compiled by the author.

The French state provides a number of direct and indirect subsidies, which totaled NF 1.7 billion in 1976. This considerable fiscal involvement of the capitalist state in press subsidies is not particular to France, as all European states provide a variety of similar aid (see Table A.12).

In this state aid, there is no discrimination among enterprises, so L'Humanité* and the far left press receive aid under the same criteria as do bourgeois-owned enterprises. Furthermore, there is no question but that without this aid there would be an acceleration in the

---

*Following the meteoric rise in newsprint costs in 1973, the state gave cash payments for several years to low circulation dailies; L'Humanité received NF 2.9 million over two years, and another sum in the "special conjunctural aid" of 1975 (Toussaint 1976, p. 39).

concentration of the press. Nonetheless, behind the magnanimity of the fiscal advantages and direct cash payments lies a hidden coerciveness, for the press has become dependent on these advantages. Even the very principle of nondiscrimination among the enterprises contains a contradiction: the smaller, independent enterprises need these extra funds to survive, while the larger corporate press groups use the funds to expand their domination through further takeovers (Boris 1975, p. 85, and Dumas 1972, p. 67).

Not every publication can receive aid, as the administrative regulatory commission, the Commission paritaire des publications et agents de presse, applies various restrictions. Qualifying publications must be of a general interest nature, aimed at the instruction, education, or recreation of the public. They must have no more than two-thirds of their total surface devoted to advertising and in no case can more than 10 percent be devoted to any single advertiser (Dumas 1972, p. 75; Pourprix 1971, p. 28). In fact, these restrictions are inadequate, as many critics point out. The phenomenon of the "free newspaper" (i.e., no charge to the reader) is in part a product of these inadequate stipulations: by making an advertising circular superficially like a newspaper, that is, by covering 33 percent of the surface space with articles, these pseudo-papers can benefit from state aid (Boris 1975, pp. 86-90). As Jean-Louis Servan-Schreiber points out, only several hundred of the more than 10,000 publications that receive the aid are really general interest information publications (1975).

Subsidies to the press take two forms: indirect and direct. The former refers to reductions in rates made available to the press in its many dealings with state monopolies (post office, transportation, telephone, and so on). These reductions are not contained in the national budget, as they do not involve cash payments. Direct aid payments make up only 10 to 15 percent of the total aid distributed, or about NF 61 million in 1976 as opposed to 1.6 billion in indirect aid (see Table 7.1).

Total 1976 state aid amounted to about 20 percent of the gross income of the average press enterprise qualifying, creating a relative financial <u>dependency</u> of the individual enterprises on the state. The threat of withdrawal of this aid has been used in a coercive fashion, for example, in 1956, to deprive <u>Le Monde</u>, which had displeased the government of Guy Mollet by its position on Algeria, of its "cultural fund" money intended to help increase foreign distribution (Association des journalistes économiques et financières 1972, p. 16).

One could also argue that state aid has been far too little to be effective and has been aimed principally at merely preserving the <u>appearance</u> rather than the reality of a pluralistic press. If the European states had been truly interested in such a press, they could

TABLE 7.1

Financial Aid to the Press by the French State, 1976
(millions of new francs)

Type of Aid	Amount
Indirect (lost revenue to the state)	
Special postal rates	1,190.00
Special telegram, telephone rates	2.67
TVA not paid	255.00
Professional taxes not paid	144.00
Article 39bis (reinvested profits)	44.00
Total	1,635.67
Direct (budgeted sums paid out)	
Telephone reimbursements	7.30
Railway reimbursements	35.00
14% fixed capital reimbursements	8.80
Funds to further international distribution	9.70
Total	60.80
Total state aid	1,696.47

Source: "La Presse quotidienne," Cahiers Français (October-December 1976): 45.

have done far more to protect the financial integrity of the small enterprises from the monopolistic practices of the larger ones. "Laissez faire" in the realm of the press is an active state policy: "laissez mourir." The aid policies of the French state have clearly served to help big capital in the sector at least as much as small and medium capital; at the same time, though, they have helped legitimate the "neutral" state apparatus. This particular mode of state intervention provides an example of what Claus Offe refers to as the capitalist state's particular ability to "convey the image of an organization of power that pursues common and general interests of society as a whole" (1975, p. 127), while in fact it operates in order to stabilize existing intraclass and interclass power relations.

AD HOC GOVERNMENT STUDY COMMISSIONS

Another subtly coercive intervention of the French state is found in government study commissions, both those in the National Assembly

and those established on an ad hoc basis. They have the air that elicits legitimacy; they seem removed, neutral, and scientific. Yet these commissions are invariably stacked from the beginning, for they are appointed by the government and there is never significant representation of the interests of either journalists or printers. Therefore, in the very structuring of an ad hoc study commission the state is, in large part, able to limit questions and thus prestructure answers.*
Let me present a few examples of just how this takes place.

In June of 1972, the powerful government agency, the Economic and Social Council, set up an ad hoc committee known as the "Drancourt Commission" to make a study of the economic situation facing press enterprises. The Drancourt commission included: (1) the minister of information (chairman); (2) six heads of organizations representing owners of papers or distributors; (3) the president of Havas (advertising corporation); (4) the president of Publicis (advertising corporation); and (5) six heads of the six journalist unions and organizations.

So the Drancourt Commission, unlike most other ad hoc study commissions, did provide for the systematic input of the journalist unions. However, upon interviewing five of the six journalist union presidents who had participated, it became apparent that they all described their involvement as merely a dependent participation. From this first meeting of the group it was evidently clear that its report would be a bland, descriptive account of the financial situation of the press—not a serious analysis of the economic factors responsible for the crisis of independent enterprises. With this prestructuring the Drancourt commission analysis could not possibly have made reference to such phenomena as Robert Hersant's illegal holding of multiple newspaper enterprises or the nefarious effects of the monopolistic practices of industries associated with the press sector. Advisory commissions, in France as in the United States, do not often lead to direct legislation; they tend to be more involved with giving the impression of remedial state intervention rather than actually being part of concrete reform programs.

It is not atypical for the French state to totally exclude representatives of the press personnel from important commissions. Take

---

*Claus Offe (1974, p. 36) provides a very useful schema of the state's ability to limit questions in its various apparatuses. Employing the concept of specificity, he analyzes the event-generating "sorting process," which structures a configuration of exclusion rules. The class character of the state, he concludes, resides in the selectivity by which the state determines what are events and what are "non-events."

the case of the Lindon Commission, set up in 1969 to study and recommend legislation on the journalist association movement, which was then in full bloom. The commission was staffed with jurists of various courts and professors from the school of law; there was no representation on the commission of journalists, or of the French Federation of Journalist Associations (FFSJ), which led the movement. Given the composition of the investigatory commission, it is hardly surprising that it concluded that it was contradictory to consider the journalists' claim to be granted a portion of (non-dividend-bearing) stock in order to allow their participation in setting editorial policy, because "their reasoning is founded on a critique of the omnipotence emanating from the rights of ownership, and a mistrust of the capitalist system" (Lindon Report 1970, p. 42).

The ad hoc study commissions have therefore been more manipulative than investigatory. They have been allowed to "study" various aspects of the press only within limits determined by the authority relations that exist generally in the state apparatus and that were purposively reproduced in the structure of the commissions by the personnel chosen to participate. The interests of workers in the sector have been occasionally represented by delegates of journalist unions, although their dependent participation has been invited more to legitimate the commissions than actually to broaden the perspective from which they have worked. The coercive aspects of such intervention techniques as ad hoc commissions are subtle compared to the forceful techniques that we shall soon observe, but they are operative nonetheless.

ADMINISTRATIVE REGULATORY AGENCIES

There are two different sources for regulatory agencies: the press bourgeoisie and the state. The agencies set up by the owner organizations are clearly designed to preempt the state's intervention; if no satisfactory private agency regulated several critical areas, the state would have brought in its own agencies. It is in the interest of the press bourgeoisie to police themselves with agencies set up from within the press sector because, if the state did the policing, it would do so from the perspective of the dominant class as a whole, which is always somewhat at odds with the bourgeoisie of any one particular sector.*

---

*The three most important "para-state" agencies are the Official Circulation Board (OJD), which keeps careful data on the circulation

There are two state-structured regulatory agencies of real importance. By far the most powerful is the Regulatory Commission for Publications and Press Agencies. Its regulatory power grows out of the state aid given each year; the state claims the right to decide which publications should have access to this aid. The commission is made up of seven representatives from various ministries and seven representatives from the "profession." These latter seven delegates are without exception from the press bourgeoisie; there is <u>no representation</u> of the artisans.

The second regulatory agency worth mentioning here is the Regulatory Commission for the Professional Journalist Card. This agency is responsible for handing out the working papers for a journalist. This is a very interesting case of labor law, for the state has essentially obtained the right to license who can and cannot write. The logic behind this intervention is similar to the previous case: since the state allows journalists to subtract 30 percent of their gross personal income before computing their income taxes, it must therefore tightly control access to this special taxation category. The 30 percent reduction is based on a late-Victorian myth that journalists are constantly buying stories and wining and dining potential sources. In reality, any funds expended by journalists are reimbursed by their papers as business expenses, as the state is well aware, since these appear as expenses on the corporate tax returns of the press enterprises. The state allows this bogus tax reduction to continue in order to have a position from which to intervene in the licensing of journalists—and hence to gain an opportunity to apply pressure.

MINISTERIAL INTERVENTION

> "General de Gaulle, what relations will you have with the press?"
> "Why relations of force, of course." (Toscan du Plantier 1974, p. 117)

The intervention of government officials in the press is constant and yet difficult to document. Most of this high-level communication takes place over the telephone, where no records are left. In any

---

of all publications, the Truth in Advertising Board (BVP), which supposedly screens advertising, and the Center for the Study of the Consumers of the Press (CESP), which performs sophisticated consumer studies each year.

case, it is not difficult for the editors of a press enterprise to know the government's view on the issue of the day: calls come in regularly from various ministerial offices. Lower-level government officials telephone directly to the journalists involved in specialized reporting. In 1976, the four unions held a warning strike to protest such calls. Specifically, there had been several calls from the Elysée (the president's offices) to Radio Télé Luxembourg and a call from the minister of the interior to a journalist at Europe No. 1 radio station <u>demanding</u> a retraction in a broadcast report about a demonstration (<u>Presse Actualité</u>, April 1977). Given this readiness on the part of French presidents and ministers to pressure journalists and editors in the electronic media, it is no surprise that de Gaulle once asked President John Kennedy, "How can you possibly manage to govern without controlling the television?" (Servan-Schreiber 1975, p. 347).

Recent ministers of labor have been extremely helpful to the press bourgeoisie as it begins to trim its work force of journalists and printers for the high-technology photocomposition and facsimile processes of today's capital-intensive press enterprises. Take, for example, the service rendered Robert Hersant by a Gaullist labor minister in 1977. The reader will remember that one of the traits of each takeover by Hersant was that he encouraged as many journalists as possible to leave, particularly union delegates. One such case, which became a national scandal, was that of François Boissarie, a journalist at <u>Le Figaro</u>. Such firings must be approved in each case by the work inspector, who in Boissarie's case <u>refused</u> Hersant's request, labeling the firing "purely political" (<u>Le Monde</u>, May 8, 9, 17, 19, 1977). Decisions of the work inspector, however, are subject to review by the minister of labor, who defiantly overturned the inspector's decision and allowed the firing. The reaction was immediate: the journalist union federation, the CFTD and CGT labor confederations, the Socialist, Communist and Left Radical parties, and the left press all formally protested what they saw to be direct ministerial intervention designed to aid and encourage union busting.

Again, I want to underline a central claim that lies at the heart of the present study: "class struggle" is not something, or some process, different from the concrete, specific instances in which it is manifested, except insofar as we use the concept to refer to the broad picture of all such instances, or, put differently, to the logic that structures them. The repression of François Boissarie mentioned above—because he was a union militant and pro-socialist journalist—was a moment, an instance, of class struggle, and can only be understood in that perspective.

LAWSUITS AGAINST PUBLICATIONS

When the state initiates legal action against press enterprises, the balance is switching in favor of force in Gramsci's dialectic of consent and coercion. With only occasional exceptions, these lawsuits have been initiated against publications on the left. Lawsuits are essentially a harassing tactic, since the time and expense of defense is burdensome for a press enterprise, even if it is eventually successful. This tactic is also aimed at coercing future consent, that is, making enterprises more circumspect in what they print in the future.

Publications of the Communist party, especially the daily L'Humanité, have been the subject of a vast number of state-initiated suits. France Nouvelle (December 1952) reported that between late 1947 and late 1952, the government undertook 750 such suits against Communist publications. Another set of figures is available for the period 1955 to 1960, when 168 government-initiated lawsuits were undertaken, and 63 more were taken out by private individuals. By late 1959, 150 of these 231 cases had been adjudicated, with L'Humanité being convicted 91 times and acquitted 59 times. Between 1956 and 1959, the 150 adjudicated cases cost the paper an average of NF 1,100 apiece, to which amount must be added the larger loss from seized (unsold) papers.*

During the Algerian war, L'Humanité was tried in court for informational offenses 209 times and seized 27 times, according to the current editor-in-chief, René Andrieu. These fines have often led to a double bind for the Communist party paper; if it did not pay them, it would be closed by the state; and when it did pay them, it was accused of receiving funds from abroad.†

THE COURTS AND THE LEFTIST PRESS

The leftist press is even more vulnerable to repression than is the press of the Communist party. One recent example is the case of La Cause du peuple (Maoist). After its fifteenth issue, La Cause

---

*Much of this information is from the extremely useful file on "The Communist Party Press" at the Institut Français de Presse, Paris.

†See the article, "Where Did the Money Come From?" Le Figaro, June 8, 1951.

was systematically seized, often before it deposited the required copies by which it was supposed to be judged. In early 1970 its director, Jean Pierre Le Dantec, and his immediate successor, Michel Le Bris, were arrested. Le Dantec was convicted for calling for various illegal street actions and was sentenced to one year of prison. Le Bris was sentenced to eight months. When Jean-Paul Sartre stepped in as managing editor following these convictions, the state backed off, preferring to seize particular issues and arrest distributors rather than risk the worldwide bad press of arresting the famous philosopher.

The state attack on La Cause du peuple is just one example of the many attacks aimed at the "revolutionary press." In June 1970, L'Humanité Rouge (pro-Peking Maoist) was convicted in a trial at Nancy and fined NF 2,000. The same year, the director of Vive la Révolution (direct action, May 1968) was also convicted of minor charges, as was Jean-Edern Hallier, creator and editor of L'Idiot International (direct action, counterculture). Eventually L'Idiot was forced to pay NF 150,000 in fines, a sum that shut down the paper for several months (Geng 1973, p. 179). Furthermore, the offices of L'Idiot were attacked and burned several times, and on one occasion its list of subscription addresses was destroyed. It is always difficult to estimate the degree of police complicity in such illegal activities. In another incident, Jean-Pierre Sallent, editor of a highly original periodical, Klapperstei 68 (direct action, counterculture), was convicted of "provoking military disobedience and desertion" (Presse Actualité, November 1973), and the local authorities in Mulhouse banned publication of the journal for having "extremist and revolutionary opinions." This ban was later overruled by the appeals court at Strasbourg (Presse Actualité, February 1976).

Another highly visible and extremely controversial case of legal repression was that of the weekly Hara-Kiri, which provided a mixture of highly politicized pornography and biting personal critiques of public officials and government policy. In late 1971, the minister of the interior ruled that the magazine could no longer (1) be sold to individuals under 18; (2) be advertised on posters; (3) receive advertising; or (4) be distributed by the cooperative press distribution company. In brief, the publication, for all practical purposes, was permanently banned. In this case, the editors and journalists were clever; rather than expend all their energies and resources in fighting the decision, they simply closed the publication and opened another, today's enormously successful Charlie Hebdo, one of the largest circulation weeklies in all of France.

I do not want to give the impression that only leftist publications are subject to expensive trials brought about by government initiation. One other category of journals often attacked are those few French publications that practice any investigative reporting. Le Canard Enchainé, on the left, and Le Crapouillot and Minute, on the right, have often been sued for revealing financial scandals and conflicts of interest of public officials (Association des journalistes économique et financières 1972, p. 14).

This harassment of the leftist press continues into the mid-1970s. Libération was the favorite target, and when Michel Poniatowski was minister of the interior he attacked it as often as possible. One case in 1977 involved an article and a drawing found in Libération (March 5, 1976) dealing with a shootout that had taken place between the police and some Southern wine growers in which one from each side was killed. The design showed a policeman standing with his foot on the chest of a fallen winegrower, pouring wine from a bottle onto the ground. There was no caption. The state prosecutor asked for a large fine on the grounds of this design and a written phrase in the text, which read, "One is dead because he wanted to live, the other because killing was his business" (Le Monde, May 11, 1977). After Poniatowski stepped down, the harassment of the successful leftist daily continued: Libération had to defend itself against 20 state-initiated lawsuits between June 1977 and February 1979 (Presse Actualité, March 1979).

The principal challenge of the left and the leftist press—and of investigative journalism in general—is their effort to expose the logic of class relations behind particular social and political events.* That is, they refuse to explain such events in the individualistic, psychologistic, ahistorical manner of the sensationalist press and insist on tracing out the elements of class structure and class struggle that lie below the surface events. One sees this most clearly in their disclosure of scandals and crises, where, as Harvey Molotch and Marilyn Lester (1973) have pointed out, the superficial gloss of everyday life has broken down and the ordinarily behind-the-scenes elements of class relations become more visible. When such scandal and crisis involves the state, they serve to reveal the class character of the capitalist state and hence to delegitimize it. In response, the state strikes back at the offending publications.

---

*Miliband (1969), Enzenberger (1974), and Wolfe (1977) have all made this point in terms of the "fragmentation of public knowledge" fostered by the capitalist state. More than anything else, they argue, the purpose of this fragmentation is to make invisible the nature and extent of the state's involvement with the corporate sector, and particularly with monopolistic corporations.

This use of the courts as a repressive state mechanism for setting limits on the press is not particular to France. In fact, the situation is far worse in contemporary West Germany (Oppenheimer 1976 and 1979). In the United States this mode of state intervention has arisen often in recent decades, and the Supreme Court has been active in determining limits to press freedom. It has consistently been the New York <u>Times</u> that has championed the cause of challenging the state in the courts; there is, among French journalists, an often expressed disappointment that <u>Le Monde</u> has always refused to play a parallel role.

CENSORSHIP AND SEIZURE

In France, formal censorship of the press is theoretically not permitted during peacetime. During the Algerian crisis, however, prior censorship <u>was</u> established beginning in April 1955. Furthermore, this case cannot be considered an anomaly because it is precisely during crises that freedom of the press becomes meaningful. If, during moments of uncertainty and heightened conflict, differing opinions, particularly differing class positions, cannot be expressed, then the formal freedom of the press during uneventful times means considerably less. The president of the French Republic recently claimed, "At the current time, France has a press regime which is entirely free, and I can say this without fear of being contradicted by anyone" (<u>L'Humanité</u>, March 23, 1977). Such a statement overlooks important periods of crisis when the French press was formally censored.

Periods of crisis, as hinted at in the previous section, are particularly fruitful times for doing critical social research. Serge Mallet (1963, p. 14) has referred to the "privileged methodological position of the 'state of emergency' and the value of crisis and class conflict as opportunities for the perception of an otherwise disguised reality." But perhaps the most insightful statement on this is found in the writings of Claus Offe:

> Political crises and conflicts . . . can be made use of as concrete proof of the class character of State power. Here, too, it is evident that this kind of proof is not to be drawn from the simple concrete state of political institutions or the day-to-day routines of the political system, but only from crisis situations and manifest class-conflicts which suspend the mechanisms of objective self-disguise and which <u>only then</u> and <u>only for this reason</u> make it possible to perceive them as such. (1974, p. 51)

When we look back at the situation in France in 1958, it is difficult for us to comprehend adequately the tense atmosphere. Although the transition from the Fourth to the Fifth Republic in fact brought about no particular loss of civil liberties, at the time there was no way to predict that outcome. On the surface, the change amounted to a fall of the Republic and a takeover by the army, in the person of General de Gaulle. De Gaulle's intentions were less than clear, and the fear was universal in the press that a liberal republican regime was quite possibly being replaced by a military form of government. Even the conservative L'Aurore, which supported a French Algeria, editorialized, "We want to believe that this will not get to the point of insurgency against republican legality" (May 13, 1958). Maurice Duverger wrote the same day in Le Monde in an article entitled "Le Rubicon," "If the Republic gives in to the rebellion, in a few days civil war would replace republican order." In contrast, several extreme right papers saw de Gaulle's investiture as the only means to preserve both a French Algeria and a unified France. Thus, Le Parisien Libéré wrote, "The call to General de Gaulle seems to be the only way out." On the left, the opposite perspective prevailed: France-Observateur's headline was: AFTER GAULLISM, DICTATORSHIP; while the Communist party's France Nouvelle called on the population to BARRICADE DE GAULLE AND DICTATORSHIP. I mention these various positions to give some indication of the political tension in France during May 1958.

Several days after these headlines, the government forced a state of emergency bill through the National Assembly. On May 18, the minister of information summoned to his office the editors-in-chief of the Parisian press: Lazareff of France-Soir, Brisson of Le Figaro, Beuve-Méry of Le Monde, Lazurick of L'Aurore, Bellanger of Parisien Libéré, and a dozen more. The editors were told that since France was in danger, the regime had decided to defend itself and that a system of a posteriori censure would be applied henceforth. The minister explained what could and could not be mentioned and warned that there was to be no mention of either the meeting or the censorship (Bellanger 1976, p. 166).

Exactly one week later, the minister called a second meeting at which he stated that he was not getting the degree of compliance he needed so the censure would be moved from a posteriori to a priori (Bellanger 1976, p. 166). Soon after, however, it became apparent that de Gaulle intended to maintain France as a liberal republic, and as a consequence both Brisson at Le Figaro and Beuve-Méry at Le Monde came out editorially in favor of accepting de Gaulle as the "least evil of the possible choices."

Many publications were seized for their positions on the Algerian situation, starting even before the above-described state of emergency was declared. In 1956, there were seizures of numerous provincial papers, and in the National Assembly the ex-governor general of Algeria called for suspension of "the four major titles of anti-French propaganda: Le Monde, France-Observateur, L'Express, and Temoignage chrétien." Since seizure amounts to stopping the distribution of a publication after it is printed, even if the censored article is replaced, the entire print run must be redone, leading to a doubling of costs. An article from a censored and redone France-Observateur (December 12, 1957) gives us some idea of the financial blow this measure represents to a press enterprise:

> Seized for the third time since the beginning of the year in Metropolitan France, France-Observateur has been seized 34 times in Algeria. . . . For a journal like ours, which lives only on the income from sales . . . 15 million [old] francs of loss in 20 months is particularly heavy. The government knows this well, and uses this arm against us more and more often and arbitrarily.

Between 1957 and 1960 the French state undertook a massive wave of seizures. In Algeria itself, L'Humanité and Libération were totally banned, and most other liberal and left publications were seized numerous times (see Table 7.2). The seizures in metropolitan France were also widespread. From 1955 to 1960, L'Humanité was seized 15 times, France-Observateur 12 times, while L'Express, Témoignage Chrétien, and even the far right Rivarol, were also seized numerous times. In his autobiography, René Andrieu, editor-in-chief of L'Humanité, writes:

> L'Humanité, which came out for a negotiated settlement and the recognition of Algerian independence, was sued 209 times and seized 27 times. For a seized issue, we had to all come back in the middle of the night and in great haste put out a special edition. We took out the censored articles, which were often either the editorial or information about torture, and left the blank space putting in the word "censored," and I would write a new editorial protesting the seizure. (1975, p. 191)

Naturally, the papers protested this intrusion on their right to publish information and opinions about the Algerian insurgency. Le Monde denounced the "degradation of civil liberties which was escalating and increasingly threatening the freedom of the press" (April 28-30, 1960). Pierre Brisson at the invariably pro-Gaullist Le Figaro

TABLE 7.2

Seizures of the French Press in Algeria, 1957-60

Newspaper	Action
L'Humanité	Banned totally
Libération	Banned totally
La Croix	40 issues seized
Le Monde	Seized 37 times in 1958 alone
France-Soir	2 issues seized
L'Aurore	6 seizures in 1960
L'Express	Banned totally May 15 to August 28, 1958
Le Canard Enchaînée	Several seizures, constant harassment
Temoignage Chrétien	50 issues seized since 1950
France-Observateur	8 issues seized May to November 1960

Source: Claude Bellanger et al., Histoire générale de la presse française, vol. 5 (Paris: Presses Universitaires de France, 1976), p. 173.

similarly made strong protests against this direct state repression (Le Figaro, June 5, 1960).

All this proved to be merely the beginning of the problems facing the French press during the Algerian war. On April 22, 1961, a second state of emergency was declared in France after the putsch of the Algerian-based generals. The minister of information called in the directors of the major French newspapers and weeklies and asked for full cooperation. In early May, the prime minister and General de Gaulle himself signed decrees formally suspending four Algerian papers that questioned the French-Algerian thesis (which held that Algeria was an inseparable part of France). Censorship was simultaneously stepped up in both Algeria and metropolitan France, with direct bans against certain kinds of information, such as news of arrests, house arrests, expulsion, and especially the genocidal, anti-guerrilla tactics of General Jacques Massu.

ARRESTS OF JOURNALISTS AND EDITORS

There were also arrests associated with the state's effort to suppress the press that supported an independent Algeria; typically these were counterproductive. They began with the arrest of a journalist named Baranès who wrote for Libération, which was followed by the conviction of Gilles Martinet, the well-known editor-in-chief of France-Observateur, who supposedly had disclosed military secrets. The arrests were initiated by the minister of the interior of Pierre Mendès France's government, none other than François Mitterrand. (Socialist governments in the Fourth Republic attacked the press almost as readily as did conservative governments.)

Mendès-France's government fell in early February 1955. Throughout the sequence of governments that followed, the arrests and convictions of journalists continued. In April, Roger Stéphane, also of France-Observateur, spent time in jail for articles he had written the year before. Robert Barrat of the same journal suffered the same fate for a report he had authored entitled, "With the Algerian Outlaws." In April 1956, Claude Bourdet, editor-in-chief of France-Observateur, was jailed, and only the unanimous support for him of the entire French press, including the conservative publications, forced the government to release him. Jean-Jacques Servan-Schreiber similarly was sentenced to a brief jail term for "attacking the morale of the army" with a series of articles published in his L'Express. These articles later came out as a best-selling and politically important book, Lieutenant en Algérie (1957). This is only a partial list of those arrested during those trying times. It does, however, demonstrate beyond any doubt that in a crisis the French state is willing to convict and incarcerate journalists and directors of publications whose opinions run counter to the incumbent government's policies. The autonomy of the press has real limits, and when it directly challenges state policy the state apparatus acts quickly to redefine the substantive limits of press freedom. State intervention is determined not only by the interplay of interclass and intraclass logics but also by the need of the state apparatus to preserve its own operational integrity and effectiveness.

It should not be thought that the French state has employed arrests to pressure the press only during periods of deep political or state crisis. Take the example of the use of this tactic in May 1952, when there was no dire threat to the state.* The setting was quite simple: the American general, Ridgeway, who had employed in Korea the genocidal tactics for which the United States was to become infamous in Vietnam, was scheduled to visit Paris. The Communist evening paper, Ce Soir, published an article saying, "The

---

*The following information is from the files on "The Communist Party Press" in the Institut Française de Presse, Paris.

people of Paris will not tolerate a war criminal in the capital."
L'Humanité ran a similar article. The next day the attorney general
(procureur general) opened an investigation against both papers for
provocation to violence, and two weeks later André Stil, the editor-
in-chief of L'Humanité, was arrested for provocation to mob action,
inciting violence, and attacks on the internal security of the state.
What he had actually done was to write the following the day after a
peaceful demonstration against Ridgeway: "That is why, encouraged
by yesterday's successes and approving the call launched by the
Peace Movement, everyone is saying, "And now, Wednesday at Place
de la République" [for another demonstration].

This arrest led to criticisms of the government's actions by
the Communist party, the CGT, and the CGT-federated journalist
union. Individuals distributing the handouts of these organizations
were arrested, and all Communist party demonstrations were banned.
Condemnations of this in the left press led to the most widespread
wave of seizures in French press history. Seven different Communist
or Party-linked papers—Les Allobroges, Le Petit Varois, Les
Nouvelles de Bordeaux et du Sud Ouest, La Marseillaise, La Voix
de la Patrie, Ouest-Matin, and Le Patriot du Sud-Ouest—were seized
in late May, and Jacques Duclos, secretary general of the CP, was
arrested. On the next day, commandos attacked delivery trucks at
Aix and Salon and burned the trucks along with copies of Le Provencal,
La France, and Le Méridional. Several days later, six individuals
were arrested for pasting a copy of L'Humanité on a wall. By the
time the week was over, there had been 160 arrests plus those of
Stil and Duclos. Furthermore, during this time there were many
police raids on press enterprises, as well as at the homes of journalists. In June the police raided the printshops of the CP weeklies
Miroir-Sprint and La Terre, and documents were seized at the seat
of the CGT in Toulon.

Although the magnitude of the above incidents stands by itself,
through the years there have been other attacks on the Communist
press. In 1951, L'Humanité and Libération were both seized when
they called for demonstrations against Eisenhower's visit. In 1952,
attention turned to the controversial play of Roger Vailland, "Colonel
Foster Will Plead Guilty," a play depicting an American colonel in
Korea who allowed shootings of civilians and burnings of buildings.*
While the left press lauded the piece, L'Aurore (May 17, 1952) wrote
that the play was a scandal and a provocation because "one does not

---

*From the file on "The Communist Party Press," at the Institut
Français de Presse, Paris.

have the right in France to insult the American army which liberated us and which is our ally." In this case, there is evidence that the police encouraged a neo-fascist shock group to attack the papers and even the theater.

In the Ridgeway, Eisenhower, and "Colonel Foster" incidents, the intervention of the state was principally determined by the intra-dominant-class relations of the era. The French bourgeoisie was deeply divided between those favoring economic and political relations with the United States and those fearing these relations of dependency and preferring to see Europe strengthened and self-sufficient as a "third way," that is, refusing the American-imposed dichotomy of world power relations. Until de Gaulle came to power in May 1968, the French state during the Fourth Republic had supported the Atlantic alliance thesis and had intervened actively with social and economic policies designed to support the important segment of the capitalist class which stood to benefit from the influx of American capital and technology. The protection of the image of the American benefactor was part and parcel of this state policy, hence the determined effort to silence the left press on such symbolic figures as Ridgeway and Eisenhower.

VIOLENCE AGAINST JOURNALISTS

Over and again throughout recent French history one finds cases of journalists being physically terrorized by the police, usually in an effort to repress left publications. What often makes this tactic backfire is that, in the heat of a demonstration, the police cannot distinguish between left journalists and establishment journalists. In any case, these beatings typically bring unanimous support from the press as a whole and an immediate condemnation of the minister of the interior. In the 1951 demonstration against Eisenhower mentioned above, five journalists were beaten up, two from Paris Presse and one each from Le Figaro, France-Soir, and Agence France Presse. Immediate protests followed the next day from the entire press as well as from all union organizations.

If one looks back through Le Journaliste, the official organ of the independent journalist union, the SNJ, one finds examples of these beatings throughout the years. The January 1934 issue speaks about beatings in the 1931 "affair of the Gare du Nord," the 1932 affair of the journalists of Ce Soir, and a 1933 affair in the corridors of the Palais de Justice. There are more cases cited in the early 1950s, as well as the 1956 incidents when Marshal Tito visited Paris. In 1959 a journalist at the Office de radio diffusion-télévision Française (ORTF) was beaten by police. In 1960, a journalist from

Parisien Libéré was wounded after incidents on the Champs-Elysées. During May 1968, journalists often had their notes and films destroyed on the spot by unidentified police. During 1971, a journalist from Politique-Hebdo and another from the Nouvel-Observateur were both harassed by police agents (Association des journalistes économique et financière 1972, p. 10). All of the above incidents are documented accounts, and hundreds of other stories circulate in the world of the press. The repressive effect of this violence is, of course, a function of the total police violence believed to occur by journalists; the exaggerated accounts and rumored events only add to the effect of documented incidents. All of this information, however, remained largely internal to the profession until the "Jaubert affair" of 1971.

Alain Jaubert, a journalist at La Recherche and a contributor to Nouvel Observateur, found himself by chance in northern Paris near a demonstration that had taken place concerning a situation in the French Antilles. The police had beaten a demonstrator and left him on the street; Jaubert helped him into a pharmacy, administered first aid to him, and also called an ambulance. When the police ambulance came, Jaubert insisted on riding in it with the wounded man and identified himself as a journalist. He was beaten by the police and thrown out the back of the moving ambulance. He was picked up by a following police vehicle and again beaten. Apart from the official inquiry into the event, the shocked Parisian intelligentsia set up its own investigative committee, including Gilles Deleuze, Michel Foucault, and Claude Mauriac. The committee substantiated the above version of Jaubert, and for once the police beating of a journalist became a national scandal (Association des journalistes économique et financière 1972, p. 12).

VIOLENCE AGAINST PRESS ENTERPRISES

Outright attacks on press enterprises became particularly visible after the escalating chain of events surrounding Algeria described above. The Algerian crisis came to a head in April of 1961 with the putsch of four generals of the sizable contingent of the French army then in Algeria. A series of bomb explosions around this time were aimed almost uniquely at publications that supported an independent Algeria. There is a general, if unconfirmed, consensus that the highly conservative, openly pro-French-Algeria police organizations encouraged these extremist bombings. There were conspicuously few arrests.

The bombings began in February 1961, when a huge bomb went off in front of Le Monde. In April, a bomb went off in the hallway of Le Meridional-La France in Marseille. In May, Louis Cardona, editor-in-chief of the only Algerian paper then allowed to appear, the Journal d'Alger, barely escaped an attempt on his life. His fellow director, Raoul Zévaco of L'Echo d'Alger, had been killed a year earlier. In mid-May, a fire was set in the offices of France-Observateur; the same day, a bomb went off in the Dépêche de l'Est, in Algeria. The next day, Le Patriote of Nice was bombed, as was Le Progrès on May 20.

Bombs exploded at the apartments of Pierre Brisson, managing editor of Le Figaro, Hubert Beuve-Méry, of Le Monde, and Pierre Lazareff, of France-Soir. Others almost killed by bomb attempts included Emile Servan-Schreiber, owner and editor of Les Echos, Claude Estier, editor-in-chief of Libération, Jean Daniel of L'Express, Gilles Martinet, of France-Observateur, Jean-Paul Sartre, Jacques Fauvet of Le Monde, and Vladimir Pozner and André Wurmser of L'Humanité. The building of Temoignage Chrétien was similarly bombed. Dozens of other bombings occurred. Most of these people escaped unhurt, but several were wounded. The Federation of the Press referred to the "dictatorship of the bomb" and condemned, helplessly, this extensive series of bombings. As it became apparent that the police were doing little to stop these attacks, vigilance committees were set up to protect press enterprises.

The French state, we have seen, makes use of a wide range of enforcement tactics available to it. At one extreme, we find enforcement techniques based on the leadership role of the state. Considerable state financial aid creates a dependency on the part of many press enterprises. Furthermore, the state also intervenes by playing a major role in the creation of news; the communiqués of state agents and bureaucracies make up a major portion of political and social news in most papers. At the other extreme, we find enforcement tactics based primarily on coercion and even violence, ranging from pressuring journalists to censoring, seizing, or suspending publications, and even to arresting and imprisoning journalists and editors of papers. State intervention in France is always a mix of leading and coercive tactics for, although the French state maintains a "free press," it will not renounce the right to intervene when it finds it necessary to do so. The French state, therefore, not only sets the rules of the game when it promulgates press law (and, of course, these rules are broader than the formally codified statutes) but also actively intervenes to enforce these laws and rules, especially during times of heightened social conflict when there is a political or state crisis. In times of crisis, evidently, the strategic importance of this intervention outweighs the ideological value of preserving the much acclaimed "freedom of the press."

8
DIRECT LINKS BETWEEN THE STATE AND THE PRESS

THE STATE AS AN ACTIVE AGENT IN THE FIELD OF INFORMATION

In the previous section we have examined how the state sets the rules by which press enterprises must operate as well as how the state then acts to enforce these rules. There is, in addition, a third mode of state intervention in this area; the French state is itself an agent in the field of information. European states are typically far more interventionist as agents in the field of information than is the case in English-speaking states, and the French state is particularly active. Although some aspects of state intervention are widely known (for example, the state ownership of the six official television and radio channels), others are relatively unknown to most people (for example, the indirect state control of the "private" radio and television stations that broadcast into France from outside her borders).

There are three principal ways in which the state intervenes as an active agent. First, the French state controls the principal news agency, Agence France Presse. Second, the state has a <u>total monopoly</u> on the electronic media through direct and indirect holding of stock in all broadcasting corporations. Finally, the state is a major purchaser of advertising, not only for its various bureaucracies (the post office, the electric and gas companies, and so on), but especially for its nationalized corporations (Air France, SNCF, Renault, and so on). Furthermore, the state holds a controlling interest in France's largest advertising agency, "Havas."

Agence France Presse

Agence France Presse (AFP) dates back to the creation by Charles Havas in 1832 of the world's first major press agency. By

1840, his control of information coming into France was so complete that Balzac himself wrote, "the public might believe that there are several newspapers, when in fact there is only one" (Cahiers Français, December 1976). The early transmission of international news was accomplished by Havas with regular carrier pigeon lines between Paris and London and between Paris and Brussels. New telecommunication technology was integrated into the system as soon as each improvement appeared. In 1848, the major papers of New York set up the cooperative effort that was to become the Associated Press, and soon afterward the Wolff news agency appeared in Germany and the Reuter agency in Great Britain. The major European nations each had their news agency; Havas represented France.

Until World War II, Havas-Information, which was only one small part of the vast Havas corporation, was an entirely private business. With the creation of the Vichy regime under the occupation, this branch of the company was sold to the French state which, by a Vichy law of November 1940, created the Office Français d'Information (OFI). The task of the OFI was stated in no uncertain terms by its director: "What the change is about, in a word, is a substitution for the liberal, capitalist type press, of a press that resembles that of Germany and Italy, which, without being directly a State press, is always at the disposition of the state" (Presse Actualité, January 1977).

The critical question today is to decide to what extent the AFP is still "at the disposition of the state." Although the AFP was created by an ordinance of September 1944, it was fully 13 years later before laws were passed to formalize its legal status. The AFP is an autonomous organization belonging neither to the state nor to the subscribing newspapers. It must support itself by the sale of its news services and is ruled over by a council, which in turn elects a president. The council is made up of the following: (1) three government representatives (from three ministeries: prime minister, foreign affairs, and economy-finance); (2) eight owners of press publications (six chosen by the provincial press syndicate, two by the Parisian); (3) two representatives of state-run radio and television (typically the president of each); and (4) two representatives of the personnel of AFP (one journalist and one employee).

The membership of the governing council is therefore firmly in the control of the press bourgeoisie and state agents, with merely a dependent participation of the working personnel. This imbalance allowed, for instance, the 1976 appointment as assistant director of a former member of Giscard d'Estaing's government. (Henri Pigeat had been a special assistant to the minister of information (1968-73) and then head of the Inter-Ministerial Committee for Information (Presse Actualité, May and June 1976). The vote was a direct polarization along class lines; the only two negative votes were those of the two AFP personnel representatives (Presse Actualité, May and June 1976). This directly political appointment caused a minor scandal, with both the Socialist and Left Radical parties lodging formal complaints in the National Assembly.

In 1978 the directorship itself of AFP came open, and the state representatives joined with those of the powerful regional press owners organization to ensure the candidacy of Roger Bouzinac, who had been director of the principal regional press organization and who was closely linked with Giscard and the Independent Republican party (Nouvel Observateur, June 5, 1978). Hubert Beuve-Méry and one of the two representatives of the Parisian press organization read a stinging denunciation of this manipulation of the supposedly independent agency, and Beuve-Méry handed in his resignation rather than cast a meaningless vote (Nouvel Observateur, June 5, 1978).

The AFP presents an interesting case of state intervention for to remain effective, it must maintain a double autonomy. First, like any state agency, it must maintain a relative autonomy with respect to specific interests of various segments of the dominant class in order to represent the general interests of the dominant class as a whole. Added to this, however, is the need to have, or at least appear to have, an autonomy with respect to the state, if its worldwide dispatches are to be considered independent news analyses and not merely governmental communiqués. This is why AFP is set up neither as a private corporation nor a public agency but lies somewhere in between. This autonomy is threatened by these recent cases of state manipulation, and hence Beuve-Méry's characterization of these power plays as "a grave attack on the statutes defining the autonomy of the agency" (Nouvel Observateur, June 5, 1978).

Of course autonomy from the state implies that the AFP must achieve fiscal stability on its own, in the "marketplace." In late capitalism, however, the myth of the marketplace has lost much of its ability to mask and obscure. In the written press, the concentration-monopolization process continually reduces the number of enterprises that subscribe to AFP wire service. Couple this with the fact that in the electronic media, the state itself is AFP's principal customer (accounting for 60 percent of the yearly budget), and it becomes clear that the state retracts with its right hand the autonomy it grants with its left.

The ideological impact of AFP is difficult to overestimate. Although there are other French news agencies, they supply only an extremely small number of dispatches to the French press. Within France, AFP is even dominant over the U.S. wire services since few enterprises can afford to subscribe to more than one news agency above and beyond AFP (Archambault and Lemoine 1977, p. 222). The provincial press relies almost totally on AFP. In the AFP, therefore, the state has a strategic emplacement from which to manipulate and manage information.

Along with the dispatches emanating directly from state agencies and state agents, the AFP also delivers communiqués given it by various social organizations. In theory such communiqués are verified and rewritten before they become AFP dispatches, but in reality there is typically far too little time and far too many communiqués to verify. Nevertheless, one does not want to fall into an instrumentalist view of AFP; its relative autonomy with respect to the state, while largely formal, becomes substantive insofar as the journalist unions act to police it.

The four journalist unions active at AFP have gathered together to form an inter-union federation that is willing to speak out and even to take strike action to protest specific instances of state pressure. On March 1, 1977, a one-hour warning strike was held to protest three such instances that occurred within a few weeks:

1. Michel d'Ornano, ex-minister and candidate for the Republican party of Giscard, protested to the director of AFP about the coverage his campaign was receiving. A new journalist was assigned to cover him.
2. Jean-Philippe Lecat, the presidential press secretary, complained about a certain dispatch on the electoral campaign. The director purely and simply annulled the dispatch.
3. Claude Bellanger, editor-in-chief of the Parisien Libéré (and one of the eight press-owner representatives to the AFP), protested to the director that certain material about the illegal management practices of the Parisien Libéré, which had been exposed in a press conference held by the printers union, ought not to be carried on the wire service. The director eliminated this material from all dispatches, although all other wire services carried the full story (Le Monde, March 3, 1977).

The issue of the right of AFP journalists to strike had been a cause célèbre since 1976, when several previous strikes called by the national union of the four principal journalist unions had closed down the AFP along with the entire French press. The issue came to a head when a Republican deputy to the National Assembly proposed legislation that would demand that a minimum skeleton crew keep AFP working even during a strike. This was immediately opposed by the Socialists and Communists for it implied that AFP was a state agency where, indeed, such skeleton crews can be required. The statute of the AFP, we have seen, defines it as an independent corporation, and, as such, under French law it cannot have such a requirement. The government had no choice but to forgo this effort to render AFP strikeproof (Le Monde, December 21, 1976, and L'Humanité, December 29, 1976).

The State Monopoly over the Electronic Media

In 1976 the French state maintained, despite increasing pressure, total monopoly over the electronic media. The fact that the monopoly is complete is not widely known for it is generally assumed that the so-called private radio and television stations that broadcast into France from around its borders (Monte Carlo, Luxembourg) are outside the state monopoly. Figure 8.1 summarizes the complex lines through which the French state maintains a controlling interest in the peripheral stations through two principal nationalized corporations, SOFIRAD and Havas. The state, therefore, has a double ideological impact on the electronic media. Besides enjoying the obvious advantages of its total monopoly, its hidden control of the "private" stations allows it to structure the output of the stations people turn to to verify what they hear on the "state-owned" stations.

With the election of Giscard d'Estaing in 1974, the question of local radio was once again raised, since his Independent Republican party was in favor of such a change. However, the opposition of the Gaullist party, joined by the Socialist and Communist parties on this issue, prevented any change. What the new president did do, however, only one month after his election, was to decentralize the state's radio and television apparatus, the old ORTF (Office de Radiodiffusion-Télévision Française). In its place he had the Council of Ministers plan a series of bodies to oversee the ORTF holdings, a plan which the National Assembly later passed into law. Besides the three corporations set up to handle each one of the three television channels, a fourth, Radio-France, was created to manage the three directly state-owned radio stations: France-Inter (popular music, sensationalist news reporting), France-Music (classical music, more rationalistic news reporting), and France-Culture (high-level informative and intellectual programming). Two other companies were formed as well, the first to produce radio and television programs, the second to foster research and innovative approaches. There has been a constant stream of criticisms of this reorganization of the ORTF, some claiming that it was done to make an informational takeover by an eventual left government more difficult, others arguing that there was no significant decentralization in authority relations involved whatsoever (see Thomas 1976). In any case, it involved the loss of some 3,000 jobs, including about 300 journalists (Rocci 1975, p. 37).

FIGURE 8.1

The French State Monopoly over the Electronic Media

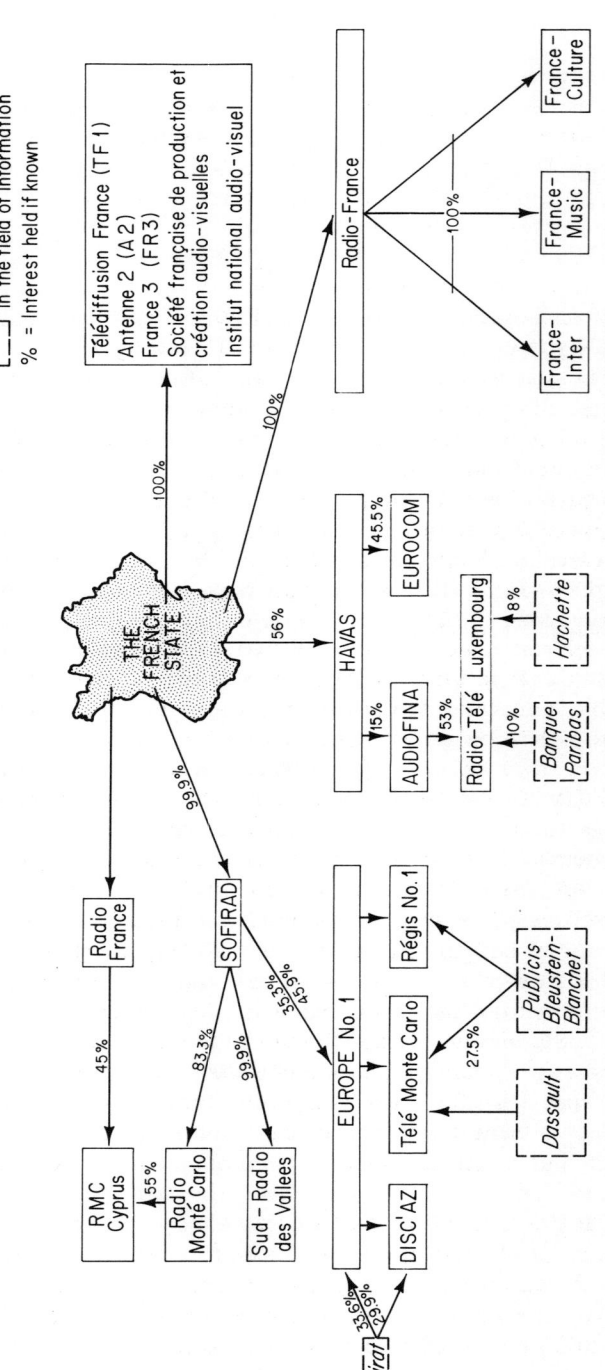

Sources: *Journal des journalistes*, May 1976; *Le Monde*, March 26, 1975; May 24-25, 1977; *Le Journaliste*, April 1976; and Jean-Louis Servan-Schreiber, *Le Pouvoir d'informer* (Paris: Robert Laffont, 1972), p. 206.

The strong role of the state in the electronic media originally demanded by de Gaulle after the war is still openly defended. When André Rossi, a government minister, was asked in 1975 what he thought about the chances of the state allowing private, local radio stations, he responded, "The government would oppose it. It is there to apply the law, and thus the monopoly" (Quotidien de Paris, September 15, 1975). Nevertheless, the lack of local radio and television in France was a controversial topic in the mid-1970s, especially after an almost identical situation was ruled unconstitutional in Italy by its Supreme Court in 1975. In less than one year after this ruling, over 250 local stations were set up, and no doubt if the French state allowed its monopoly to be broken there would be numerous stations created throughout France. The vigilance of the state is strict on this issue; when various "pirate" stations have opened they have been closed down quickly. For instance, when Jean-Edern Hallier, ex-publisher of l'Idiot International, began broadcasting "Radio-Green" (ecology-oriented) from his apartment in the Place des Vosges in May 1977, he was quickly threatened with legal action (International Herald Tribune, May 15, 1977).

Clearly the decision to forbid local radio and television is not only political. It is also a response to pressure from the press bourgeoisie, particularly those in the provinces (Presse Actualité, April 1975 and September 1976). These provincial monopolistic press enterprises have a vested interest in maintaining the total monopolies they have on both local news and local advertising. A recent government report looking into the question of local radio, while suggesting first steps toward the funding of several small scale "experiments," noted that "the government and the parliament have refused to allow anarchy to enter this realm. They will continue to do so" (Presse Actualité, January 1980, my emphasis).

The highly political use of the television under Gaullist and Republican regimes has come under direct attack from the left. The "Programme Commun" of the Union of the Left took a strong position on this issue and promised major changes. The matter came into the public arena in 1977, when Gaston Defferre, mayor of Marseille and head of the Socialist group in the National Assembly, mounted a major attack and outlined the perspective of the Socialist party:

1. Since the coming of de Gaulle's Fifth Republic to power, the television has been put at the service of the government. The monopoly has become a political monopoly, a synonym for "abuse, exclusive use, and an instrument of domination."
2. "The Programme Commun is very explicit. The radio and television will become a true public service at the disposal of the nation."

3. "The expression and confrontation of ideas will be guaranteed by the equitable attribution of antenna time to not only the government but also to political parties, unions, representative organizations, and other entities."
4. The resources for television will come from the television tax paid by each consumer and also from a tax on the industries involved in the radio and television field. Advertising will be banned (Le Monde, May 4, 1977).

The state maintains a strict, if indirect, control on the editorial positions of its stations. The following example exposes the degree of censorship that takes place in these state-owned stations.

In August 1976, Michel Lemerle, a journalist at France-Culture, wrote a story on Robert Hersant's takeover at France-Soir which the editor-in-chief banned from being read over the air. Lemerle in response, acting through the federation of journalist unions, sent the paper with an explanation of what had happened to the press. L'Humanité, La Croix and several other papers picked up not only the original story on Hersant, but also the censorship at France-Culture. In response, Lemerle received a letter from the president of Radio-France, the holding company of all three public radio stations, advising him that he had put his job in jeopardy by having sent the article to other papers without authorization. This response was in turn protested by the journalist unions, for it was one incident among many in a tightening picture of increased control by the state at Radio-France (Le Journaliste, November 1976, p. 14; and L'Humanité, April 16, 1977).

The HAVAS Advertising Corporation

If the state monopoly on French-based radio and television is controversial, it is far less well known that the French state also has controlling interest in the non-France-based "private" stations that broadcast into France. Even as astute a student of the French media as Ruth Thomas (1976), although knowing that the French state has "acquired shares" (p. 102) and "has considerable opportunities for control" (p. 105), reports that the state's "jealously guarded monopoly is broken in practice by the privately run radio and television stations operating on France's borders" (p. 102). The state's control is exercised indirectly through holding companies, one of which is the vast advertising and travel-industry corporation, Havas. Havas, a private corporation before World War II, was nationalized at the liberation. Its news agency functions became Agence France Press, and 56 percent of its advertising and travel interests are held by the French state. Havas today is bigger than ever, with a gross income of over NF 1.2 billion per year in its advertising wing alone (see Figure A.3) (Archambault and Lemoine 1977, p. 199).

What I am interested in tracing here is the use made of Havas to control the important peripheral radio station Radio-Télé Luxembourg (RTL). Until recently this station was controlled by a "French group" made up of Jean Prouvost (13 percent), Banque Paribas (about 10 percent), Compagnie de Compteurs (10 percent), and Havas (15 percent). Although Jean Prouvost served as president for many years, the group was actually led by the French state through its controlling interests in Havas.

It is impossible to know precisely why the "French group" at CLT-RTL broke up, but it is known that the 1974 move was initiated by Havas (that is, by the state) (Le Monde, April 27, 1975). Havas joined with several Belgian corporations to take immediate control of the station out of French hands (Le Monde, March 26, 1975). Some contend that Giscard d'Estaing, then minister of finance, effected the changes in order to be able to name a new director. Others believe, and I think more reasonably, that the move was part of a series of moves to eliminate the <u>direct</u> involvement of the French state in setting political policy for the stations. Why do this? Because during this period, the allied left parties were rapidly expanding at the expense of the deeply divided right; more subtle means of controlling information became preferable to block the degree of control an eventual left government would have over this important radio station.

The SOFIRAD Holding Company

To understand the manner in which the French state holds controlling interest in the remaining peripheral, "private" radio and television stations, one must take a look at the structure and holdings of the Société Financière de Radio-Diffusion (SOFIRAD). This company, which is owned 99.9 percent by the state, has several subsidiaries, among them two radio stations: Radio Monte Carlo (RMC) and Sud-Radio des Vallées. It also holds 35.3 percent of the shares (but a controlling 46.9 percent of the votes) of the most important "private" station, Europe #1, which, in turn, holds a controlling interest in Télé Monte Carlo, which broadcasts television into southeastern France.

SOFIRAD was constituted in 1942 by the Vichy government to assure French control over the peripheral radio stations. SOFIRAD obtained 50 percent of the shares of Radio Monte Carlo during the war and bought the remaining part from German holders after the war. Thereafter SOFIRAD was used as a base to acquire shares in foreign radio ventures for clearly political reasons. For example, the station held highly unprofitable but politically useful shares of: Andorradio in Andorra, Radio Sarrebrück in the Sarre, Radio France-Asie in Saigon, Radio Brazzaville in the Congo, and, finally, La Compagnie Libanaise de Télévision (Presse Actualité, February 1977). In 1979, SOFIRAD extended its influence into Africa by joining the government of Gabon in the creation of a new station, "Afrique No. 1" (Presse Actualité, January 1980).

The men placed at the head of SOFIRAD are indicative of the control the government maintains over this important holding company. In 1973, the director, Pierre LeFranc, was simultaneously president of the National Association for the support of General de Gaulle. His successor, Dennis Baudouin, had previously been the chief press secretary for President Pompidou, who had openly expressed displeasure at Radio-Monte Carlo's provocative May 1968 "direct from the barricades" broadcasts. As Pompidou phrased it, "It is necessary to establish a certain policy in regard to information" (Presse Actualité, February 1977). SOFIRAD is run by an administrative council on which there is no representation whatsoever of the personnel (Thomas 1976, p. 104).

Another example of the long reach of the French state in the realm of the audio-visual media was a project begun in the early 1970s to build a transmitter on Cyprus that would send French-language programs to the Middle East. By 1973, a large and effective station had been installed which soon increased its audience by broadcasting in Arabic. During the 1973 and subsequent wars between Israel and her Arab neighbors, this station was one of the most listened to (Presse Actualité, February 1977). Only the political importance of this station to the French state can explain its willingness to cover the considerable yearly operating deficit (Presse Actualité, February 1977).

SOFIRAD's most important holding, however, is its controlling interest in "Europe #1," a major and highly profitable radio station with one of the largest audiences in France (Presse Actualité, February 1974, June 1976, and February 1977). It has numerous holdings of interest, since they once again exhibit private sector-public sector interlocks. In Europe #1 itself, the state is linked with the major industrialist Sylvian Floirat, a member of the press bourgeoisie as well (Lui, numerous free-distribution weeklies, and so on). Europe #1 is also a holding company with a controlling interest in Télé Monte Carlo. Here the state is interlocked with Marcel Bleustein-Blanchet (principal holder of the monopolistic Publicis advertising corporation) and Marcel Dassault (industrialist and owner of Jours de France) (Presse Actualité, June 1976).

Besides the class character of the state's monopolization of the electronic media, one also wants to see the role of the logic of the state's self-interest. Only this can explain the fact that the French state is as vehement about denying a private broadcasting license to elements of the bourgeoisie as it is consistent in utilizing immediate police intervention to close "pirate" radio stations opened by elements of the left.

STATE PERSONNEL INTERLOCKS WITH THE PRESS BOURGEOISIE

We have noted before that personnel interlocks exist between various information-related corporate units and the state apparatus. Often one finds a former ministerial-level press secretary serving as an executive in a press enterprise, and, in the other direction, many of the most important personalities of the press bourgeoisie have successfully run for office and held important political positions. What distinguishes interlocks from ministerial intervention is that personnel interlocks represent an unofficial, off-the-record interpretation of state agents with the bourgeoisie of an economically minor but ideologically important industrial sector, the press.

In and of themselves, personnel interlocks between the press bourgeoisie and the state are reasonably minor phenomena. Far more important, for instance, are the private sector-public sector media partnerships that are formed. But in neither case can one assume that the state is directly manipulated by the interests and influence of the press bourgeoisie. Besides safeguarding its own particular interests, the state must be responsive to far broader and more general interests than those of the press owners. Although personnel interlocks demonstrate the class character of state intervention in the press, they do not imply either that the press loses its operative autonomy relative to the state or that the state apparatus, in those agencies and offices which concern themselves with the press, is overrun by and dependent upon the representatives and interests of the press bourgeoisie.

Personnel Interlocks

At least one major personnel interlock has been arranged by each of the recent presidents and prime ministers of France (see Table A.13). Most of these were handled quietly, and the public remained unaware of the nature of the linkages being forged. Le Monde, in announcing public or private sector appointments, always includes a small biography of the individual involved, but other newspapers make little or no mention of the appointee's background. Some of the appointments, however, were so blatantly political as to lead to scandals. For example, when Giscard appointed a personal lieutenant, Henry Pigeat, as assistant director of Agence France Presse in 1976, the personnel called a strike, and the left press, political parties, and unions vociferously condemned the appointment. This particular appointment represented an escalation in the politics of interlocks; never before had a purely political appointment been made to head the supposedly independent news agency (Le Journalist, April 1976, p. 10).

A far greater scandal arose from Prime Minister Jacques Chaban-Delmas's appointment of Simon Nora and Gérard Worms as directors of the Hachette corporation. Given the extensive role of Hachette in both the written and electronic media, there is good reason for both a particular government and the state itself to want to have channels by which to influence decisions in the corporate giant of the information sector. Influence, however, is based on exchange, and Hachette also meant to benefit from allowing the penetration of former state agents. This became a national scandal in the present case when Nora and Worms proceeded to arrange for Hachette to have exclusive access to the state's entire radio and television archives for the production of future cable television and cassette programming. When the role of the two appointees became public knowledge, it served as one principal factor leading Chaban-Delmas to resign (Presse Actualité, September 1971 and December 1972; Le Monde, October 22, 1974; and Enkiri 1972, p. 108; see also below on Hachette).

President Pompidou placed Jean Meo at the head of France-Soir, but the most important Pompidou interlock was his placement of Xavier Marchetti at Le Figaro. At the time it was not clear whether the prestigious newspaper would remain Gaullist or would be taken into the Independent Republican camp of Giscard d'Estaing. Clearly Marchetti's role was to work within the paper to assure its continued presence in the Gaullist camp. Several years later Gaullist Prime Minister Jacques Chirac arranged to have Le Figaro sold to Robert Hersant, and Marchetti played an important role in convincing Le Figaro's major journalists (Raymond Aron, Jean d'Ormesson, and others) to continue writing for the paper; their initial response had been to announce their resignations.* The continued presence of Le Figaro's best-known editorialists was a critical element in masking the transition of the newspaper into the Hersant chain.

---

*Interview with Jean d'Ormesson, March 7, 1977.

Political Offices for the Press Bourgeoisie

Above and beyond the interlocks of a traditional nature, as described above, another powerful link between the press bourgeoisie and the state is made when press owners hold political office. Since they control their local paper, often in a monopoly situation, they are in a unique position to further their own candidacy. Table 8.1 gives a list of political offices held by some of the press bourgeoisie whose names have come up repeatedly throughout this study.

Back in 1951, Robert Hersant clearly stated why he was running for office: "I will enter politics to protect my business interests. . . . I will be a deputy to guard my flanks. . . . One thinks twice before attacking a man who is a Parliamentarian rather than simply another businessman." By 1976, Hersant had confirmed what he had merely theorized about a quarter of a century earlier: "I have to say that the reactions of the men in power are different when a press magnate is also a Parliamentarian. . . . Certainly, I am a deputy, but I cannot say that I am a politician, as I have never done it for the career of it" (Pons 1977, p. 41).

One principal role these important members of the press bourgeoisie have been able to play in the National Assembly in regard to the press is in contributing to the legislative efforts to block promul-

TABLE 8.1

Political Offices Held by the Press Bourgeoisie, 1977

Name	Press Position	Political Office
Robert Hersant	Head of Hersant chain	Deputy to National Assembly
André Audinot	Head of *France-Soir*	Deputy to National Assembly
Gaston Defferre	Head of *Provençal* group	Deputy to National Assembly
J.-J. Servan-Schreiber	Head of *L'Express* group	Deputy to National Assembly
Marcel Dassault	Head of *Jours de France*	Senator
Dominique Pado	Editor-in-chief of *L'Aurore*	Senator

Source: Compiled by the author.

gation of the press statutes promised at the liberation. They have acted in every way possible to promote the monopolization and centralization tendencies in the press, from which their particular enterprises benefit (Le Monde, April 18, 1975; Durand 1974; Pons 1977, p. 57).

It is no surprise to find high-level linkages between state personnel and the press bourgeoisie. Given that France is split down the middle politically,* the ideological support of the press is critical for the ruling center-right political alliance. This support is readily forthcoming, since the press bourgeoisie in turn is in need of state aid for its technological transfer from lead-based to computer-based technology, that is, from labor-intensive journalism to highly centralized, capital-intensive journalism. In this revolution in the mode of production in the press enterprises, a great number of journalists and printers will be laid off, and the press bourgeoisie will need state help of several kinds. They will need permission for the lay-offs from the minister of labor and police protection from the minister of the interior during the inevitable strikes and protests. They will also need state financial assistance with reconversion programs aimed at reducing their labor force (early retirement, retraining programs, de-skilling indemnity payments, and so forth). In short, the symbiotic relationship between the state personnel and the press bourgeoisie should be at least as important in the coming decade as it has been in the past.

The documentation of interlocks does not, however, imply that there has been an effective __breaching__ of the relative autonomy of the state. State agents can only favor a given industrial sector to a limited extent before they begin to violate the interests of the bourgeoisie of other sectors.

The state, regardless of its penetration by representatives of the press bourgeoisie, cannot act exclusively in their favor in deciding questions relevant to the press sector.

The relative autonomy of the capitalist state is thus in part a __structural necessity__, given the often opposed interests of the bourgeoisie of different industrial sectors, not to mention the conflicting interests among the industrial bourgeoisie taken as a whole, the commercial bourgeoisie, the financial bourgeoisie, and so forth. It is essential to see that the "relative autonomy" of the state is not merely a theoretical abstraction, but a practical and quite necessary

---

*In the second round of the 1978 legislative elections, the right received 12.9 million votes, the left 12.5 million (Le Monde, March 16-22, 1978).

<u>operational space</u> in which intra-dominant-class struggle and negotiation about state policy making and implementation takes place.

CONCLUSION TO PART III

Part III has attempted to trace concrete moments of state intervention in the media. State intervention, however, cannot be viewed as a simple affair since there are multiple logics structuring the state's purposes in its intervention. The so-called instrumentalist view of the state, in which the state is seen as essentially a tool of the dominant class, is therefore an inadequate conceptual model. The capitalist state does, of course, act on behalf of the general interests of the bourgeoisie with respect to the interests of the dominated classes, but it does so with varying degrees of dependent representation of popular class interests in various state agencies. Thus the capitalist state serves in part as a site of interclass struggle and negotiation where working-class interests are represented and responded to.

In the press sector one can see this first logic of state intervention. We found many examples of the French state serving the interests of the press bourgeoisie relative to the interests of the journalists and printers. For instance, it was shown that the state regulatory commissions, investigative committees, and administrative agencies in the press sector were consistently set up with no representation, or at best a meager and dependent representation of press workers that was aimed more at protecting the image of state "neutrality" than at encouraging serious input from the workers in the sector. There are contradictory examples, however, when the state has acted to encourage the institutionalization of popular class interests, particularly in the social-democratic legislation of the liberation era. On the whole, it would seem that adequate documentation has been presented to demonstrate that the intervention of the state in affairs of the press is by and large in favor of the press bourgeoisie relative to the workers of the sector.

But the capitalist state is not merely an arena of interclass confrontation; it also is deeply involved in intraclass relations, acting to balance the sometimes opposed interests of different segments of the bourgeoisie. The state must weigh the sometimes contradictory interests of different industrial sectors. We saw this in the case of newsprint: the paper bourgeoisie pleaded for the deregulation of newsprint prices, whereas the press bourgeoisie simultaneously favored continued price controls on newsprint. State policy could not serve the interests of both sectors simultaneously.

Second, the state acts to promote the general interests of the bourgeoisie against the particularistic interests of a given industrial sector. We saw an interesting example of this in the legislation introducing paid television advertising, which almost instantly reduced newspaper advertising by 25 percent. The press bourgeoisie, for obvious reasons, were strongly opposed to the policy change, but a wide range of bourgeoisie from more powerful economic sectors lobbied successfully in favor of the new legislation.

Third, one must recognize that the contemporary capitalist state in the core societies intervenes in a given sector in favor of big capital against small and medium capital. Numerous examples were brought up documenting the state's central role in promoting the monopolization and concentration process in the press sector. Furthermore, the state has taken no action to prevent the reduction in overall productive capacity that has accompanied monopolization in both the printing and paper-producing sectors, a state policy which has encouraged rising unemployment, the externalization of a great deal of printing and paper production to other Common Market countries, and the increased concentration of the remaining firms in these two sectors.

Finally, we have also seen how the state jealously guards its own corporate self-interests with respect to the private sector. This is particularly clear in France, where the total monopoly on the electronic media held by the state is merely an electronic-age manifestation of classical French étatism. This étatism is also evident in the direct state intervention to set limits on the editorial freedom of the press, particularly during times of political crisis and especially as regards the left press.

PART IV

MODES OF JOURNALISM AND CLASS RELATIONS IN CAPITALIST SOCIETY

INTRODUCTION TO PART IV

Dieter Prokop (1974, p. 61) has argued, "The center of mass communication research lies outside the media," and Oskar Negt (1978) has stressed the same point: "The media do not constitute the core of a critical media theory." Clearly my own agreement with this approach is apparent in that only now, at the end of this report, do we turn to look at the media as such, in other words, at the <u>content</u> of the articles and programs. Up until now the analysis has dealt with the political economy of the organizational restructuring of the press sector in France since World War II, the effects this has had on labor and labor organization within the sector, and the role of the French state in promoting these structural shifts. Now I want to turn briefly to observe the changes in the content of the press that have resulted from this process.

Of course, an analysis of the content of the press in France is open to the complexities involved in determining the role of the press in ideological relations in capitalist society. Such an effort must deal with the theoretical difficulties of a doubly autonomous process: To what extent do the press bourgeoisie and the wider segments of the bourgeoisie on whom they are dependent purposively structure (deform) information in the press in light of their interests? In what way and to what extent do the media have an ideological impact on their consumers? The theoretical difficulty of such an undertaking is evident in that even as insightful a thinker as Ralph Miliband produces a thoroughly inadequate model which ignores the double autonomy of the media:

> Whatever else the immense output of the mass media is intended to achieve, it is <u>also</u> intended to help prevent the development of class-consciousness in the working class and to reduce as much as possible any hankering it might have for a radical alternative to capitalism. The ways in which this is attempted are endlessly different; and the degree of success achieved varies considerably from country to country and from one period to another—there are other influences at work. But the fact remains that "the class which has the means of material production at its disposal" does have "control at the same time of the means of mental production": and that it does seek to use them for the weakening of opposition to the established order. (1977, p. 50)

Nicholas Garnham has criticized Miliband's position as reductionist since it is based on an economic determinism which ends up <u>assuming</u> the very relationships between the economic and the ideological which need to be held open and investigated in concrete, historical cases. Garnham (1979, p. 12) argues that Miliband's analysis precludes investigations into "the specificities of the varying and shifting relationships between economic, ideological, and political levels within actual concrete historical moments."

It is equally unfortunate that the occasional references to "ideological state apparatuses" in the writing of Louis Althusser (1971) and Nicos Poulantzas (1975) make a similar economistic reduction of the media. If these two theorists criticize Miliband's "instrumentalism" on the issue of the capitalist state, they proceed to produce an equally instrumentalist theory of the media: they proclaim the "relative autonomy" of the state and conceive it as a site of class conflict, but when they treat ideological apparatuses they inexplicably picture them as closed, impervious to struggle and directly manipulated by the dominant class.*

A more adequate critical theory of the ideological role of the media would do better to start with the sentiment of Theodore Adorno and Max Horkheimer that "under the private culture monopoly, it is a fact that 'tyranny leaves the body free and directs its attack at the soul.'" Capitalist societies do not experience a closed ideological universe, and while this seems patently evident in liberal capitalist state structures, one could argue that it is, if in a more hidden fashion, still the case in totalitarian capitalist state structures, where the populace has long since learned to "translate" the official version of events and read between the lines of censored information. (Obviously this also takes place in totalitarian socialist societies). Ideological processes, particularly in the liberal forms of capitalist society, are mediated far more complexly than the instrumentalist model of a heavy-handed, intentional information manipulation suggests.

Given the absence of an adequate general model from which to study ideological relations, the present effort will be quite modest in scope. In fact, Part IV is structured around one principal hypothesis, namely, that <u>the contribution of the mass media to ideological relations in capitalist society is principally a function of their partici-</u>

---

*See Paul Hirst's (1976, p. 394) criticism of the concept of "ideological state." He points out that while Althusser and Poulantzas correctly criticize Miliband for assuming a unity of state <u>structure</u>, they proceed to assume a unity of state <u>function</u>, and hence a unity to the ideological output of all media.

pation in the reproduction of basic class divisions. Along with other cultural institutions—especially the family structure and the educational system—the media serve to differentiate the life experiences of different classes and class segments. The effectiveness of these institutions is in large part a function of their multiple reinforcement of the determination of these divisions. Writing about Sweden, Jan Ekecrantz (1974, p. 400) notes:

> The impact of ideological apparatuses is strengthened by the fact that they operate in combinations. We can conclude, e.g., that the family, the school, and the mass media together make up an extremely forceful combination in a country like Sweden, where these institutions are relatively integrated compared to many other countries (high use of TV, radio and daily papers in schools, large-scale family-school organizations, a considerable portion of mass media material of "family" type, and so forth).

Put in other terms, the basic thesis being argued is that the mass media form part of a two-tier cultural system which participates in the complex process of dividing social agents along class lines.* In any capitalist society, part of the population must be readied for and kept satisfied with low-paying, low-prestige, often strenuous occupations, while others must be prepared for routine white collar work. At the other extreme, a small part of the population must be formed to execute high-level management positions and to accept and defend the highly visible inequalities of capitalist society, which form the basis of their privileged position. The operational contribution of the media and other culture institutions to the reproduction of existing class relations is what Poulantzas has in mind when he insists that "the exact role of the ideological apparatuses in the reproduction of social relations . . . is, in fact, of supreme importance: for it is their reproduction which dominates the process of

---

*Ithiel de Sola Pool, Harold D. Lasswell, and David Lerner (1970, p. 62) came close to recognizing this when they wrote, "In each major power one newspaper stands out as an organ of elite opinion. Usually semiofficial, always intimate with the government, these "prestige papers" are read by public officials, journalists, scholars, and business leaders." Their lack of a class perspective, however, led them to conclude that "there is no inherent reason why such a paper should exist."

reproduction as a whole, particularly the reproduction of the labour force and the means of labour" (cited in Ekecrantz et al. 1976, p. 20).

Analyses of the ideological functions of the media must always be undertaken from within a framework sensitive to the differential relations between the media and different social classes. When one forgoes this framework, one succumbs to the (elitist) culture critique typical of the Frankfurt School, that is, to a general cretinization thesis which forgets that, while some classes indeed experience mostly informational and aesthetic banality in their media consumption, others experience sophisticated printed, filmed, and recorded information about socioeconomic and political trends and cultural events occurring throughout the world. Take, for example, the otherwise brilliant work of Armand Mattelart (1974b), which fails to make any differentiations when claiming that sensationalism is the key structure of the mass culture of advanced capitalist society. Similarly, Yrjo Littunen of Finland (1978, p. 174) writes that "knowledge as a resource is being drowned in the very flow of mass communication, in the escapist, non-informational or even anti-informational programme content of the Western cultural market." Exactly the same shortcoming appears in the work of Jan Eckecrantz of Sweden (1976, pp. 15ff.), who speaks of the "escapist," "illusory" nature of the contemporary media without any reference to those media programs which certainly cannot be described in that fashion. In the United States, Herbert Schiller (1973, pp. 8 ff.) provides an insightful analysis of the "myths" and delivery techniques that characterize the manipulation of information, that is, individualism, pseudo-neutrality, absence of social conflict, fragmentation of events, and overconcentration on immediacy; but he too fails to trace the class factors involved.

What these otherwise useful analyses of sensationalist journalism lack is an awareness that they are dealing with only _part_ of media output: they do not distinguish that part of the media which is _not_ sensationalist in the sense they describe. One does not want to ignore the New York _Times_, the London _Times_, _Le Monde_, _La Stampa_, and other high-quality newspapers, to say nothing of the dozens of informative and politically sophisticated periodicals found in each advanced capitalist society.

What I hope to do in the following pages, accordingly, is to demonstrate how in France there is not a unified media system, supplying alternative written and electronic material to _individuals_ according to their personal tastes but rather a two-tier media system, which is used differentially by different _social classes_. Thus two separate claims must be documented: the question of the existence of two distinguishable media tracks, and a consistent recourse to these different tracks by different social classes.

9
THE SENSATIONALIST PRESS

Several central characteristics of sensationalist journalism, especially its overt depoliticization, its inherent conservatism, its informational vacuity, and its crisis orientation, interest us at this juncture. It is these traits (although one could extend the analysis and locate others) that distinguish the sensationalist press from the "informational" press which was dominant in France at the liberation but now is found in only a handful of publications. Others have worked with this distinction before, although seldom has it been argued along lines of class relations. Michael Schudson (1978) has analyzed in detail the distinctions in both form and content between "information news" and "telling stories" but does not link his study to a political-economic analysis of the origin of the disjunction. Helen Hughes's (1940) contribution to this distinction is still of value; in analyzing the impact of the human interest story she concludes, "Its invasion of the newspaper and final adoption as a policy of news-writing were accompanied by changes in every aspect of the newspaper's organization." Her insistence that the key to understanding sensationalist journalism and the "yellow press" is to be found in an analysis of the human interest story seems to me to be entirely correct. She writes (p. 67), "The human interest story is not news; the test of it is not in action . . . in contradistinction to news, it has no urgency, and no practical consequences."

OVERT DEPOLITICIZATION AND INHERENT CONSERVATISM

The relative and absolute column inches given to political reporting and analysis has decreased precipitously since the liberation. According to one study of French daily papers of the late 1960s, the percentage of surface space devoted to national or international political coverage ranged from 6 to 13 percent in the sensationalist papers, as compared to 14 to 35 percent in the informational press (Pourprix 1971, p. 71).

The French sociologist Francis Balle has produced several studies on the depoliticization phenomenon and has argued that the relative presence of political coverage has dropped in _all_ papers since the liberation. Figure 9.1 shows the relative drop in space devoted to political coverage as well as the relative rise in other topics that have supplanted it. This graph of the evolution of the space devoted to different sections allows us to discover which sections are filling the gap resulting from the relative decline in political news present in all four papers. L'Humanité has allowed its political news to slip from 75 percent of its written surface just after the war to only about 11 percent today. It should be noted that papers today are far bigger than they were just after the war, when newsprint was scarce, so the drops in percentage of space given over to political discussion are not necessarily drops in an absolute sense. Nevertheless, for L'Humanité there is an _absolute_ drop between 1944 and 1964. Le Monde and Figaro have increased, and France-Soir has remained about the same in absolute terms (Balle 1968, p. 298).

L'Humanité has also lost space in economic and financial news, while there has been an appreciable expansion in the coverage of human interest stories, leisure, culture, and sports. So even the official C. P. organ, L'Humanité, has become progressively depoliticized by this trivialization process. In Le Figaro and Le Monde the considerable drop in the proportion of political news is clearly _not_ a function of trivialization; there is little or no growth in the relative presence of human interest stories, sports, general news, leisure, or culture. What accounts for the depoliticization at Le Figaro is increased advertising.

Has there been a depoliticization of Le Monde ? In relative terms, yes; in absolute terms, certainly not. The sheer quantity of political news and analysis carried by Le Monde coupled with the quality of the documentation and research used in writing the articles leads one to find that, in fact, Le Monde has held firm against the trend. As Balle concludes:

> Le Monde is the only French daily to offer a real resistance to the "lucrative" rubrics and to bet on a substantial growth of serious articles. . . . Le Monde is by far the paper which offers the most substantial quantity of truly political information. (Balle 1968, p. 306)

FIGURE 9.1

Evolution of Number of Pages Devoted to Various Rubrics, 1946-65
(percentages)

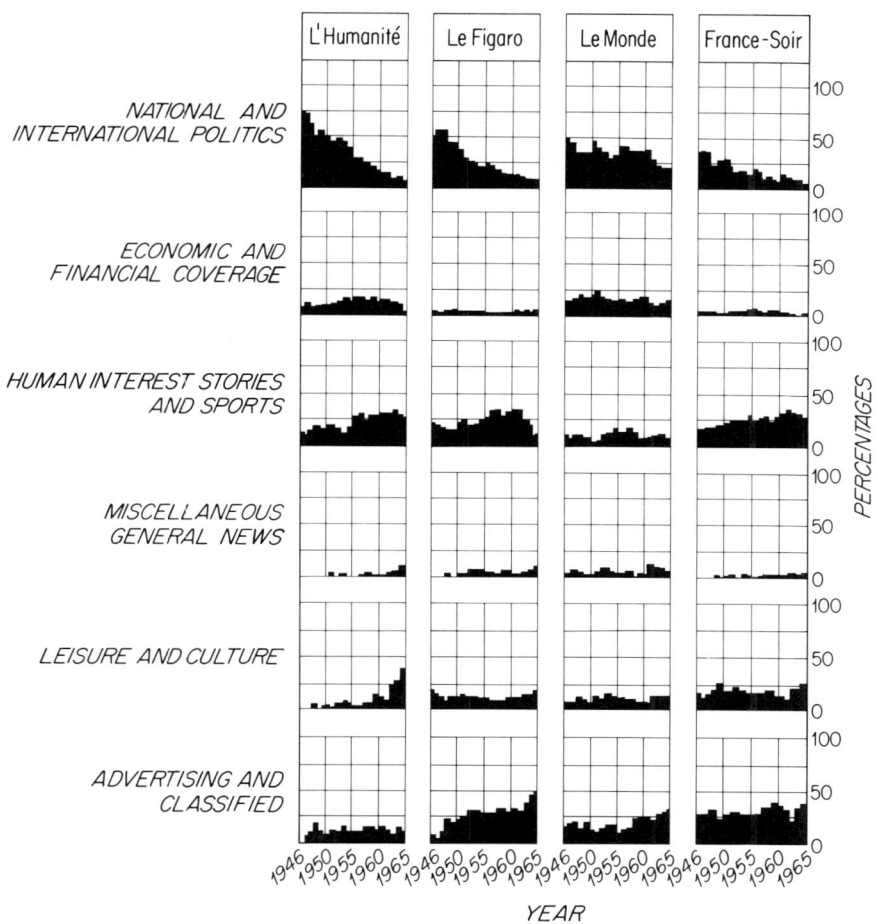

Source: Francis Balle, "Les grands quotidiens français sont-ils dépolitisés?" Annals (March-April 1968).

A comparative look at the newsworthiness of the sensationalist and informational modes of journalism can be had by looking at the sources of information used by the small but important daily publication, L'Index. This publication is created each night from the evening press and the first editions of the next morning's papers; by 10 AM it is on the desk of every government official, as well as many others throughout Paris. Its job is to summarize the French press, that is, to present concisely and accurately what is happening in France and in the world. Looking at the sources used by L'Index for the entire month of September 1976, gives us a reasonably accurate profile of the newsworthiness of the French press from the perspective of L'Index. For that month, there were 835 informational and 207 sensationalist newspaper citations.*

The process of depoliticization extends even into the few remaining overtly political articles in the sensationalist press. This "trivialization" of political reporting takes several forms, two of the most common of which are excessive concentration on merely formal or incidental aspects, and excessive concentration on the personal lives of individual political personalities. In an extensive content analysis study, Violette Morin (1969, p. 47) documented just this point. She counted the ten most mentioned aspects of Nikita Khrushchev's visit to Paris in the seven Parisian dailies and nine weeklies of the era. Incidental aspects (decor, gastronomy, and so forth) accounted for 58 percent of all topics covered, while personal aspects (Khrushchev the individual, his wife Nina) accounted for another 27 percent. Only the remaining 15 percent of the topics covered were political in nature (reaction of the French CP to the visit, disarmament, and so on).

THE INHERENT CONSERVATISM OF THE HUMAN INTEREST STORY

Although the sensationalist press, which makes up a great proportion of the French press, minimizes reporting having direct reference to political, social, and economic events, it does not follow, however, to say that it is apolitical. In fact, the sensationalist press is at once both "depoliticized" and yet still heavily conservative in its implicit logic. Herbert Schiller (1973) has analyzed the assump-

---

*Informational papers are Le Monde, Le Figaro, L'Humanité, Libération, and La Croix; sensationalist papers are L'Aurore, France-Soir, Parisien Libéré, and all the provincial papers.

tions of the world view in which sensationalist journalism is conceived and written: (1) reporting is invariably in terms of individuals, the world is seen as one of personal choice, and therefore psychological explanations are used to explain away structural determinations; (2) the neutrality of the state is assumed, and its agents and particularly its highest officials are seen as embodying the national will; (3) there is an assumption of an absence of class conflict, disorder is a function of individual deviants and a sign of the need for increased social repression; (4) human nature is taken to be essentially unchangeable, hence the world is seen not as problematic and open to intervention and reform but as a given to be adapted to; and (5) the social world is conceived of and presented as <u>fragmented</u>, and there is no effort to understand the interrelatedness of the seemingly disparate events that make up the day's news. These assumptions, to name a few, are inherently conservative because they reproduce the principal ideological categories of the bourgeois world view: individualism, psychologism, unconditional free will, the division of the state from the civil society, and society as unified by shared values and implicit social contracts. This world view is present both in the sensationalist press and in the sensationalist programming of the electronic mass media as well.

As Hughes (1940, pp. 62, 68, 114) suggests, the overt depoliticization and inherent conservatism of the sensationalist press are particularly visible in one of its central elements, the "human interest story," which is invariably individualistic, ahistorical, and episodic. The ideological conservatism of the human interest story, however, goes far deeper than this, and in one valuable monograph on the subject Georges Auclair (1970) has argued that sensationalist journalism is actually predicated upon entirely different epistemological assumptions than is informational journalism. Auclair claims that the latter is based upon linear, scientific (Levi-Strauss would say "domesticated") information. Informational journalism, on the contrary, conceives the world, both natural and social, as understandable and hence as manageable. Informational journalism is based on a demystified, Enlightenment view of the power of knowledge and expertise. Sensationalist journalism, on the contrary, reveres the mysterious, the inexplicable, and the passionate. Auclair (1970, p. 37) finds that human interest stories are seldom based on either "facts" or "concepts" but instead on "sympathetic resonances and affective participation." The logic of emotion, not the logic of cognition, is at work here. According to Jacques Lacan (1966, p. 47) human interest stories take us into the realm of the symbolic surrounding the field of our more normal activity in everyday life. The human interest story presents symbols, not arguments; it deals in images, not concepts.

The opposed epistemological assumptions of the two modes of journalism are especially visible in the contradictory notions of causality with which each works. Whereas informational journalism bases its discussion on scientific notions of causality, sensationalist journalism, especially in human interest stories, seeks out antiscientific, nonlinear causal chains. Bizarre motives, for example, are a favorite because they represent a scandal to the logic of the "quotidien" in industrial society. Thus the headline, "HE KILLS FOR A FISHING SPOT."* What is searched for here, or in many other cases (HE KILLS FOR 1 FRANC), is a nonequivalence of cause and effect. Roland Barthes (1964, p. 193) underlines this point in his perceptive essay on human interest stories:

> Here, once again, one finds most of the time the deceived causality which is for the human interest story a shocking spectacle. A TRAIN IS DERAILED IN ALASKA: A BUCK HAS BLOCKED THE SWITCH. AN ENGLISHMAN JOINS THE FOREIGN LEGION: HE DID NOT WANT TO SPEND CHRISTMAS WITH HIS MOTHER-IN-LAW. . . . All these examples illustrate the rule: small causes, large effects.

Coincidence, chance, bad luck—these are major themes in human interest stories, whereas they are absent from informational journalism. Chance occurrences are particularly savored, as in THE SAME JEWELER IS ROBBED THREE TIMES. Or consider the following gem: THE EXECUTIONER LOSES HIS LIFE AS HE LEFT TO PERFORM AN EXECUTION IN HIS NATIVE VILLAGE. "Providence," said France-Soir. In these chance events, the lack of an obvious linear causality allows the sensationalist press to structure its own hidden causalities—fate and destiny.

Along with chance, paradox is a sensationalist theme of central importance. One comes across headlines over and again that clearly delight in the paradoxical inversion of normal social order: THE AMBULANCE KILLS THE DOCTOR. THE THIEVES ARE SURPRISED AND SCARED OFF BY ANOTHER THIEF. AN OLD MAN IS STRANGLED BY THE CORD OF HIS HEARING AID. A JUDGE DISAPPEARS AT PIGALLE. THIEVES UNLEASH A POLICE DOG ON THE NIGHT WATCHMAN. In its use of paradox, the sensationalist press presents the world as irreducibly mysterious; events do not go as planned and

---

*All phrases in full capitals were actual headlines in major French sensationalist newspapers.

can even have the opposite effect: an ambulance causes death, a robbery is stopped by a thief, a medical aid becomes a murder weapon, a judge seeks deviant pleasure, a police dog works for the thieves. It is an image of a topsy-turvy world beyond the control of social intervention.

There are, therefore, a number of ways in which human interest stories are inherently conservative. They displace the informational function of the press: social, political, and economic reporting and analysis is replaced by discussions of human interest trivia. Furthermore, the deep structure of human interest stories assumes and reproduces the basic ideological categories of the bourgeois world view. On an epistemological level, human interest stories are profoundly antirational: the world is pictured as a product of chance, mystery and paradox and hence beyond amelioration through policy intervention and social change.

A SHIFT TO THE RIGHT

As a good deal of the clandestine press was written and edited by Socialists, left Christians, and Communists, and as it was these clandestine journalist teams to whom the sequestered press enterprises were given, it is hardly a surprise that the left press was dominant after the war. Table 9.1 presents information on the French daily press of 1947, and 1976.*

The shift in the political spectrum of the daily press is actually somewhat greater than these figures indicate. The Parisian daily press of the Communist party has been reduced from four publications to one while the press of the Socialist party as such has totally disappeared. I have classified Le Monde and Le Quotidien de Paris as "socialistic" to indicate that these papers are totally independent from (and not always in agreement with) the Socialist party. If Le Monde had not begun to take a pro-socialist position in 1968, the left press would consist only of the CP's one Parisian and three provincial dailies plus a handful of small-circulation socialistic and far left dailies. The same pattern can be found in the postwar fate of the provincial daily press. In 1947 there were 52 CP or near-CP dailies, 32 Socialist or near-Socialist, and 27 left Christian dailies linked to the MRP (Bellanger et al. 1976, p. 315). By 1976 this left press had practically been eliminated from provincial France: there were

---

*See Tables A.15 and A.16 for a title-by-title analysis of the political spectrum in the Parisian daily press in these two periods.

TABLE 9.1

The Political Spectrum of the French Daily Press, 1947 and 1976
(percentages)

1947		1976	
Left	66.7	Left	12.9
Communist	22.0	Communist	2.9
Socialist	14.8	Socialist	9.4
Radical	13.6	Far Left	.6
M.R.P.	16.3		
Center and Right	30.9	Conservative	87.4
Moderate and Right	10.9		
General Information	20.0		

Sources: Mottin (1949, p. 143); these figures are confirmed in Bellanger et al. 1976, pp. 309, 315, 356. Presse Actualité, May 1977.

three small CP papers remaining, two medium-sized and two small Socialist party-linked publications, and no MRP press left whatsoever (Presse Actualité, February and May 1977).

This considerable shift to the right in the political ideology found in the daily press, however, has not been accompanied by a parallel shift in the political ideology of the French electorate. On the contrary, there has been no shift in the latter sphere; in the 1970s the French left and right split almost precisely fifty-fifty, as they did directly after the war. This unchanged ratio implies an intriguing point: clearly a good portion of the left-voting French electorate today reads conservative newspapers. Furthermore, the news available on television and radio, which we have seen are tightly controlled by the state, is also politically conservative. This tells us that the ideological impact of the mass media must never be assumed or implied: obviously, in the French case, there are many other mediating factors involved in the formation of political consciousness than the conservatively biased information available to media consumers.

INFORMATIONAL VACUITY

The sensationalist press that has developed in France since World War II is characterized by the strict minimum of social, political, economic, and cultural information it prints. This claim can be confirmed by observing (1) how the sensationalist press allocates its surface space; (2) to what extent it provides "hard" as opposed to "soft" news; and (3) to what extent it is selectively silent on important social and political issues. It is also important to notice the effect of this insipid media content on reducing the consumer's demand for hard news coverage.

On the issue of space allocation, the two modes of journalism differ radically in the percentage of a paper given over to advertising, headlines, and photographs. In 1976, France-Soir devoted 52.6 percent of its total surface to advertising alone, while Le Monde used 36.7 percent (Thibault 1976, p. 16). Le Monde has purposely kept its relative advertising space at this limit, despite a large increase in the absolute amount of advertising carried: for every page of advertising it has added in the last decade, it has added an additional page of news coverage (Presse Actualité, February 1978).

Standing in front of a news kiosk in France, one is immediately aware of the different amounts of space devoted to headlines in different papers. Le Monde uses only about 11 percent of its total surface space for headlines and bylines, while certain sensationalist papers use as much as 20 percent of their space (Thibault 1976, p. 19). Similarly, the differentials in the presence of photographs are quite striking: Le Monde is extreme in having a policy of never printing any photographs and using only 0.9 percent of its surface for illustrations and political drawings. France-Soir, in contrast, uses 11.5 percent of its surface for visual presentations, and Le Parisien Libéré devotes 17.4 percent.

It is interesting to total the space allotted for advertising, headlines, and photographs for this is essentially lost space as far as communicating information is concerned. In 1976 France-Soir consumed 73.2 percent of its surface area on these, in contrast to Le Monde's 48.6 percent. Even in the informational press, one sees, almost one-half of the surface space is lost before any news reporting or analysis has begun.

With the remaining space, each newspaper must then allocate a proportion of column inches to "soft" news, for readers expect a certain amount of coverage of films, television, sports, and the like.*

---

*Actually the distinction between hard and soft news is not as simple as I assume here. Molotch and Lester (1975) have shown

Again, there is a significant difference between the two modes of journalism: France-Soir devotes 35.1 percent of its total printed space to soft news, and Le Monde restricts this coverage to 10.2 percent (Pourprix 1971, p. 73). (See Table A.16 for further details.)

These differences mean that reading such widely varying newspapers must provide very different experiences for their respective clientele. In fact, one cannot really "read" Parisien Libéré or France-Soir; "read" is simply not the right verb. Mostly the "reader" is looking at comics, pictures, serialized photo-novelettes, sports scores, and banner headlines. Furthermore, the little hard news that is presented is schematized and simplified; there are seldom political analyses or opposing points of view. This experience has little in common with the studious attitude needed to comprehend the serious and subtle treatments of diplomatic and socioeconomic events in Le Monde.

The issue of content is not simply a question of what is present but also of what is absent. When less than 10 percent of a newspaper is devoted to coverage of social, political, and economic events, many important issues are necessarily left uncovered. One might assume that there is no binding unity to what is not printed, that this is merely the dross, the bits and pieces that are chipped away in the sculpting of the final paper. But insofar as there is an essential disunity and isolation to the human interest type of sensationalist journalism, one could claim that this anarchy of petty information can be contrasted to the essential unity of the sociopolitical information such papers refuse to cover. The French sociologist, Maurice Mouillaud (1976, p. 19), has written that, in the Western press, ideology appears less and less as explicit opinion and has taken the form of a series of filters that decide the relative importance and meanings of events. This "silent ideology," he argues, is all the more effective in that it remains hidden and unsuspected.

The sociological meaning of silent ideology can be found only by tracing the actual process of filtering and censorship whereby the silences are produced. In other words, the meaning of the absences will be found in the logic of the power relations of the institutions and hierarchies that are able to determine what will and will not be printed. We have seen earlier in this study how press owners, advertisers, social elites, and political agents intervene in the flow

---

how the sensationalist press can at times purposely translate hard news items into soft news reporting in order to obfuscate their social and political implications. This only exaggerates the distinction I am making.

of information by determining the parameters within which journalists must write.

The socialistic weekly <u>Le Nouvel Observateur</u> (September 18, 1972) undertook a study of this journalistic technique of selective reporting and criticized the sensationalist press for the practice. The article, appropriately entitled "La Presse du Silence," includes a long list of examples, among which one finds the following:

1. <u>La Montagne</u> of Clermont-Ferrand never once published a word or an ad on the film "The Sorrow and the Pity" because the film contains a powerful analysis of the collaboration in this city during the war.
2. <u>Nice-Matin</u> never mentions periods of bad weather on the Côte d'Azur.
3. <u>Ouest-France</u> does its best to maintain a minimum mention of the Breton separatist movement; for years it kept an absolute silence.

These examples of total silence are extreme cases. Far more often one finds a subtle gradation of coverage given to a topic, from extensive coverage in some papers to bare mention in others.*
One of the most powerful manipulative techniques a newspaper has is to (relatively) ignore—or expand—coverage given to a hard news item. The power of the press owners, therefore, extends even into the relatively mandatory coverage of a given day's major wire-service stories.

The ideological impact of the pervasive silence of the sensationalist media on sociopolitical issues operates to diminish and deform the social and political curiosity of consumers. Recent studies have shown that readers tend to selectively avoid politicizable rubrics (that is, political, economic, social, and financial coverage), and to spend the greatest part of their reading time (about 20 minutes per day in France) on service columns and soft news (Toussaint 1976, p. 54). Furthermore, it is not only the consumers of the sensationalist press who progressively ignore the hard news items.

---

*See J. W. Lapierre's (1968) extensive study of the differential coverage of events in Israel during an entire year by the Parisian press. Among other findings, he creates an "index of regularity" which proves a powerful tool for distinguishing sensationalist and informational journalism, for although all papers cover hot crisis situations, only the informational press provides continual, non-crisis-oriented coverage as well.

Le Figaro is certainly an "informational" newspaper, but a recent study found that only 13 percent of its readers even looked at articles on French and international politics (Brunois 1973). The only articles receiving attention from more than 30 percent of the readers were those that began on the front page and the TV listings.

Communication requires not only that something be said but also that it be listened to. Insofar as the great majority of French media consumers progressively manifest less interest in obtaining hard news, the media, which must sell to survive, will increasingly displace social, political, and economic coverage with an ever escalating proportion of soft news, or "filler" as it is known in the profession. In other words, there is a cyclical aspect to this: consumers (particularly those of the sensationalist media) become increasingly de-skilled as readers and increasingly unaware of the non-newsworthiness of much that is presented as news. The decreasing presence of hard news decreases the demand for it, which leads to further introduction of soft news, or filler.

I have hypothesized earlier that history is going in the direction of a popular demand for the "right to information." There is, however, no evidence that this demand will develop spontaneously on a mass level. On the contrary, it will become a widespread demand only insofar as it is linked to future times of heightened social crisis and class conflict. A decentralized, self-management, democratic-socialist society would need not only radically different media than exist in contemporary capitalist society but radically reformed media consumers as well.

THE CRISIS ORIENTATION

The sensationalist paradigm of journalism thrives on crises. This crisis reporting carries its own coded message, independent of the given content in a particular article. Hubert Beuve-Méry (1956, p. 6), creator of Le Monde, insists that the overabundance of crisis information and the excessive rapidity of its transmission is detrimental to the quality of information provided. He raises the question of the ideology of the "cult of the instantaneous." The coded message of instantaneous information, he writes, is that in-depth coverage is not as important as is the near simultaneity of event and news. The "news flash," Beuve-Méry continues, can go so far as to remove all intelligibility from information. It also serves to detach information from its antecedent events. With the electronic media this distortion is played out to its logical extreme: one is actually carried to the event, and what is only a secondary and highly manipulated experience takes on the appearance of firsthand experience.

In the "news flash," information is rushed to consumers before there is time to verify it or put it in perspective. This largely unintelligible and often erroneous information is only later confirmed or disconfirmed by further investigation. One humorous twist resulting from this phenomenon occurred in France when a sensationalist Sunday newspaper (falsely) reported the death of Maurice Chevalier five full days before he did; the story was hastily retracted several hours after the newspapers had been delivered to the press kiosks (Presse Actualité, February 1972).

Serious informational abuses can also be produced by the "news flash" mentality of the crisis-oriented press. In one recent case, the sensationalist press reported a multiple rape of a young woman by four Algerians before taking the time to confirm the story. In fact, this was an openly racist use of the first police reports; the rape itself was disproved by police within several hours, but little effort was made to retract the information disseminated. The racist ideology tied up with such reporting could in any case not be undone by a printed statement of the facts of the case appearing in the next day's paper, and several newspapers did not even print a formal retraction (Presse Actualité, December 1968).

The ideology of the "news flash" leads to competitive endeavors in which journalists of different papers pay off their sources to be the first or the exclusively informed. The police, in turn, know how to put this practice to great advantage; papers that present the police version of the petty events that make up a good portion of the sensationalist news are the first to be given the "scoops" on the next day's sordid trivia. These same links are readily used by the police to impose on the press their version of confrontations with political militants during demonstrations and political events.

The sensationalist crisis paradigm destroys the unity of the social world. Events and processes are presented as independent of the context in which they develop. There is no history to the day's crises; they are presented as unexpected, sudden eruptions. Sensationalist journalism is therefore mystifying because it portrays history as a daily compendium of unrelated crises. Furthermore, it is not possible, if one's information is restricted to sensationalist sources, to understand even these crisis events, since there is little or no presentation of the background situation in which they developed. One sociologist analyzes this aspect of the temporal and historical isolation typical of sensationalist journalism by comparing it to the transitory character of consumer objects in an economy based on planned obsolescence (Mattelart 1974a, p. 144).

In the sensationalist press, natural disasters, social and political conflicts, and shifts in the careers of the famous and infamous are all covered in precisely the same tone, rendering the sensationalist press incapable of distinguishing social and political crises from natural disasters. The ideological implication is clear: the contradictions and conflicts of class relations that bring about <u>social</u> turmoil are confounded with the fires and floods that bring about natural turmoil. The identical handling of both social and natural crises implies that society is conceived of as unified; just as we are all inconvenienced by a major storm, so we are all equally troubled by inflation, unemployment, and high property taxes. The image is that of "mankind" or "civilization," or, more often, "society," as being threatened by both natural and social chaos. There are no social classes in this world view and no class conflict. Social disorder is a product of deviance, which will be eradicated only if and when adequate repression is applied.

One could analyze further the sensationalist press that has developed since World War II, but the three characteristics discussed above adequately distinguish it from the informational press for our purposes. In the following chapter I want to glance briefly at the surviving informational press and make some predictions about its short-term future.

10
THE PERSISTENCE OF AN INFORMATIONAL PRESS

There is still an informational press in France, although it is clearly on the defensive and the prognosis for its future is certainly not very bright. The informational press falls into three principal categories: rationalistic, propagandistic, and expressionistic. The <u>rationalistic</u> press employs a method of news reporting and analysis that is characterized by its carefully postured tone of neutrality, objectivity,* and removal; <u>Le Monde</u> is, of course, the extreme case of this type. In contrast to this, the <u>propagandistic</u> press rejects the tone of "neutrality" and openly adopts partisan stances, as in the CP's <u>L'Humanité</u>. Recently, the May 1968 events led to the creation of an underground press (<u>presse parallel</u>), which attempted to forsake the objectivistic tone of the rationalistic press while not limiting itself a priori to the political aspect of all issues, as is typical of the propagandistic publications. These <u>expressionistic</u> publications (which parallel the "new journalism" trend in the United States), in fact, have attempted to forge a new type of informational press, one that provides information while taking a political stance that is sensitive to cultural problems as well. Here the contemporary Parisian archetype is <u>Libération</u>.

---

*Gaye Tuchman (1972) has argued that there is an objectified form of writing scientific articles that has its own inherent logic based on a reverence for "facticity." She (1972) notes the presence of a "rhetoric of objectivity" that is imposed on rationalistic newspaper reporting independently of the quality of information on which the article is based

The rationalistic press is small, particularly among dailies. Apart from Le Monde, there are no more than three or four other such publications in France, and all of these are financially threatened since the independent enterprises that publish them experience increasing fiscal difficulties each year. This is true for Le Monde, too, which had some lean years in the late 1970's. The new Parisian rationalistic daily Le Matin, despite an increasing readership, can only balance its fiscal accounts with input from the successful newsweekly that launched it, Nouvel Observateur. Le Quotidien de Paris, a small rationalistic daily, was forced to close its doors altogether in 1978.

The rationalistic press is in some senses structured by an eighteenth-century philosophy of enlightenment and intellectualism. Far more than propagandistic and expressionistic publications, it assumes that "the truth shall set us free." In tone and usually in content, this press presents information in the guise of a political vacuum; what is done with this information is left up to the individual reader. The rationalistic press therefore addresses its readers as isolated individuals rather than as political movements or cultural units as in the other two types of informational journalism. The rationalistic press promotes understanding for its own sake and, except in times of crisis, maintains an aloofness from direct political action. It prefers to analyze rather than to advocate.

Critics of the rationalist press have argued that it is, in the final analysis, more objectivistic than objective, that is, its air of removal and neutrality is used purposively to mask its political positions. One recent Communist critic of Le Monde analyzed the four basic operational components of this masking technique: (1) pseudo-scientific objectivity; (2) purposive passionlessness; (3) superfluity of descriptive detail; and (4) a refusal of political polemics (Guedj and Girault 1970, p. 131). A recent conservative critic of Le Monde claimed:

> The liberal and the Marxist can both find Le Monde in agreement with their views, and a Gaullist can also find much to agree with. But behind this composite facade, capable of seeming reasonable to such diverse perspectives, the successor to Le Temps seldom misses the occasion to extend the Socialist cause (Hostert 1973, p. 112).

From both the left and the right, therefore, the criticism of Le Monde exposes the deceptive nature of rationalistic reporting: the implicit claim to objectivity and neutrality is false. Perhaps nowhere is this more clear than in the rationalistic newsweeklies, as American readers know perfectly well of Time magazine, whose glib and graceful prose and self-conscious distance from partisan politics mask a consistently conservative political and social outlook. The French equivalent to Time is L'Express, whose principal owner and editor, Jean-Jacques Servan-Schreiber, has often served as head of the Radical party. L'Express was developed in the 1950s to fight against the government position in pressing ahead with the Algerian war. The magazine was politically committed and often censored by the state for its publication of material documenting torture and genocide on the part of the occupying French army. In 1964, Servan-Schreiber decided to transform his magazine from a propagandistic, action-oriented publication to a rationalistic, more neutral-sounding type of journalism. The change was probably motivated in large part by the great differential in attractiveness to advertisers between propagandistic and rationalistic journalism. In any case, we know that the state-owned, monopolistic advertising agency, Havas, was deeply involved in this change and was probably the major source for the several million francs spent in the creation and promotion of the "new" L'Express (Boris 1975, p. 165).

The propagandistic press rejects the superficial neutrality and pseudo-objectivity of the rationalistic press and takes ideological positions on the information it presents. Among weeklies, for example, L'Humanité-Dimanche openly argues the CP line; Nouvel Observateur presents a socialistic interpretation of the events of the week; and Minute speaks from the far right. These highly successful newsweeklies actually give a false impression of continued and open political commitment in the French press for in fact the propagandistic type of informational publication has otherwise all but disappeared. Nowhere is this more clear than in the case of the formal publications of the various political parties.

THE DEMISE OF THE POLITICAL PARTY PRESS

One might expect the left political press to have suffered a harder fate than the right, but in fact this is not the case: political propaganda organs of all parties have nearly disappeared. Those that persist are supported by external funds, with the exception of the successful L'Humanité-Dimanche. The figures in Table 10.1 tell the story at a glance: as the political press of the liberation disappeared, its place was taken by the sensationalist general information newspapers, which alone have demonstrated an impressive survival rate.

Of the three ruling left parties of the liberation, all have lost their press. The heart of the MRP press had been Francisque Gay's

TABLE 10.1

The Disappearance of the Political Press, 1944-70

Newspaper	Number of titles	
	1944	1970
Left dailies	10	1
Center dailies	8	2
Right dailies	9	1
General information dailies	5	4

Source: Bellanger et al., Histoire générale de la presse francaise, vol. 4 (Paris: Presses Universitaires de France, 1976), pp. 309, 315, 356.

L'Aube in Paris; it closed its doors in 1951. The Socialist party lost its principal voice, Le Populaire de Paris, in 1962, although even by 1950 it was reduced to a very few pages and circulated almost exclusively among party officials and militants. The Communist press has not fared much better, although the extreme efforts of its dedicated militants have allowed it to preserve a few effective titles. In 1945 there were 19 CP dailies in the provinces and three in Paris; by 1951 this was reduced to 13 and two, respectively; and by 1974, to three and one. In 1945 every department of France was served by a local Communist weekly; in 1974 only four departments were covered (Gaborit 1974, p. 12).*

It is not only the left, however, that has lost its political press. Gaullism has had similar problems in trying to maintain a political press. Its La Nation has never circulated more than 20,000 copies, and this circulation is only by subscription among party militants. In similar fashion the Radical party, which had 29 provincial dailies in 1946 (Bellanger et al. 1974, p. 315), today has only the limited

---

*For a general discussion of the CP press, see also Presse Actualité, January 1967 and September 1976, and Nouvelle Critique, December 1976. The CP perspective is available in Etienne Fajon's (1964) small book, and the perspective of the right is available in L'Echo de la presse et de la publicité, March-April 1977. In the final analysis, there is a serious absence of scholarly work on the venerable press of the French CP.

commitment of the Dépêche du Midi, which is highly sensationalist, that is to say, seldomly overtly political and occasionally in open disagreement with Jean-Jacques Servan-Schreiber, head of the Radical party.

THE RELATIVE SUCCESS OF THE FAR LEFT PRESS

Only the far left in France has been relatively successful at maintaining an active propagandistic press. In 1976, one found publications from seven branches of Trotskyists, three anarchist tendencies, Maoists, and several independent groups. What was truly singular about 1976, however, was the existence of four daily leftist newspapers. The launching of these dailies took considerable funds, and one sociologist traced an initial capital input of over NF 2 million into just one of these publications (Dartville 1976, p. 223). This ability to raise such hefty contributions was indicative of both a reasonably widespread support and a following among the privileged classes.

One of these daily newspapers, Libération, serves as the best example of the third type of informational press, the expressionistic publications. It attempts to combine the informational wealth of the rationalistic model, the political commitment of the propagandistic publications, and the cultural sensitivity of the short-lived publications of the May 1968 era. It employs the designs, humor, and spicy classified ads we know so well from the U.S. underground press, which clearly served as a model.

Expressionistic Libération has an interesting background. After the 1971 police beating of Alain Jaubert (see Chapter 7), disillusionment among many young reporters with the pro-police news dispatches of the AFP led to their forming an alternate news agency, Agence Presse Libération. This effort lasted only a year, but it played a highly visible role in being the exclusive news agency to deliver accurate information on a sensitive event of that year, the killing of a Maoist militant worker by a plain-clothes officer at a state-owned automobile assembly plant. The next year, Serge July and several other central journalists from the agency parlayed this notoriety into the successful launching of a new daily paper—Libération.

Libération has prospered, as have many other publications of the expressionist "parallel press."* This press is in almost every

---

*Libération circulated 43,000 copies by 1979; the satirical weeklies Le Canard Enchaîné and Charly-Hebdo each sold over 400,000 each week.

TABLE 10.2

Extent of the Parallel Press: Numbers of Regular, Periodical Publications, 1973

Type of Publication	Number of Periodicals
Anti-militarist	9
Comic format	35
Counter-information:	
National	16
Regional	50
Ecology	26
Education	8
Critique of science and technology	2
Cultural themes	37
Medicine and society	6
Social minorities	9
Regionalism (regional separtist movements)	24
Sexual issues	7
Miscellaneous	27+
Total	258+

Source: Claude Boris, Les Tigres de papier (Paris: Seuil, 1975), pp. 230 ff.

case highly political, despite the countercultural mode in which its positions are often presented. One should certainly not underestimate the extent and importance of the parallel press, for its many different titles are widely read. These titles tend to be organized around topical issues; one researcher has listed 258 publications in 1973, whose content can be categorized as shown in Table 10.2. This list is certainly incomplete, and it is probably safe to imagine that the number of regular periodical publications of the parallel press total nearly 500 (Bercoff 1975, pp. 326 ff.). I was shown a dozen titles in Grenoble that simply were not known in Paris. While the circulation of many of these journals is small indeed, others have an appreciable distribution. One can conservatively estimate their total circulation at 700,000, and it is also clear that each copy is read by many different individuals, probably even more so than the already multiple readership per copy of the grande presse. It is also reasonably safe to make an estimation in the other direction: there are probably very few French teenagers in cities of any fair size who have <u>not</u> had some contact with publications of the parallel press.

CONCLUSION

There is a persistent informational press in France, although, whether measured in terms of circulation or in terms of the financial soundness of the enterprises involved, these cannot compete with the sensationalist press. Furthermore, one must see that the disproportionately large circulation of the sensationalist press is reinforced by the sensationalist mode of news reporting in the electronic media. The reporting and analysis broadcast over the airwaves is as overtly depoliticized, inherently conservative, informationally vacuous, and crisis-oriented as the written sensationalist press. The overall amount of informational reporting reaching the French population is, therefore, quite small. The question of just what ideological impact this state of affairs has on class relations in France is a subtle and difficult problem, but I would like to propose some tentative hypothetical remarks in the following chapter.

11
ON THE ROLE OF THE MEDIA IN CLASS RELATIONS

The present study is based on the assumption that critical media studies must analyze the media as a sphere of production of surplus value, while also considering the contribution of the media to more general processes of social reproduction. Insofar as the media have a relative autonomy with respect to the state, their ideological functions operate only in and through their particular corporate structures. To ignore the real and operative relative independence of media enterprises, and particularly the privately owned press enterprises, is to lose the ability to posit and study the media enterprises as sites of ideological struggle.

In the writings of Louis Althusser, there is as much confusion as enlightenment introduced on the topic of "ideology." But what is truly a contribution is his insistence "that to adopt the point of view of reproduction is therefore in the last instance, to adopt the view of class struggle: because this reproduction (stability, duration, security) is obtained by a permanent class struggle which must be fought."* As soon as we conceive of social reproduction as a <u>necessarily ongoing</u> problematic for any dominant class, we lead ourselves to consider the equally perennial susceptibility of social reproduction to conflict and crisis. This conflict can be studied in many concrete manifestations, and the media enterprises are no exception, as Hans Magnus Enzenberger points out:

---

*Quoted and insightfully discussed in McLennan, Gregor and Petos 1977, p. 92.

A "critical" inventory of the status quo is not enough.
There is danger of underestimating the growing conflicts
in the media field, of neutralizing them, of interpreting
them merely in terms of trade unionism or liberalism,
on the lines of traditional labor struggles or as the
clash of special interests (program heads/executive
producers, publishers/authors, monopolies/medium-
sized businesses, public corporations/private companies,
etc.). An appreciation of this kind does not go far
enough and remains bogged down in tactical arguments.
(1974, p. 96)

Enzenberger concludes, "So far there is no Marxist theory of the media," and this does seem to be the case. We have bits and pieces of media research, but it has never been formulated in any more systematic and satisfactory a fashion than has the general theory of ideology. What seems clear, however, are several potential pitfalls that a general theory of the media would do well to avoid.

First, a critical theory of the media must reject economic determinist approaches, which assume that the media have no autonomy from the dominant class. Although the organizational structure and editorial line of the media will certainly reflect dominant class interests (to different extents in different enterprises), the irreducible differences in interests between various segments of the dominant class ensure that the media will be organized with an operational autonomy from any given segment.

Second, a critical theory of the media in capitalist society must also reject political determinism, or <u>instrumentalism</u>. We cannot assume that the media are necessarily a wing of the <u>state</u> ideological apparatus. It is an <u>empirical</u> question to what extent the capitalist state permeates and attempts to control the sphere of the media. Certainly we want to be able to distinguish between the ability of the state to intervene in state-regulated (or, in many societies, even state-owned) electronic media, on one hand, and the privately owned press enterprises, on the other. Even state-owned media enterprises are typically set up with a degree of autonomy that is not mere window dressing. This autonomy represents a concrete degree of compliance on the part of the capitalist state with its discourse of "neutrality" and "freedom of the press."*

---

*One is only "free" <u>from</u> some given constraint; "freedom of the press" historically meant freedom <u>from the state</u>. In a democratic socialist society it would also mean freedom <u>from the intervention of capital</u>.

A capitalist state that transgresses certain thresholds of intervention in the media takes the risk of delegitimating its communiqués and news dispatches by contradicting its own discourse too transparently.

But surely the most important reason not to fall into a political determinism in considering the relation between the state and the media is that the concept of "state" amenable to such a reductionism ignores that the "state" is itself not unified. The capitalist state is infused with the multiple conflicts inherent in the intraclass contradictions of the dominant class. Furthermore, there is a certain degree of institutionalization of popular-class interests, often representing negotiations from past moments of open interclass conflict. Insofar as the state <u>cannot</u> achieve an internal unity of purpose and insofar as contradictory class interests reappear as policy contradictions in the programs of the capitalist state, the state cannot be seen as monolithic. A nonmonolithic concept of the state has the advantage of discouraging one from seeing the media (or the educational system, and so on) as directly manipulated by the state, for a state with perpetual internal discord along class and class-segment lines must be seen as being largely incapable of taking overt manipulative control of information enterprises. Furthermore, insofar as a capitalist state does attempt direct management of the media, it will only introduce its internal contradictions into these enterprises, politicizing them internally. Both interclass and intraclass conflict are endemic to capitalist society. As Alain Touraine (1976) has convincingly argued (and as the political instability and ultimate bankruptcy of the postwar southern European fascist capitalist states has confirmed), interclass and intraclass conflicts will either be allowed to express themselves in an open, pluralistic political forum, or, if repressed as in the fascist states, will disappear from the political horizon only to reappear inside state institutions as debilitating, highly politicized debates over operational policies.

Third, a critical media theory must reject the "cretinization" hypothesis. The error in this thesis is that such a general culture critique misses the identification of the two parallel but separate media systems and the consistent class determination of the two separate consumer groups. The fact that part of the population is informationally impoverished by the sensationalist media should not make us forget that other parts are relatively enriched by the informational publications and programming, where the ideology process takes on altogether different forms. We need to determine <u>empirically</u> which classes and class segments are being systematically misinformed, and just what role this plays in the general process of social reproduction.

Fourth, a critical media theory must also abandon the "one-dimensionality" approach. This thesis erroneously proposes, in both its left version (Marcuse 1964) and its right version (Bell 1962) that capitalist society is reaching a period of ideological calm. One would think that the <u>worldwide</u> events of 1968, which neither Marcuse nor Bell saw as even being <u>possible</u>, would have taught all of us about the inadvisability of ever making such a claim. Capitalist society by its very nature is perennially in a state of tension; both interclass and intraclass struggles are ineradicable, even if, as Touraine (1970a, 1976) reminds us, the specific agents and forms of this struggle undergo historical transformations. Furthermore, since these two modes of class struggle do not occur in the abstract but, on the contrary, are found only in their concrete manifestations in each and every organization and institution of capitalist society, the task of critical media theory is to locate the specific contradictions and struggles within the corporate and state media structures.

Fifth, a critical theory of the media must not exaggerate the ideological impact of the media; political ideology is not the monopoly of the formal communication media. Every class and class segment is constantly producing political ideology from its own perspective, and no degree of media control or state suppression of ideological pluralism can escape this rediscovery of political understanding and strategy at the base. There is no evidence to show that either the most stringent of fascist regimes or their Stalinist equivalents succeed in manipulating the minds of the great mass of people. When information is reduced to propaganda, its principal effect is probably counterproductive; when there is little worth reading <u>on</u> the lines, media consumers quickly learn to read <u>between</u> the lines.

THE ROLE OF THE MEDIA IN SOCIAL REPRODUCTION

Given the absence of an adequate general model to employ in assessing the contribution of the media to the reproduction of existing class relations, the present study will take for itself a modest goal, namely, the investigation of a single hypothesis: <u>The principal ideological function of the media in capitalist society is their contribution to the social process of the division of social classes and the production and distribution of social agents to their respective positions</u>. Such a claim is interesting only insofar as the concrete social processes involved can be analyzed empirically in specific case studies, and the French case seems indeed to lend credence to this hypothesis.

In contemporary France, there is no unified media system from which individuals choose programming according to their personal taste. On the contrary, there is evidence (far from conclusive, but I would say compelling) of a <u>two-tier media system</u>, providing in each medium a choice between sensationalist and informational programming. Thus, some newspapers, television channels, radio programming, films, and so on, share common elements in their world views and myth structures, while they stand in contrast with another set of media products that approach information and even entertainment in an essentially different fashion.

Furthermore, these two media systems are used systematically by different social classes and class segments. The former claim, of the existence of these two media systems in the press, has been argued in the two preceding chapters. The latter claim is largely an empirical question, and in the following pages I would like to present some data demonstrating class differentials in media usage.

Other researchers have located a similar divisive role in other French cultural institutions. Pierre Bourdieu and Jean-Claude Passeron (1970), in a major study entitled simply Reproduction, have located a pervasive differential along class lines of the "cultural capital" that is transmitted to children. Working-class children, they conclude, emerge from their first years of socialization at home with a consistently inferior "linguistic capital" compared to children of middle- and upper-strata homes.* This wide differential in the linguistic capabilities of different classes of children entering the educational system determines different reactions on their part to the "pedagogical action" they encounter. Bourdieu and Passeron (p. 9) see this as a type of general "symbolic violence" used by the dominant class to impose its official culture. Their study proposes that the principal role of the educational system is to compel a cultural unity on an otherwise divided society. As they put it, "In a given social formation, pedagogical work imposes the legitimacy of the dominant culture on dominated groups or classes" (p. 56).

This thesis of the unifying action of the French educational system has been criticized by the study of Christian Baudelot and Etienne Establet (1972). They have argued that the class content of the educational system is less a product of its forceful inculcation of the dominant culture (which they agree does happen) than it is a product of the effective separation of schoolchildren along class lines. They report that, in the very first year of school, six-year-old children are divided into "strong" and "weak" readers, and this division is almost precisely along class lines: three-fourths of middle-strata children pass the reading test, and two-thirds of

---

*Basil Bernstein (1974) makes the same conclusion for Great Britain, as does Claus Mueller (1973) for West Germany; and Bowles and Gintis (1976) for the United States.

working-class children fail it (Baudelot and Establet 1972, p. 209). Therefore, according to the controversial thesis argued by Baudelot and Establet, the educational system does not act to lessen the differences in reading and conceptual skills of the children entering the system with different amounts of "cultural capital" but in fact ends up reinforcing these differences.* If this were true, it would be a partial explanation of the differential use made of the media by these same people as adults. One could argue that the different social classes emerge from the education system with widely variant information and recreation needs and tastes. Children of dominant class backgrounds, having been disproportionately present in the advanced sections, are more likely to have been introduced to the historical and philosophical subtleties of European culture and hence to continue to seek similarly structured experiences in the media. On the other hand, popular-class children, having been disproportionately tracked into remedial and "practical" subjects, are more likely to emerge without the reading and cultural skills necessary to take advantage of the informational media. Of course, this would be only a partial explanation; many other variables are at work which together structure the preference of the different class for their characteristic media consumption (different amounts of leisure time, differing degrees of fatigue after work, and so forth).

THE TWO-TIER MEDIA SYSTEM AND THE LEGITIMATION PROCESS

If it is true that (1) children arrive at the beginning of their educational experience with large differentials among different social classes in "cultural capital," that (2) the educational system acts to reinforce rather than equalize these differences, and also that (3) the two-tier media system (among other cultural institutions) acts to reinforce and reproduce these differentials along class lines, then surely we need to ask ourselves the meaning and social purpose of all this divisiveness.

---

*Until the mid-1950s, Western European countries provided higher education for only 2 to 5 percent of their young people, while by the 1970s this had reached 15 to 20 percent. Nonetheless, a recent study by the Organization for Economic Cooperation and Development showed that the expanded enrollment "has mainly been to the benefit of the middle class" (New York Times, December 27, 1978). Herbert Gintis and Samuel Bowles have demonstrated the class character of differential educational success in the United States (1976).

It is not surprising that France has such extensive cultural divisiveness, given that <u>the inequalities in income and wealth in France are greater than in any other advanced capitalist society</u> (<u>Le Monde</u> 1976, p. 117). In 1975, the top 10 percent of French incomes were 22 times greater than the lowest 10 percent. The top 20 percent of French households owned 47 percent of all private property, while the bottom 20 percent owned only 4 percent. Only 15.4 percent of all full-time workers of all categories earned more than about $750 per month, while more than one-third of all workers earned less than about $380. In 1976, France had the highest percentage of official "poverty-level" individuals of any advanced capitalist society: fully 16 percent of the population (<u>Le Monde</u> 1976, pp. 54, 127).

Social reproduction has two principal thrusts: the reproduction of the social structure itself (the hierarchy of "places," with their attendant rights and powers), and the reproduction of new generations of social agents (the individuals who enter and act (not without a certain autonomy) in the structure with which they are confronted. Multi-leveled reinforcing cultural inequalities are, I want to propose, part of the latter aspect of the reproduction process: they are active in the division and appropriate training of agents for given places in the production system. Some agents must be conditioned to do manual labor and to accept its meager rewards in a society where the de-skilling process has removed a good deal of self-respect (and also of bargaining power) for these laborers. Others must be convinced of the value of the low-level managerial tasks they will be asked to undertake; and still others must be trained to defend the propriety of their private ownership of the means of production and the morality of the exploitative extraction of surplus value that takes place therein. The divisive family, education, and media systems (among others) play a role in social reproduction insofar as they legitimate this necessary "division of labor" in the populace. These divisive cultural institutions operate, if I may use a metaphor, like a tailor: however, instead of fitting the suit to the person, they fit the person to suit his task.

I would like to turn at this point to some data which, while far from conclusive, do seem to indicate strongly the divisive nature of the press and, for that matter, the media in general in France.

MEDIA USAGE AND CLASS ORIGINS

A study of the relation between social class and mass media consumption patterns ideally would consist of a large-scale interview of a representative, stratified sample of the French population. As this was impossible to undertake, given that the main thrust of the present study was to complete the institutional analysis of the press presented earlier, we must make do with existing data. One such source of information are the "consumer profile" studies of particular publications, although these do not give quite the information we need. Nonetheless, especially since the reliability of these readership statistics is extremely high,* they do provide us with hints at what a proper study of reading habits of different social classes would discover.

Table 11.1 presents information on the occupations of the readerships of four major Parisian newspapers, two of which are informational (Le Monde and Le Figaro) and two of which are sensationalist (France-Soir and L'Aurore). This information includes several important findings. We have an approximation of the bourgeoisie in the first category: they make up the greatest part of the readership of the informational papers, just as the petty bourgeoisie and traditional working class account for much of the readership of the sensationalist newspapers. What is rather surprising is that the upper reaches of the new middle strata (middle-level management) do not prefer the informational to the sensationalist papers; I would have predicted this incorrectly. Nonetheless, as one descends the occupational ladder, the choice of sensationalist over informational newspapers increases. The figures are far from conclusive, but they do give us a first approximation.

An interesting source of confirmation for this data can be found by observing the fate of the sensationalist press in Paris over the last 15 years. Manuel Castells (1973; 1975) and Jean Lojkine (1973), among others, have documented the "deproletarianization" of Paris during this period due to the "gentrification" movement in former working-class neighborhoods. ("Gentrification" refers to the out-movement of traditional working-class families and the influx of middle-strata, especially professional, personnel into central Paris.) One would predict that the sensationalist press as a whole would find it increasingly difficult to maintain its former large Parisian sales levels, if the hypothesis is correct that a good portion of its readership is among the traditional working class. Conversely, one would

---

*Each year the Center for the Study of Advertising Media performs a massive, methodologically sophisticated study of the adult French population to gather quite detailed information on the readerships of most daily and periodical publications. I am grateful to CESP for the data, which they so generously shared with me for use in this study.

TABLE 11.1

Occupations of Readers of Four Major Parisian Dailies, 1975 (thousands)

Occupation, Head of Household	Total Number of Readers of Le Monde and Le Figaro (informational dailies)	Total Number of Readers of France-Soir and L'Aurore (sensationalist dailies)	Ratio of Informational to Sensationalist Readers
Businessman; upper management	285	116	2.5:1.0
Middle-level management	186	182	1.0:1.0
White collar employees	66	121	1.0:2.0
Small business owner	22	78	1.0:3.5
Skilled workers	45	148	1.0:3.3
Unskilled workers	33	129	1.0:4.0
Farmer, farm worker	14	7	2.0:1.0

Source: Center for the Study of Advertising Media (CESP), "CESP Readership Study" (Paris: CESP, 1975); and Presse Actualité, May 1977.

TABLE 11.2

Circulations of Sensationalist and Informational Newspapers in Paris, 1961-76 (thousands)

Newspapers	1961	1976
Three most sensationalist[a]	2,259	1,244
Three most informational[b]	648	947

[a] Parisien Libéré, France-Soir, and L'Aurore.
[b] Le Monde, Le Figaro, and La Croix.
Source: Presse Actualité, March 1972, April 1974, and May 1977.

expect a concomitant rise in the circulation of the informational press, as the figures in Table 11.2 confirm, although there are certainly other factors at work as well.

In many, if not most spheres, the different consumption patterns of social classes are in large part a function of price differences between high- and low-quality products. It is hardly mysterious that Mercedes sell better among the dominant classes than among the popular classes. But daily newspapers all cost the same price, and since by law every newsstand carries every national newspaper and magazine, there are interesting lessons about French social relations to be learned in looking closely at the consumption patterns that emerge.

Given the hypothesis of class determination of media consumption patterns, and given the strong correlation of social class and educational achievement, one would expect a strong relationship between the amount of education received, and the choice of journalistic mode. Indeed, this is the case: those who have had superior education are more than three times as likely to choose the informational over the sensationalist papers, while those with technical, commercial, or only primary education are more than twice as likely to make the opposite choice (see Table A.19) (CESP 1975). These strong differentials in consumer patterns between different social classes are partly determined by the widely variant reading skills imparted—along class lines—in the divisive educational system. Reading as such is a more or less easy and enjoyable activity according to one's education.

TABLE 11.3

Classified Job Advertising in the Parisian Press, 1976
(in thousands of column millimeters)

Job	Le Monde	Le Figaro	France-Soir
Management positions	409	250	51
White collar employees	1,071	840	104
Minor positions and maintenance	134	203	367

Source: Le Monde internal document, April 25, 1977.

One final piece of information about the differential class makeup of the readerships of the two journalistic modes is available in their respective "help wanted" sections. Given the different readerships hypothesized, and given a sensitivity to this on the part of firms advertising for personnel, one would expect to find class-specific personnel ads in the informational and the sensationalist press. This is borne out by Table 11.3.

SOCIAL CLASS AND THE USE OF PERIODICALS

According to a very useful study of the Office for Cultural Affairs (Secrétariat d'Etat à la Culture) done in 1974, only 16.6 percent of Frenchmen regularly read a political, social, or economic magazine. The question then becomes, what is the class makeup of this 16 percent? Figures are available on this subject and they bear out the thesis that class membership is strongly related to habits in information consumption, since these informational publications are disproportionately read by the dominant classes (see Table 11.4). Note that newspaper readership does not show this pattern; all classes seem to be about equally attracted to daily papers (albeit to different modes of journalism, as we have seen).

The information in Table 11.4 on daily and periodical publications, while far from conclusive, does lend some weight to the hypothesis that there is not a unified press system, with various titles appealing to different tastes and different political perspectives, but a two-tier press system, with an identifiable elite press disproportionately consumed by the dominant classes, and an equally identifiable popular press disproportionately bought by the traditional petit bourgeoisie and different segments of the working class.

The informational press, I would hypothesize, is chosen for its informative content at the surface level but also for its particular set of class-based codes and myth structures. In other words, the informational press, particularly the non-opposition rationalist press, is also deeply involved in the reproduction of existing class relations, although it is concerned with reproducing quite a different class segment than is the sensationalist press. Agents must be reproduced to fill management positions in the private sector, official positions in the state bureaucracy, and the like. Successful social reproduction is as much a function of reproducing the "superiority complex" of the dominant agents as of reproducing the convictions of inferiority among the dominated. The informational press plays a role in inculcating a sense of significant social and political participation onto its readers; as such, they identify more readily with government and corporate decisions into which, in reality, they have no input.

A clear example of this is found in Ithiel de Sola Pool et al.'s classic study (1952) by content analysis of the key terms in the "prestige" newspapers in several advanced capitalist societies.

TABLE 11.4

Regular Readership of Periodical Magazines, by Occupational Categories, 1973
(percentage)

Occupational Category of Head of Household	Regularly Read a Political or Social Magazine	Regularly Read a Daily Newspaper
Upper management	44.9	65.4
Middle management	28.7	58.9
White collar employees	20.5	68.1
Owner of a business	16.2	65.0
Skilled worker, foreman	9.8	57.6
Unskilled worker	6.9	56.7
Farmers and farm labor	18.2	63.2
Retired, unemployed	14.3	72.1

Source: Secrétariat d'état à la culture, Service des études et de la recherche, Pratiques culturelles des français (December 1974): 134.

Fortunately for our purposes, the study did analyze <u>Le Temps</u>, the
prewar predecessor of its more liberal replacement, <u>Le Monde</u>.
The study found that in the 1920s and 1930s, rationalist <u>Le Temps</u>
concentrated on the repeated usage of a small set of terms in its
political analyses and editorials: crisis, security, order, Bolshevism,
Communism, war, left, allies. After the war, although <u>Le Monde</u>
was written by precisely the same journalists who had written <u>Le
Temps</u> (see Chapter 3), "there was a significant decrease in these
security symbols" (Sola Pool et al. 1952, p. 140). It is clear in
retrospect that <u>Le Temps</u>, organ of the steel trust and deeply involved
in the ideological struggles of its time, presented the "Popular Front"
of the United French left as a greater threat than Nazi Germany.
The informational press, in sum, is as involved in the ideology
process as is the sensationalist press.

I would hypothesize that the sensationalist press must be
analyzed in altogether different terms, for it is probably chosen by
its readership more for entertainment and distraction than for its
political ideology. One informal interview study of traditional working-
class readers found that they read it "for the horseracing column,"
"for Lucky Luke" (a cartoon character), "to pass the time on the
subway," and so forth (FFTL 1976, p. 94). There is, it seems,
little ideological commitment on the part of many of these readers
to the political content of their sensationalist papers, probably in
contrast to the readers of informational newspapers. One hint at
this is the fact that the circulation of the sensationalist press in Paris
is strongest in the neighborhoods that invariably vote for the Communist party. (<u>Le Monde</u> internal document, December 5, 1977).
In fact, the low circulation of <u>L'Humanité</u> (about 185,000 in the mid-
1970s) and the high proportion of the Communist party's vote that
came from the traditional working class, probably combine to tell
us that most people who voted Communist in France read the sensationalist press. Determining that there is a two-track press system,
therefore, is a far different matter from determining its impact on
the electorate.

IS THE TWO-TIER PRESS SYSTEM PART OF A
TWO-TIER MEDIA SYSTEM?

The press is just one medium among several, although it is
not unimportant: about 70 percent of Frenchmen read a paper at
least occasionally, and the circulation of major dailies can soar
during important crises and politically hot moments. Nevertheless,
what needs to be done now is to link the hypothesized two-tier press
system to a more general, two-tier media system. To do so requires

at least a brief look at the consumption patterns of television, radio, and books.

Television Viewing

Roughly 90 percent of Frenchmen now have access to a television set, although the popular classes are more likely to own a set than are the elite classes. Over 93 percent of the readers of France-Soir and L'Aurore, for example, have television sets in their home, while only 81 percent of the readers of Le Monde do (CESP 1975). Since readers of Le Monde have higher-paying jobs than do readers of the two popular titles and since readers of Le Monde are far more likely to have telephones, automobiles, and other consumer items than the readers of France-Soir and L'Aurore (CESP 1975), it follows that Le Monde's clientele has chosen to moderate its use of television. This data matches other available information on the differential use of television along class lines, which show that traditional blue collar workers are 50 percent more likely to watch television every day than are managers and professionals (see Table 11.5). That the bourgeoisie and new middle strata watch less television can be confirmed by observing differential TV viewing in respect to educational

TABLE 11.5

Television Watching, by Occupational Category, 1973

Occupational Category	Percent Watching Some TV Every Day
Higher management, self-employed professionals	44.8
Middle management	51.0
Owners of businesses and companies	60.8
Employees	63.7
Foremen, skilled labor	66.1
Unskilled labor	68.3
Farmers, agricultural labor	71.6
Retired, unemployed	75.9

Source: Secrétariat d'état à la culture, Service d'étude et de la recherche, Pratiques culturelles des français (1974): 66.

TABLE 11.6

Television Programs Offered and Seen, 1973

Type of Program	Percent of Programs Offered	Percent of Programs Seen
Underwatched		
Cultural reports	13	7
Political, social reports	6	4
Documentaries	10	3
Youth programs	4	2
Offerings Equal Reception		
National and local news	18	17
Sports	5	4
Games	4	4
Religious programs	2	1
Overwatched		
Variety shows	13	18
Weekly serials	11	15
Films	10	18
Soap operas (melodramas)	3	7
Total	100	100

Source: Presse Actualité, April 1975.

background: those with university degrees view 8.7 hours per week; those with high school degrees 11.2 hours; and those with no diplomas view 18.1 hours (Secrétariat d'état à la culture 1974; 1973 data).

It is also informative to take a look at the programming offered on French television. If one contrasts the number of hours of various types of programs that are aired with the number of hours these are actually viewed, one finds some interesting disjunctions, as illustrated in Table 11.6. Cultural reports, documentaries, and political and social reports are underseen as compared with their air time. These are the more educational, informational programs. On the other hand, it is the films, variety shows, weekly half-hour series, and soap operas that are relatively overconsumed. It is probably the case that the relative overrepresentation of popular classes in the television audience accounts for these disjunctions.

Interestingly, there are data that show that this class differential in program selection does not hold for one important type of program: popular viewers of the television are just as likely as elite viewers to watch the news programs (Toussaint 1976, p. 59). Here more than in any other informational medium there is a unified consumption by nearly all classes and class segments. For television news the thesis of Bourdieu and Passeron (1970), even if developed for the educational system, becomes useful. They speak of the "pedagogical action" encountered by the students and of the general "symbolic violence" used by the dominant class to impose an official culture. This describes perfectly French television news, for both radio and television news production has been under the consistent and tight control of the office of the minister (or secretary, in some governments) for information (Thomas 1976, p. 82). One clear example of this is the 1972 appointment of Arthur Conte, a Gaullist deputy, as president of ORTF. Soon after the appointment, the television news was "reorganized," and commentators complained of a return to pre-1968 extremes of censorship (Le Monde, December 9, 1972). Furthermore, we know that Conte had secret, weekly breakfast meetings with Prime Minister Messmer during this period (Thomas 1976, p. 89). If television news programs are, therefore, one medium in which serious information can be imparted to the popular classes, the French state is manifestly present to determine the tone and bias of the news broadcasting.

Radio Listening

Quite a similar case can be made for radio listening, for as one analyst of the French media argues:

> This division of labor attains a sort of perfection in the organization of the audio-visual press. The structuring of national radio into three channels, one called "popular," and having an extremely strong signal, the others called "cultural" and difficult to receive unless one has an FM radio, gives a valuable piece of evidence as to the desires of those in power to educate: that which is cultural is not popular, and vice-versa. (Lepape 1972, p. 69)

Sociologist Jean Cazeneuve makes the same point: the informational broadcasts are almost all grouped on "France-Culture," and this is certainly not the channel chosen by the popular classes (1974, p. 63). If this is true, then radio listening does feed into the two-tier media system because those members of the ruling strata who do listen are drawn off into several special stations, "France-Culture" and "France-Music," while the popular audience listens either to the intellectually low-level broadcasts of "France-Inter" or any one of the similar peripheral stations broadcasting from outside of France.

Quantities of radio listening vary inversely with education, as one would predict. About 72 percent of Frenchmen listen to the radio daily, while the average weekly listening amounts to 18 hours among those with no school diplomas, in contrast to 13.4 hours for those holding bachelors and advanced degrees (Toussaint 1970, p. 183).

Book Reading

Certainly few will be surprised to learn that there are class differences in the reading of books. Nevertheless, this adds another important facet to the thesis that the media in France are divided into two opposed, class-determined systems, and therefore it deserves at least passing documentation. The pattern in the consumption of books has changed appreciably since the introduction of paperbacks, but a recent government report finds no increase in the number of people buying books—only an increase in the number of books owned by those who were already purchasers of books (Secrétariat d'état à la culture 1974, p. 45). Among unskilled labor, for example, the percentage of homes with no books at all remains 33.8 percent. Furthermore, 85 percent of those who have read no books in the last year also never read a political or social magazine (and 24 percent never read a newspaper). There clearly are appreciable numbers of people in France who simply never read. This, of course, brings one again to a qualitative question, For those who do read books, just which books do they choose? The same government report allows us to see the very considerable class differentials that exist in the readership of informative books. Individuals in management were more than twice as likely to have read a historical, social, or political text than were unskilled laborers during the year of the study (Secrétariat d'état à la culture 1974, p. 47).

Conclusion

The report of the Office of Cultural Affairs ends by noticing and openly reporting the "extremely privileged position of the milieux of upper management and the liberal professions as to the general level of their activity in the field of cultural activities." Of course this is the case, but the study dares not investigate why this class differential in media usage is so persistent. Although the evidence presented in this chapter is far from being sufficient to confirm the hypothesis of the existence of a two-tier media system, it does begin to support the claim that the "privileged position" is not to be understood in terms of the greater use of the dominant class of <u>the</u> media, but rather the predetermined use by different classes of <u>different</u> media systems.

The mass media, contrary to what many thought they would be—the great levelers that would make culture available to everyone—have become divisive cultural institutions which are deeply involved in the production of social agents with appropriate social and political knowledge and epistemological categories for the tasks they are largely determined to fulfill by their social origins. Of course, this has nothing to do with the media as such, as technological means, but with the use to which they fall in a class society.

CONCLUSION

The liberation gave birth to a new press in France. The large pre-World War II press groups and oligopolistic press enterprises, owned and controlled by the industrial bourgeoisie, were confiscated at the liberation and given over to teams of journalists who had risked their lives by publishing clandestine works during the war. For several years thereafter France had what must stand as one of the most exciting periods in journalism in all history; in Paris alone, several dozen daily and periodical publications, written from every imaginable social and political perspective, openly debated the great issues of the day.

Today these enterprises are gone. They have either closed or been absorbed into press groups or monopolistic cartels. Those that remain no longer belong to the journalists who first managed these enterprises after the war but have been bought out by the industrial bourgeoisie. They are no longer edited by the strong-willed individuals who characterized the heroic era but by corporate men who report directly to the owners. They are no longer written by highly skilled, specialized journalists but by teams of anonymous press employees who take neither responsibility nor pride in their articles. They are no longer typeset by anarchosyndicalist, labor aristocrat printers but by secretaries seated at photocomposition typewriters.

These changes, while internal to the press sector, have been introduced by more general economic and social developments in French society. Throughout the economy the concentration-monopolization process, the centralization trend, the internationalization of production, and the deindustrialization of particular economic sectors have worked together so as to alter totally the organizational topography of French industry in the 35 years since World War II.

The French state has played a complex role in promoting these transformations. Through its multileveled intervention in the media, the state has aided the industrial bourgeoisie in their reconquest of the private press enterprises and has been particularly useful to the larger corporate units at the expense of the smaller. While the French state has guaranteed the formal existence of a "free press," its concrete media policies have acted more to restrict than to enhance the continuity of a substantive pluralism in the media. This is arguably the case in the press, as I have attempted to document, but it is absolutely and without question the case in the electronic media.

These structural transformations, exacerbated by state intervention, have very considerably altered the content of the French press since the war. Today, as before the war, the press is dominated by large-circulation, sensationalist newspapers, which are typically overtly apolitical, inherently conservative, and informationally vacuous. What is left of the informational press that was dominant in the years following the war is highly threatened. The press of the political parties has disappeared altogether, with the exception of remnants of the CP press. The rationalist, highly politicized papers have disappeared, with only a few anachronistic independent enterprises still weathering the storms mentioned above. The high visibility of these few enterprises, especially Le Monde, gives us the rather false impression that there is still a viable alternative to the sensationalist, conservative press in France. Closer scrutiny finds the situation far more problematical.

Insofar as there do exist two distinguishable journalistic modes in the French press—sensationalist and informational—this study has argued that there is a class-specific use of them, with the former being disproportionately chosen by the working classes and the latter by the dominant classes. This discovery leads to a hypothesis, one I hope to take up in future work, namely, that the principal ideological function of the media in capitalist society is their contribution to the social process of the formation and distribution of social agents to positions in the social hierarchy.

A NOTE ON RESEARCH METHODS

I like to think of critical social research as a branch of "investigative reporting." One does <u>whatever</u> is called for to gain access to the necessary information. At times, in the present study, this merely involved running down out-of-print books, searching through dusty archives, piling through dossiers, or reading through the yellowing pages of forgotten newspapers. At other times it involved undertaking a broad range of interviews with individuals and organizational spokesmen in the press sector. But at times it also meant a far more direct involvement, as in a number of mini-apprenticeships in editorial offices, newsrooms, and print shops, as well as attendance as an observer at demonstrations and strike activities. I am afraid that my simple notions of sociological method have little in common with the complex techniques marketed under the label "methodology," but I would still like to discuss very briefly several aspects of this research that might be of interest to others.

In a study such as this, the researcher's greatest assets are the individuals involved in the corporate entities, state agencies, and, given my critical perspective, especially in the union organizations. Naturally, one reads everything previously published on the topic, but what makes this literature hang together and what forms a critical ability in the researcher to be able to distinguish the contributions from the mystifications found in earlier works is the living dynamic he can currently experience in the sector involved.

<u>Interviewing must be undertaken along oppositional axes</u>. One needs to set up interviews with representatives of various opposing parties. Furthermore, there is no better source of questions than across oppositional lines. It was union militants who supplied me with the truly interesting queries to pose to newspaper owners—and vice versa. In interunion struggles, especially among the five journalist unions, I learned a great deal, just as I did in the criticisms launched by both press management and the unions against the state regulatory agencies—and vice versa.

My ability to have people on all social and political sides tell me their point of view was in large part a function of my speaking French without being French. I was outside the game, neither placable nor threatening. Had I been French, I would have had to label myself convincingly and hence cut off many informative sources. Perhaps only this circumstantial element was responsible for the success of the oppositional interviewing technique.

My interviewing was also influenced by the anthropological technique of searching out <u>informants</u>, principal agents in particular spheres to whom I could turn for interpretation and especially for further introductions. I rarely interviewed anyone whom I did not ask to introduce me to others; this snowball technique led me to make almost 150 interviews with individuals from all levels in the sector. I also made a point of supplementing interviews with official spokesmen with interviews from rank-and-file individuals in the same organization. The two perspectives were not always in complete accord.

There is no point in my expressing gratitude to 150 individuals by name; in any case, my editor would not permit it. There are, however, several principal informants who really must be mentioned, and, besides delivering my acknowledgements, the network linkages might be of methodological interest for those wanting a more concrete example of what I mean by "oppositional" and "snowball" interviewing.

I first met Jean-Marie Dupont of <u>Le Monde</u>, who opened the doors for me to both his enterprise and the independent journalist union. I spent the better part of two months at <u>Le Monde</u>, interviewing its founder, Hubert Beuve-Méry, its current managing editors, Jacques Fauvet and Jacques Sauvegeot, the heads of its major departments, numerous journalists, printers, cadres and employees, as well as the union representatives for all of the latter four groups. Often representatives of one union would seek me out, stating that they knew I had spoken with the heads of other unions. This provided a splendid learning experience. I am also deeply grateful to <u>Le Monde</u> for the access it gave me to its remarkable collection of dossiers in which one can find all articles having appeared in <u>Le Monde</u> (or in other Parisian publications) on any given individual or topic.

Dupont's introduction to the independent union led me to its vice president, Claude Prunier, who in turn gave me contacts with his local representative at any press enterprise I wished. This led me to François Boisarie and Denis Perier-Daville, both late of <u>Le Figaro</u>, who supplied copious information on the Prouvost years and the takeover by Robert Hersant. They arranged for me to make several clandestine visits to an enterprise Hersant had turned into a police-guarded stronghold. I was also able to interview <u>Le Figaro</u>'s editor-in-chief, Jean d'Ormesson, who was remarkably frank about its owner; he was to quit only a few months later.

Prunier, of the independent journalist union, gave me the crucial questions to pose to Gerard Gatinot, president of the CGT-affiliated journalist union, who in turn provided an introduction, and again a set of sensitive questions, to pose to Noel Monnier, president of the CFDT equivalent. Each of these gentlemen arranged interviews

for me with their union delegates in particular enterprises of my
choosing, such as Paul Parisot, who led me through both the hallways
and recent history of Hersant's then newest acquisition—<u>France-Soir</u>.

During my stay at <u>Le Monde</u>, I spent nearly as much time with
the printers as with management and the journalists, and I grew to
know, among others, Gilbert Trappier and Christien Gerard. Not
only did they explain to me the details and ramifications of the workshop transformations discussed in this study, but they also led me
to important contacts within the printers unions. I was able to interview leaders of the union (Roger Lancry, Roger Coquelin, and Emilien
Spaziro were especially informative). They in turn made contacts
for me with printers in particular enterprises I wished to visit,
particularly the <u>Parisien Libéré</u>, then in the twenty-third month of
its 29-month strike. There, Jean Bodin and several others explained
the great strike from the printer's point of view and invited me to
observe firsthand the furious struggle as it approached its acme.
I undertook to do this in the spirit of a war correspondent, and,
besides attending dozens of meetings and demonstrations, I was
invited to go along as an observer on various tactical maneuvers,
including commando attack sorties that searched out and destroyed
delivery trucks. From this close-up observation came the interest
in the interplay of tactics and strategy in labor strife evident in my
analysis of the <u>Parisien Libéré</u> strike. I also met journalists from
the embattled paper and am particularly indebted to Marc Moulin,
a proud man who, after setting up a house union at the paper, realized
his mistake and courageously spoke out. He was immediately fired.
He led me to other journalists, and I was eventually able to meet
with Claude Bellanger, editor-in-chief of the paper.

I could name so many more who were of help, but let me
mention only four. Gilbert Guilleminault, chief of the editorial staff
of <u>L'Aurore</u>, told me much about his paper, although I cannot say
that I ended up agreeing with him that "<u>L'Aurore</u> is not a newspaper
of the right, but of the center." Réné Andrieu, editor-in-chief of
<u>L'Humanité</u>, spoke frankly with me about the Communist press and
opened up the documentation center of the enterprise for me to use.
Finally, I need to express my deepest gratitude to one of the great
journalists of the clandestine press—Pierre Hervé. Now retired
and living in central France, Hervé brought the era of the 1940s to
life for me, with tales of close calls and lost comrades. He introduced me to others who had been part of the heroic era, including
Jules Mercillion, who passed on to me many historical documents
from the war period.

Besides reading and interviewing individuals and representatives, I consulted various press-related institutions which were of
great help, particularly the French Press Institute, whose files were

made available as were the knowledge and advice of its two directors, Francis Balle and Pierre Albert. Various regulatory agencies allowed me access to their data, especially the Center for the Study of Advertising (CESP). Yves L'Her of <u>Presse Actualité</u> was also a great help.

I have admiration and even awe for historians and archaeologists, for in general they must work to understand past eras with only written documents and material artifacts; seldom can they find living informants. But I also pity my colleagues in these sister disciplines, for they lose the thrill of coming to know firsthand the individuals involved. This personal involvement, for me, was a wonderfully enrichening experience, for three quite different reasons. First, the direct contact allowed me to keep confirming and disconfirming my understanding of events and structures by posing questions. Second, the "oppositional" interviewing technique allowed me to control for the bias of particular informants by purposively posing the same questions to other individuals holding structurally opposed positions. Third, the direct contact brought the events and organizations to life and infused them with the dignity and tragedy, the pride and pathos with which they were lived. Hopefully my "academic" style of writing has not totally stifled or hidden from view my excitement about the importance of the events I relate and the issues involved. If I speak strongly, for example, about the issue of the de-skilling of labor in the sector, it is because I grew to know the well-founded pride of the traditional journalists and printers in their considerable skills. De-skilling is a terrible human tragedy; it is not <u>merely</u> a trend to be coldly analyzed as one aspect of the political economy of late capitalism.

APPENDIXES

TABLE A.1

Daily Circulation Controlled by Largest Press Groups, 1969 (percentage)

Country	Four Biggest Enterprises	Eight Biggest Enterprises	Twenty Biggest Enterprises
Ireland	81	100	—
Great Britain	60	77	89
Austria	52	71	97
Denmark	50	64	84
Belgium	49	69	94
West Germany	42	50	62
Holland	39	55	82
Italy	30	47	75
France	30	46	73
Spain	29	43	55

Source: R. B. Nixon, "Concentration of Press Ownership," Journalism Quarterly 48, no. 1 (Spring 1971).

TABLE A.2

Origins and Life Spans of All General Information Newspapers Appearing in Paris, World War II to 1977

Origin	No Longer Existing	Still Existing in 1977
Newspapers existing before World War II	L'Intransigeant: 1880-1948 L'Information: 1899-1942, 1949-67 Le Populaire de Paris: 1916-66 L'Ordre: 1929-48 L'Aube: 1932-51 L'Epoch: 1937-50 Ce Soir: 1937-53	Le Figaro: 1866- La Croix: 1883- L'Humanité: 1904-
Clandestine and liberation newspapers	Combat: 1941-74 Libération: 1941-64 Paris-Presse: 1944-70 16 short-lived (to 1947) 3 medium-lived (to 1958)	France-Soir: 1941- L'Aurore: 1942- Le Monde: 1944 Parisien-Libéré: 1944-
Later efforts to start new newspapers	Paris-Jour: 1957-72 8 ephemeral efforts (less than 1 year)	Libération: 1973- Le Quotidien de Paris:* 1974- Le Quotidien du Peuple:* 1975- Rouge:* 1976- L'Humanité-Rouge:* 1976- Le Matin de Paris: 1977-

*Closed, or reduced to a weekly by 1979.
Source: Compiled by the author.

TABLE A.3

Newspapers Held Directly by the Industrial Bourgeoisie Just Before World War II

Title	Remarks
Le Temps and Le Journal des Débats	Both held by the steel lobby, the Comité des Forges, presided over by the Wendel and Schneider families, who had controlled French steel since before the Revolution.
Paris–Soir, Match, and other journals	All owned by Jean Prouvost, France's major wool magnate.
Le Petit-Parisien, Siècle, and Excelsior	All owned by the Depuy family, who own Papéteries de la Seine (paper), Cie Européene de Petroles (oil), and Cie Général d'Energie Radio-Electrique (electricity).
Le Journal	Held by Havas corporation, the Banque Paribas, and the Darblay family, who have controlled French wheat production since the seventeenth century (Darblay Mills), also paper holdings, and so on.
Le Figaro	Owned by François Coty, billionaire from domination of perfume industry.
Quotidien	Owned by the Hennessy family, producers of cognac.
Candide and Je Suis Partout	Owned by Artheme Fayard, publishing fortune.

Source: Compiled by the author.

TABLE A.4

Newspapers and Newsweeklies Held Directly by the Industrial Bourgeoisie in 1975

Title	Remarks
Le Figaro, Paris-Match, and other journals	Held by Jean Prouvost and Fernand Béghin; in 1973 Prouvost's wool interests grossed F1.4 billion. Béghin is a major industrialist in paper, sugar, and the Credit du Nord (bank).
L'Aurore Paris-Turf	Owned by Marcel Boussac, the "King of Cotton"; owns Comptoir de l'Industrie Cotoniere, Dior, and so on. 1975 group grossed F800 million.
Jours de France, Vingt-Quatre Heurs, and Télé Monte-Carlo	Owned by Marcel Dassault, wealthiest individual in France (?); Société des Avions Marcel Dassault produces the major French airplanes; 30% of Banque Vernes; Avions Marcel Dassault-Breguet grosses about F2 billion per year.
France-Soir Le Point, and other journals	Held by Hachette corporation; monopoly on educational books and press distribution, owns six major publishing houses, and so on. Hachette did F4.4 billion of business in 1975.

Nouvelle Observateur (and Le Matin in 1977)	Claude Perdriel, industrial fortune from production of health care equipment for hospitals, modern high-technology hospital equipment.
Province No. 1, Le Progres de Lyon, and Le Dauphinée Libéré	Schneider family holds 30 percent of this largest French provincial press monopoly; also steel interests and banking.
Un Jour, a chain of free weeklies, Lui, Playboy, and Europe #1 (radio)	Partially held by Sylvian Floirat, whose industrial base was in aviation; principal owner of Breguet Aviation; built the French atomic "force de frappe."

Source: Much of this is from Henri Coston's Dictionnaire des Dynasties Bourgeoises et du Monde des Affaires. Paris: Editions Alain Moreau.

TABLE A.5

Changes in Commercial Advertising in Parisian Dailies

Daily	Percentage Change: 1971-76	1976 Million MM per column	1976 Millions NF
Gainers			
L'Humanité	+21	1.1	—
Le Monde	+11	7.3	122
Losers			
Le Parisien-Libéré	-39	1.7*	25
Le Figaro	-21	8.8	138
L'Aurore	-16	2.6	26
France-Soir	-15	5.8	91
La Croix	-10	0.9	—

*Low due to strike.
Sources: Le Monde internal document, February 22, 1977; Presse Actualité, February 1978.

TABLE A.6

Sources of External Financing in the Press and Publishing Industry (millions of francs)

Source	1965	1971	Change (percentage)
Short-term debt	701	1,460	208
Medium- and long-term debt	264	599	226

Source: INSEE, "Industries polygraphiques, presse-edition" (Paris: INSEE, 1974), table 9.

TABLE A.7

Hachette's Principal Press Holdings, Late 1976
(thousands)

Subsidiary	Titles Held	Circulation
France Editions et Publications (80%)	Le Journal du Dimanche	334
	France-Dimanche	752
	Elle	403
	Jardin des Modes	71
Edi-Monde	Confidences	283
	Le Journal de Mickey	306
Cogipresse (40%)	Paris-Match	564
Télé-7 Jours (60%)	Télé-7 Jours	2,125
Presse et Information	Le Point	255
Prominfo	Le Nouvel Economiste	128
Edifrabel (Belgium)	Belge Edition of Elle	
Edipac		
Editions du Henin		
Paris Graphic	Graphics	
Publicité d'Aujourd'hui	Publicity agent	
Total		5,000+

Sources: Les Cahiers de la Presse Française, no. 131 (October 1976): 23; Gabriel Enkiri, Machette la pieuvre . . . témoinages d'un militant CFDT (Paris: La Commune, 1972), p. 63.

TABLE A.8

Hachette's Principal Publishing Holdings, 1972

Subsidiary	Nature of Publications
Fayard Grasset Stock Albin Michel	Major, general publishing houses
Comptoir International du Livre	General books
Librarie des Champs-Elysées	Police novels; luxury books
Livre de Paris ODEGE	Youth books (Tout l'Univers)
Librarie Général Française	"Livre de Poche" series
Librarie Pédagogique du Centre	School books and teaching material
Rossignol	School books and teaching manuals
Maison du Livre	Distribution of books
Edicef	Books sent to French-speaking world
Edito	Luxury books
Tallandier	General books

Source: Gabriel Enkiri, <u>Machette la pieuvre . . . temoinages d'un militant CFDT</u> (Paris: La Commune, 1972), p. 70.

FIGURE A.1

Organigram and Top Management of Le Monde, 1976

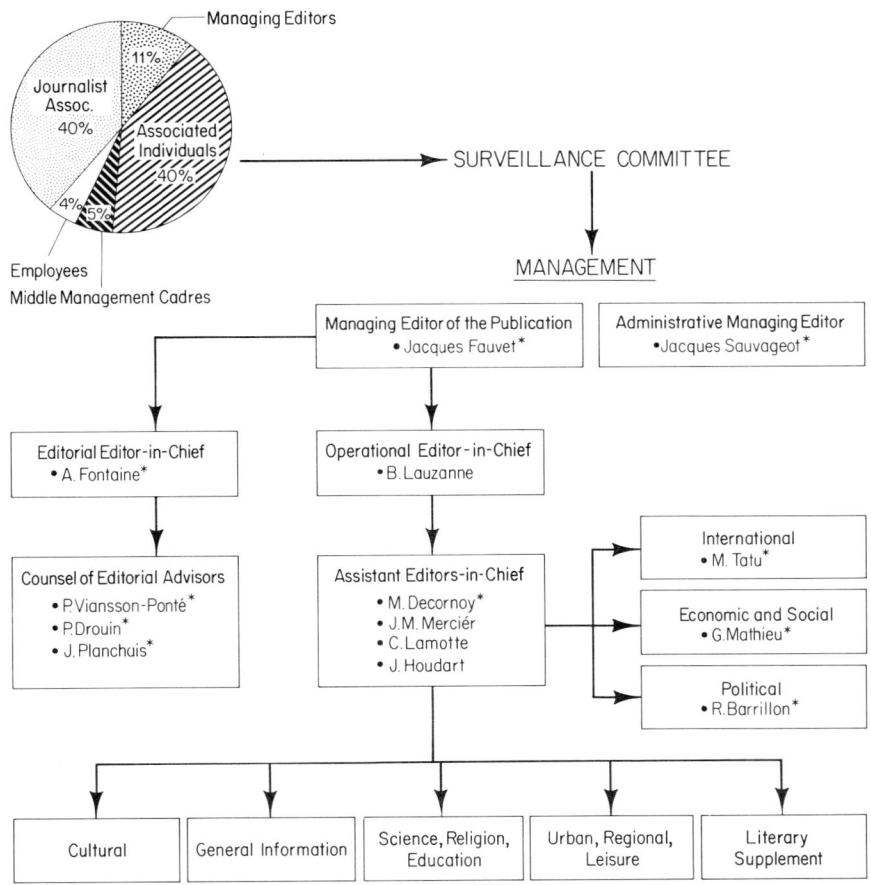

* = Was active in left Christian movement.
Sources: Le Monde internal documents and interviews.

TABLE A.9

Book-Length Critiques of Le Monde

---

1. Aimé Guedj and Jacques Girault. Le Monde: humanism, objectivité et politique. Paris: Editions Sociales, 1970.
Guedj and Girault are Communist party intellectuals. They find that Le Monde is leftist, since it sided with the students in 1968 and condemned the CP for supporting the government. They accuse Le Monde of a false objectivity, as for example in its support of the CFDT union over the CGT union. Le Monde, they conclude, is deeply anti-Communist.
2. Guy Hostert. Le Journal. Le Monde et le Marxisme. Paris: La Pensée Universelle, 1973.
Hostert condemns Le Monde for wanting "revolution by law." He condemns Le Monde's anti-Franco position and claims that the paper sells itself by including itself in the "charms of socialism." He sees the paper as "socio-Communist," as witnessed by its support of the students in 1968. He argues (quite cogently) that there has been a progression from Beuve-Méry's "revolution by law" to Fauvet's 1973 position paper: "In voting in the first round for one of the socialist currents, one puts oneself on the side of change and justice; in risking a change, one gives freedom a chance."
3. Michel Legris. Le Monde tel qu'il est. Paris: Plon, 1976.
Legris, for years a reporter at Le Monde, argues that the paper has changed greatly since the days of Beuve-Méry, when it was "objective, serious, honest, and well informed." But since Fauvet's takeover in 1968, coupled with the entry of young journalists deeply affected by the 1968 events, he claims that the paper has become increasingly superficial, leftist, and deceitful. It is superficial since coverage on a given topic is less in-depth than in the earlier Le Monde. It is leftist in that it supported the CGT-federated printers union over the owner of the Parisien Libéré, Amaury. It also attacked Solznenytsin, supports the CERES end of the Socialist party, is not anti-Communist, and supported the Khmer Rouge in Cambodia. It is deceitful in that while pretending to be neutral and objective in fact Le Monde is constantly biasing its articles in favor of the left.

Table A.9 (continued)

4. Philippe Simonnot. *Le Monde et le pouvoir*. Paris: Presses d'Aujourd'hui, 1977.
   Simonnot describes how Fauvet bent to ministerial pressure in firing him from his position of *Le Monde*'s journalist on oil issues. He describes the internal hierarchy of *Le Monde* and how it acts to filter the articles produced by the young journalists. He finds that *Le Monde* is in many ways similar to *Le Figaro*; the advertisers are mostly the same. He performs an experiment in content analysis: from August 18 to September 24, 1976 he found that of the outside papers accepted by Le Monde for publication, there were 15 from the Gaullist-Republican side, and only 9 from the opposition, with none at all from either the CP or the CGT. *Le Monde*, he concludes, is deeply anti-Communist.

FIGURE A.2

Structure of the Printers Union (Press Sector)

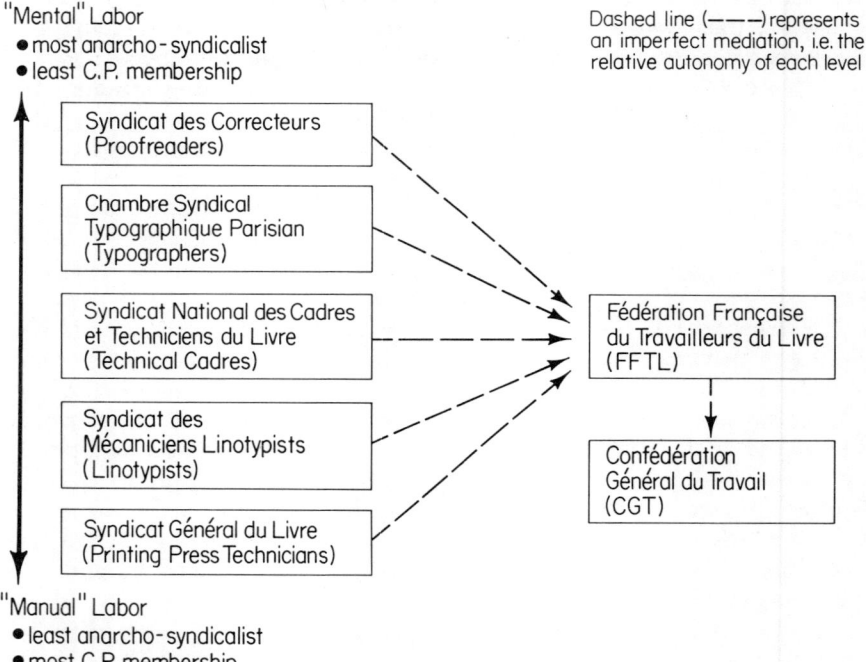

Source: Compiled by the author.

TABLE A.10

Summary of the Agreement Between the Parisian Press Owners Syndicate and the Comité-Inter (Negotiating Committee) of the Parisian Printers. July 1976

Chapter I: The Reduction of Labor Hours
  a. Such a reduction is necessary with the modern equipment; the details must be worked out between the Comité-Inter and the management of each particular enterprise, as the equipment will vary from one print shop to the next.
  b. There will be a revision of work norms for each category of work. The notion of "work on one title only" will be dropped.

Chapter II: The Reduction of Currently Employed Printers
  a. Conditions of early retirement, starting at 57, are worked out with the help of the state agencies involved.
  b. The number of "services" per month will be increased to 26, with no extra pay.
  c. No individual will be required to leave the profession, although printers are encouraged to do so and are guaranteed 90 percent of their salary for the first year, retraining programs, and so forth.
  d. Some printers will be required to change subspecialties, and no more hiring will take place whatsoever in subspecialties defined as overmanned; if such a change involves a dequalification, a forfeit will be paid by the paper to the individual involved.
  e. There is a possibility that some printers might be sent to work in the new facsimile receiving print shops being set up in the provinces.

Chapter III: Hiring Priorities
  a. Each enterprise must first hire their own printers to man the new equipment.
  b. Highly specialized positions can be filled by management with non-printer-derived personnel.

Chapter IV: Particular Problems
  a. <u>Parisien Libéré</u> printers will not be hired by other enterprises until an agreement is reached between the <u>Parisien</u> and its printers.
  b. The <u>Parisien Libéré</u> must reintegrate its printers who are on strike.

(continued)

Table A.10 (continued)

---

   c. The <u>Parisien Libéré</u> printers must have the same early retirement conditions, leaving-the-profession conditions, and retraining rights as do all other printers in Paris.
   d. After the <u>Parisien Libéré</u> has hired back all of its printers that it can, the rest will be hired by other Parisian enterprises.

Chapter V: Mode of Application
   a. This agreement is only valid for the printers working full time in the enterprises signing this agreement and at the time of its being put into action.

    <u>Source</u>: Comité intersyndical du livre Parisien, "Les Accords-Cadres." Mimeographed. Paris: CTLP, 1976.

TABLE A.11

An Outline of Current French Press Law

I. Creation of a Paper or Periodical
No restrictions, except that a legal declaration of title, name and address of managing editor, and identification of the printer must be given.
II. Managing editor of the Publication
No restrictions, except that the editor must be an adult enjoying full civil rights who had not been previously convicted by a court and deprived of these rights. The managing editor is civilly and criminally responsible for what his paper prints. He must be French (exceptions are made for foreign publications). In dailies and weeklies, the director must be the principal owner of the publication. If the publication is not structured in terms of owners, then he must be the president or head of the administration. For dailies printing over 10,000 copies and weeklies over 50,000 copies, the managing editor may not derive his main income from other positions held. No one can be the managing editor or owner of more than one daily.
III. Ownership of the Publication
Any type of corporate structure is acceptable.
IV. Title of the Publication
Any title not already being used is acceptable, except those of the papers having collaborated with the Germans.
V. Obligatory Information to Be Printed
Every day: the name of the managing editor; the identification of the printer; the number of copies printed; the price.
Every year: the financial accounts for the fiscal year.
VI. Legal filing of copies
Fifteen copies of every issue must be filed with administrative and judicial authorities. This must be done before the publications are distributed for sale.
VII. Civil and Criminal Responsibility
For common law infractions, only the author of the offending article is responsible. But in certain misdemeanors linked to the publication itself (provocation of mobs, outrage to morals, attacks on people's private lives, and so on), the managing editor and even the printer can be legally prosecuted.

(continued)

Table A.11 (continued)

> For infractions of press law, the editor is responsible. Civil responsibility leading to damage suits are the responsibility of the author. These can become criminal offenses under certain circumstances, and the victim can ask for criminal prosecution, and this is required if the printed, illegal attacks are against state bodies or public functionaries.

VIII. Seizure of a Newspaper or Periodical

> Judicially ordered seizure can be undertaken for numerous reasons, among them: offenses to foreign sovereigns or their diplomatic agents; provocation to steal, murder, pillage; bombing or applauding such acts; applauding war crimes or collaboration with the enemy; provoking military disobedience; provoking unlawful assembly; attacks on national security elements or on the honor of the nation; outrages to proper morals; exposure of private lives. Whereas for press infractions in respect to the above, the seizure must be court ordered; for common law violations in respect to the above, the police can act before obtaining a judicial order.
>
> Administratively ordered seizure, which is completely separate from the above criminal procedures, can be ordered when the minister of the interior or the "préfets" esteem that there is a clear and present danger, or in cases of exposures of military secrecy. These administrative seizures can occur at the print shop before any distribution.

IX. The Suspension of a Publication

> A publication can be suspended for a period not to exceed three months for: complicity in crimes or misdemeanors; provocation to violence, bombing, military disobedience; publication in bad faith of false news which troubled or might have troubled the public peace, or publication of material that leads to stirring up military discipline or that shackles the war effort of the country. Such suspension by law in no way affects the labor and other contracts for which the publisher is held totally accountable.

X. Foreign Publications

> The minister of the interior can himself ban any single issue of any foreign publication; the Conseil des Ministres must decide upon total illegalization. Propaganda of foreign origin which threatens national security is illegal.

(continued)

Table A.11 (continued)

XI. Special "Exceptional States of Affairs"
During a legally declared state of war, siege, or emergency, all freedom of the press recognized by common law is suspended, and the executive and particularly the military authorities are given extremely broad authority with which to: forbid publication, censure content, and seize papers and pursue those responsible in legal conditions wholly outside of common law. At the end of the exceptional state, there is a return to the normal press law.

Note: Much of this information is drawn from Fernand Terrou, L'Information (Paris: Presses Universitaires de France, 1974), and especially in Terrou's contributions on press law throughout the five volumes of Claude Bellanger et al., l'Histoire générale de la presse française, 5 vols. (Paris: Presses Universitaires de France, 1969-76).

TABLE A.12

Different Forms of Press Subsidies in European Countries

Type of Subsidy[a]	France	West Germany	Italy	Sweden	Norway	Denmark	Finland	Holland	Belgium	Switzerland	Austria	Ireland	Great Britain
VAT concessions	x	x	x	x	x	x	x	x	x	x	x		x
Other tax concessions	x												
Direct grants	x		x	x	x				x				
Low-interest loans	[b]	x	x	x	x	x		x	x				
Postal concessions	x	x	x	x	x	x	x	x	x	x	x		x
Telephone and telegraph concessions	x	x	x	x	x	x	x	x	x	x	x		
Rail concessions	x		x						x	x	x		
Transport subsidies							x				x		
Government advertising	[c]		x	x		x	x		x				
Training and research grants					x		x						
Newsagency subsidies				x	x								
Subsidies to political party organizations	x		x	x	x		x					x	
Subsidies for joint distribution				x	x								
Subsidies for joint production				x									

[a] The "cultural fund" subsidies for foreign distribution are a type of aid not mentioned in this table.
[b] Such loans were available 1957-63 (Bellanger 1976, p. 121).
[c] There is important state advertising in France.

Source: Anthony Smith, "Subsidies and the Press in Europe." Political and Economic Planning 43, no. 569 (1977):110.

FIGURE A.3

The Havas Advertising Empire, 1976

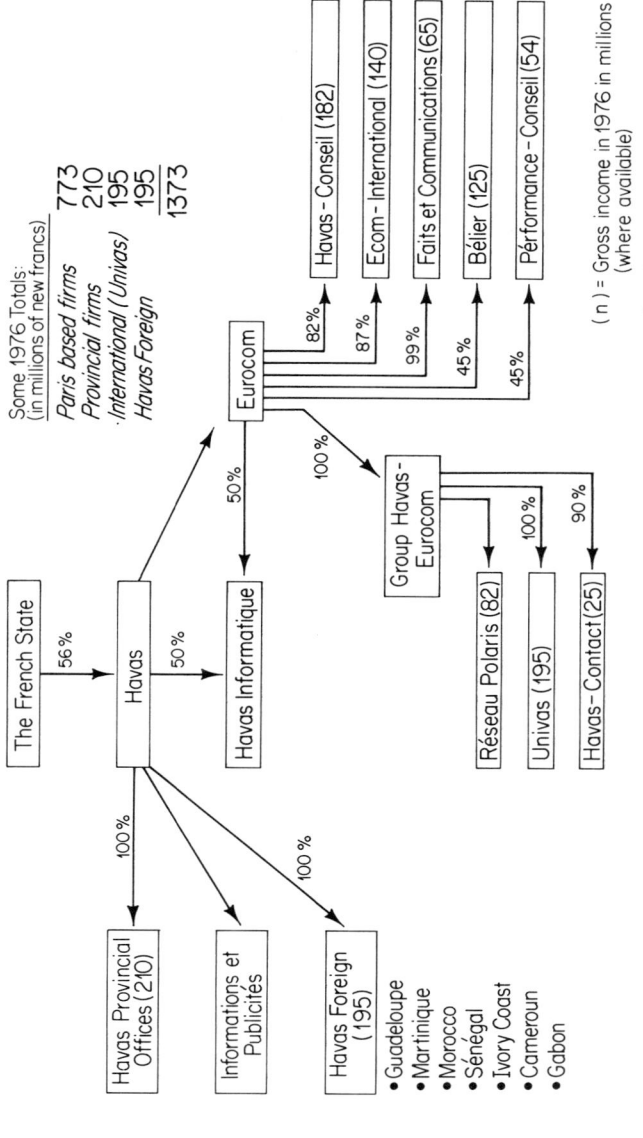

Source: Compiled by the author from data from François Archambault and Jean-François Lemoine, 4 Milliards de journaux (Paris: Alain Moreau, 1977), p. 199.

TABLE A.13

Examples of the Flow of State Personnel into Information Enterprises

State Personnel Represented	Agents	Previous Government Position	Information Enterprise Position
Georges Pompidou	Xavier Marchetti	Advisor to Pompidou at the Elysée	Editor-in-chief of <u>Le Figaro</u>
	Jean Meo	Cabinet of de Gaulle; at Elysée with Pompidou	PDG* of <u>France-Soir</u>; then PDG (adjoint) of Havas
Jacques Chaban-Delmas	Simon Nora	Charge de mission of Chaban-Delmas	PDG of Hachette
	Gérard Worms	Cabinet of Chaban-Delmas	PDG of Hachette
	Jacques Marchandise	Conseil d'état (honorary): legal advisor to Conseil des Ministres	VPDG of Hachette
	Henri Amouroux	Chaban was mayor of Bordeaux when H.A. was PDG of Bordeaux's only paper, <u>Sud-Ouest</u>	PDG of <u>France-Soir</u>
	Arthur Conte	Gaullist deputy to National Assembly	President of ORTF

Jacques Chirac	Denis Baudouin	Advisor to Chirac on problems of information	PDG SOFIRAD
Giscard d'Estaing	Xavier Grouyou-Beauchamp	Head press secretary for Giscard	PDG SOFIRAD
	Henri Pigeat	Headed ministry office of press relations, television branch. Was lieutenant to Grouyou-Beauchamp	Assistant director of Agence France Presse
	Françoise Giroud	Named Secretary of State for Culture	Had been one of the originators of L'Express

*PDG = Président directeur général (chairman of the board and chief executive officer); VPDG = Vice Président directeur général.

Sources: Presse Actualité, September 1971 and December 1972; Gabriel Enkiri, Machette . . . CFDT (Paris: La Commune, 1972), pp. 108–21; L'Humanité, April 14, 1977; Pierre Lepape, La Presse (Paris: Deroel, 1972), passim.; Ruth Thomas, Broadcasting and Democracy in France (London: Bradford University Press, 1976), p. 89.

TABLE A.14

The Political Spectrum of the Parisian Daily Press at the Liberation

Political Orientation	Parisian Daily	Thousands of Copies Printed		
		January 1945	April 1947	
Ruling "Tripartite Parties" Communist party and near CP	L'Humanité*	326	450	(56 papers = 23.5%)
	Ce Soir*	288	448	
	Libération	196	180	
	Front National	172	[100]	
Socialist party and near CP	Le Populaire*	235	159	(37 papers = 15.5%)
	Combat	185	128	
	Résistance	160	[100]	
	France-Tireur	182	350	
	Libé-Soir	250	[50]	
MRP (left Christian)	L'Aube*	148	125	(28 papers = 2.3%)
Center	L'Intransigeant*	—	200	(= 16.2%)
	La Croix*	—	162	
	Le Monde	150	174	
	Ce Matin	—	200	
	4 others	—	(75)	

282

Right	L'Epoch*	—	97
	L'Aurore	90	205
	La Nation	—	[20] (= 8.9%)
	France-Libre	194	122
	5 others		
General information	Le Figaro*	231	399
	L'Ordre*	15	[5]
	Parisien Libéré	222	340 (= 35.9%)
	France-Soir	264	578
	Paris-Presse	200	478

Note: The print runs of the liberation papers were particularly large for several reasons. First, the papers were only four pages long at first, that is, one sheet of newsprint folded twice. Only in 1949 was the paper shortage solved to the point where six pages were allowed. Readers therefore often bought and read numerous papers. Asterisks indicate prewar papers allowed to reopen at the liberation. Estimated figures are in brackets, while dashes indicate an absence of data.

Source: Claude Bellanger et al., Histoire générale de la presse française, vol. 5 (Paris: Presses Universitaires de France, 1976), pp. 309, 356, 315.

TABLE A.15

The Political Spectrum of the Daily Press in 1976

Newspaper	Average Copies Actually Sold Per Day		
Paris			
Conservative and reactionary press			
L'Aurore	300,500		
Le Figaro	382,200	1,626,200	1,626,200
Parisien Libéré	310,400		
France-Soir	633,100		
Socialistic press*			
Le Monde	439,900	459,900	
Le Quotidien de Paris	20,000		
CP press			
L'Humanité	151,000	151,000	660,000
Far left press			
L'Humanité Rouge	4,000		
Libération	23,500	50,000	
Le Quotidien du Peuple	12,500		
Rouge	10,000		
Provinces			
Conservative			
(In some senses, all the highly depoliticized papers of the provinces play this role, but far less openly than in Paris)		6,126,000	6,126,000
Socialistic press*			
Nord Matin	108,000		
Le Populaire du Centre	53,000	369,700	
Libération-Champagne	26,800		474,000
Le Provençal	181,900		
CP press			
L'Echo du Centre	30,000		
Liberté (Lille)	25,000	105,000	
La Marseillaise	50,000		
Far left press			
(no dailies, but significant contributions to the parallel press in periodicals)		Total	
		Conservative:	7.8 million
		Left:	1.1 million

*Socialist leaning, but not linked formally or financially to the Socialist party.

Source: Press Actualité, February and May 1977.

TABLE A.16

The Content of Five Major Newspapers, 1969
(% of total printed surface)

Content	Parisien Libéré	France Soir	Le Figaro	Le Monde	Progrés (Lyon)
Hard news					
National politics	3.2	8.5	8.4	12.0	5.5
International politics	1.0	4.1	9.0	18.0	4.0
French economy	0.5	1.2	5.0	10.6	3.0
Regional news	1.5	1.5	0.0	0.0	25.0
Social problems	2.5	1.8	1.0	2.0	1.0
Total	8.7	17.1	23.4	42.6	38.5
Soft news					
Movies and TV	6.0	7.5	6.1	4.7	5.2
Miscellaneous news	10.5	10.6	3.5	1.5	1.0
Society news	3.5	2.5	3.5	1.5	1.0
Comics, recipes	7.3	5.0	1.1	0.0	1.5
Sports	7.0	5.0	2.2	1.5	10.0
Racing	3.8	2.0	1.5	0.0	2.5
Fashion, beauty	4.0	2.5	2.4	1.0	1.5
Total	42.1	35.1	20.3	10.2	22.7

Source: Bernard Pourprix, La Presse gratuite (Paris: Editions Ouvrières, 1971), p. 73.

TABLE A.17

The Education of Readers of Four Parisian Dailies, 1975
(thousands of readers)

Education of Head of Household	Le Monde and Le Figaro (informational)	France-Soir and L'Aurore (sensationalist)
Superior	354	107
Secondary	216	179
Technical/commercial	103	214
High primary	60	88
Primary and less	100	405

Source: CESP, 1975 and Presse Actualité, May 1977, and Centre d'étude des supports de publicité (Paris) 1975. "Études du centre d'étude des supports de publicité: La Presse quotidienne," Photo copies of bound reports.

BIBLIOGRAPHY

A number of references in the text are to daily newspapers and periodicals that the reader will not find referenced below. Among the dailies, Le Monde proved the most useful, but there are also citations from L'Humanité, Le Figaro, La Croix, Le Populaire, L'Aurore, Quotidien de Paris, International Herald Tribune, and L'Index. Among the periodicals, Presse Actualité, a monthly specializing in candid reporting of the minutiae of daily happenings in the press, was enormously useful, as were other magazines specializing in affairs of the media such as Correspondance de la presse, Le Journalist, Journal des Journalistes, and L'Echo de la presse et de la publicité. There are also many references to general information magazines, such as Nouvel Observateur, L'Expansion, La Vie française, L'Express, Que Choisir, La Nation, Riverol, France Nouvelle, Cahiers française, and Aprés Demain. All other cited sources are found in the following bibliography:

Adorno, Theodor. 1969. Negative Dialectics. New York: Seabury Press.

Agnés, Yves, and Croissandeau, Jean-Michel. Lire Le Journal. Paris: Editions F. P. Lobies.

Albert, Pierre. 1976. La Presse. Paris: Presses Universitaires de France.

____, and Terrou, F. 1974. Histoire de la presse. Paris: Presses Universitaires de France.

Alberts, Jurgen. 1972. Die Massenpresse als Ideologiefabrik: An Beispiel "Bild." Frankfurt/Main: Athenaum Fischer.

Althusser, Louis. 1971. Lenin and Philosophy and Other Essays. London: New Left Books.

Anders, Gunter. 1968. "Berlin und Jerusalem." Deutsche Volkszeitung 9, no. 1.

Andrieu, René. 1975. Du bonheur et rien d'autre. Paris: Stock.

Archambault, François, and Ambault, Michel. 1966. Un journal pour 30 centimes: Mythes et réalités de la presse moderne. Paris: Juillard.

Archambault, François, and Lemoine, Jean-François. 1977. 4 Milliards de journaux. Paris: Alain Moreau.

Aronowitz, Stanley. 1973. False Promises: The Shaping of American Working Class Consciousness. New York: McGraw-Hill.

Aronson, James. 1973. Packaging the News. New York: International.

"Aspects de la propagande allemande en zone interdite: L'Echo de Nancy." 1976. Bulletin du centre d'histoire du socialisme et du centre d'études socialistes des relations internationales (July).

Association des journalistes économiques et financières. 1972. Les atteintes à la liberté des journalistes. "Livre Blanc" no. 2. Paris: AJEF.

Auclair, Georges. 1970. Le mana quotidien: Structures et fonctions de la chronique des faits divers. Paris: Editions Anthropos.

Bagdikian, Ben H. 1972. The Effete Conspiracy and Other Crimes by the Press. New York: Harper & Row.

Balle, Francis. 1973. Institutions et publics des moyens de l'information. Paris: Editions Mont Christien.

_____. 1968. "Les grands quotidiens français sont-ils dépolitisés?" Annales (Paris) (March-April).

Barou, Jean-Pierre. 1972. Luttes actuelles: De la liberté de la presse à la presse de la liberté. Brussels: Editions La Taupa.

Barsalou, Joseph. 1954. Histoire de la Quatrième République. Vol. 8. Paris: Presses Universitaires de France.

Barthes, Roland. 1972. Mythologies. New York: Hill and Wang.

_____. 1967. Writing Degree Zero and Elements of Semiology. Boston: Beacon Press.

_____. 1964. Essais critiques. Paris: Editions du Seuil.

Baudelot, Christian, and Establet, Roger. 1972. L'Ecole capitaliste en France. Paris: François Maspero.

___, and Malemort, Jacques. 1975. La petite bourgeoisie en France. Paris: François Maspero.

Baudrillard, Jean. 1972. Pour une critique de l'économie politique du signe. Paris: Gallimard.

___. 1967. "Marshall McLuhan: Understanding Media." L'Homme et la société (July-September).

Bell, Daniel. 1962. The End of Ideology. New York: Free Press.

Bellanger, Claude, et al. 1976. Histoire générale de la presse française. Vol. 5. Paris: Presses Universitaires de France.

___. 1975. Histoire générale de la presse française. Vol. 4. Paris: Presses Universitaires de France.

___. 1974. Histoire générale de la presse française. Vol. 3. Paris: Presses Universitaires de France.

Bercoff, André. 1975. L'Autre France: L'Underpresse. Paris: Stock.

Berelson, Barnard, and Janowitz, Maurice, eds. 1966. Reader in Public Opinion and Communication. 2nd ed. Glencoe, Ill.: Free Press.

Bernstein, Basil. 1974. Class, Codes and Control. New York: Schocken Books.

Bertaux, Daniel. 1977. Destins personels et classes sociales. Paris: Presses Universitaires de France.

Beuve-Méry, Hubert. 1956. "Du Temps au Monde, ou la presse et l'argent." Paris: Reprint of a speech given for Les Conférences des Ambassadeurs.

Boris, Claude. 1975. Les Tigres de papier. Paris: Seuil.

Bourdieu, Pierre, and Passeron, Jean-Claude. 1970. La Réproduction. Paris: Editions de Minuit.

Bowles, Samuel, and Gintis, Herbert. 1976. Schooling in Capitalist America. New York: Basic Books.

Braverman, Harry. 1974. Labor and Monopoly Capital. New York: Monthly Review Press.

Brimo, Nicolas. 1977. Le Dossier Hersant. Paris: François Maspero.

Brown, Les. 1971. Television: The Business Behind the Box. New York: Harcourt Brace Jovanovich.

Bruhat, Jean, and Piolot, Marc. 1966. Esquisse d'une histoire de la CGT. Paris: CGT Press.

Brulé, E. 1976. "From the Editor-in-Chief to all Journalists." Internal document of Ouest France.

Brunois, Richard. 1973. Le Figaro face aux problèmes de la presse quotidienne. Paris: Presses Universitaires de France.

Cahiers d'étude de presse. 1968 and 1963. Paris: Institute de Presse.

"Cahiers du centre d'études et de recherches sur la presse et le personnel politique de la France contemporaine." 1975 and 1973. Mimeographed colloquia proceedings.

Cahiers du Rhone. 1945. De la résistance à la révolution. Boudry: Editions de la Baconnière-Neuchatel.

Castells, Manuel. 1977. The Urban Question. Cambridge, Mass.: MIT Press.

____. 1975. Sociologie de l'espace industriel. Paris: Anthropos.

____. 1973. Luttes urbaines. Paris: François Maspero.

Cau, Jean. 1976. Lettre ouverte à tout Le Monde. Paris: Albin Michel.

Caute, David. 1964. Communism and the French Intellectuals, 1914-1960. New York: Macmillan.

Cayrol, Roland. 1973. La Presse: Ecrite et audio-visuelle. Paris: Presses Universitaires de France.

Cazeneuve, Jean. 1974. Sociologie de la radio-télévision. Paris: Presses Universitaires de France.

Centre d'étude des supports de publicité (Paris). 1975. "Etudes du Centre d'études des supports de publicité: La Presse quotidienne." Photocopies of bound reports. CESP.

Centre d'étude et de recherches sur la presse et le personnel politique de la France contemporaine. 1976. "Press et politique: La Libération et la IVe République." Mimeographed. Paris: CERPPPFC.

Centre d'étude et de recherches sur les qualifications. 1974. "Les journalistes: Etude statistique et sociologique de la profession." Dossier no. 9. Mimeographed. Paris: CERQ.

Centre de formation et de perfectionnement des journalistes. 1976. Guide du droit de la presse. Paris: CFPJ.

Champeix, Pierre. 1968. "Le pouvoir, la publicité et la télévision. Economie et politique (January).

Charlot, Jean. 1970. Repertoire des publications des partis politiques français: 1944-1967. Paris: Presses de la Fondation Nationale des Sciences Politiques.

Chatelain, Abel. 1962. Le Monde et ses lecteurs. Paris: Armand Colin.

Chauvet, Paul. 1971. Les ouvriers du livre et du journal. Paris: Les Editions Ouvrières.

Cherry, Colin. 1971. World Communications: Threat or Promise? London: Wiley Interscience.

Coffey, Peter. 1973. The Social Economy of France. London: Macmillan.

Cohn-Bendit, Daniel. 1968. Obsolete Communism. The Left Wing Alternative. New York: McGraw Hill.

_____ et al. 1968. The French Student Revolt. New York: Hill and Wang.

Comité intersyndical du livre parisien. 1976. "Les Accords-Cadres." Mimeographed. Paris: CILP.

Commission de la carte d'identité des journalistes professionnels. 1966. "Enquête statistique et sociologique de la liste des titulaires de la carte professionnelle au 1ere juillet." Mimeographed. Paris: CCIJP.

Communist Party. Livre: Les Travailleurs luttent contre la crise, les gâchis, les monopoles, l'autoritarisme. Paris: CP Press.

Coquelin, Roger. 1976. "Le retour des travaux d'expression française confectionnés à l'étranger." Press conference, November 29, Paris. Mimeographed.

Coston, Henri. 1977. Lectures françaises (Paris) (October).

_____. 1975. Dictionnaire des Dynasties Bourgeoises et du monde des Affaires. Paris: Editions Alain Moreau.

Crozier, Michel. 1970. La Société bloquée. Paris: Seuil.

Dagnaud, Monique. 1978. Le Mythe de la qualité de la vie, et la politique urbaine en France. Paris: Mouton.

Dartville, Bernard. 1976. "Etude economique sur le lancement de Liberation et de Rouge." Ph.D. dissertation, Université de Paris.

Debord, Guy. 1967. La Société du spectacle. Paris: Editions Buchet/Chastel.

Derieux, Emmanuel, and Texier, Jean C. 1974. La Presse quotidienne française. Paris: Armand Colin.

Domhoff, G. William. 1967. Who Rules America. Englewood Cliffs, N.J.: Prentice-Hall.

Dorfman, Ariel. 1974. Ensayos quemados en Chile: Inocencía y neocolonialismo. Buenos Aires: Ediciones de la Flor.

_____, and Jufre, Manuel. 1974. Superman y sus amigos del alma. Buenos Aires: Ediciones Galerna.

Douffiagues, Jacques, and Peltier, Roger. La France contemporaine. Vol. 6. Monoco: L'Union Européenne d'Editions.

Drancourt, Michel. 1974a. "L'Economie d'une entreprise de presse." Problèmes Economiques, March 27.

_____. 1974b. "Rapport présenté au nom du Conseil économique et social par M. Michel Drancourt." Paris: Conseil Economique et Social.

Dumas, Evelyn. 1974. La Crise de la presse en France. Ottawa: Editions Lemeac.

Durand, Pierre. 1974. "La Presse et l'argent." L'Humanité, March 26-28.

Durieux, Claude. 1976. La Télécratie. Paris: Téma-Editions.

Duverger, Maurice. 1977. L'Autre Côté des choses. Paris: Albin Michel.

Eco, Umberto. 1972. La Structure absente: Introduction à la recherche semiotique. Paris: Mercuro de France.

Ehrenreich, John, and Ehrenreich, Barbara. 1976. "Work and Consciousness." Monthly Review (July-August).

_____. 1969. Long March, Short Spring. New York: Monthly Review Press.

Ekecrantz, Jan. 1974. "Mediating Factors in the Production of Systematic Ignorance Under Late Capitalism." In Der Anteil der Massenmedien bei der Herausbildung des Bewusssteins in der sich wandelnden Welt. Leipzig: Sektion Journalistik der Karl Marx Universität.

_____, et al. 1976. "The Politics of Information." Manuscript of the Universitat van Amsterdam, Seminarium voor de Leer der Communicatiemiddelen.

Enkiri, Gabriel. 1972. Hachette la pieuvre . . . témoignage d'un militant CFDT. Paris: La Commune.

_____, et al. 1970. Hachette: Une Experience syndicale CGT-CFDT. Paris: François Maspero.

Enzenberger, Hans Magnus. 1974. The Consciousness Industry. New York: Seabury Press.

_____. 1970. "Constituents of a Theory of the Media." New Left Review (November).

Eversole, J. 1971. "Concentration of Ownership in the Communication Industry." Journalism Quarterly, 48 (Spring), no. 1.

Ewen, Stuart. 1976. Captains of Consciousness: Advertising and the Social Roots of the Consumer Culture. New York: McGraw-Hill.

_____. 1973. "Herbert Schiller: The Mind Managers." Telos, no. 17.

Fajon, Etienne. 1964. En Feuilletant L'Humanité. Paris: L'Humanité.

Faucier, Nicolas. 1964. La Presse quotidienne. Paris: Les Editions Syndicalistes.

Fédération Française des Sociétés de Journalistes. 1976. "Pour un statut de la presse: Le Droit de citoyens a l'information." Mimeographed. Caen: Centre d'études et de documentation sur l'information de l'Université de Caen.

Fédération Française des Travailleurs du Livre (FFTL). 1976. Le Putsch d'Amaury. Paris: Editions Sociales.

Fekete, John. 1973. "McLuhancy: Counterrevolution in Cultural Theory." Telos, no. 15.

Finkelstein, Sidney. 1968. Sense and Nonsense of McLuhan. New York: International.

Freiberg, J. W. 1981. "Towards a Structuralist Model of State Intervention in the Mass Media." In Political Power and Social Theory, edited by Maurice Zeitlin. Vol. 4. Greenwich, Conn.: JAT Press.

Freiberg, J. W. 1979. "The Capitalist State and the Information Media: The Case of France." Media, Culture and Society, no. 1.

Friere, Paulo. 1970. Pedagogy of the Oppressed. New York: Seabury Press.

Gaborit, Pierre. 1974. "La Presse Communiste." Projet (November).

Gabriel-Robinet, Louis. 1961. Histoire de la presse. Paris: Hachette.

Galtung, Johan. 1965. "The Structure of Foreign News." Journal of International Peace Research, no. 1.

Garnham, Nicholas. 1979. "Towards a Political Economy of Mass Communications." Media, Culture and Society, no. 1.

Geng, J. M. 1973. Information, mystification. Paris: Epi.

Gerreton, Manuel A., ed. 1974. Ideologia y medios de communicación. Buenos Aires: Amorrortu.

Glasgow Media Group. 1976. "Bad News." Theory and Society 3, no. 3.

Goldmann, Lucien. 1974. The Enlightenment. Cambridge, Mass.: MIT Press.

Grafteaux, Serge. 1975. Le Marbre et al plume: Le Conflict du Parisien Libéré. Paris: Tema.

Gramsci, Antonio. 1974. Prison Notebooks. New York: International.

Granou, André. 1977. La Bourgeoisie financière au pouvoir. Paris: François Maspero.

Guedj, Aimé, and Girault, Jacques. 1970. Le Monde. Paris: Editions Sociales.

Guillauma, Yves. 1973. "La Presse quotidienne politique et d'information générale en France de 1944 à 1972: Naissance, vie, et mort des quotidiens." Paris: Institut National de Techniques de la Documentation, Conservatoire National des Arts et Metiers.

Guillo Lohan, Georges. 1970. "Les Concentrations dans la presse quotidienne et leurs incidences sur les marchés de l'information et de la publicité." Paris: Université de Paris I.

Habermas, Jurgen. 1975. Legitimation Crisis. Boston: Beacon Press.

Hall, Stuart. 1977. "Culture, Media and the Ideological Effect." Center for Contemporary Cultural Studies, University of Birmingham. Mimeographed.

———, Lumley, Bob, and McLennan, Gregor. 1977. "Politics and Ideology: Gramsci." Working Papers in Cultural Studies, no. 10. Birmingham: University of Birmingham, Centre for Contemporary Cultural Studies.

Harris, André, and de Sédouy, Alain. 1974. Voyage à l'intérieur du Parti Communiste. Paris: Seuil.

Hauser, Eugen. 1974. "Falk for ever: Statt einer sozialistischen Pressepolitik." Weiner Tagebuch (March).

Hervé, Pierre. 1945. La Libération trahie. Paris: Editions Bernard Grasset.

Hirst, Paul Q. 1976. "Althusser and the Theory of Ideology." Economy and Society 5, no. 4.

Hoffman, Stanley. 1974. Decline or Renewal? France Since the 1930s. New York: Viking Press.

Horkheimer, Max and Adorno, Theodore. 1972. Dialectic of Enlightenment. New York: Herder and Herder.

Hostert, Guy. 1973. Le Journal Le Monde et le marxisme. Paris: La Pensée Universelle.

Hughes, Helen MacGill. 1940. News and the Human Interest Story. Chicago: University of Chicago Press.

Institut National de la Statistique. 1974. "Industries polygraphiques, press-édition." Status dossier prepared for the Commissariat Général au Plan. Paris: INSEE.

Institut National de L'Audiovisual. 1976. "Cinque monopoles de l'information." Mimeographed. Paris: INA.

Jeanneney, Jean-Noël, and Juliard, Jacques. 1979. Le Monde de Beuve-Méry ou le métier d'Alceste. Paris: Seuil.

Johnson, Dale L. 1978. "Strategic Implications of Recent Social Class Theory." The Insurgent Sociologist 8, no. 1.

"Journaliste communiste vous dites?" 1976. <u>La Nouvel Critique</u> (December).

Kayser, Jacques. 1963. <u>Le Quotidien français</u>. Paris: Armand Colin.

Kervevan, Pierre. 1975. "La Contre-révolution culturelle." <u>Le Monde</u>, September 11.

Krieghbaum, Hillier. 1972. <u>Pressures on the Press</u>. New York: Thomas Y. Crowell.

Lacan, Jacques. 1966. <u>Ecrits</u>. Paris: Editions du Seuil.

Landis, Fred. 1975. "Psychological Warfare in Chile: The C.I.A. Makes Headlines." <u>Liberation</u>, March 3.

Lapierre, J. W. 1968. "L'Information sur l'état d'Israel dans les grands quotidiens français en 1958." Paris: Editions de CNRS.

Lawson, John Howard. 1953. <u>Film in the Battle of Ideas</u>. New York: Masses and Mainstream.

Lebel, Jean-Patrick. 1971. <u>Cinema et idéologie</u>. Paris: Editions Sociales.

Lecat Report (Rapport du groupe de travail sur la situation et les perspectives de l'imprimerie française, présenté par Lecat, J.-Ph.). 1975. Paris: Ministère de l'Industrie et de la Recherche.

Lefebvre, Henri. 1969. <u>The Explosion</u>. New York: Monthly Review Press.

Legris, Michel. 1976. <u>Le Monde tel qu'il est</u>. Paris: Plon.

Le Monde. 1978. "Supplement à Dossiers et documents." Paris: Le Monde.

Le Monde. 1977. "Dossiers et documents du Monde." Paris: Le Monde. (Pamphlet about the enterprise.)

Le Monde. 1976. <u>L'année économique et sociale</u>. Paris: Le Monde.

Le Monde. 1973. "Le Monde." Paris: Le Monde. (Pamphlet about the enterprise.)

"Le Monde . . . ses methodes." 1976. Association pour une lecture critique de la presse. Paris: ALCP.

Lepape, Pierre. 1972. La Presse. Paris: Denoel.

Libération. 1943. Les Cahiers de Libération. Clandestine publication.

Liebling, A. J. 1975. The Press. New York: Ballentine.

Lindon Report (Rapport sur les problèmes posés par les sociétés de rédacteurs). 1970. Paris: Documentation Française.

Litterman, Bob. 1973. "Who Owns the Media? Pacific Research and World Empire Telegram. East Palo Alto, Cal.: Pacific Studies Center. (Pamphlet.)

Littunen, Yrjo. 1978. "Information in the Welfare State: Problems and Approaches." Acta Sociologica (supplement).

"Livre blanc du Figaro." 1969. (Pamphlet by the journalists about their strike.) Paris: Syndicat National des Journalistes.

"Livre noir de Paris-Normandie." 1975. Rouen: The Journalists of Paris-Normandie.

Lojkine, Jean. 1973. La Politique urbaine dans la région parisienne, 1945-1972. Paris: Mouton.

Machiavelli, Niccolo. 1961. The Prince. London: Penguin.

Maire, Edmond, and Juillard, Jacques. 1975. La CFDT d'aujourd'hui. Paris: Seuil.

Mallet, Serge. 1963. La Nouvelle classe ouvrière. Paris: Plon.

Marcuse, Herbert. 1964. One-Dimensional Man. Boston: Beacon Press.

Mattelart, Armand. 1976. Multinationales et systèmes de communication: Les Appareils idéologiques de l'impérialism. Paris: Anthropos.

_____. 1975. "Vers la formation des appareils idéologiques de l'état multinational." Politique Aujourd'hui (January).

____. 1974a. "Appareils idéologiques d'état et luttes de classes: Chile 1970-73." Cahiers du Cinema (December).

____. 1974b. Mass media, idéologies et mouvements révolutionnaires. Paris: Anthropos.

____. 1971. Donald l'imposteur, ou l'impérialisme raconté aux enfants. Paris: Moreau.

____, Castillo, Carmen, and Castello, Leonardo. 1970. La ideologia de la dominación en una sociedad dependiente. Buenos Aires: Editiones Signos.

____, Piccini, Mabel, and Mattelart, Michelle. 1970. Los Médios de communicación de masas: La ideología de la prensa liberal en Chile. Santiago de Chile: Cuadernos de la Realidad Nacional.

McLennan, Gregor, Molina, Victor, and Peters, Roy. 1977. "Althusser's Theory of Ideology." Cultural Studies, no. 10. Birmingham: University of Birmingham, Centre for Contemporary Cultural Studies.

Miliband, Ralph. 1977. Marxism and Politics. Oxford: Oxford University Press.

____. 1969. The State in Capitalist Society. New York: Basic Books.

Modiano, René. 1935. La Presse pourrie aux ordres du capital. Paris: Editions du Parti Socialiste (SFIO).

Molotch, Harvey L., and Lester, Marilyn. 1975. "News as Purposive Behavior." American Sociological Review, no. 39.

____. 1973. "Accidents, Scandals and Routines: Resources for Insurgent Methodology." Insurgent Sociologist 3, no. 4.

Morin, François. 1974. La Structure financière du capital francaise. Paris: François Maspero.

Morin, Violette. 1969. L'Ecriture de presse. Paris: Mouton.

Mottin, Jean. 1949. Histoire politique de la press, 1944-49. Paris: Editions Bilans Hebdomodaires.

Mouillaud, Maurice. 1976. "L'Etude de contenu." Cahiers Francais (supplement) (Octobre).

Mueller, Claus. 1973. The Politics of Communications: A Case Study in the Political Sociology of Language, Socialization and Legitimation. New York: Oxford University Press.

Murdock, Graham. 1973. "Political Deviance: The Press Presentation of a Militant Mass Demonstration." In The Manufacture of News, edited by S. Cohen and J. Young. London: Constable.

____, and Golding, Peter. 1973. "For a Political Economy of Mass Communications." In The Socialist Register, edited by Ralph Miliband and J. Saville. London: Merlin Press.

Negt, Oscar. 1978. "Mass Media: Tools of Domination or Instruments of Liberation? Aspects of the Frankfurt School's Communications Analysis." New German Critique, no. 14.

Nixon, Raymond. 1968. "Trends in U.S. Newspaper Ownership." Gazette, no. 3.

____. 1971. "Concentration in Press Ownership." Journalism Quarterly 48 (Spring), no. 1.

____, and Hahn, Tae-youl. 1971. "Concentration of Press Ownership: A Comparison of 32 Countries." Journalism Quarterly (Spring).

Novick, Peter. 1968. The Resistance Under Vichy. London: Chatto and Windus.

O'Connor, James. 1973. The Fiscal Crisis of the State. New York: St. Martins.

Offe, Claus. 1975. "The Theory of the Capitalist State and the Problem of Policy Formation." In Stress and Contradictions in Modern Capitalism, edited by L. Lindberg et al. Lexington, Mass.: Heath.

____. 1974. "Structural Problems of the Capitalist State. Class Rule and the Political System. On the Selectiveness of Political Institutions." In German Political Studies, edited by Klaus von Beyme. Vol. 1. London: Sage.

Oppenheimer, Martin. 1979. "West German McCarthyism." The Nation, March 17.

———. 1976. "The New German Repression." The Nation, September 11.

Padioleau, Jean G. 1976. "Systèmes d'intervention et rhetoriques journalistiques." Sociologie du Travail (July-September).

Parisien Libéré. 1976. Livre blanc du journal Le Parisien Libéré. Paris: Le Parisien Libéré.

Paulu, Burton. 1967. "Public and Private Corporations: France, the Netherlands, Italy and Sweden." In Mass Communications: A World View, edited by Alan Wells. Palo Alto, Calif.: Mayfield.

Paxton, Robert O. 1972. Vichy France. New York: W. W. Norton.

Pember, Don R. 1974. Mass Media in America. Chicago: Science Research Associates.

Perier-Daville, Denis. 1976. Main basse sur Le Figaro. Paris: Tema.

Pons, Dominique. 1977. Dossier "H" comme Hersant. Paris: Alain Moreau.

Poulantzas, Nicos. 1975. Classes in Contemporary Capitalism. London: New Left Books.

———. 1974. Fascism and Dictatorship. New York: Schocken Books.

Pourprix, Bernard. 1971. La Presse gratuite. Paris: Editions Ouvrières.

"Pratiques culturelles des français." 1974. In Report of the Secretariat d'état à la culture. 2 vols. Paris: Service des études et de la recherche (December).

"Presse et statistique." 1974. (Statistical government data published by the Service Juridique et Technique de l'Information.) Paris: Ministre de l'information.

Priaulx, Allan and Ungar, Sanford J. 1969. The Almost Revolution. New York: Dell.

"La Presse, outil d'information et d'éducation?" 1976. Pour (September-October).

Prokop, Dieter. 1974. Massenkultur und Spontaneitat: Sur veranderten Warrenform des Massenkommunidation im Spatkapitalismus (Aufstze). Frankfurt/Main: Suhrkamp.

Prunière, Bernard. 1964. La Presse sans politique. Paris: Librarie General de Droit et de Jurisprudence.

Read, William H. 1976. America's Mass Media Merchants. Baltimore: John Hopkins University Press.

Reynaud, Jean Daniel. 1975. Les Syndicats en France. 2 vols. Paris: Seuil.

Rocci, Jean. 1975. La Télévision malade du pouvoir. Paris: Editions Sociales.

Santini, André. 1966. L'Aide de l'état à la presse. Paris: Presses Universitaires de France.

Schiller, Herbert I. 1973. The Mind Managers. Boston: Beacon Press.

———. 1971. Mass Communications and American Empire. Boston: Beacon Press.

———, Mattelart, Armand, and Texcier, Jean C. 1974. "Impérialisme culturelle." Le Monde Diplomatique, no. 249.

———, and Smythe, Dallas W. 1973. "Chile: An End to Cultural Colonialism." Society (March).

Schramm, Wilbur. 1973. Men, Messages, and Media. New York: Harper & Row.

Schudson, Michael. 1978. Discovering the News: A Social History of American Newspapers. New York: Basic.

Schwoebel, Jean. 1968. La Presse, le pouvoir, et l'argent. Paris: Seuil.

Seale, Patrick and McConville, Maureen. 1968. Red Flag, Black Flag. New York: Ballentine.

Seppanen, Esko. 1974. "Mass Media in the Nordic Countries." Mimeographed. Available at the International Mass Media Research Center in Bagnolet, Paris.

Serisé Report (Rapport du group de travail sur les aides publiques aux entreprises de presse). Cahiers de la presse Française (September).

Servan-Schreiber, Jean-Jacques. 1957. Lieutenant en Algérie. Paris: Plon.

———. 1969. The Spirit of May. New York: McGraw-Hill.

Servan-Schreiber, Jean-Louis. 1975. "La Presse de qualité en France." Pamphlet. Paris: n.p.

———. 1972. Le Pouvoir d'informer. Paris: Robert Laffont.

Silva, Ludovico. 1970a. La plusvalia ideologica. Caracas: Universidad Central de Venezuela.

———. 1970b. Teoría y pratica de la ideología. Mexico City: Editorial Nuestro Tiempo.

Simmonot, Philippe. 1977. Le Monde et le pouvoir. Paris: Presses d'Aujourd'hui.

Sinclair, Upton. 1920. The Brass Check: A Study of American Journalism. Pasadena, Calif.: Upton Sinclair.

Smith, Anthony. 1977. "Subsidies and the Press in Europe." Political and Economic Planning 43, no. 569.

———. 1973. The Shadow in the Cave: The Broadcaster, the Audience and the State. London: Quartet Books.

Sola Pool, Ithiel de, Lasswell, Harold D., and Lerner, Daniel. 1970. The Prestige Press: A Comparative Study of Political Symbols. Cambridge, Mass.: MIT Press.

———, et al. 1952. The "Prestige Papers": A Survey of Their Editorials. Palo Alto, Calif.: Stanford University Press.

———, eds. 1973. Handbook of Communication. Chicago: Rand McNally.

Stein, M. L. 1974. Shaping the News. New York: Washington Square Press.

Suzuki, Shiro. 1974. "The Situation of the Japanese Press and Mass Media." The Democratic Journalist 12.

Syndicat National des Journalistes. 1976. "Analysis des elections au Congres national des journalistes." Mimeographed circular. Paris: SNJ.

Tebbel, John. 1974. The Media in America. New York: Mentor.

Terrou, Fernand. 1974. L'Information. Paris: Presses Universitaires de France.

Therborn, Goran. 1978. What Does the Ruling Class Do When it Rules? London: New Left Books.

Thibault, Danièle. 1976. Explorer le journal. Paris: Hatier.

Thibault, Jacques. 1978. Le Monde: Histoire d'un journal, un journal dans l'histoire. Paris: Jean-Calude Simoën.

Thomas, Ruth. 1976. Broadcasting and Democracy in France. London: Bradford University Press.

Toscan du Plantier, Daniel. 1974. Donnez-nous notre quotidien. Paris: Olivier Orban.

Touraine, Alain. 1976. The Self-Production of Society. Chicago: University of Chicago Press.

_____. 1970a. The May Movement. New York: Random House.

_____. 1970b. Post-Industrial Society. New York: Random House.

Toussaint, Nadine. 1975. "Economie de l'Information." Mimeographed. Paris: Institut Français de Presse.

_____. 1970. "La Consumation de presse, de radio et de télévision en France 1950-65." Paris: Université de Paris.

_____, ed. 1976. "La Presse quotidienne." Cahiers Français (October-December).

____. 1973. "La crise de la presse." Problèmes Politiques et Sociaux, no. 205-6.

Tuchman, Gaye. 1978. Making News: A Study in the Construction of Reality. New York: Free Press.

____. 1972. "Objectivity as Strategic Ritual." American Journal of Sociology (January).

____, ed. 1974. The T.V. Establishment: Programming for Power and Profit. Englewood Cliffs, N.J.: Prentice-Hall.

Tunstall, Jeremy. 1977. The Media Are American. New York: Columbia University Press.

Vernon, Raymond. 1977. "Storm over the Multinationals: Problems and Prospects." Foreign Affairs (January).

Vidal, Daniel. 1971. Essai sur l'idéologie: Le Cas particulier des idéologies syndicales. Paris: Anthropos.

Voyenne, Bernard. 1972. L'Information en France. Paris: Ediscience.

____. 1971. La Presse dans la société contemporaine. Paris: Armand Colin.

____. 1970. Le Droit à l'information. Paris: Aubier.

Wallez, Paul. 1976. "Enquête a l'intérieur de la presse régionale: Hiérarchie et travail en équip." Le Journaliste (January).

Wells, Alan. 1974. Mass Communications: A World View. Palo Alto, Calif.: Mayfield.

____. 1972. Picture-Tube Imperialism? The Impact of U.S. Television on Latin America. New York: Orbis Books.

Will, Nicolas. 1976. Essai sur la presse et le capital. Paris: 10/18.

Williams, Raymond. 1977. Marxism and Literature. Oxford: Oxford University Press.

____. 1976. Communications. London: Penguin Books.

Winston, Brian, et al. 1975. "Television Coverage of Industrial Relations: Evidence Presented to the Committee on the Future of Broadcasting." Mimeographed. London: SSRC Media Project, Glasgow.

Wolfe, Alan. 1977. The Limits of Legitimacy. New York: Free Press.

INDEX

accumulation, 158
Action, 38n
Action Chrétienne Jeunesse Française, 85
ad hoc government study commissions, 172-73 (see Drancourt, Lindon, Neuwirth, Vedel and Lecat commissions)
administrative regulatory agencies: state agencies, 171, 174-75; para-state agencies, 174n
Adorno, Theodore, 210
advertising: agencies, 7; and American firms, 43, 45n; booking agencies (régis), 27, 45, 51 (see Régis-Presse and Havas-Régis); commercial and classified, 41; development of in France, 42n; in different media, 42n; dilemma of, 43; effect on content, 46-49; in Le Figaro, 55, 214; and the French state, 189 (see Havas); growth of, 42n; impact on press sector, 45-46; income, 20-21; legal requirement, 48; monopolistic firms, 40, 41-46 (see Publicis and Havas); pooling, 28; report on by Drancourt Commission, 45
"Afrique No. 1," 198
L'Agence et Messageries de Presse, 60 (see Hachette)
Agence France Presse: 7, 12, 186, 189-93, 200; budget of, 191; compromise of autonomy of, 190-91; derivation from Havas Information, 189-90, 196; journalist unions at, 192
Agence générale de presse et d'information (AGPI) 69, 73, 79
Agence Presse Libération, 228 (see Libération)
Agfa Gavaert, 113
Albin Michel, 60
Algerian Crisis, 180, 187
Les Allobroges, 185
Alsace, 28
Althusser, Louis, 3, 92n, 157, 209, 234
Amaury, Emilien: 74, 126, 127, 141; close links with state, 134; director of Havas, 127; double life during occupation, 127
American Association for Free Enterprise, 95
anarchist press, 231
anarcho-syndicalism: and the Parisien-Libéré strike, 125; of the printers, 120-21
Anders, Gunter, 6
Andorradio (Andora), 198
Andrieu, René, 38, 138n, 171, 182
Anger, 128
Aragon, Louis, 38
Aron, Raymond: 70, 72-74, 200; criticism of Beuve-Méry, 93
Aronson, James, 83
arrests of journalists and directors, 183-86
Associated Press, 190
Association of Aeronautical Journalists: and link with Dassault, 48
Atlantic-Alliance Thesis: 54; and

Le Monde, 86
L'Aube: demise of, 229-30
Auclair, Georges, 217
Audinot, André, 201
Auriol, Vincent, 86
L'Aurore: 7, 20, 25, 55, 168, 181, 185-86, 241, 247; Hersant takeover, 77-79; resignation of principal personnel, 78
Austria, 6, 7
authority relations: 20, in press enterprises, 33-38
L'Auto Journal, 66

Bagdikian, Ben, 6
Balle, Francis, 214
Balzac, Jean-Louis, 190
Banque Nationale de Paris, 71
Banque Paribas (Banque de Paris et de Pays-Bas): 95n; early links with Hachette, 58; and Expeditive, 58; holdings, 51-53; holdings in Hachette, 62-63; holdings in paper sector, 114
Banque Suez, 114
Banque Vernes, 71
Banque Worms: 95; holdings in Hachette, 62
Barrat, Robert, 184
Barre, Raymond, 133
Barthes, Roland, 218
Baudelot, Christien, 15, 238-39
Baudouin, Dennis, 198
Béghin, Fernand: 32, 51; at Le Figaro, 56; as spokesman for paper industry, 114
Belgium: 60, 112n; printing of scab Parisien-Libéré in, 131
Bell, Daniel, 237
Bellanger, Claude, 181, 192, 256
Bernstein, Basil, 238n
Bertaux, Daniel, 33

Beullac, Christian, 135
Beuve-Méry: 31, 55, 81n, 95, 181, 188, 191, 224; against "Atlantic alliance" thesis, 86; and Christian-liberalism, 85; criticism of for support of May '68 students, 93; and Resistance movement, 85; retirement of, 87, 89
Blanc, Louis, 29
Bleustein-Blanchet, Marcel: 167; at Télé-Monte Carlo, 198 (see Publicis)
Blum, Léon, 166
Boisarie, Francois, 70n, 72n, 176
Bordeaux, 28
Bourdieu, Pierre: 15, cultural capital, symbolic violence, 238; pedagogical action, 249
bourgeoisie: 5; effort to launch J'Informe, 95, 95n; industrial, 7, 13-14, 19, 21, 31-33, 167, 252; instrumentalist image of, 159; liberal, 32; Le Temps and the steel trust, 84
Bourrellis, Jean, 95n
Boussac, Marcel, 32, 78
Bouzinac, Roger, 191
Bowls, Samuel, 238n
Braverman, Harry, 10, 21, 105, 135
Brazzaville Radio (Congo), 198
Le Bris, Michel, 178
Brisson, Pierre, 53-56, 181, 183, 188
Brive-Informations, 66n
Buob, Jacques, 75

Camus, Albert, 1, 2
Le Canard Enchaîné, 81, 179, 231
capital intensive production: 21; effect on competition, 46; and new press empires, 50

Cardona, Louis, 188
Carrefour, 74, 128
Castells, Manuel, 241
Cau, Jean, 93
causality, 218
La Cause du peuple, 177-78
Caute, David, 37
Cazeneuve, Jean, 249
censorship: 180-83; Hersant at France-Soir, 77; of journalists, 33-38; at ORTF, 249; at Radio-France, 196
Center for the Education of Journalists, 147
centralization: 21, 27, 113; in CP press group, 37-38; and Hersant's empire, 51; in Le Monde, 37
Center for the Study of Advertising Bearing Publications (CESP), 241n
Centre-Presse, 28, 66, 66n
Ce Soir, 184-85, 186
Ceyrac, Francois, 70
Chaban-Delmas, Jacques: 58; links with Hachette, 60; placement of his men at Hachette, 63n, 200; scandal at ORTF and resignation as Prime Minister, 64n
Chaix printing plant, 115, 118
Champs-Elysées: during Parisien-Libéré strike, 132
Charlie-Hebdo, 178, 231n
Charpentie, Yvon, 151
Chartres, 131, 134
Chevalier, Maurice, 225
Chirac, Jacques: 71, 76, 200; and CGC, 151; influences sale of Le Figaro to Hersant, 70; influences sale of France-Soir to Hersant, 76
clandestine publications, 27, 142
Clarté, 38
class origins: and media usage,
237; of press workers, 33
class struggle/class relations: 7, 8; and the capitalist state, 160; the concrete nature of, 92, 176; inter-class and intra-class, 13, 159, 165; and the reproduction of class divisions, 210; the role of the media in, 234; visibility in crisis, 179, 180
Clazel, Jean, 96n
Clerc, Yann, 73
Cohn-Bendit, Daniel, 148n
Colas, Michel, 99n
collaboration: 5, 31; conviction of Hersant for, 64-66; in Clermont-Ferrand and silence of local paper about a film on, 223; conviction of Prouvost for, 53; and Hachette, 58
Combat, 1, 2, 25
Comité des Forges (steel trust): 30; and Le Temps, 84; and modern equivalent, 95
Commercial Court (Tribunal de Commerce): and Le Figaro case, 54, 56
Commission for Press Operations (Commission des opérations de presse): proposal for, 77-78
Common Market (EEC): 46, 107; and duty free status of printed material, 116
Communist Party: 1, 5, 10, 27, 31, 33, 37-38, 167, 176, 181, 192, 229; closing of publications, 229-30; criticism of Le Monde, 228; demise of press, 219; documentation on press of, 230n; influence at Havre Libre, 67; press of, 37-38, 177n; program to nationalize Hachette, 64; Secretary General Duclos arrested,

185; state lawsuits against publications of, 177
Communist Student Union (UEC), 38
Compagnie Financière "Paribas" International (Hachette international financing company), 62, 63
La Compagnie Libanaise de Télévision (Beirut), 198
concentration process: 6, 8-9, 19, 23-25, 28, 29-30, 45, 46, 113; and fall in productive capacity, 107; induction of concentration, 43
Confédération fédérale du travail (CFDT): 80, 109, 176; grouping at Le Monde, 89; journalist union, 80; general policies, 149
Confédération générale des cadres (CGC): 73; journalist union, 151
Confédération générale du travail (CGT): 109, 112, 176, 185; analysis of printer's crisis, 116; attack of printing bourgeoisie on CGT monopoly, 123; founding unions, 121; journalist union, 80, 185; and Moissant law, 123; monopoly among Parisian printers, 112 (see French Federation of Printers)
conservative shift of post-war press, 219
consumerism, 8
Conte, Arthur, 249
Coquelin, Roger, 113n, 116n, 117n
corporatism: of early SNJ, 89; and economism, 125; end of, 137, 149; movement away from of journalists, 109; of printers, 111

Cotneareanu, Madame, 54
Coty, Francois, 53
Courtin, René, 85
Le Crapouillot, 179
cretinization thesis: 212, need to reject, 236
crisis: of hegemony, 5, 8, 13, 157; orientation of sensationalist press, 224-25; of the state, 5, 8, 179-80
La Croix, 47, 196

Daniel, Jean, 188
Le Dantec, Jean-Paul, 178
Darblay family, 30
Dartville, Bernard, 231
Dassault, Marcel: 32, 48, 71, 71n, 81, 198; Hersant blocks article critical of, 77
Debré, Michel, 53
Défence de la France, 167 (see France-Soir)
Defferre, Gaston, 28, 81, 167, 195
de Gaulle, Charles, 55, 56, 85, 165, 175-76, 181, 183, 186, 195, 198
deindustrialization, 9, 46
Deleuze, Gilles, 187
Denmark, 6, 25
Dépêche de l'Est, 188
Dépêche du Midi, 231
dependent participation, 13, 159, 173
depoliticization, 7, 8, 29, 213-16
deproletarianization of Paris, 128
de Roquemaurel, Ithier, 60
Deroy, Henri, 63
de-skilling: 11, 21, 106, 108, 118-19, 136, 160; of journalists, 139; of press readers, 224
de Sola Poole, Ithiel, 211n, 246

devaluing of capital (dévalorization), 117
de Villefosse, Louis, 93
dialectic of consent and coercion, 169
Diligent, Senator, 64n
dominant class: 13, 20-21, 40, 235; reproduction of superiority complex of, 249
d'Ormesson, Jean, 70, 72-73, 200
d'Ornano, Michel, 192
Douce, Jacques, 76
Drancourt Commission, 45, 173
Droit, Michel, 48
Drouin, Pierre, 85n
Duclos, Jacques, 185
Duhamel, Georges, 54
Dupont, Jean-Marie: 94; role in Le Monde transition to third generation, 90-91
Dupont de Nemours, 113
Dupuy, Jacques and family, 30, 32, 95
Duverger, Maurice, 37, 181

L'Echo d'Alger, 188
L'Echo de Paris, 31
Eclair du Berry, 66n
Economic and Social Council (Conseil économique et social), 77, 173
Edi-Monde, 76
education: of Le Monde readers, 96; and radio listening, 250; relation to TV watching, 247-48
Ehrenreich, John, 10, 148n
Ekecrantz, Jan, 4n, 211-12
Elf-Aquitaine, 35
Elleinstein, Jean, 92n
Ellul, Jacques, 93, 93n
Empain Schneider, 113
Enzenberger, Hans Magnus, 179n, 234-35

L'Epoque, 31
Esso Standard, 95
Estier, Claude, 188
Europe #1: 197; state co-ownership with press bourgeoisie, 198
Eurocommunism, 73
L'Eveil Normand, 80
Ewen, Stuart, 15, 45n
L'Expansion, 93
L'Express: 37, 70, 182, 184; history of depoliticization, 229; how advertising changed it, 47; and link with Havas, 229
expressionistic press, 227 (see informational press)
external influences on press enterprises, 39-45

far left press: 33; extent of, 232; relative success of, 231
fascism, 40, 237
Faure, Roland, 78
Fauvet, Jacques: 85, 87, 94, 188; appointment of, 87, 89
Fayard, 60
Le Figaro: 7, 20, 40, 41, 71, 96, 142, 145, 183, 186, 208, 214, 241; advertising income, 97n; Figaro-Madame, 74; Figaro-Magazine, 74-75; Hersant's purchase, 70, 168; more liberal inside than on page one, 70; under Prouvost, 53-57; drop in quality, 73; study of readership's column choices, 224; repression of unions by Hersant, 73
Figaro-Magazine: 74-75; importance to the New Right, 75
financial aid of state to the press: 169-72
Finaly, Horace, 58
Floirat, Sylvian: 198

Florence conventions (UNESCO), 116
Fontaine, André, 85n
Force Ouvrière (FO): journalist union, 80; and Parisien-Libéré strike, 131-32
Foucault, Michel, 187
Fouret, Edmond, 62-63
La France, 185
France-Antilles, 78
France-Asie Radio (Saigon), 198
France-Nouvelle, 38n, 177, 181
France-Observateur, 181, 182, 188 (see Nouvel-Observateur)
France-Soir: 7, 20, 32, 55, 72, 96, 167, 168, 186, 200, 214, 218, 241, 247; advertising income, 97n; cost of composing, 112; sale by Hachette, 60; Hersant's takeover, 75; prevalence of soft news, 222; use of surface space, 221
Frankfurt School, 15, 212
Franpresse, 78-79 (see Hersant)
Free French Zone, 31, 54, 65
free press, 161, 163-64
French Federation of Journalist Associations (Fédération Française des sociétés des journalists): absence from Lindon commission, 174; creation of, 142
French Federation of Printers (Fédération française des travailleurs du livre) (FFTL): call off of strike at France-Soir, 76; one of founding unions of CGT, 121; control over foremen, 124; double independence of, 121; the four unions which compose the federation, 121
Funck-Brentano, F., 86

Gabon, 198

Le Gaillard, 66n
Gambetta, 29
Garaud, Marie-France, 76
Garçon, José, 138n
Garnham, Nicholas, 3-4, 210
Gasset, 60
Gaudard, J. P., 38
Gaullist press, 230
Gay, Francisque, 58, 229
General Motors, 106-7
Georges Lang print shop, 116
German occupation of France, 5, 27, 31
Germany, 6-7, 24-25
Gide, André, 54
Giscard d'Estaing, Valery, 37, 77, 165, 190-91, 193, 200
giveaway newspapers, 171, 198
Glucksman, André, 75
Gramsci, Antonio, 12, 157, 169
Grenoble, 28, 232
Guehenno, 38n
Guilleminault, Gilbert, 8n, 78
Guillené-Brulen, Jacques, 79

Hachette: 20, 21, 50, 51, 57, 82-83; estimation of recent earnings, 61; Edi-Monde subsidiary, 76; sale of France-Soir, 75; history of, 57-64; international holdings, 60; Le-Point, 60; monopoly on press delivery, 58-59; Presse-Routage subsidiary, 60; principal stockholders, 62; publishing holdings, 60; scandal at ORTF, 200; secret purchase of France-Soir, 167, 150 subsidiaries of, 61; today, 59; threatened by the united left, 60
Hachette-Litérature, 60
Hachette, Louis, 57, 60
Hall, Stuart, 3
Hallier, Jean-Edern, 178, 195

Hara-Kiri, 178
Harris Corporation, 113
Hauser, Eugen, 6
Havas: and Amaury, 127; earnings, 196-97; and L'Express conversion, 229; Havas-Régis, 45; history of, 29, 43, 196-97; as a state holding company, 193, 196-97
Havas, Charles, 190
Havas-Information (see AFP)
Havas Régis, 45 (see Havas)
Le Havre, 67
Havre Libre, 67
Havre Presse, 67
headlines: space devoted in different modes of journalism, 221
Helio-Cachan print shop, 116
Henri-Lévy, Bernard, 75
Hersant, Jacques, 133
Hersant, Robert, 20, 21, 50, 57, 81-83, 141, 176, 200-1; AGPI, the group's newsagency, 69; takeover of L'Aurore, 77-79; collaborationist background, 64; conviction for collaboration, 65; as deputy to National Assembly, 79; his editorial in Le Figaro, 73-74; takeover of Le Figaro and France-Soir, 70-77; history of, 64-81; invalidation of his election, 79; lawsuits by journalist unions against, 80; repression of journalist unions at Le Figaro, 73
Hervé, Pierre, 38n
historical specificity, 5
Hoffman, Stanley, 31n, 84n
Horkheimer, Max, 210
Hughes, Helen, 213, 217
human interest story: 213; inherent conservatism of, 216-19

L'Humanité: 27, 38, 60, 95, 142, 164, 170, 170n, 182, 185, 196; low circulation of, 246; depoliticization of, 214; as propagandistic press, 227; state law suits against, 177
L'Humanité-Dimanche, 229
L'Humanité-Rouge, 178
Hutin, Francois, 55

IBM, 113
ideological relations: 14; situational, 109; importance of not overestimating the effectiveness of, 237
L'Idiot International, 195
Independent Republican Party, 191, 193, 200
L'Index, 214
induced reproduction, 20
industrial sectors, 14
inequality, 15, 240
L'Information, 95
informational press: 40, 214, 227-33; why selected, 245
instrumentalism, 8, 159, 210, 235
internationalization of production, 115, 160
investigative reporting, 40, 92, 164, 165, 179, 254
Italy, 24

Jeanneney, Jean-Noël, 85
Janrot, Pierre, 78
Jansenism, 85
Japan, 6
Jaubert, Alain, 187, 231
Jaurès, Jean, 29
Jeunes Forces, 65
J'Informe: 25, 32; sources of funding, 95
Journal d'Alger, 188
journalist association movement (société de rédacteurs); failure

312

of, 144; at Le Figaro, 56; beginning at Le Monde, 86; and the SNJ, 142; contrasted with syndicalism, 146
Le Journaliste, 186
journalists: from professionalistic to socialistic, 148; salaries of, 138; specificity of, 141; unemployment among, 138
journalist unions: at AFP, 191-92; suits against Hersant by, 79, 80-81; National Syndicate of, 147, 176, 196; politicization of, 146; history of SNJ, 141
Jours de France, 7
Julien, Claude, 91
July, Serge, 231

Kennedy, John Fitzgerald, 176
Khrushchev, Nikita, 216
Klapperstei 68, 178
Kodak, 113

labor-aristocracy, 120, 122, 125 (see printers)
labor law, 175
Lacan, Jacques, 217
laissez-faire policy for the press, 172
Lapierre, J. W., 223n
lawsuits against publications, 177
Lazareff, Pierre, 55, 75, 181, 188
Lazurick, Francine, 78
Lazurick, Robert, 55, 78, 181
Lecanuet, Jean, 68
Lecat Commission, 118
Lecat, Jean-Philippe, 168, 192
Lefebvre, Henri, 148n
Lefranc, Pierre, 198
left-Christian movement: 19, 31; demise of press of, 219-20;

and Le Monde, 85; and Nord-Eclaire, 67
leftist press (see far left press)
Left-Radical Party, 33, 176
Lemerle, Michel, 196
Lepape, Pierre, 139-40
Leroy, Roland, 38
Les Lettres Francaises, 38
Lévi-Strauss, Claude, 217
liberal orientation: 76
liberation, the (1944), 2, 6, 13, 15, 19-20, 25, 27, 31-32, 67, 84, 127, 142, 152, 157, 164, 166, 213-14, 229
Libération (1941-1964), 182, 184, 185
Libération (1973-   ): 25, 164, 179; as an expressionistic publication, 227; history of, 231
Lille, 36, 67, 90, 147
Lindon Commission: 56, 57, 145-46, 174; creation of, 144
linotype machine, 118
Littunen, Yrjo, 212
local elites (notables), 39n
local news, 28
Lojkine, Jean, 241
London Times, 112n
Louis Napoleon, 57
Lui, 198
Lyon, 28

Machiavelli, Niccolo, 169
Maire, Edmond, 80
Mallet, Serge, 180
Le Mans, 128
Maoist, 38, 177-78, 231
Marchais, Georges, 38
Marchetti, Xavier, 72, 200
Marcuse, Herbert, 237
La Marseillaise, 185
Marseille, 28, 29, 167, 187
Martinet, Gilles, 184, 188
Massu, General Jacques, 183
Le Matin (pre-war), 31, 65

Le Matin, (1977-   ), 25, 33
    78, 228
Mattelart, Armand, 45n, 83,
    212
Mauriac, Claude, 187
Mauriac, Francois, 54, 70
May, 1968 events: 56, 146, 198;
    and the expressionistic press,
    227; effect on Le Monde, 89;
    Le Monde's support of, 93
Meaulle brothers, 80 (see
    L'Eveil Normand)
mediating processes, 5
Mendès France, Pierre, 63n,
    184
mental labor and manual labor:
    10, 15, 106, 108; division
    exacerbated by monopoliza-
    tion process, 105-6; and CP
    membership of printers, 121
Meo, Jean, 200
Le Méridional, 185
Le Meridional-La France, 188
Messmer, Pierre, 249
Michelin family, 95, 95n
middle-strata, 19, 32, 76, 136
Miliband, Ralph, 3, 15, 161,
    179n, 209
milk trust, 95
Minister: 192, 195; intervention
    by, 175
Minister of Economy and Fi-
    nance, 35, 190,
Minister of Foreign Affairs, 190
Minister of Information: 173;
    censorship by, 181; Secre-
    tary of State for Information,
    167
Minister of the Interior: 163,
    179, 186; Mitterand's repres-
    sion of press as, 184; Ponia-
    towski and Amaury, 134
Minister of Labor: 73, 176;
    Beullac on Parisien-Libéré
    settlement, 135

Minister, Prime: 183, 190, 200;
    Barre captured by printers
    during Parisien-Libéré strike,
    133; Chaban-Delmas and the
    Hachette-ORTF scandal, 63n,
    64n, 200; Chirac and the sale
    of Le Figaro, 70; Chirac and
    the sale of France-Soir, 76;
    Messmer's control over
    ORTF, 249
Minute, 74, 75, 179, 229
Miror-Sprint, 185
Mitterand, Francois, 37, 70,
    147, 184
modernization process, 109
modes of journalism, 209-12,
    253 (see sensationalist press,
    informational press)
Moisant law, 123
Mollet, Guy, 171
Molotch, Harvey, 179
Le Monde: 15, 22, 26-27, 31,
    32, 37, 41, 42, 142, 171,
    180, 182, 183, 187, 214, 228,
    241, 247; advertising income,
    54, 97, 99; attacks on Le
    Monde, 92; not depoliticized,
    214; foreign sales, 96; history
    and corporate structure, 84-
    91; objectivistic reporting,
    228; as a rationalistic publica-
    tion, 227; satellite publications,
    98n; as socialistic, 219; mini-
    mum of soft news, 222; use of
    surface space by, 221
Le Monde Diplomatique, 91, 98n
Monik, Emmanuel, 63
monopolistic corporate units: 19,
    21, 27n, 113, 116; in adver-
    tising, 29-30; Hachette and
    Hersant, 82; and monopoly
    capital, 160; in related indus-
    tries, 107
monopolization process: 6-7,
    160; three case studies, 50-83;

induction of, 45; effect on labor relations, 105; strategies of, 83
monopoly: vertical and horizontal, 21, 50, 59-60; Hachette's early efforts at, 58-60
La Montagne, 223
Montenay, Michel, 95n
Morin, Violette, 216
Mottin report, 134
Mouillaud, Maurice, 222
Moustier law, 168 (see press laws)
Mouvement Republican Populair (MRP): 5, 31, 58, 85; demise of press of, 219-20, 229-30; influence at Havre Libre, 67; influence at Paris-Normandie, 67-68
Mueller, Claus, 238n
multinational firms, 160 (see Hachette)
Munich agreements, 85
Murdock, Graham, 3, 6

Nader, Ralph, 47
La Nation, 230
National Assembly: 6, 159, 167, 181-82, 192, 193, 195, 201-2; Hachette's collaboration, 58; anti-Hersant speeches, 81; first journalist work codes, 141; legislative blockage of press statutes, 166
National Association for the Support of General de Gaulle, 198
National Committee of Manufacturers (Comité national du Patronat Francais), 70, 151
National Resistance Committee (Comité national de la Résistance), 127
National Consumers Union (L'Union Féderale des Consommateurs), 80

nationalization, 60, 144
National Journalist's Union (Syndicat National des journalists) (SNJ): 80, 186; history of, 141; and journalist association movement, 144; after its politicization, 146
National Student Union (Union national des étudiants francais) (UNEF), 90
National Syndicate of Journalist Unions (Union national des syndicats des journalists) (UNSJ), 147, 176, 196 (see journalist unions)
Negt, Oscar, 3, 209
Neuwirth Commission, 144
news flash: 224-25; causes dependency on police, 225 (see crisis orientation, sensationalist journalism)
Newspaper Preservation Act, 165n
New Philosophers, 75
New Right, 75
New York Times, 15, 112n, 165, 180
Nice-Matin, 223
Noirot, Paul, 38
Nora, Simon: 70; links to Hachette, 63n; scandal at ORTF, 64n, 200
Nord-Eclair, 67, 71
Nord-Matin, 67
Notre Dame Cathedral, 133
La Nouvelle Critique, 38n
Nouvel Observateur, 20, 43, 92, 145, 187, 223, 228; as socialistic, 229
Les Nouvelles de Bordeaux et du Sud Ouest, 185

O'Connor, James, 161
Offe, Claus, 12, 157, 158, 159, 161, 172, 180

Office Francais d'Information (OFI), 190
Office de Radio-Télévision Française (ORTF): 186; breakup of, 193; appointment of Conte as Director, 249
oppositional interviewing, 254
Ouest France: 2, 20, 28, 36, 55, 142; silence on Brittany separatist movement, 223
Ouest-Matin, 185
ownership of press enterprises, 30-31

Padioleau, Jean, 139n
Pado, Dominique, 78
paper industry: 21; Béghin as spokesman for, 114; dismantling of, 46; rise in newsprint cost, 114
paradox, 218
Paribas, (see Banque Paribas)
Paribas Corporation, 88
Paribas International, S.A., 62-63
Parisian press: 2, 20, 24, 25, 32; of CP, 219; comparative study of coverage of events in Israel, 223n
Le Parisien-Libéré: 55, 127, 181, 187; the great strike, 126-35; Mottin Report on settlement, 134-35; extreme sensationalism of, 222; strategies and tactics of the great strike, 128-35; use of surface space by, 221; urban guerilla tactics against, 132
Paris-Jour, 145
Paris-Match, 47
Paris-Normandie: 28, 76, 145; Hersant's conquest of, 67-69
Parisot, Paul, 77n
Paris-Presse, 186
Paris-Soir, 54

Paris Stock Exchange, 133
Paris-Turf, 78
participation: de Gaulle's policy, 56; Pompidou's displeasure with, 145
Le Patriot de Nice et du Sud-Est, 185, 188
Pauwels, Louis, 73, 75
Paysant, André, 143
Pedraglio, Gerard, 95n
Pentagon Papers, 165
Perdriel, Claude, 76, 77, 145
Perier-Daville, Denis, 70, 71, 145, 147n
Pétain, Maréchal, 31n, 65
Le Petit Journal, 31
Le Petit Varois, 185
photocomposition: 10, 118-19; effect on Canadian press, 119
photographs: space devoted to in different modes of journalism, 221
Pigeat, Henri, 190, 200
pirate radio stations, 195, 199
La Plaine Saint-Denis, 78
Planchais, Jean, 85n
Le Point, 20, 60, 73
political party press, 231
politicization, 146
Politique-Hebdo, 187
Pompidou, Georges, 56, 76, 120, 165, 198, 200
Poniatowski, Michel, 134, 179
Pope John XXIII, 143
Le Populaire de Paris, 230
Port Royal, 85
Poulantzas, Nicos, 3, 10n, 157, 159, 210, 211
Power Corporation, 62
Pozner, Vladmir, 188
President of the Republic: 165, 180, 190, 198, 200; Giscard and Amaury, 134; Giscard's news conference on Hersant's takeover of L'Aurore, 77;

appeal by Le Monde's journalists to, 86; switch on "participation" policy from de Gaulle to Pompidou, 56; Pompidou on breaking the printer's union, 120
press bourgeoisie: 5, 19, 30, 33, 39-40, 51, 109, 111, 134, 135, 146, 148, 167; and AFP, 190; and Europe #1, 198; threatened by journalist association movement, 144; misuse of Florence Convention loophole, 116; owner syndicates, 123; Parisian and regional press owner's syndicates, 128; political offices held by, 201-2; state interlocks with, 199
press delivery companies (messageries): confiscation of MPP by Liberation authorities, 58; "Expéditive" of Hachette, 58; Hachette's early monopoly, 58; creation of NMPP, 59; NMPP and Parisien-Libéré strike, 132
press employee (employee de presse), 140
"presse d'opinion," 168
Presses de la cité, 48
press laws: 163-65; anglo press law, 165, 166; legal status of sequestered enterprises after 1944, 167; legislative blockage of press statutes, 32, 166, 168, 268; Moustier law, 168; right of rectification, 166; right of response, 166
Priaulx, Allan, 148n
printers, 10, 33; their anarcho-syndicalism, 120-21; as a labor aristocracy, 120; salaries of, 124-25
printing industry: 21; dismantling of, 115; endangered and closed shops, 115-16; Hachette's holdings, 61; strategies of the printing bourgeoisie, 117
printing sector, 111
productive capacity: 107, decrease in paper sector, 115; monopolization causes drop in, 46
productivity, 113; large printing enterprises versus small, 107; and profitability, 117
profitability, 46, 69, 117
Le Progrès de Lyon, 29, 188
Prokop, Dieter, 209
propagandistic press, 227, 229, (see informational press)
Prouvost, Jean: 21, 30, 32, 50, 60; collaboration conviction, 53; at Le Figaro, 53; sale of Le Figaro, 70; at RTL, 197
Le Provencal, 28, 185
Province No. 1, 28-29, 142
provincial press, 2, 19-20, 23, 27
Prunier, Claude, 79
Publicis: 29, 43; partial ownership of Régis-Presse, 45
public's right to information, 142-44

Quasimodo, 133
Québec, 62
Que Choisir?, 80
Le Quotidien de Paris: 25; bankrupt and closed, 228; as rationalistic, 228; as socialistic, 219
Le Quotidien du Peuple, 25

racist ideology, 225
Radical Party: 29, 47, 70, 229; failure of press of, 230-31
Radio-France, 193, 196
Radio Monte Carlo, 197

Radio-Télé Luxembourg: Hachette's involvement, 60, 62; Prouvost's involvement, 53
rationalist press, 227 (see informational press)
Read, William H., 45n, 83
readership: as class specific, 32
Rebois, Charles, 73
La Recherche, 187
Régis-Presse: 29, 43; Publicis subsidiary, 45; Hachette subsidiary, 61
relations of production, 105
relative autonomy: of the state, 160, 191; of state media apparatuses, 191, 210, 235
Rennes, 28
Républicain Lorrain, 112
resistance movement: 1, 85; and Amaury's apartment, 127; and Prouvost's donation, 53; and left-Christian movement, 85
restoration of the bourgeoisie, 19, 32, 53
Reuter news agency, 190
rhetoric of objectivity: 227n; analysis of Le Monde, 228
Ridgeway, General, 184
right of conscience (clause de conscience): 34; Hersant's use of at Le Figaro, 72; Hersant's use of at France-Soir, 76; legal creation of, 141
Riverol, 182
Rossi, André, 195
Rouen, 28, 65, 67
Rouge, 25
Rouzier, Marc, 79
Ruberol, François, 80

St. Etienne, 29
Saint-Ouen, 131, 134
Sallent, Jean-Pierre, 178

Sarrebrück Radio (Sarre), 198
Sartre, Jean-Paul, 54, 178, 188
Sauvageot, Jacques, 73, 73n, 85n, 87, 89, 93n, 94n
Scandinavia, 6
Schiller, Herbert, 45n, 83, 91, 212, 216-17
Schneider family, 30
School of Journalism, Bordeaux, 147
School of Journalism of Lille, 147
Schudson, Michael, 213
Schwoebel, Jean, 142-45
SDF-Neogravure: 116, 117; Hachette subsidiary, 61
Seale, Patrick, 148n
Secretary for Cultural Affairs (Secrétariat d'Etat à la culture), 244, 247-48, 250
Séguy, Georges, 122
seizure of publications, 163, 180-82, 185
sensationalist press: 1, 7, 15, 24, 29, 179, 212, 213-26; confusion of natural and social disasters, 226; crisis orientation of, 224; as informationally vacuous, 221; use of paradox, 218; why selected, 246; worldview of, 217
Seppanen, 6
Servan-Schreiber, Emile, 188
Servan-Schreiber, Jean-Jacques, 37, 70, 81, 86, 148n, 184, 229
Servan-Schreiber, Jean-Louis, 93, 171
Signal, 58
silent ideology, 222
Simmonnot, Philippe, 35, 36
Smadja, Jean-Claude, 76
social-democratic legislation, 13, 164
socialistic orientation: 223; of

Havre Libre, 67; among journalists, 148; of Le Matin, 77; of Le Monde, 85, 219; of Nord Matin, 67; of Nouvel Observateur, 229
Socialist Party: 1, 6, 29, 31, 33, 176, 192; Leon Blum, 166; demise of press of, 219-20, 229-30; program to nationalize Hachette, 64; influence at Havre Libre, 67; independence of Le Monde from, 219; influence at Paris-Normandie, 67-68
social reproduction: 12; different processes for different classes, 245; role of the media in, 210, 237; principal tasks of, 240; of superiority and inferiority, 249
SOCPRESS: 71; in the takeover of L'Aurore, 78
SOFIRAD: 193; foreign media holdings, 197-98; formation under Vichy, 197-98; subsidiaries and holdings, 197-98
soft news and hard news: 223; soft news and the de-skilling of readers, 224 (see sensationalist and information press)
"The Sorrow and the Pity," 223
Spaziro, Emilien, 127
specialization, 140
specificity of journalists, 141
S. S. France, 133
Stalinist, 237
La Stampa, 15
state: 3, 4, 5, 172, 174, 188, 191; arrests of journalists, 184; class character of, 179; financial aid to the press, 169-72; lack of unity in, 235; lawsuits against publications, 177-79; monopoly on electronic media, 193-96; structuralist analysis of, 157
statism (étatism), 163
steel industry lobby (Groupement de L'Industrie Siderurgique): 95
Stéphane, Roger, 184
Still, André, 185
Stock, 60
Sud-Ouest, 2, 20, 29
Sud-Radio des Vallées, 197
surplus value, 33
suspension of publications, 163n
Suzuki, Shiro, 6
Sweden, 24, 112n, 211

Télé-Monte Carlo, 197, 198
Télé- 7 Jours, 53
Temoignage Chrétien, 182, 188
Le Temps: 31, 93; analysis of content, 85; owned by steel trust, 84
Le Temps de Paris: 32; origins of funds, 95
tendency of the rate of profit to fall, 118
La Terre, 185
Therborn, Göran, 10n, 159
Third Republic, 30
Thomas, Ruth, 195, 196
Tito, Marshal, 186
Touraine, Alain, 148n, 159, 236
"Tour de France," 133, 134
trivialization of political reporting, 216
Trotskyist: 38; seven branches represented in the press, 231
Tuchman, Gaye, 34n, 139n, 165n, 227n
Tunstall, Jeremy, 41, 45n
two-tier cultural system: 15, 211, 237-38, 246-50, 251; and book reading, 250; relation of education to, 247-48; and the

legitimation process, 239; and the press, 244; and radio listening, 249-50

unemployment: 9, 21, 135, 146; among journalists, 108, 138, 140; and the Lecat Commission, 118; among printers, 108, 122
union of the left (union de la gauche): 33, 195; plans for Hachette, 60
Union of Parisian Insurance Companies, 62
Union of Swiss Banks, 62
United Kingdom, 6-7, 24
urban guerilla attacks on scab delivery trucks, 132

Vailland, Roger, 185
Van den Esch, José, 78
Vedel Georges, 77
Vendredi, 38n
Viansson-Ponté, Pierre, 68, 75n, 85n
Vichy government, 1, 31, 53, 65, 190, 199
Vingt-Quatre Heures, 32
violence against press enterprises, 187-88
Vive la Révolution, 178
La Voix du Nord, 67
La Voix de la Patrie, 185

Wendel family, 30
white collar workers, 10
Willemot-Roussel, 95n
Williams, Raymond, 2-3
Winkler, Paul, 76
Wolf, Pierre-René, 68
Wolfe, Alan, 179n
Wolff news agency, 190
work inspector (Inspecteur du travail), 79, 176
Worms, Gerard: links to Hachette, 63n; scandal at ORTF, 64n, 200
Wurmser, André, 188
"yellow press" 213 (see sensationalist press)
Zévaco, Raoul, 188
Zola, Emile, 29

ABOUT THE AUTHOR

J. W. FREIBERG received his Ph.D. from UCLA and the Ecole pratique des hautes études in Paris. He is a member of Alain Touraine's Centre d'étude des mouvements sociaux in Paris. He has published <u>Critical Sociology: European Perspectives</u> with Irvington/John Wiley, and has had articles appear in such journals as <u>Bulletin of Concerned Asian Scholars</u>, <u>Dialectical Anthropology</u>, <u>Insurgent Sociologist</u>, <u>Sociological Inquiry</u>, <u>Sociological Analysis</u> (US); <u>Sociologie du Travail</u>, <u>L'Homme et la société</u>, <u>Le Mouvement Social</u> (France); <u>Media, Culture and Society</u> (United Kingdom); <u>Dialectica</u> (Columbia); <u>City Magazine</u> (Hong Kong); and <u>Critica sociologica</u> (Italy).

THE LIBRARY
ST. MARY'S COLLEGE OF MARYLAND
ST. MARY'S CITY, MARYLAND 20686